The Epistle of Barnabas

The Epistle of Barnabas

A Commentary

Jonathon Lookadoo

FOREWORD BY
James Carleton Paget

Apostolic Fathers Commentary Series

Paul A. Hartog and Shawn J. Wilhite
Series Editors

CASCADE *Books* • Eugene, Oregon

THE EPISTLE OF BARNABAS
A Commentary

Apostolic Fathers Commentary Series

Copyright © 2022 Jonathon Lookadoo. All rights reserved. Except for brief quotations in critical publications or reviews, no part of this book may be reproduced in any manner without prior written permission from the publisher. Write: Permissions, Wipf and Stock Publishers, 199 W. 8th Ave., Suite 3, Eugene, OR 97401.

Cascade Books
An Imprint of Wipf and Stock Publishers
199 W. 8th Ave., Suite 3
Eugene, OR 97401

www.wipfandstock.com

PAPERBACK ISBN: 978-1-5326-6070-2
HARDCOVER ISBN: 978-1-5326-6071-9
EBOOK ISBN: 978-1-5326-6072-6

Cataloguing-in-Publication data:

Names: Lookadoo, Jonathon, 1987– [author] | Paget, James Carleton [foreword writer].

Title: The Epistle of Barnabas : a commentary / by Jonathon Lookadoo ; foreword by James Carleton Paget.

Description: Eugene, OR: Cascade Books, 2022 | Apostolic Fathers Commentary Series | Includes bibliographical references and index.

Identifiers: ISBN 978-1-5326-6070-2 (paperback) | ISBN 978-1-5326-6071-9 (hardcover) | ISBN 978-1-5326-6072-6 (ebook)

Subjects: LCSH: Epistle of Barnabas—Commentary | Epistle of Barnabas—Criticism, interpretation, etc. | Epistle of Barnabas—Theology

Classification: BS2900.B3 L66 2022 (print) | BS2900.B3 (ebook)

06/06/22

To Joel

Contents

Series Preface | ix
Foreword by James Carleton Paget | xvii
Preface | xxiii
List of Abbreviations | xxv
Translation of the Epistle of Barnabas | xxxiii

Part I: Introductory and Critical Articles

1. Introduction to the Epistle of Barnabas | 3
2. The Epistle of Barnabas and Scripture | 33
3. Toward a Theology of the Epistle of Barnabas | 51

Part II: Commentary

Barnabas 1.1–8:   Greetings and Introduction | 71
Barnabas 2.1—16.10: Revealing Knowledge in Scripture | 85
Barnabas 17.1–2:   Transition | 191
Barnabas 18.1—20.2: Section Body Section: Two Ways | 194
Barnabas 21.1–9:   Closing | 216

Bibliography | 225
Author Index | 247
Scripture Index | 253

Series Preface

"Introduction to the Apostolic Fathers Commentary Series"

Who Are the Apostolic Fathers?

THE LABEL "APOSTOLIC FATHERS" reflects a narrow collection of early Christian texts that generally date from the first and second centuries CE.[1] The works of the Apostolic Fathers offer a remarkable window into early (especially second-century) Christianity, as communities forged their religious and social identities within the broader Graeco-Roman culture.[2] As these early authors defined themselves and their readers in relationship to pagan culture, Jewish religiosity, and internal rivals, they ultimately influenced Christian movements for generations to come. Each book within the collection sheds unique light on the diversity of theology, worship, and life within nascent Christian communities.

The collection of "Apostolic Fathers" is an "artificial corpus" and a "modern construct."[3] Authors in antiquity did not use the label to describe such a collection.[4] Some of the Apostolic Fathers appear in the fourth-

---

1. Clayton N. Jefford, *Reading the Apostolic Fathers: A Student's Introduction*, 2nd ed. (Grand Rapids: Baker Academic, 2012), xvii. Some scholars have dated the Letter to Diognetus or the Martyrdom of Polycarp into the third century. See Candida R. Moss, "On the Dating of Polycarp: Rethinking the Place of the *Martyrdom of Polycarp* in the History of Christianity," *EC* 1 (2010) 539–74.

2. Clayton N. Jefford, *The Apostolic Fathers: An Essential Guide* (Nashville: Abingdon, 2005).

3. Paul Foster, "Preface," in Paul Foster (ed.), *The Writings of the Apostolic Fathers*, T. & T. Clark Biblical Studies (London: T. & T. Clark, 2007), vii.

4. According to Robert Grant, the term "Apostolic Fathers" was employed by the Monophysite Severus of Antioch in the sixth century, but not of a collection of writings as now recognized. See Robert M. Grant, "The Apostolic Fathers' First Thousand Years," *CH* 31, no. 4 (1962) 21, 28.

century Codex Sinaiticus (Barnabas and Hermas) and the fifth-century Codex Alexandrinus (1 Clement and 2 Clement).[5] Some were read in public worship, were cited as "scripture," or were mentioned in the context of early canonical discussions.[6] Codex Hierosolymitanus (1056 CE), which was discovered in 1873, contains the Didache, Barnabas, 1 Clement, 2 Clement, and a long recension of the Ignatian epistles.

Jean-Baptiste Cotelier produced the first printed edition of a collection akin to the Apostolic Fathers in 1672.[7] Cotelier's Latin collection was titled *SS. patrum qui temporibus apostolicis floruerunt; Barnabae, Clementis, Hermae, Ignatii, Polycarpi*.[8] Inclusion within the collection was thus associated with an assumed historical connection to the times of the apostles (*temporibus apostolicis*). Within the text of his work, Cotelier spoke of an *Apostolicorum Patrum Collectio*.[9] In 1693, William Wake put forth an English edition of the Apostolic Fathers: *The Genuine Epistles of the Apostolical Fathers: S. Barnabas, S. Ignatius, S. Clement, S. Polycarp, the Shepherd of Hermas, and the Martyrdoms of St. Ignatius and St. Polycarp*.[10] In 1699, Thomas Ittig abbreviated Cotelier's Latin title to *Bibliotheca patrum apostolicorum Graeco-Latina*.[11] Early commentators continued to insist that at least some of the Apostolic Fathers had contact with the original apostles.[12]

Andreas Gallandi added the Letter to Diognetus, extant material from the Apology of Quadratus, and the Papias fragments to the corpus

---

5. Dan Batovici, "The Apostolic Fathers in Codex Sinaiticus and Codex Alexandrinus," *Bib* 97 (2016) 581–605.

6. See D. Jeffrey Bingham, "Senses of Scripture in the Second Century: Irenaeus, Scripture, and Noncanonical Christian Texts," *JR* 97 (2017) 26–55; M. C. Steenberg, "Irenaeus on Scripture, *Graphe*, and the Status of *Hermas*," *SVTQ* 53 (2009) 29–66.

7. David Lincicum, "The Paratextual Invention of the Term 'Apostolic Fathers,'" *JTS* 66 (2015) 139–48.

8. J. B. Cotelier, *SS. Patrum qui temporibus apostolicis floruerunt; Barnabae, Clementis, Hermae, Ignatii, Polycarpi: opera edita et inedita, vera et supposititia* . . . (Paris: Petri Le Petit, 1672).

9. For this and related history, see J. A. Fischer, *Die ältesten Ausgaben der Patres Apostolici: ein Beitrag zu Begriff und Begrenzung der Apostolischen Väter* (Munich: Alber, 1974).

10. William Wake, *The Genuine Epistles of the Apostolical Fathers: S. Barnabas, S. Ignatius, S. Clement, S. Polycarp, the Shepherd of Hermas, and the Martyrdoms of Ignatius and St. Polycarp* (London: Ric. Sare, 1693).

11. Clare K. Rothschild, *New Essays on the Apostolic Fathers*, WUNT 375 (Tübingen: Mohr Siebeck, 2017), 9. See Thomas Ittig, *Bibliotheca Patrum Apostolicorum Graeco-Latina* (Leipzig: J. H. Richter, 1699).

12. Jefford, *Reading the Apostolic Fathers*, xvii.

of the Apostolic Fathers in 1765.[13] The Didache, since its rediscovery in the nineteenth century, has regularly accompanied the collection as well.[14] The scholarly work of J. B. Lightfoot, Theodore Zahn, and others elevated the "middle recension" of Ignatius's epistles as the preferred form of the Ignatian correspondence.[15]

In the Anglophone world, the "most readily available" and "widely used" editions of the Apostolic Fathers are Bart Ehrman's entry in the Loeb Classical Library (2003) and Michael Holmes's thorough revision of Lightfoot and Harmer's work, now in its third edition (2007).[16] Both Ehrman and Holmes include the Didache, 1 Clement, the fragment of Quadratus, the seven letters of the middle recension of the Ignatian correspondence, Polycarp's *Epistle to the Philippians*, the fragments of Papias, the Epistle of Barnabas, 2 Clement, the Shepherd of Hermas, the Martyrdom of Polycarp, and the Epistle to Diognetus. This list of eleven has attained somewhat of a quasi-canonical status within Apostolic Fathers studies, though a few works float in and out of the boundaries of investigations within the field.[17] Although early modern scholars tended to insist upon the direct contact of the Apostolic Fathers with the apostles, contemporary scholars recognize the phenomenon of pseudepigraphal attribution within the corpus, and they acknowledge a diverse notion of "apostolicity" within the primary source texts themselves.[18]

---

13. Andreas Gallandi, *Bibliotheca veterum partum antiquorumque scriptorium ecclesiasticorum* (Venice: Joannis Baptistae Albritii Hieron Fil., 1765).

14. Jefford, *Reading the Apostolic Fathers*, xix.

15. J. B. Lightfoot, *The Apostolic Fathers* (London: Macmillan, 1890); Theodore Zahn, *Ignatius von Antiochien* (Gotha: Friedrich Andreas Perthes, 1873). For a history of this debate, see Paul A. Hartog, "A Multifaceted Jewel: English Episcopacy, Ignatian Authenticity, and the Rise of Critical Patristic Scholarship," in Angela Ranson, André A. Gazal, and Sarah Bastow, *Defending the Faith: John Jewel and the Elizabethan Church*, Early Modern Studies Series (University Park, PA: Pennsylvania State University Press, 2018), 263–83.

16. Jefford, *Reading the Apostolic Fathers*, xiii. See Bart D. Ehrman, *The Apostolic Fathers*, 2 vols., LCL (Cambridge: Harvard University Press, 2003); Michael W. Holmes, *The Apostolic Fathers: Greek Texts and English Translations*, 3rd ed. (Grand Rapids: Baker Academic, 2007).

17. See Wilhelm Pratscher, "The Corpus of the Apostolic Fathers," in Wilhelm Pratscher (ed.), *The Apostolic Fathers: An Introduction* (Waco, TX: Baylor University Press, 2010), 1–6.

18. Taras Khomych, "Diversity of the Notion of Apostolicity in the Apostolic Fathers," in Theresia Hainthaler, Franz Mali, and Gregor Emmenegger (eds.), *Heiligkeit und Apostolizität der Kirche* (Innsbruck: Tyrolia, 2010), 63–81.

Why Are the Apostolic Fathers Important?

The works of the "Apostolic Fathers" represent a spectrum of literary genres, including a church manual (Didache), occasional letters (1 Clement, the Ignatian correspondence, Polycarp's *Epistle to the Philippians*), a theological tractate in epistolary form (Barnabas), apocalyptic and visionary materials (Hermas), a martyr narrative in epistolary form (Martyrdom of Polycarp), a homily (2 Clement), an apology with appended homiletic material (Diognetus), and fragments of both expositional and apologetic works (Papias and Quadratus).[19] The Apostolic Fathers also represent a wide range of geographical provenance and intended audience, pointing interpreters to early Christian communities in locations scattered throughout the Roman Empire, such as Corinth, Philippi, Rome, Asia Minor, Egypt, and Syria.[20]

The Apostolic Fathers reflect variegated facets of early church life and organization, theological and liturgical development, spirituality and prayer, moral instruction and identity formation.[21] The Apostolic Fathers are important witnesses to the transmission and consolidation of earlier traditions, including the reception of the scriptures (both the Hebrew Scriptures and works now found in the New Testament).[22] A number of the Apostolic Fathers draw from Jesus traditions and especially the Pauline letters.[23] For example, Papias hands on traditions concerning the origins

---

19. Simon Tugwell, *The Apostolic Fathers*, Outstanding Christian Thinkers (London: Continuum 2002); Jefford, *Reading the Apostolic Fathers*.

20. See Christine Trevett, *Christian Women and the Time of the Apostolic Fathers (AD c 80–160): Corinth, Rome and Asia Minor* (Cardiff: University of Wales Press, 2006).

21. Helmut Koester, "The Apostolic Fathers and the Struggle for Christian Identity," in Foster (ed.), *Writings of the Apostolic Fathers*, 1–12; Kenneth Berding, "'Gifts' and Ministries in the Apostolic Fathers," *WTJ* 78 (2016) 135–58; Clayton N. Jefford, "Prophecy and Prophetism in the Apostolic Fathers," in Joseph Verheyden, Korinna Zamfir, and Tobias Nicklas (eds.), *Prophets and Prophecy in Jewish and Early Christian Literature*, WUNT 2/286 (Tübingen: Mohr Siebeck, 2010), 295–316; C. F. A. Borchardt, "The Spirituality of the Apostolic Fathers," *Studia historiae ecclesiasticae* 25 (1999) 132–52.

22. Wilhelm Pratscher, "Die Rezeption des Neuen Testament bei den Apostolischen Vätern," *TLZ* 137 (2012) 139–52; Clayton N. Jefford, *The Apostolic Fathers and the New Testament* (Peabody, MA: Hendrickson, 2006); Andrew F. Gregory and Christopher M. Tuckett, *The Reception of the New Testament in the Apostolic Fathers* (Oxford: Oxford University Press, 2005); Richard A. Norris, "The Apostolic and Sub-Apostolic Writings: The New Testament and the Apostolic Fathers," in Frances M. Young, Lewis Ayres, and Andrew Louth (eds.), *The Cambridge History of Early Christian Literature* (Cambridge: Cambridge University Press, 2004), 11–14; Oxford Society of Historical Theology, *The New Testament in the Apostolic Fathers* (Oxford: Clarendon, 1905).

23. Stephen E. Young, *Jesus Tradition in the Apostolic Fathers: Their Explicit Appeals to the Words of Jesus in Light of Orality Studies*, WUNT 311 (Tübingen: Mohr Siebeck,

of the Gospels, and Polycarp seemingly provides evidence of the reception of 1 Timothy, 1 Peter, and 1 John.[24] The Apostolic Fathers provide insights into biblical interpretation, as well as valuable assistance with linguistic and philological investigations.[25]

The Apostolic Fathers do not delve deeply into philosophical theology but rather address specific pastoral concerns in particular contexts.[26] They reflect a diversity of theological perspectives and emphases, although sharing a common yet malleable core kerygma. The works assume the role of the one God as Creator and Ruler, and they proclaim Jesus Christ as the crucified, risen, and exalted Lord.[27] Relatively fewer texts discuss the Holy Spirit's continuing work in the *ekklesia*, while some warn of the continuing threats of satanic opposition.[28] The Apostolic Fathers underscore future resurrection and judgment. They center salvation in the person and work of Christ, although differing in their explanations of grace and human response.[29]

2011); Andreas Lindemann, "The Apostolic Fathers and the Synoptic Problem," in Paul Foster, Andrew F. Gregory, John S. Kloppenborg, and Joseph Verheyden (eds.), *New Studies in the Synoptic Problem* (Leuven: Peeters, 2011), 689–719; Todd D. Still and David E. Wilhite (eds.), *The Apostolic Fathers and Paul*, Pauline and Patristic Scholars in Debate 2 (London: T. & T. Clark, 2017).

24. Jonathon Lookadoo, "Polycarp, Paul, and the Letters to Timothy," *NovT* 59 (2017) 366–83; Paul A. Hartog, "The Opponents in Polycarp, *Philippians*, and 1 John," in Andrew F. Gregory and Christopher M. Tuckett (eds.), *Trajectories through the New Testament and the Apostolic Fathers* (Oxford: Oxford University Press, 2005), 375–91.

25. Joseph W. Trigg, "The Apostolic Fathers and Apologists," in J. Alan Hauser and Duane Frederick Watson (eds.), *A History of Biblical Interpretation*, vol. 1 (Grand Rapids: Eerdmans, 2003), 304–33. A valuable linguistic tool is Daniel B. Wallace, *A Reader's Lexicon of the Apostolic Fathers* (Grand Rapids: Kregel Academic, 2013).

26. J. Lawson, *A Theological and Historical Introduction to the Apostolic Fathers* (New York: Macmillan, 1961).

27. A. R. Stark, *The Christology in the Apostolic Fathers* (Chicago: University of Chicago Press, 1912); John A. McGuckin, "Christ: The Apostolic Fathers to the Third Century," in D. Jeffrey Bingham (ed.), *The Routledge Companion to Early Christian Thought* (New York: Routledge, 2010), 256–70.

28. I. Howard Marshall, "The Holy Spirit in the Apostolic Fathers," in Graham N. Stanton, Bruce W. Longenecker, and Stephen C. Barton (eds.), *The Holy Spirit and Christian Origins* (Grand Rapids: Eerdmans, 2004), 257–69; Jonathan Burke, "Satan and Demons in the Apostolic Fathers: A Minority Report, *SEÅ* 81 (2016): 127–68; Thomas J. Farrar, "Satanology and Demonology in the Apostolic Fathers: A Response to Jonathan Burke," *SEÅ* 83 (2018) 156–91.

29. Christopher Todd Bounds, "The Understanding of Grace in Selected Apostolic Fathers," StPatr 48 (2013) 351–59; Michael R. Whitenton, "After ΠΙΣΤΙΣ ΧΡΙΣΤΟΥ: Neglected Evidence from the Apostolic Fathers," *JTS* 61 (2010) 82–109; Christopher Todd Bounds, "The Doctrine of Christian Perfection in the Apostolic Fathers," *WesTJ* 42 (2007) 7–27. See also the influential but now dated Thomas F. Torrance, *The Doctrine of Grace in the Apostolic Fathers* (Edinburgh: Oliver and Boyd, 1948).

The Apostolic Fathers serve as a window into theological trajectories and themes that emerged in early Christianity. Specific developments include the incorporation of the "Two Ways" literary tradition (Didache, Barnabas), apostolic succession (1 Clement), the Eucharist as sacrifice and medicine (Didache, Ignatius), a three-fold ministry resembling monoepiscopacy (Ignatius), emphatic Sunday observance (Didache, Ignatius, Barnabas), baptism as a seal (2 Clement), stipulations concerning post-baptismal sin and repentance (Hermas), the metaphor of the church as the "soul" within the world (Diognetus), references to the "catholic church" (Ignatius, Martyrdom of Polycarp), and an incipient veneration of martyrs (Martyrdom of Polycarp). The Apostolic Fathers confronted so-called "docetic" and "judaizing" opponents (Ignatius, Polycarp), as well as pagan critics (Quadratus, Diognetus). The Apostolic Fathers illuminate differing courses of the "parting of the ways" between Judaism and Christianity.[30]

What is the Apostolic Fathers Commentary Series?

The Apostolic Fathers Commentary Series (AFCS) proposes to offer a literary and theological reading of individual works among the Apostolic Fathers corpus. Although the compositional development and textual history of some of the texts are quite complex, the series offers a literary and theological reading of the final form text in an intelligible fashion for a broad audience.

Each volume in the series will offer a similar, two-part structure. Part one will include introductory essays, and part two will consist of exegetical, theological, and historical commentary on the final-form text in a section-by-section format. In the first part, each volume will include an essay on preliminary matters, such as historical placement, provenance, and social setting; an essay on the use of scripture; and an essay on themes and theology. All volumes will offer a fresh and readable translation of the text, along with brief textual notes.

The AFCS is designed to engage historical-critical scholarship and to synthesize such material for a wide range of readers. The series will make use of international scholarship, ancient languages (with English co-translations), and primary research, aiming to elucidate the literary form of the

---

30. Thomas A. Robinson, *Ignatius of Antioch and the Parting of the Ways: Early Jewish-Christian Relations* (Peabody, MA: Hendrickson, 2009); Pierluigi Lanfranchi, "Attitudes to the Sabbath in Three Apostolic Fathers: *Didache*, Ignatius, and *Barnabas*," in Rieuwerd Buitenwerf, Harm W. Hollander, and Johannes Tromp (eds.), *Jesus, Paul, and Early Christianity*, NovTSup 130 (Leiden: Brill, 2008), 243–59.

text for students and scholars of earliest Christianity. The exegesis of AFCS will engage grammatical, rhetorical, and discourse features within the given work. In particular, the series will expansively discuss the elements relevant to theological interpretation of the texts. The AFCS thus seeks to fill a niche by offering a theological and literary reading of the Apostolic Fathers in both an economical and accessible form for a wide readership.

Paul A. Hartog
Shawn J. Wilhite
AFCS Series Editors

Foreword

IN THE PAST THREE decades the Epistle of Barnabas has stimulated a good deal of scholarly interest. At least four monographs have appeared together with a major commentary and a healthy number of articles. This, of course, barely compares with the plethora of publications on the books of the New Testament during the same time (thankfully, in many ways) but it marks a relatively fecund period in the history of *Barnabas* studies. This growth of interest may in part be explained by the fact that *Barnabas* touches, in a distinctive way, upon a subject that has witnessed a considerable renewal of interest during the same period, namely the Jewish origins of Christianity and the so-called parting of the ways. No document from the early second century seems as concerned as *Barnabas* with marking out distinctions between Jews and Christians, though he does not use these terms; and no document appears to do this in such a distinctively polemical way, while at the same time betraying a strongly Jewish character. Scholars who have concentrated on this matter have diverged considerably in their understanding of the meaning and significance of this aspect of *Barnabas*, particularly as it relates to any mooted purpose of the document, but all have had to contend with it; and many have made it the major concern of their engagement with the epistle. Discussion of this subject has inevitably led scholars to discuss *Barnabas*' hermeneutical profile, that is, how he goes about interpreting the Jewish scriptures, a subject that has also witnessed ever more intensive discussion in recent times, and about which *Barnabas* has much to say, again of a distinctive kind.

Given that, for whatever reason, the Epistle of Barnabas has elicited a good deal of comment over the past thirty years, it is an opportune time for a new commentary in English to appear. A weighty commentary in German was published in 1999 by Ferdinand Prostmeier in the HNT series, here replacing Windisch's succinct and brilliant commentary of some eighty or so years earlier, which did so much to stimulate new avenues of discussion concerning this work.[1] Prostmeier's commentary is very much a contribution for the scholarly community alone as well as being formidably long. Jonathon Lookadoo's commentary, which is the first to appear in English since R. A. Kraft's publication of 1965,[2] is learned (his reading in the scholarship on *Barnabas* is extensive, as is his knowledge of relevant subjects in the wider Christian and Jewish world) but one that is both more accessible and considerably shorter than Prostmeier's, and should therefore do much to familiarise a wider audience with the striking contents of this early piece of Christian literature.

Lookadoo, who has already written extensively on the so-called Apostolic Fathers, in whose collection *Barnabas* is traditionally placed, writes in an uncluttered style. His introduction covers the usual ground effectively and succinctly, adopting a measured view of what can be said about the date and provenance of *Barnabas*. He includes helpful discussions of both the text of *Barnabas* as well as of its theology, especially as this manifests itself in Barnabas' view of scripture, which he quite rightly places at the center of the epistle's concerns. By and large Lookadoo sees the text as a letter and emphasizes its argumentative coherence over against a developed tendency in the history of scholarship to see signs of interpolation or certainly of an underdeveloped and disjoined structure. In this context one might point in particular to his discussion of the transition between chapter 14 and 15, and the so-called Two Ways section as this is introduced in chapter 17. Following the work of Hvalvik and Rhodes, he is able to show the way in which the language and atmosphere of the Two Ways pervades the whole text, and to argue against the view that chapters 18 to 20 are a kind of add on or afterthought.[3]

Lookadoo's commentary is not driven by an overarching thesis about the purpose of the text he is discussing and, strikingly, he avoids detailed discussion of that subject in his introduction. At one point he notes that "(t)he letter appears to be written for multiple purposes"; and he sees these as bound up both with a desire to promote covenantal faithfulness, understood here in ethical terms, as well as a need to oppose what the author takes to be false interpreters of the Jewish scriptures. These opponents he assumes to be Jews, though he never discusses how Barnabas understood his own identity, that is, did the author of the epistle think of himself as non-Jewish? Or put another way, Lookadoo never states explicitly whether Barnabas assumes a debate with his opponents which is *intra muros* or *extra muros*. This is, of

---

1. Prostmeier, *Barnabasbrief*; Windisch, *Barnabasbrief*.
2. Kraft, *Barnabas*.
3. Hvalvik, *Struggle for Scripture and Covenant*; Rhodes, "Two Ways Tradition."

course, a complex matter, made more so by Barnabas' failure to use either the word "Christian" or "Jew," preferring what Lookadoo calls "pronominal deictic markers," or the terms "them" and "us."

Lookadoo's view of multiple purposes for the epistle is in many ways a sensible one and reflects different strains in the history of the epistle's interpretation. Rhodes' view that *Barnabas* is a "Deuteronomistic" work in which the author uses the example of the Jews to warn Christians from moral backsliding is an extreme version of the more ethically oriented view of the epistle; but it certainly has the advantage of taking seriously both the heavy emphasis on moral interpretations of the Torah, which are the other side of *Barnabas*' attack upon false interpretations, and the broadly non-polemical content of the opening and closing chapters of the epistle.[4] Although the polemical side of the work is striking and remains, as already stated, the main ground for scholars' ongoing interest in the epistle (an interest, intriguingly, not reflected in the ancient reception of the work, which Lookadoo highlights in his introduction), it probably should not be emphasized at the expense of the rest of its content. Indeed, the fact that Lookadoo eschews an exclusive view of the epistle's purpose helps him in his effort to present a more rounded commentary in which the epistle's variegated theological implications can be examined and in which its individual arguments can be explained without having to be placed within the shade of an overarching thesis about the document's origins.

Lookadoo emphasizes a number of features of the epistle. *Barnabas* is in many ways a soteriological work with a strong emphasis on the means by which those he is addressing have been redeemed. Christ's death as well as his incarnation are focal concerns in this respect, as is baptism as the means by which the benefits of those events are mediated to Christians. Christians as a result are the new covenantal people, and the concept of the covenant plays a strikingly significant role in the epistle (in fact, the concept appears far more frequently in *Barnabas* than anywhere else in the writings of the Apostolic Fathers). As the covenant people, Christians are obliged to behave ethically, in contrast to Israel in the wilderness when they worshipped the golden calf (in this context Lookadoo interprets the use of the golden calf incident in chapter 4 as primarily a warning to ethically complacent Christians), and according to *Barnabas*, in a piece of extra-scriptural innovation, forfeited their covenantal status.

Related to an emphasis on soteriology and ethics is the importance for the author of eschatology. *Barnabas* sees the present times as critical (Lookadoo is ambivalent as to whether this is the result of events associated

---

4. Rhodes, *Epistle of Barnabas*.

with the Bar Kokhba revolt, though he seems clear that a Hadrianic date for the epistle best accounts for the reference to a building of a temple in Jerusalem, either pagan or Jewish, in 16.3-4). Although Barnabas is keen to emphasize the present benefits of redemption, even utilizing exodic vocabulary in this vein, he is clear that ultimate salvation is in the future as becomes especially clear in chapter 4 and chapter 15. Connected with the epistle's emphasis on eschatology, Lookadoo notes how language of what one might term an apocalyptic kind permeates the letter, and can be said to unite different facets of the text's theology.

Significant in this context is the language of revelation. Correctly Lookadoo notes that the center of revelation is the incarnation, in which God is revealed through Christ. Such a revelation has as one of its most significant consequences the fact that Christians now understand scripture, conceived of by Barnabas, in broad terms at least, as what Christians came to call the Old Testament. This is not surprising as scripture has as its central referent Jesus and so commitment to Jesus will necessarily lead to a right understanding of scriptural texts; and as Lookadoo shows, it is scriptural texts and their interpretation that dominate the epistle, giving it a strikingly hermeneutical aspect. But the tone is not blandly instructive. As Lookadoo notes: "The scriptural discourse in Barnabas functions as a social identity marker by which Barnabas separates his audience from his opponents. As a result of their understanding of scripture, Barnabas and his readers are set apart from other mistaken readers of the Jewish scriptures as a distinct community of covenantal heirs." *Barnabas* achieves this by what Lookadoo terms the use of pronominal deictic markers, that is, the use of language related to "us" and "them," with "them," because of their failure to embrace Christ, constantly incapable of interpreting the scriptures as they should be, whether that relates to an apprehension of their Christocentricity or a clear and proper understanding of the Torah, which involves an understanding of the non-literal meaning of prescriptions held by Jews to have a literal meaning (e.g., language relating to the temple and sacrifice, circumcision and the sabbath, etc.). In seeking to achieve this, *Barnabas* adopts a distinctive position in two ways. First, in spite of his Christocentricity and in spite of his mention of a law of Christ at 2.6, Barnabas never directly, as is the case with Paul, aligns his view of the Torah with Christ. This is linked to what Lookadoo emphasizes at a number of points and has always been at the center of Barnabean studies, namely that Barnabas does not think that the Torah, as seen through its ritual prescriptions, should ever have been interpreted literally. Interestingly, Lookadoo never attempts to show whether this was a position that originated with *Barnabas* or was inherited, though his commentary contains discussions of parallels to *Barnabas*' hermeneutical assumptions as these relate to the law, especially as we find these in the *Letter of Ptolemy to Flora*, though ultimately and rightly, Lookadoo is clear that there are differences between these two texts. I say "interestingly" because ever since the work of Windisch, which was greatly extended by R. A. Kraft and by other means, by Klaus Wengst, scholars have wanted to see *Barnabas* as little more than the tradent of sources, a view that is supported, apparently, by, inter alia, his reference at 1.5 where he talks about handing on what he has received, and by the possibility that some of his combination of scriptural texts imply access to pre-existing testimony collections.[5] Lookadoo alludes to the latter point but nowhere deals with the admittedly murky question of *Barnabas'* originality. The question is not easily resolvable, however, and given Lookadoo's concern to follow the arguments of *Barnabas* as closely as possible and make sense of the letter's structure, such a concern would have greatly lengthened the commentary and detracted from its major aim to elucidate the contents of the epistle.

One other reason for thinking that Barnabas used sources lies in his use of the so-called Two Ways tradition, especially as we find this in chapters 18–20. Lookadoo accepts that Barnabas is making use of a well-known Jewish tradition, also witnessed in Christian sources such as the Didache and Apostolic Constitutions, but rather than becoming caught up in a dull debate about how, for instance, *Barnabas* relates to the Didache, he spends more time showing how this section of the epistle, often thought of as something that was slapped on at the end without real reference to what precedes, informs other parts of the epistle, especially *Barnabas'* concern with "a way of righteousness," which is present right at the beginning of the text, and encourages the idea of covenantal faithfulness. In the same context, Lookadoo is keen to show how the Two Ways informs *Barnabas'* attempt to separate this people from another people. As he writes: "Although Barnabas does not mention Israel in 18.1—20.2 and employs traditional forms that are used without reference to Israel elsewhere in early Christian literature, he associates the way of light with the audience and himself, while connecting the opponents to the way of darkness. Israel's idolatry that was typified at Sinai has resulted in them walking along the path of darkness under the influence of Satan's angels and the ruler of the present age." In part, then, the Two Ways section of the epistle becomes an extension of elements of *Barnabas'* polemic, a point that emerges from a careful reading from within the epistle, without any need to refer to externals.

The many riddles and difficulties that are raised by the Epistle of Barnabas will never be solved, though reflection upon them will continue

---

5. Windisch, *Barnabasbrief*; Kraft, *Barnabas*; Wengst, *Tradition und Theologie*.

to prove stimulating. Lookadoo's commentary, the first to appear in English for almost sixty years, adopts a suitably sober view of what can and cannot be established about this text. Learned, thoughtful, betraying good knowledge of a wide range of sources, it will be an excellent starting point from which to study a text that Philipp Vielhauer described as the strangest document to emerge from early Christianity.

James Carleton Paget
January 13th, 2022

Preface

WRITING A COMMENTARY PRESENTS a unique set of challenges as one seeks to offer a clear interpretation that enables readers to engage usefully with the text under discussion. While attempting to comment on the Epistle of Barnabas, I have been fortunate to receive help along the way in multiple forms and from various corners.

I am grateful to Paul Hartog and Shawn Wilhite for the invitation to participate in the Apostolic Fathers Commentary Series and for the editorial support that they have offered to me along the way. It has been an immensely rewarding experience to pore over the Epistle of Barnabas, to consider its intricate scriptural interpretations, and to engage with the scholarly literature on the topic. The book is better as a result of the encouragement, suggestions, and advice that both Paul and Shawn have given.

Thank you to James Carleton Paget for his interest in my commentary and for his willingness to contribute the foreword to the book. I am grateful to be the beneficiary both of his prodigious scholarship on the Epistle of Barnabas and of the much-needed aid that he provided to a junior researcher.

I would like to say thanks as well to Robin Parry for his keen editorial attention. It is a pleasure to work with you again. The team at Cascade Books has been a model of generosity, timeliness, and professionalism that I have appreciated throughout the publication process.

This book would not have been possible without the Presbyterian University and Theological Seminary in Seoul. In addition to providing me with a wonderful environment in which to teach and conduct research, I very much appreciate the staff at the PUTS library who have contributed to this book by maintaining a strong collection in the stacks, by carefully considering my sometimes disparate purchase requests, and by quickly obtaining hard-to-find resources through Interlibrary Loan.

Finally, the humor, support, and thoughtfulness of my family in Korea and in the US has sustained me not only in the writing process but in all areas of life. While studying the Epistle of Barnabas with its thoroughgoing interest in biblical texts, chats with my brother, Joel, about scripture, education, and the Christian life have come repeatedly to mind. I have been sharpened during these discussions, and the book is dedicated to him with such conversations in mind.

Jonathon Lookadoo
Seoul
All Saints' Day 2021

Abbreviations

1. Ancient

Acts Barn.	Acts of Barnabas
Acts John	Acts of John
Adv. Jud.	Tertullian, *Adversus Judaeos*
Agr.	Philo, *De agricultura*
A.J.	Josephus, *Antiquitates judaicae*
Antichr.	Hippolytus, *De Christo et Antichristo*
Apoc. Ab.	Apocalypse of Abraham
Apos. Con.	Apostolic Constitutions
Apol.	*Apology*
Autol.	Theophilus, *Ad Autolycum*
b. Ned.	Babylonian Talmud, Nedarim
b. Yoma	Babylonian Talmud, Yoma
2 Bar.	2 Baruch
Barn.	*Epistle of Barnabas*
B.J.	Josephus, *Bellum judaicum*
C. Ap.	Josephus, *Contra Apionem*
C. Gent.	Athanasius, *Contra Gentes*
Cels.	Origen, *Contra Celsum*
1 Clem.	1 Clement
2 Clem.	2 Clement
Comm. Dan.	Hippolytus, *Commentarium in Danielem*
Comm. Jo.	Origen, *Commentarium in evangelium Joannis*

Congr.	Philo, *De congressu eruditionis gratia*
Cor.	Tertullian, *De corona militis*
Decal.	Philo, *De decalogo*
Dial.	Justin, *Dialogus cum Tryphone*
Did.	Didache
Didasc.	*Didascalia*
Diogn.	Epistle to Diognetus
Doctr.	*Doctrina apostolorum*
1 En.	1 Enoch
2 En.	2 Enoch
Epid.	Irenaeus, *Epideixis tou apostolikou kērygmatos*
Flor.	Ptolemy, *Epistula ad Floram*
Fort.	Cyprian, *Ad Fortunatum*
frag.	fragment
Fug.	Philo, *De fuga et inventione*
Gen. an.	*De generatione animalium*
Gen. Rab.	Genesis Rabbah
Gos. Pet.	Gospel of Peter
Gos. Thom.	Gospel of Thomas
Haer.	Irenaeus, *Adversus haereses*
Her.	Philo, *Quis rerum divinarum heres sit*
Herm. *Mand.*	Shepherd of Hermas, *Mandate(s)*
Herm. *Sim.*	Shepherd of Hermas, *Similitude(s)*
Herm. *Vis.*	Shepherd of Hermas, *Vision(s)*
Hist.	Dio Cassius, *Historia romana*
Hist. eccl.	Eusebius, *Historia ecclesiastica*
Hom. Jes. Nav.	Origen, *In Jesu Nave homiliae*
Ign. *Eph.*	Ignatius, *To the Ephesians*
Ign. *Magn.*	Ignatius, *To the Magnesians*
Ign. *Phld.*	Ignatius, *To the Philadelphians*
Ign. *Pol.*	Ignatius, *To Polycarp*
Ign. *Rom.*	Ignatius, *To the Romans*
Ign. *Smyrn.*	Ignatius, *To the Smyrnaeans*

Ign. *Trall.*	Ignatius, *To the Trallians*
In Metaph.	Alexander of Aphrodisias, *In Aristotelis* Metaphysica *Commentaria*
Inst.	Lactantius, *Divinarum institutionum libri VII*
Jub	Jubilees
Ker. Petr.	Kerygma Petri
LAB	*Liber antiquitatum biblicarum*
Leg.	Philo, *Legum allegoriae*
Let. Aris.	Letter of Aristeas
LXX	Septuagint
m. 'Abot	Mishnah 'Abot
m. Menaḥ.	Mishnah Menaḥot
m. Yoma	Mishnah Yoma
Marc.	Tertullian, *Adversus Marcionem*
Mart. Ascen. Isa.	Martyrdom and Ascension of Isaiah
Mart. Pol.	Martyrdom of Polycarp
Mem.	Xenophon, *Memorabilia*
Metam.	Ovid, *Metamorphoses*
Migr.	Philo, *De migratione Abrahami*
Mos.	Philo, *De vita Mosis*
MT	Masoretic Text
Nat.	Pliny the Elder, *Naturalis historia*
Nat. an.	Aelian, *De natura animalium*
Odes Sol.	Odes of Solomon
Op.	Hesiod, *Opera et dies*
Opif.	Philo, *De opificio mundi*
Or. Graec.	Tatian, *Oratio ad Graecos*
P.Berol.	Papyrus Berolinensis
P.Fay.	Papyrus Fayum
P.Flor.	Papyrus Florentia
P.Oxy.	Papyrus Oxyrhynchus
P.Rein.	Papyrus Reinach
Paed.	Clement of Alexandria, *Paedagogus*

Pasch.	Melito, *Peri Pascha*
Physio.	*Physiologus*
Pol. *Phil.*	Polycarp, *To the Philippians*
Praem.	Philo, *De praemiis et poenis*
Praep. ev.	Eusebius, *Praeparatio evangelica*
Prax.	Tertullian, *Adversus Praxean*
Princ.	Origen, *De principiis*
Ps.-Clem. *Hom.*	Pseudo-Clement, *Homilies*
Ps.-Clem. *Rec.*	Pseudo-Clement, *Recognitions*
Pud.	Tertullian, *De pudicitia*
QG	Philo, *Quaestiones et solutiones in Genesin*
Rust.	Varro, *De re rustica*
Sacr.	Philo, *De sacrificiis Abelis et Caini*
Sib. Or.	Sibylline Oracles
Spec.	Philo, *De specialibus legibus*
Strom.	Clement of Alexandria, *Stromateis*
T. Ash.	Testament of Asher
T. Benj.	Testament of Benjamin
T. Jos.	Testament of Joseph
T. Levi	Testament of Levi
Tab. Ceb.	*Tabula Cebetis*
Tg. Ps.-J.	*Targum Pseudo-Jonathan*
Trad. ap.	*Traditio apostolica*
Vir.	Jerome, *De viris illustribus*
Zach.	Didymus the Blind, *Commentarii in Zachariam*

2. Modern

AFCS	Apostolic Fathers Commentary Series
AGJU	Arbeiten zur Geschichte des antiken Judentums und des Urchristentums
AKG	Arbeiten zur Kirchengeschichte
ANRW	Aufstieg und Niedergang der römischen Welt

ANTC	Abingdon New Testament Commentaries
BAC	Biblioteca de autores cristianos
BASP	*Bulletin of the American Society of Papyrologists*
BETL	Bibliotheca Ephemeridum Theologicarum Lovaniensium
BETS	*Bulletin of the Evangelical Theological Society*
BFCT	Beiträge zur Förderung christlicher Theologie
BG	Biblische Gestalten
BHT	Beiträge zur historischen Theologie
Bib	*Biblica*
BMSEC	Baylor-Mohr Siebeck Studies in Early Christianity
BNTC	Black's New Testament Commentaries
BRLA	Brill Reference Library of Judaism
BSGRT	Bibliotheca Scriptorum Graecorum et Romanorum Teubneriana
BTB	*Biblical Theology Bulletin*
BWA(N)T	Beiträge zur Wissenschaft vom Alten (und Neuen) Testament
BZNW	Beihefte zur Zeitschrift für die neutestamentliche Wissenschaft
CAG	Commentaria in Aristotelem Graeca
CanCul	*Canon & Culture*
CBQ	*Catholic Biblical Quarterly*
CCSA	Corpus Christianorum: Series Apocryphorum
CRINT	Compendia Rerum Iudaicarum ad Novum Testamentum
CSCD	Cambridge Studies in Christian Doctrine
CSCO	Corpus Scriptorum Christianorum Orientalium
CSEL	Corpus Scriptorum Ecclesiasticorum Latinorum
CUASEC	CUA Studies in Early Christianity
EC	*Early Christianity*
ECAM	Early Christianity in Asia Minor
EKK	Evangelisch-katholischer Kommentar zum Neuen Testament
ESCJ	Études sur le christianisme et le judaïsme
ÉTH	*Études de Théologie Historique*

EvQ	*Evangelical Quarterly*
FKDG	Forschungen zur Kirchen- und Dogmengeschichte
FO	*Folia Orientalia*
FonChr	Fontes Christiani
FRLA(N)T	Forschungen zur Religion und Literatur des Alten (und Neuen) Testaments
GCS	Die griechischen christlichen Schriftsteller der ersten (drei) Jahrhunderte
GSECP	Gorgias Studies in Early Christianity and Patristics
HNT	Handbuch zum Neuen Testament
HTR	*Harvard Theological Review*
IDS	*In die Skriflig*
IkaZ	*Internationale katholische Zeitschrift*
JBL	*Journal of Biblical Literature*
JBTS	*Journal of Biblical and Theological Studies*
JEA	*Journal of Egyptian Archaeology*
JECS	*Journal of Early Christian Studies*
JETS	*Journal of the Evangelical Theological Society*
JJS	*Journal of Jewish Studies*
JP	*Journal of Philology*
JSNT	*Journal for the Study of the New Testament*
JSP	*Journal for the Study of the Pseudepigrapha*
JSPSup	Journal for the Study of the Pseudepigrapha Supplement Series
JTS	*Journal of Theological Studies*
KAV	Kommentar zu den apostolischen Vätern
KfA	Kommentar zu frühchristlichen Apologeten
KNTS	*Korean New Testament Studies*
LBRS	Lexham Bible Reference Series
LCL	Loeb Classical Library
LNTS	The Library of New Testament Studies
LSTS	The Library of Second Temple Studies
MH	*Museum Helveticum*
MVS	Menighedsfakultetets Videnskabelige Serie
Neot	*Neotestamentica*

NHS	Nag Hammadi Studies
NovT	*Novum Testamentum*
NovTSup	Supplements to Novum Testamentum
NTGF	New Testament in the Greek Fathers
NTOA	Novum Testamentum et Orbis Antiquus
NTS	*New Testament Studies*
NTTS	New Testament Tools and Studies
NTTSD	New Testament Tools, Studies, and Documents
OECT	Oxford Early Christian Texts
OrChr	*Oriens Christianus*
OrChr NS	*Oriens Christianus* New Series
OSTLT	Oxford Studies in Typology and Linguistic Theory
OTLing	Oxford Textbooks in Linguistics
PPS	Popular Patristics Series
PPSD	Pauline and Patristic Scholars in Debate
PTS	Patristische Texte und Studien
RB	*Revue biblique*
RHPR	*Revue d'histoire et de philosophie religieuses*
RQ	*Römische Quartalschrift für christliche Altertumskunde und Kirchengeschichte*
RTL	*Revue théologique de Louvain*
SAC	Studies in Antiquity and Christianity
SAPERE	Scripta Antiquitatis Posterioris ad Ethicam REligionemque pertinentia
SBLDS	Society of Biblical Literature Dissertation Series
SBLSBS	Society of Biblical Literature Sources for Biblical Study
SBR	Studies of the Bible and Its Reception
SBS	Stuttgarter Bibelstudien
SC	Sources chrétiennes
SCJ	Studies in Christianity and Judaism
SCS	Septuagint and Cognate Studies
SEÅ	*Svensk exegetisk årsbok*
SecCent	*Second Century*
SIJD	Schriften des Institutum Judaicum Delitzchianum

SJLA	Studies in Judaism in Late Antiquity
SLAG	Schriften der Luther-Agricola-Gesellschaft
SNTSMS	Society for New Testament Studies Monograph Series
SR	*Studies in Religion*
SSR	*Studi storico-religiosi*
StPatr	Studia Patristica
StPB	Studia Post-biblica
SUC	Schriften des Urchristentums
SVTG	Septuaginta Vetus Testamentum Graecum
SVTP	Studia in Veteris Testamenti Pseudepigraphica
TBN	Themes in Biblical Narrative
TC	Traditio Christiana
TDÉHC	Textes et documents pour l'étude historique du Christianisme
ThQ	*Theologische Quartalschrift*
TENTS	Texts and Editions for New Testament Study
TRE	*Theologische Realenzyklopädie*
TS	Texts and Studies
TU	Texte und Untersuchungen
TUGAL	Texte und Untersuchungen zur Geschichte der altchristlichen Literatur
UTB	Uni-Taschenbücher
VAWJ	Veröffentlichungen der Akademie für die Wissenschaft des Judentums
VC	*Vigiliae Christianae*
VCSup	Supplements to Vigiliae Christianae
VT	*Vetus Testamentum*
WUNT	Wissenschaftliche Untersuchungen zum Neuen Testament
ZAC	*Zeitschrift für antikes Christentum*
ZNW	*Zeitschrift für die neutestamentliche Wissenschaft und die Kunde der älteren Kirche*
ZWT	*Zeitschrift für wissenschaftliche Theologie*

Translation of the Epistle of Barnabas

1

1. Greetings in peace, sons and daughters, in the name of the Lord who loved us.

2. Since God's requirements are great and rich toward you, more than anything I am exuberantly and excessively overjoyed over your blessed and glorious spirits. You have thus received the implanted grace of the spiritual gift.

3. For this reason, I also rejoice all the more in myself, hoping to be saved because I truly see in you the Spirit that has been poured out on you from the wealth of the Lord's spring. I was thus overwhelmed on your account by the desire to see you.

4. Therefore, I have been convinced of this and have become aware that, having said many things among you, I know that the Lord travels together with me in the way of righteousness. I am also completely compelled to this—to love you more than my own soul because great faith and love indwell you in the hope of his life.

5. So, when I reckoned that there will also be a reward for me because I minister to such spirits, if I was concerned enough about you to send part of what I received, I hurried to send you a short piece so that you might have perfect knowledge with your faith.

6. There are, then, three doctrines of the Lord: the hope of life, which is the beginning and end of our faith; righteousness, which is the beginning and end of judgement; and love of gladness and exultation, which is a witness of works in righteousness.

7. For through the prophets the Master made known to us things that are past and present, and has given us a taste of the firstfruits of the things that will come. As we see how things are being effected one after the

8. I, then—not as a teacher but as one of you—point out a few things through which you will be glad about present matters.

2

1. Because the days are evil and the one who is working has authority, we ought to be on the alert and seek the requirements of the Lord.
2. The aides of our faith, then, are fear and endurance, and our allies are patience and self-control.
3. Accordingly, when these things remain in purity in matters related to the Lord, wisdom, understanding, intelligence, and knowledge rejoice with them.
4. For he has revealed to us through all the prophets that he does not need sacrifices, whole burnt offerings, or general offerings. For he said somewhere,
5. "'What is your multitude of offerings to me?' says the Lord. 'I am full of your burnt offerings and the fat of lambs. I do not want the blood of bulls and goats—not even if you come to appear before me. For who sought these things from your hands? Do not continue to trample my court. If you bring fine wheat flower or futile incense, it is an abomination to me. I have had it with your new moons and sabbaths.'"
6. Therefore, he destroyed these things in order that the new law of our Lord Jesus Christ, which is without the yoke of compulsion, might have an offering that is not made by human beings.
7. But it says somewhere to them, "'Did I command your ancestors to offer whole burnt offerings and sacrifices to me when I brought them out of the land of Egypt?'
8. Instead I commanded them, 'Let none of you remember an evil deed in their heart against a neighbor, and do not love a false oath.'"
9. Therefore, because we do not lack understanding of our Father's good purpose, we ought to notice that he speaks to us and wants us to seek how we should bring him an offering while not being deceived like them.
10. He thus speaks to us in this way, "A sacrifice to God is a broken heart; a sweet fragrance before the Lord is a heart that glorifies the one who

has formed it." We ought then to be accurate, brothers and sisters, concerning our salvation in order that the evil one not sling us away from our life by planting deceit in us.

3

1. Then he speaks again to them about these things: "'Why do you fast to me,' says the Lord, 'so that your voice is heard shouting today. I did not choose this fast,' says the Lord, 'not a person humbling their soul.

2. Not even if you bow your neck like a ring and wear sackcloth and sit in ashes—not even then will I call the fast acceptable.'"

3. But to us he says, "'Behold, this is the fast that I have chosen,' says the Lord. 'Break the bond of injustice. Break up the bonds of violent agreements. Send the oppressed out in freedom, and tear apart every unjust contract. Break your bread for the hungry, and, if you see someone naked, clothe that person. Bring the homeless into your house, and, if you see someone humiliated, do not overlook them—neither you nor anyone from the household of your child.'

4. Then your light will break forth like the dawn, and your garments will rise up quickly. Righteousness will go before you, and the glory of God will clothe you.

5. Then you will cry out, and God will hear you; while you are still speaking, he will say, 'Behold, I am here'—if you remove every bond, threatening gesture, and word of grumbling and give your bread to the hungry from your soul and have mercy on the soul that has been humiliated."

6. Therefore, brothers and sisters, the one who is patient looked ahead to this—how the people whom he prepared for his beloved will believe in innocence—and revealed to us beforehand concerning all things in order that we might not be broken to pieces against that law like the proselytes.

4

1. Therefore, we ought to seek the things that can save us by extensively investigating present matters. Let us flee completely, therefore, from all works of lawlessness lest the works of lawlessness overtake us. Let

us hate the deceit of the present age in order that we can be loved in the coming age.

2. Let us not give relief to our own soul so that it has license to consort with sinners and those who are evil, lest we become like them.

3. The final stumbling block has drawn near, concerning which it is written, as Enoch says, "For the Master has cut short the ages and days for this reason, that his beloved will be quick and will come into the inheritance."

4. And so also the prophet says, "Ten kings will rule over the earth, and a small king will arise after them who will humiliate three of the kings at once."

5. Daniel likewise says about this, "And I saw the fourth beast, evil and strong and worse than all of the beasts of the sea, and how ten horns rose up from it, and a small horn from them—an offshoot—and how it humbled three of the great horns at once."

6. Therefore, you ought to understand. Moreover, I ask you as one of you, who loves you all more than my own life, to be on the alert for yourselves and not to be like some by accumulating your sins, saying that the covenant remains ours.

7. But they lost it completely in this way, even though Moses already received it. For scripture says, "And Moses was on the mountain fasting forty days and forty nights, and he received the covenant from the Lord—stone tablets that had been written by the finger of the Lord's hand."

8. But when they turned to idols, they lost it. For the Lord says this, "Moses, Moses, go down quickly because your people, whom you led out of the land of Egypt, broke the law." And Moses understood and threw the two tablets out of his hand. The covenant was broken so that the covenant of his beloved Jesus might be sealed into our heart in the hope of his faithfulness.

9. Although desiring to write many things—not as a teacher but as is fitting for someone who does not like to leave out anything that we have—I, your devoted servant, hurried to write to you. Consequently, let us be on the alert in the last days. For all the time of our faith will not benefit us at all unless we resist the coming stumbling blocks now in the lawless age, as is fitting for children of God, so that the Black One does not have an opportunity to sneak in.

10. Let us flee from all futility. Let us hate completely the works of the evil way. Do not retire within yourselves and live alone like you were already justified. Instead, as you meet together in the same place, seek for what is beneficial to the common good.

11. For scripture says, "Woe to those who are understanding in their own view and those who are wise in their own presence." Let us be spiritual. Let us be a complete temple to God. In as much as we can, let us attend to the fear of God and let us struggle to keep his commandments in order that we can rejoice in his requirements.

12. The Lord will judge the world without favoritism. Each will receive just as they have done. If it is good, their righteousness will precede them. If it is evil, the wage of evil is before them.

13. As if we who are called have reason to rest, let us not fall asleep in our sins, lest the evil ruler take authority over us and push us away from the kingdom of the Lord.

14. Moreover, consider this as well, my brothers and sisters. Whenever you see that, after such great signs and wonders have happened in Israel and they are thus forsaken, let us be on the alert lest we be found, as it is written, "many are called, but few are chosen."

5

1. For it was for this reason that the Lord endured to give his flesh up to corruption, so that we might be cleansed by forgiveness of sins, which is by the sprinkling of his blood.

2. For some things are written about him to Israel, others to us. And it says thus: "He was wounded because of our lawless deeds and was afflicted because of our sins. By his wound we are healed. He was led before the slaughter like a sheep and like a lamb was silent before his shearer."

3. So then we ought to be extraordinarily thankful to the Lord that he has made known to us things that are past, has made us wise in things that are present, and we are not without understanding into things that are coming.

4. Now the scripture says, "Nets are not unjustly spread out for birds." This means that a person dies justly who mixes themselves into the way of darkness even though they have knowledge of the way of righteousness.

5. Moreover, my brothers and sisters, if the Lord endured to suffer for our soul even though he was Lord of all creation—the one to whom God said at the establishment of the world, "Let us make human beings in our image and likeness"—how then did he endure to suffer at the hands of people? Learn.

6. The prophets had grace from him, and they prophesied about him. But he himself endured in order that he might make death ineffective and exhibit resurrection from the dead since he had to be revealed in the flesh,

7. and he endured in order that he might make good on the promise to the ancestors and show, while he was on the earth and preparing the new people for himself, that he will judge when he enacts the resurrection.

8. In addition, by teaching Israel and doing such great wonders and signs, he preached and loved them exceedingly.

9. And when he chose his own apostles who were about to preach his gospel—they who were more lawless than all sin so that he could show that he did not come to call the righteous but sinners—then he revealed himself to be Son of God.

10. For if he did not come in the flesh, how would people ever be saved by seeing him? When they look at the sun, which will not exist and is a work of his hands, they are not able to look directly at its beams.

11. So then, the Son of God came in the flesh for this reason: to bring the completion of sins together for those who persecuted his prophets to death.

12. So then, he endured for this reason. For God says that the bruise of his flesh is from them: "Whenever they strike their own shepherd, then the sheep of the flock are destroyed."

13. But he wanted to suffer in this way. For it was necessary that he suffer on a tree. For the prophet says about him, "Spare my soul from the sword" and "Pierce my flesh because a synagogue of evildoers have risen up against me."

14. And again he says, "Behold, I have offered my back for lashes and my cheeks for blows, but I have set my face like a solid rock."

6

1. Then when he gave the commandment, what does he say? "Who is the one who judges me? Let that one oppose me. Or who is the one who justifies me? Let that one draw near to the Lord's servant.

2. Woe to you because you all will grow old like a garment and moth will consume you." And again, since he was set like a mighty stone to crush, the prophet says, "Behold, I will put into the foundations of Zion a cornerstone that is costly, chosen, and precious."

3. Then what does it say? "And the one who will hope on him will live forever." Is our hope then on a stone? By no means. But he says this, since the Lord established his flesh in strength. For he says, "And he established me like a solid rock."

4. Now the prophet says again, "The stone that the builders rejected, this became the head of the corner." And again it says, "This is the great and marvelous day that the Lord has made."

5. I, a devoted servant of your love, write to you more simply in order that you may understand.

6. What, then, does the prophet say again? "A synagogue of evildoers surrounded me. They surrounded me like bees around honeycomb, and they cast lots for my clothing."

7. Therefore, as he was about to be revealed and to suffer in the flesh, the suffering was revealed beforehand. For the prophet says about Israel, "Woe to their soul because they take wicked counsel against themselves, saying, 'Let us bind the righteous one because that one is useless to us.'"

8. What does the other prophet, Moses, say to them? "'Behold,' thus says the Lord God, 'enter into the good land which the Lord swore to Abraham, Isaac, and Jacob, and inherit it, a land flowing with milk and honey.'"

9. Now what does knowledge say? Learn. "'Hope,' it says, 'on Jesus who is about to be revealed to you in the flesh.'" For a human being is suffering earth, since the formation of Adam came from the face of the earth.

10. What, therefore, does "into the good land, a land flowing with milk honey" mean? Blessed is our Lord, brothers and sisters, who has set the wisdom and understanding of his secrets in us. For the prophet

speaks a parable of the Lord: "Who will understand except the one who is wise and understanding and loves their Lord?"

11. Therefore, since he renewed us by the forgiveness of sins, he made us into a different model so that we may have the soul of children, as indeed he is reforming us.

12. For scripture speaks about us when he says to the Son, "Let us make human beings in our image and likeness, and let them rule over the beasts of the earth and the birds of the air and the fish of the sea." And when he saw our good formation, the Lord said, "Increase and multiply and fill the earth." He said these things to the Son.

13. I will show you again how the Lord speaks to us. He made a second formation at the end of all times. Now the Lord says, "Behold, I am making the last things as the first things." Therefore, it was for this reason that the prophet proclaimed, "Enter into the land flowing with milk and honey, and rule over it."

14. See, now, we are being reformed just as it says again in another prophet, "'Behold,' says the Lord, 'I will extract stony hearts from them'"—that is, from those whom the Spirit of the Lord saw beforehand—"'and I will place fleshly hearts within.'" For he was about to be revealed in the flesh and to dwell among us.

15. For the habitat of our heart, my brothers and sisters, is a holy temple to the Lord.

16. For the Lord says again, "And how will I appear to the Lord my God and glorify him?" He says, "I will confess you in the congregation of my brothers and sisters, and I will psalm you in the midst of the congregation of the saints." Therefore, we are those whom he led into the good land.

17. What, then, are the milk and honey? Since the child is first made alive by honey then milk, so also, therefore, when we are made alive by the faith of the promise and the word, we live ruling over the earth.

18. Now it said above, "Let them increase and multiply and rule over the fish." Who, then, is the one who is presently able to rule over the beasts, the fish, or the birds of heaven? For we ought to perceive that "to rule" is characterized by authority so that someone giving commands is the master.

19. Therefore, if this is not the case presently, then he has told us when it will be: whenever we ourselves are completed to become heirs of the covenant.

7

1. So then, children of gladness, understand that the good Lord has revealed all things to us beforehand in order that we may know to whom we ought to give thanks and praise in all things.

2. Therefore, if the Son of God, although he was Lord and about to judge the living and the dead, died so that his wound could make us alive, we ought to believe that the Son of God could not suffer except on our account.

3. Moreover, when he was crucified he was drinking sour wine and gall. Hear how the priests of the temple have revealed something about this. When the commandment was written that "whoever does not keep the fast will certainly die," the Lord commanded it because he himself was about to offer the vessel of the spirit as a sacrifice for our sins to complete the model that was made when Isaac was offered on the altar.

4. What, then, does it say in the prophet? "And let them eat of the goat that was offered in the fast for all sins." Pay careful attention. "And let all the priests alone eat the unwashed intestines with sour wine."

5. Why? "Because you are about to give me gall with sour wine, even though I am about to offer my flesh for the sins of my new people, you alone eat while the people fast and lament in sackcloth." This was to show that it was necessary for him to suffer at their hands.

6. Pay attention to the things that were commanded. "Take two goats—fine and alike—and offer them and let the priest receive one as a whole burnt offering for sins."

7. But what do they do with the other? "That one is cursed." Pay attention to how the model of Jesus is revealed.

8. "And all of you shall spit on the goat and pierce it and place scarlet wool around its head. Let it be cast into the desert in this way." And whenever this happened, the one who carried away the goat leads it into the desert and takes away the wool and places it in the shrub that is called Rachē—the flowers of which we are accustomed to eating when we find them in the country. Only the fruit of the Rachē is sweet.

9. What, then, does this mean? Pay attention: one is for the altar, while the other is cursed, and the one that is cursed is crowned. For they will see him then on that day wearing a long scarlet robe around his flesh, and they will say, "Is this not the one whom we once crucified,

despising, piercing, and spitting on him? Truly, this is the one who was then saying that he himself was the Son of God."

10. For how is he like that one? The goats are similar, fine, and equal for this reason: so that whenever they see him coming then, they will be astonished at his similarity to the goat. So then, see the model of Jesus, who is destined to suffer.

11. What does it mean, then, that the wool is set in the midst of the thorns? It is a model of Jesus being set in the church, since whoever wants to take up the scarlet wool must suffer many things because the thorn is fearful and possesses it through affliction. "Thus," he says, "those who want to see me and touch my kingdom ought to receive me by being oppressed and suffering."

8

1. Now what do you think the model signifies that was commanded to Israel, that men who are completely sinful should offer a heifer and burn it after they slaughter it? Children should then take the ash, put it into a jar, and wrap scarlet wool and hyssop around a piece of wood (notice again the model of the cross and scarlet wool). And thus the children should sprinkle the people individually in order to purify them from their sins.

2. Understand how he is speaking to you single-mindedly. The calf is Jesus. The sinful men who bring the offering are those who offered him for slaughter. Then the men are no longer; the glory of sinners is no longer.

3. The children who sprinkle are those who brought the good news of forgiveness of sins and purification of the heart to us. He gave the authority of the good news to them to preach, while they are twelve as a witness to the tribes since there were twelve tribes of Israel.

4. Why then are there three children who sprinkle? To bear witness to Abraham, Isaac, and Jacob because these were great before God.

5. What about the wool on the wood? It is because the kingdom of Jesus is on the wood, and those who hope in him will live forever.

6. Why, then, are there wool and hyssop together? Because in his kingdom the days will be evil and filthy during which we will be saved, and because the one who experiences pain in the flesh is healed by means of the hyssop's filth.

7. Because of this, the things that have happened are open to us, but they are dark to them because they did not listen to the Lord's voice.

9

1. For he speaks again about the ears, describing how he circumcised our heart. The Lord says in the prophet, "They obeyed me because they heard with their ear." And again he says, "Those who are far away will surely hear; they will know the things that I have done." And, "'Circumcise,' says the Lord, 'your hearts.'"
2. And again he says, "Hear, Israel, for thus says the Lord your God: Who desires to live forever? Let that one surely listen to the voice of my servant."
3. And he says, "Hear, heaven, and give ear, earth, because the Lord spoke these things for a testimony." And again he says, "Hear the word of the Lord beginning from this people." And again he says, "Hear, children, a voice crying out in the wilderness." So then, he circumcised our hearing in order that we might believe by hearing the word.
4. Moreover, the circumcision in which they have confidence is destroyed, for he said that circumcision is not for the flesh. But they were transgressed because an evil angel made them wise.
5. He says to them, "Thus says the Lord your God"—I find here a commandment—"do not sow among thorns; be circumcised to your Lord." And what does he say, "Circumcise your hard heart, and do not stiffen your neck." Take this again: "'Behold,' says the Lord, 'all gentiles are uncircumcised with respect to their foreskin, but this people is uncircumcised in the heart.'"
6. But you will say, "Yet surely the people were uncircumcised for a seal." But every Syrian, Arab, and the all the priests of the idols are also circumcised. Therefore, are they also members of their covenant? Moreover, the Egyptians are circumcised!
7. Learn about all things richly, then, children of love, because Abraham—who first gave circumcision—was circumcised when he looked ahead in the Spirit to Jesus, receiving the doctrines of three letters.
8. For it says, "And Abraham circumcised eighteen and three hundred men from his house." What, then, was the knowledge given to him? Learn that he first says "eighteen" and then, making space, "three hundred." Regarding the eighteen, *iōta* (I) is ten, while *ēta* (H) is eight. You

have Jesus. Now because the cross was about to have grace in the *tau* (T), he also says three hundred. Therefore, he discloses Jesus in two letters and the cross in one.

9. The one who set the implanted gift of his covenant within us knows these things. No one has learned a more reliable word from me, but I know that you are worthy.

10

1. Now when Moses said, "You will not eat a pig, a vulture, a hawk, a crow, or any fish that does not have scales on it," he received three doctrines in understanding.

2. In addition, he says to them in Deuteronomy, "And I will make a covenant with this people about my requirements." Therefore, then, God's ordinance has nothing to do with not eating, but Moses spoke in the Spirit.

3. He spoke about the pig for this reason: Do not be associated, he says, with people who are like pigs. That is, whenever they live in luxury, they forget the Lord. But whenever they have need, they remember the Lord just as the pig does not know its master whenever it is eating but cries out in hunger only to become silent again after receiving food.

4. "You shall not eat the vulture, the hawk, the kite, or the crow." Do not, he says, be associated or be like people who do not know to procure food for themselves through toil and sweat but instead lawlessly snatch things that belong to others. While walking innocently and looking around, they are watching out for someone whom they can strip because of their greed, just as these birds alone do not procure food but sit idly seeking how they can eat another's flesh—they are pestilent in their evil.

5. "And do not eat," he says, "the sea eel, the octopus, or the cuttlefish." Do not, he says, be like these people who are completely godless and have already been judged for death just as these lonely, cursed fish swim in the deep, not joining with the rest but dwelling in the mud underneath the depth.

6. Moreover, "do not eat the hare." Why? Do not become, he says, a child-corrupter or be like people like this, because the rabbit annually adds an anus. For it has as many orifices as years it has lived.

7. "Neither eat the hyena." Do not, he says, become an adulterer or a seducer or be like people like this. Why? Because this animal changes its nature annually, becoming male at one time and female another.

8. Moreover, he rightly hated the weasel. Do not, he says, become like those whom we hear about doing lawlessness with their mouth due to their impurity, and do not associate with the impure who commit lawlessness with their mouth. For this animal conceives with its mouth.

9. Moses, receiving three doctrines, spoke in the Spirit about food, but they, in accordance with the lust of the flesh, received it as about food.

10. Now David receives knowledge of the same three doctrines and says, "Blessed is the man who does not walk in the will of the godless"—as also the fish walk in darkness in the depths—"and does not stand in the way of sinners"—like those who sin seeming to fear the Lord like the pig—"and does not sit on the seat of the pestilent"—like birds sitting for plunder. You also have it completely when it comes to food.

11. Again Moses says, "Eat everything that has a divided hoof and chews the cud." Why does he say this? Because the one who receives food knows the one who feeds them, and seems to rejoice as they rest in him. He speaks well when looking at the commandment. What, then, does he mean? Associate with those who fear the Lord, with those who meditate on the special meaning that they received in their heart, with those who speak and keep the Lord's requirements, with those who know that meditation is a work of gladness, and those who chew on the Lord's word. Now, why the "divided hoof?" Because the righteous walks in this world and receives the holy age. See how well Moses legislated.

12. But how can these things be known or understood by them? Yet because we know the commandments rightly, we speak like the Lord desired. Because of this, he circumcised our hearing and hearts in order that we might understand these things.

11

1. Now let us seek whether it was a concern for the Lord to reveal anything beforehand about the water and about the cross. Regarding the water, it is written about Israel how they will not receive the baptism that carries forgiveness of sins but will construct something for themselves.

2. For the prophet says, "Be amazed, heaven, and let the earth shudder greatly over this, because this people has done two evil things. They abandoned me, the fountain of life, and they dug a pit of death for themselves.

3. My holy mountain Sinai is not a deserted rock. For you will be like hatchling birds fluttering about when taken away from the nest."

4. And again the prophet says, "I am going before you, and I will level mountains and crush bronze gates and smash iron bars. I will give to you dark, hidden, invisible treasures in order that they may know that I am the Lord God."

5. And, "you will dwell in a high cave of solid rock, and its water will be trustworthy. You will see a king with glory, and your soul will meditate on the fear of the Lord."

6. And he says again in another prophet, "And the one who does these things will be like a tree planted by outlets of water that will bear its fruit in its season. Its leaves will not fall away, and all that it does will prosper.

7. Not so the ungodly, not so. Rather, they will be like chaff that the wind blows up from the face of the earth. Because of this the ungodly will not be raised in judgement, nor the sinners in the counsel of the righteous. For the Lord knows the way of the righteous, and the way of the ungodly will perish."

8. Understand how he declares the water and the cross in the same place. For he says this, "Blessed are those who hope in the cross and descend into the water," because he describes the wage "in its season." Then, he says, "I will repay." But now he says, "the leaves will not fall away." This means that every word that comes out of you through your mouth in faith and love will bring conversion and hope to many.

9. And again another prophet says, "And the land of Jacob will be praised by the whole earth." This means that he will glorify the vessel of his spirit.

10. Then what does he say? "And there was a river flowing from the right, and beautiful trees were growing up out of it, and whoever eats from one of them will live forever."

11. This means that we go down into the water full of sins and filth, and we come up bearing fruit in our heart, having fear and hope in Jesus in the Spirit. "And whoever eats from these will live forever."

This means: "Whoever," he says, "hears these people speaking and believes will live forever."

12

1. Again, likewise, he declares about the cross in another prophet who says, "'And when will these things be completed?' The Lord says, 'Whenever the tree is laid down and raised up and whenever blood drips from the tree.'" Again you have something about the cross and the one who was about to be crucified.

2. But when Israel was being attacked by foreign tribes, he speaks again to Moses also to remind those who were being assaulted that they were handed over to death because of their sins. The Spirit speaks to Moses's heart in order that he might make a model of the cross and the one who was about to suffer. "Because," he says, "they will be at war forever unless they hope in him." Therefore, Moses set weapons one on top of the other in the middle of the fight, and he stretched out his hands while standing at a higher place than everyone else. And thus Israel was victorious again. Then, whenever he lowered his hands, they began to die again.

3. Why? In order that they might know that it is impossible to be saved unless they hope in him.

4. Again he says in another prophet, "I stretched out my hands all day to a people that is disobedient and antagonistic to my righteous way."

5. As Israel is falling, Moses again forms a model of Jesus showing that he, whom they will think they have destroyed, had to suffer and will give life. For the Lord caused every snake to bite them, and they died—since the transgression came in Eve through the snake—in order that he might convince them that they will be handed over to the distress of death because of their transgression.

6. In addition, although Moses himself commanded them, "You shall have no molten or carved images as a god," he made one in order to exhibit a model of Jesus. Therefore, Moses makes a bronze serpent, sets it up prominently, and calls the people with a proclamation.

7. Therefore, when they came together, they were asking Moses to offer prayers about them for their healing. But Moses said to them, "Whenever," he says, "one of you is bitten, let that one come to the serpent that is laid upon the wood and let that one hope, believing that although

he is dead, it is possible to be made alive, and he will immediately be saved." And they did exactly this. You have again the glory of Jesus in these things, because all things are in him and for him.

8. Again, what does Moses say to "Jesus," the son of Nave, who was a prophet, when he gave this name to him in order that all the people would listen to him alone that the Father reveals all things about Jesus the Son?

9. Therefore, when he gave this name and sent him as a spy of the land, Moses says to "Jesus," the son of Nave, "Take a book in your hands and write what the Lord says, for the Son of God will cut off the entire house of Amalek from the root in the last days." See again that Jesus is not the son of man but the Son of God, though he was revealed as a model in the flesh.

10. Therefore, since they are about to say that the Christ is the son of David, David himself prophecies because he is afraid and understands the deceit of the sinners: "The Lord said to my lord, 'Sit at my right hand until I place your enemies as a footstool for your feet.'"

11. And again Isaiah says it in this say: "The Lord says to Christ my Lord, 'I took hold of his right hand so that the nations listen to him, and I will break the strength of kings.'" See how David calls him Lord and does not call him son.

13

1. But let us see whether this people or the first will inherit and whether the covenant is for us or for them.

2. Hear, therefore, what the scripture says about the people. "Now Isaac was praying for Rebecca, his wife, because she was barren. And she became pregnant." Then, "Rebecca also went out to inquire of the Lord, and the Lord said to her, 'Two nations are in your womb and two peoples in your belly. One people will be superior to the other, and the greater will serve the lesser.'"

3. You ought to ask who Isaac is, who Rebecca is, and about whom he has shown that this people is greater than that.

4. In another prophecy, Jacob says more clearly to Joseph his son, "Behold, the Lord did not deprive me of your presence. Bring your sons to me so that I may bless them."

5. So he brought Ephraim and Manasseh, desiring that Manasseh should be blessed because he was older. For Joseph brought him to the right hand of his father Jacob. But Jacob saw in the Spirit a model of the coming people. And what does it say? "And Jacob crossed his hands, and he set his right hand on Ephraim's head—the second and younger—and blessed him. And Joseph said to Jacob, 'Switch your right hand to the head of Manasseh, because he is my firstborn son.' Then Jacob said to Joseph, "I know, child, I know. But the greater will serve the lesser, and it is this one who will be blessed."'

6. See, he has set this people over others to be the first and the heir of the covenant.

7. Therefore, if it is recalled even through Abraham, we receive the completion of our knowledge. What does he say to Abraham when he only believed and it was established for righteousness? "Behold, I have established you, Abraham, as the father of the gentiles who believe in God while uncircumcised."

14

1. Yes. But let us see whether the covenant—which he swore to the fathers to give to the people—let us seek whether he has given it. He has given it, but they were not worthy to receive it because of their sins.

2. For the prophet says: "And Moses was fasting for forty days and forty nights on Mount Sinai in order to take the covenant of the Lord to the people. And Moses received two stone tablets from the Lord that were written in the Spirit with the finger of the Lord's hand. And when Moses received them, he brought them down to give to the people.

3. And the Lord said to Moses, 'Moses, Moses! Go down quickly because your people, whom you led out from the land of Egypt, broke the law.' And Moses understood that they had again made molten images for themselves. He threw the tablets from his hands, and the tablets of the Lord's covenant were broken." While Moses received the covenant, they were not worthy.

4. But how did we receive the covenant? Learn. Although Moses received it as a servant, the Lord himself gave it to us to be the people of inheritance when he endured on our account.

5. Now, he was revealed in order that they also may be completed with respect to their sins and that we may receive the covenant through the

Lord Jesus, the heir. He was prepared for this reason, namely, in order that when he was revealed, he might make a covenant in us by his word after he redeemed our hearts from darkness, which were indentured to death and handed over to the lawlessness of deceit.

6. For it is written how the Father commanded him to redeem us from darkness and to prepare a holy people for himself.

7. Therefore, the prophet says: "I, the Lord your God, called you in righteousness. I will take hold of your hand and strengthen you. I gave you as a light for the gentiles, to open the eyes of the blind, to lead out those who are bound from their chains and who are sitting in darkness from their prison house." Therefore, we know from where we were redeemed.

8. Again the prophet says: "Behold, I have established you as a light for the gentiles so that you will be for salvation to the end of the earth. Thus says the Lord God who redeemed you."

9. Again the prophet says: "The Spirit of the Lord is on me because he anointed me to proclaim the good news of grace to the humble and because he has sent me to heal those who have been crushed in their hearts, to preach forgiveness to the captives and sight to the blind, to call for the favorable years of the Lord and the day of recompense, to comfort all who mourn."

15

1. Moreover, therefore, it is written about the Sabbath in the Ten Words in which he spoke on Mount Sinai face-to-face with Moses: "And sanctify the Lord's Sabbath with pure hands and a pure heart."

2. And in another place he says, "If my sons keep the Sabbath, then I will bestow my mercy on them."

3. He speaks about Sabbath at the beginning of creation: "And God made the works of his hands in six days, and he finished on the seventh day. And he rested on it and sanctified it."

4. Pay attention, children, to what it means by "he finished in six days." This means that the Lord will finish all things in six thousand years, for a day with him means one thousand years. And he himself testifies for me, saying: "Behold, the day of the Lord will be like one thousand years." Therefore, children, he will finish all things in six days, that is, in six thousand years.

5. "And he rested the seventh day." This means that whenever his Son comes and makes the time of the Lawless One ineffective, judges the ungodly, and changes the sun, the moon, and the stars, then he will truly rest on the seventh day.

6. In addition, he says: "You will sanctify it with pure hands and a pure heart." Therefore, if some person currently is able to sanctify the day that God sanctified by being pure in heart, we have been deceived in all things.

7. But if that is not the case, then we will consequently rest and sanctify it truly when we ourselves will be capable to do so—after being justified and receiving the promise, when lawlessness is no more but all things are made new by the Lord. Then we will be able to sanctify it because we ourselves have been sanctified first.

8. In addition, he says to them: "I have had it with your new moons and Sabbaths." See how he speaks. The current Sabbaths are not acceptable to me but the one that I have made, in which I will set all things at rest and make a beginning for the eight day, which is the beginning of another world.

9. For this reason, we also spend the eight day in gladness in which Jesus also raised from the dead and rose into the heavens after he was revealed.

16

1. Moreover, then, I will speak about the temple, how, because they were deceived, the lousy people hoped in a building as if it was God's house and not on their God who made them.

2. For they consecrated him in the temple almost like the gentiles. But how does the Lord speak while he destroys it? Learn. "'Who measured the heaven with the span of their hand or the earth with their palm? Is it not I?' says the Lord. 'The heaven is my throne, and the earth is the footstool for my feet. What sort of house or what place for my rest will you build for me?'" You have known that their hope was futile.

3. Moreover, he says again, "Behold, those who tore down this temple will rebuild it."

4. It is happening. For because they went to war, it was torn down by the enemies. And now those who are servants of the enemies will rebuild it.

5. Again, when the city, the temple, and the people of Israel were about to be handed over, he was revealed. For the scripture says: "And it will be during the last days that the Lord will hand over the sheep of the pasture, the fold, and their tower to destruction." And it happened according to what the Lord said.

6. But let us seek whether there is a temple of God. There is, where he himself says he will make and construct it. For it is written, "And it will be, when the seventh day is completed, that the temple of God will be gloriously built in the name of the Lord."

7. Therefore, I find that there is a temple. How, then, will it be built in the name of the Lord? Learn. Before we believed in God, the dwelling of the heart was corrupt and weak like a temple constructed by hand, for it was full of idolatry and was a house of demons since its making was opposed to God.

8. "But it will be built in the name of the Lord." Now, pay attention so that God's temple may be gloriously built. How? Learn. We became new by receiving forgiveness of sins and hoping in the name, resulting in our being created again from the beginning. Therefore, God truly dwells in our dwelling in us.

9. How? By his word of faith, his call of promise, the wisdom of the requirements, the commandments of the teaching—he is prophesying in us, he is dwelling in us, opening the door of the temple to us, who have been enslaved to death—by giving us repentance, he enters into the incorruptible temple.

10. For the one who longs to be saved looks not to a person but to the one who dwells and speaks in them and is amazed that they have never heard such words from the speaker or ever desired to hear such words. This is the spiritual temple that is being built for the Lord.

17

1. Insofar as it was possible single-mindedly to clarify to you, my soul hopes not to have left anything out.

2. For if I write to you about present or future matters, you will by no means be able to understand because they are found in parables. So much for these things.

18

1. Now let us move on to another knowledge and teaching. There are two ways of teaching and authority—one of light and one of darkness. There is a great difference between the two ways. For God's light-bearing angels are in charge over one, while Satan's angels are over the other.

2. And, on the one hand, is the Lord from eternity and for eternity; on the other hand, is the ruler of the present age of lawlessness.

19

1. This, then, is the way of light. If someone wants to walk the way to the determined place, let that person be eager for his works. Therefore, the knowledge that was given to us so that we may walk in it is such as follows.

2. You will love the one who made you, fear the one who formed you, and glorify the one who redeemed you from death. You will be single-minded in heart and rich in spirit. You will not be joined with those who walk in the way of death. You will hate everything that is not pleasing to God. You will hate all hypocrisy. You will not forsake the commandments of God.

3. You will not exalt yourself, but you will be humble in every way. You will not take glory upon yourself. You will not accept evil counsel against your neighbor. You will not give arrogance to your soul.

4. You will not engage in sexual immorality. You will not commit adultery. You will not corrupt children. The Word of God shall by no means go out in the impurity of some. You shall not show favoritism when you reprove someone for a transgression. You will be gentle. You will be quiet. You will tremble at the words that you hear. You will not hold a grudge against your brother.

5. You will not be double-minded about whether something will happen or not. You will not take the name of the Lord in vain. You will love your neighbor more than your soul. Do not murder a child in corruption or kill it after it is born. You will not take your hand from your son or your daughter, but you will teach the fear of God from youth.

6. You will not desire your neighbor's belongings. You will not be greedy, nor will you be joined by your soul to those who are exalted. Rather,

you will associate with the humble and the just. Receive what happens to you as good things, knowing that nothing happens apart from God.

7. You will not be double-minded or double-tongued. You will submit to masters in fear and modesty like a pattern of God. Lest they no longer fear the God of you both, you will not bitterly order your male slave or female slave, who hope on the same God, because he came not to call according to reputation but those whom the Spirit prepared.

8. You will share with your neighbor in all things, and you will not claim things to be your own. For if you are sharers in what is incorruptible, how much more in things that are corruptible. You will not be quick to speak, for the mouth is a trap of death. Insofar as you are able, you will be pure for the sake of your soul.

9. Do not be one who stretches the hands to receive but draws them back from giving. You will love all who speak the Word of the Lord to you like the pupil of your eye.

10. You will remember the day of judgment night and day. You will seek the faces of the saints each day, whether laboring by word, walking to encourage, and meditating to save the soul by word, or whether you work with your hands for the ransom price of your sins.

11. Do not be hesitant to give or grumble when giving, but know who is the good paymaster. You will keep what you received, neither adding nor taking away from it. You will hate evil completely. You will judge righteously.

12. You will not cause division, but you will make peace by bringing together those who are fighting. You will confess your sins. You will not come to prayer with an evil conscience.

20

1. The way of the Black One is crooked and full of cursing. For it is a way of eternal death with punishment in which are the things that destroy their soul: idolatry, audacity, the elevation of power, double-mindedness, adultery, murder, robbery, pride, transgression, deceit, evil, contumacy, magic, sorcery, greed, and no fear of God.

2. There are persecutors of the good, haters of truth, lovers of lies, those who do not know the wage of righteousness, who do not join with the good, who do not judge with justice, who do not attend to the widow and orphan, who stay alert not to the fear of God but to what

is evil, who are far and distant from gentleness and endurance, who love emptiness, who pursue recompense, who have no mercy on the poor, who do not work on behalf of those who are worn down, who do not know the one who made them, who murder children, who corrupt what God has formed, who turn away from someone in need, who wear down the oppressed, encouragers of the rich, lawless judges of the poor, all-sinful.

21

1. Therefore, it is good, having learned the requirements of the Lord that have been written, to walk in them. For the one who does these things will be glorified in the kingdom of God. The one who chooses those things with their works will destroy themselves. For this reason, there is resurrection. For this reason, there is recompense.

2. I ask those in high positions if you will accept my well-intentioned advice: You have with you those to whom you will do good; do not fail.

3. The day is near in which all things associated with the evil one will be destroyed. The Lord and his wage are near.

4. Again and again I ask you: be good lawgivers among yourselves. Remain faithful advisers among yourselves. Remove all hypocrisy from you.

5. May the God who rules over all the world give you wisdom, understanding, intelligence, knowledge of his requirements, and endurance.

6. And be God-taught. Seek out and do what the Lord seeks from you in order that you may be found on the day of judgment.

7. But if there is any remembrance of what is good, remember me, meditating on these things in order that both desire and sleeplessness may lead to something good. I ask you, requesting a favor.

8. As long as the good vessel is still with you, do not fail with regard to any of these things, but continually seek out these things and fulfill every commandment. For it is worthy.

9. For this reason, I hurried all the more to write based on my abilities in order that you may rejoice. Farewell, children of love and peace. May the Lord of glory and all grace be with your spirit.

Part I

Introductory and Critical Articles

1

Introduction to the Epistle of Barnabas

WITHIN THE PAGES OF the New Testament, and particularly within the Acts of the Apostles, Barnabas is depicted as a generous patron, an energetic preacher, and a trusted mediator.[1] Yet Barnabas is ultimately overshadowed by the towering figures of Peter, Paul, and others. Within the collection of documents known as the Apostolic Fathers, the Epistle of Barnabas is in danger of a similar fate. Unlike the sayings of Papias or the letters of Ignatius, Polycarp, and possibly Clement, the Epistle of Barnabas has been transmitted in the name of someone who is known from the New Testament but is unlikely to have been its author. *Barnabas* contains a Two Ways Tradition that is closely related to the Didache but has not received the same level of scholarly attention in recent years.[2] The transformative elements within the apocalyptic story of the Shepherd of Hermas give readers a handhold to grasp as they make their way through its occasionally repetitive allegorical teachings that the epistolary nature of *Barnabas* does not easily allow. Barnabas's attempt to distinguish early Jesus-followers from his Jewish opponents has made the document of interest to those who study the partings of the ways, but the severity of Barnabas's polemic and the deftness with which the author of the Epistle to Diognetus writes of Christians as a third race and the soul of the world

---

1. A word about orthography should be given from the outset. Within the pages of this commentary, the Epistle of Barnabas may also be identified by the italicized *Barnabas*. Although this commentary follows the majority opinion in arguing that the historical Barnabas was not the author of the letter studied here, I will sometimes refer to the author of the Epistle of Barnabas as Barnabas. These alterations are purely stylistic in order to limit repetition. Thus, *Barnabas* refers to the Epistle of Barnabas, while Barnabas refers to the author of the letter or, at times in the introduction, to the historical figure as he is remembered elsewhere in early Christian literature.

2. A similar point has been made by Draper ("Barnabas," 89–90). Since then, the studies of Rhodes ("Two Ways Tradition," 797–816) and Smith ("The *Epistle of Barnabas*," 465–97) have also focused on the Two Ways Tradition in *Barnabas*.

(Diogn. 5.1—6.10) makes the latter an easier point of entry to discussions about Jewish-Christian relations in the second century.

Despite the possibility that the Epistle of Barnabas may be overshadowed by other texts in the Apostolic Fathers, it remains the case that readers who study the letter carefully are likely to find both a rich text to engage on its own merits and points of connection between the letter and other early Jewish and Christian literature from the first and second centuries CE. This commentary will focus on the first matter, that is, on the interpretation of the Epistle of Barnabas as a single text. The primary aim of the commentary is to offer a clear interpretation of the text with a view to its historical, literary, and theological contexts. At times, I will also look further afield to compare *Barnabas* to other early Christian texts in order to better situate the letter. In so doing, this volume hopes to illustrate the benefit of devoting focused attention to the arguments within *Barnabas*, of noting the letter's unique contributions to the interpretation of scripture, and of wrestling with Barnabean teaching alongside other expressions from the Jesus movement of the first and second centuries. In order to accomplish these tasks, it will be helpful to set out key introductory matters that are assumed and argued for within the pages of the commentary. Before proceeding to critical questions about the letter's provenance, date, and authorship, it will be useful to outline the manuscripts and translations in which the letter remains extant.

Manuscripts and Versions of the Epistle of Barnabas

Although most readers will engage the Epistle of Barnabas through critical editions and modern translations, such publications are attempts to reconstruct and communicate the text based upon the best available witnesses.[3] The most important manuscripts for the Epistle of Barnabas are the Greek witnesses and the Latin translation.

---

3. The editions and translations that have been regularly consulted in the course of writing this commentary include Ehrman, *Apostolic Fathers*; Holmes, *Apostolic Fathers*; Lindemann and Paulsen, *Apostolischen Väter*; Prigent and Kraft, *Épître de Barnabé*; Prinzivalli and Simonetti, *Seguendo J*; Prostmeier and Lona, *Epistola Barnabae*; Wengst, *Didache*. Although all translations of the Epistle of Barnabas are my own and I have regularly checked textual variants listed in textual apparatuses with photographs of the manuscripts when they are available online, I have relied most heavily on the recent critical editions of Prinzivalli and Simonetti, *Seguendo Gesù*; Prostmeier and Lona, *Epistola Barnabae*.

INTRODUCTION TO THE EPISTLE OF BARNABAS   5

Greek Manuscript Witnesses

Codex Sinaiticus (S)

Codex Sinaiticus was brought to the public's attention by Constantine Tischendorf after he found it at St. Catherine's Monastery on Mount Sinai.[4] Tischendorf published his find in 1862, and the manuscript is now housed at the British Library, the Leipzig University Library, the National Library of Russia (St. Petersburg), and St. Catherine's Monastery.[5] S is a parchment codex comprised of more than 400 leaves. It dates to the fourth century and is written in an uncial hand with each page divided into four columns of text.[6] Most important for the purposes of this book, S contains the Epistle of Barnabas and the Shepherd of Hermas in its final pages.[7]

The Epistle of Barnabas is located between Revelation and the Shepherd of Hermas. The entire letter is extant in S, beginning in the second column of folio 334ʳ with Barn. 1.1 and ending on the third column of folio 340ᵛ with Barn. 21.8. The title given at the start of the work is "Epistle of Barnabas" (ΒΑΡΝΑΒΑΕΠΙΣΤΟΛΗ), while the scribe marked the end of the work with a coronis to the left of the column and a three-line subscription again reading "Epistle of Barnabas" (ΕΠΙΣΤΟΛΗ / ΒΑΡΝΑ / ΒΑ). The headings on the intervening pages read "of Barnabas" (ΒΑΡΝΑΒΑ). The text was copied by Scribe A.[8] Since it provides an early and complete witness to the Epistle of Barnabas, S is an immensely valuable manuscript for textual criticism. However, New Testament scholars who are accustomed to viewing S as a reliable text should not assume without warrant that the same thing holds when it comes to the Epistle of Barnabas.[9] The text of S must be compared closely to the texts of the other Greek witnesses and versions.[10]

---

4. For a concise account of the drama surrounding Tischendorf's initial discovery in 1844 through publication and the subsequent controversy, see Porter, *Constantine Tischendorf*, 24–29, 40–54.

5. Constantine Tischendorf, *Bibliorum Codex Sinaiticus Petropolitanus*. The manuscript can be viewed online at codexsinaiticus.org (accessed March 3, 2020).

6. Prigent and Kraft, *Épître de Barnabé*, 49; Parker, *Codex Sinaiticus*, 27–42.

7. Batovici, "Apostolic Fathers," 581–605; Batovici, "Less-Expected Books," 39–50.

8. On the scribes in Sinaiticus, see Batovici, "Two B Scribes," 197–206; Hernández, *Scribal Habits and Theological Influences*, 49–95; Jongkind, *Scribal Habits*, 9–18; Milne and Skeat, *Scribes and Correctors*, 1–86; Myshrall, "Codex Sinaiticus," 40–48; Myshrall, "Presence of a Fourth Scribe?" 139–48.

9. See similarly Prostmeier, *Barnabasbrief*, 14; Prostmeier, "Einleitung," 14.

10. On the correctors that have also worked on the Epistle of Barnabas in S, see Batovici, "Textual Revisions," 443–70; Malik, "Earliest Corrections," 207–54; Malik, "Corrections of Codex Sinaiticus," 595–614; Milne and Skeat, *Scribes and Correctors*, 1–86; Myshrall, "Codex Sinaiticus," 65–92, 533–703.

Codex Hierosolymitanus 54 (H)

Codex Hierosolymitanus was discovered in 1873 by Philotheos Bryennios in the Library of the Holy Sepulcher in Constantinople.[11] Bryennios arranged to have portions of the manuscript published in 1875 and 1883.[12] The Epistle of Barnabas was printed in the 1883 volume along with the Didache and the long recension of Ignatius's letters. The manuscript is now kept in the Library of the Greek Patriarchate in Jerusalem.[13] H is a parchment manuscript comprising 120 leaves and is written in a cursive hand with no columns dividing the pages. The end of the manuscript is significant for codicological studies of H because the scribe signs their name and dates the manuscript (folio 120r). The codex has been copied "by the hand of Leon, notary and sinner" (χειρὶ Λέοντος νοταρίου καὶ ἀλείτου) and was completed on June 11, 1056.[14] The codex contains several early Christian texts but, differently from S, none that have been included in the New Testament.[15]

The Epistle of Barnabas begins on folio 39ʳ and comes to a close on folio 51ᵛ. The text is preceded by a work attributed to Pseudo-Chrysostom and is followed by 1 Clement. The title given at the inscription of the letter is "Epistle of Barnabas" (ΒΑΡΝΑΒΑ ΕΠΙΣΤΟΛΗ). No subscription is given at the end, nor is there any indication of the name of the text given in the headings of intervening pages. However, the Epistle of Barnabas is marked off from the work that follows it by a colon and the indentation of the title of 1 Clement. The text is significant because it provides only the second complete Greek text of the Epistle of Barnabas. The precise planning of the whole manuscript may lead one to think that the scribe was careful in the copying of individual texts.[16] Although the evidence of H should be weighed judiciously when

---

11. On the discovery of H, see Lightfoot, *Apostolic Fathers*, 1.1.121–23.

12. Bryennios, Τοῦ ἐν ἁγίοις πατρὸς ἡμῶν Κλήμεντος ἐπισκόπου Ῥώμης; Bryennios, Διδαχὴ τῶν δώδεκα Ἀποστόλων.

13. Images of the manuscript can be viewed online through the Library of Congress at www.loc.gov/item/00279389694-jo (accessed March 3, 2020). The manuscript has been designated by various abbreviations in modern scholarship. For example, Wilhite (*Didache*, 7) refers to the manuscript as H54, thereby helpfully recognizing its number within the papyrological collection in which it is found. I have followed Prinzivalli and Simonetti (*Seguendo Gesù*) as well as Prostmeier and Lona (*Epistola Barnabae*) in referring to the manuscript as H.

14. Schaff (*Oldest Church Manual*, 7) offers a fuller translation of the colophon: "Finished in the month of June, upon the 11th (of the month), day 3d (of the week, *i.e.*, Tuesday), Indiction 9, of the year 6564. By the hand of Leon, notary and sinner."

15. For a complete list of texts contained in H, see Wilhite, *Didache*, 7.

16. Prostmeier, *Barnabasbrief*, 17; Prostmeier, "Einleitung," 15.

discrepancies appear in the manuscript tradition, it provides an important witness for textual criticism of the Epistle of Barnabas.

Codex Vaticanus Graecus 859 and Its Descendants (G)

G is a collective symbol for the text of *Barnabas* as it is witnessed in ten manuscripts.[17] The most important of these manuscripts is Codex Vaticanus Graecus 859 (v), an eleventh-century minuscule. These manuscripts are typically grouped into three families as follows.[18]

Family G¹

1. Vaticanus gr. 859 (v): Folios 198^r–211^v
2. Ottobonianus gr. 348 (o): Folios 66^v–84^r

Family G²

1. Florentinus Laurentianus plut. 7.21 (f): Folios 59^v–75^r
2. Parisinus Bibl. Nat. gr. 937 (p): Folios 50^v–63^v

Family G³

1. Andros Hagias 64 (a): Folios 120^r–126^v
2. Romanus Bibl. Casanatensis 334 (c): Folios 335^r–353^v
3. Vaticanus gr. 1655 (d): Folios 301^v–311^r
4. Neopolitanus Bibl. Nat. Borbonicus 17 (n): Folios 535^v–546^v
5. Vaticanus gr. 1909 (r): Folios 70^r–75^v [19]

---

17. Lightfoot (*Apostolic Fathers*, 2.1.549, 2.3.319) lists a manuscript not included here. He refers to this manuscript as Salmasianus and gives it the siglum "s." This manuscript appears to have been used indirectly by James Ussher in his edition of Polycarp's *Philippians* and seems to have been included in the count of manuscripts in Holmes, *Apostolic Fathers*, 375. However, Kraft notes that he has been unable to find anything about the manuscript (Prigent and Kraft, *Épître de Barnabé*, 52 n 1). The manuscript is not listed in Lindemann and Paulsen's edition (*Die apostolischen Väter*, 24) or in Prostmeier's fuller study ("Zur handschriftlichen Überlieferung," 48–64).

18. On this grouping, see Hartog, *Polycarp*, 26–27; Kraft, *Barnabas*, 17–18; Prigent and Kraft, *Épître de Barnabé*, 50–53; Prostmeier, "Zur handschriftlichen Überlieferung," 55–57. The folios following the list of manuscripts indicate the folios in the manuscripts that contain the Epistle of Barnabas.

19. Notably, this manuscript begins only at Barn. 10.3. Folios 68–69 are missing in this manuscript. They most likely contained earlier portions of the Epistle of Barnabas. Polycarp's *Philippians* is not contained in this manuscript, so r does not follow the pattern of the other manuscripts in G in which Pol. *Phil.* 9.2 abruptly gives way to Barn. 5.7. See further Prostmeier, "Zur handschriftlichen Überlieferung," 52–53.

8 PART I: INTRODUCTORY AND CRITICAL ARTICLES

6. Vaticanus Reginensis Pii gr. 2.11 (t): Folios 236ᵛ–257ʳ

The unique element of v and all of its descendants is that Polycarp's *Philippians* immediately precedes the Epistle of Barnabas. An even more unusual trait is that v ends abruptly in Pol. *Phil.* 9.2 and passes seamlessly into Barn. 5.7: ἀποθανόντα καὶ δι' ἡμᾶς ὑπό (from Pol. *Phil.* 9.2) τὸν λαὸν τὸν κενὸν (from Barn. 5.7).[20] The transition is made seamlessly and without any indication that there has been a change in texts. The best explanation for this peculiarity is that either the exemplar used by the scribe of v or an exemplar used by another scribe further back in the stemma of v was missing a group of pages containing Pol. *Phil.* 9.2—14.1; Barn. 1.1—5.7. This manuscript was copied by the scribe and incorporated into v. This manuscript then became the progenitor of a series of manuscripts that contain the same defect.

These manuscripts are not exactly identical, but it will be sufficient to refer to G as a single witness for the purposes of this commentary. While a more detailed textual study of *Barnabas* may be a desideratum, F. X. Funk's conclusion is appropriate for this volume: "The truth is, despite the presence of four or even more manuscripts, we will only have to refer to v, since this is the archetype of all the others."[21] While the manuscripts date between the eleventh and seventeenth centuries, the text contained in these manuscripts may reflect a third- or fourth-century provenance.[22]

Papyrus PSI 757 (P)

Papyrus PSI 757 is a fragment from a papyrus codex that contains Barn. 9.1–6 currently housed in Florence at the Biblioteca Medicea Laurenziana.[23] It is 6.3 x 11 cm, is written in semi-uncial letters, and is dated between the late-third and early-fifth centuries.[24] The papyrus is written on both sides. 9.1–3a

---

20. A variant appears within some of the manuscripts related to v in which καινόν may be read instead of κενόν, the latter of which is the reading in v.

21. "In Wahrheit werden wir uns in Zukunft trotz des Vorhandenseins von vier, bezw. noch mehr weiteren Handschriften ausschließlich an V halten müssen, da dieser sich als das Archetyp aller übrigen darstellt" (Funk, "Codex Vaticanus gr. 859," 637).

22. Prostmeier, "Einleitung," 37–38.

23. Images of the papyrus can be viewed online at http://www.psi-online.it/documents/psi;7;757 (accessed February 2, 2020).

24. Vitelli (*Papiri greci e latini VII*, 40–41) and Kraft ("An Unnoticed Papyrus Fragment," 153) date the papyrus to the late-fourth or early-fifth centuries. However, Kraft modified his view in his 1971 introduction to the Sources Chretiennes edition of the Epistle of Barnabas. On the basis of correspondence with C. H. Roberts, he posits a date in the late-third or early-fourth century (Prigent and Kraft, *Épître de Barnabé*, 53 n 3).

is on the verso side, while the recto contains 9.3b–6. Although the papyrus was published and identified as a fragment of Barn. 9.1–6 in 1925,[25] its text seems to have gone largely unnoticed by scholars until Robert Kraft drew attention to its existence in 1967.[26] His study of the manuscript highlights similarities between the text of P and readings found in G. This provides confirmation that, although the text of G is only witnessed in manuscripts that are relatively late, its *Vorlage* likely dates to the fourth century.[27]

Versions

As one moves from Greek witnesses to the versions of the text that likewise impact text-critical judgements, three translations should be mentioned: the Latin translation, Syriac translation, and a possible Coptic translation.[28]

Latin Translation (L)

The most important early translation of the Epistle of Barnabas was into Latin. The Latin translation is attested in only one manuscript that is written in a minuscule hand and is alternatively known as Codex Corbeiensis Q.v.I. 38/39 or Codex Petropolitanus Lat. Q.v.I. 38–39. The manuscript is usually dated to the ninth century, and the Epistle of Barnabas is sandwiched between Pseudo-Tertullian's *De cibis Iudaicis* and the New Testament letter of James.[29] The origins of the translation are likely to be found at the end of the second century or early in the third.[30] One reason for dating

---

More recently, Rachel Yuen-Collingridge dates the papyrus to the third century (Yuen-Collingridge, "Hunting for Origen," 55 n 67). I have followed Prostmeier ("Einleitung," 24), the most recent editor of a text of the Epistle of Barnabas, in giving a range of dates for the papyrus.

25. Vitelli, *Papiri greci e latini VII*, 40–43. The papyrus was transcribed by Raffaello Bianchi, while S. G. Mercati identified it as a portion of the Epistle of Barnabas.

26. Kraft, "An Unnoticed Papyrus Fragment," 150–63.

27. Kraft, "An Unnoticed Papyrus Fragment," 157; Prostmeier, "Einleitung," 37–38.

28. Prostmeier ("Zur handschriftlichen Überlieferung," 61 n 22) notes that there is a reference to an Armenian translation at the end of the Epistle of Barnabas as contained in v. Although v appears to have served as the Vorlage for an Armenian translation, no manuscript evidence has been found that would allow one to know anything further about its date, the translation technique, or its value for textual criticism. It has thus not been included in this introduction.

29. Cunningham, *Dissertation*, viii; Dentesano, "La versione latina," 135; Heer, *Versio Latina* xii–xv; Prigent and Kraft, *Épître de Barnabé*, 53; Prostmeier, "Einleitung," 24.

30. Bardy, *La question des langues*, 107; Dentesano, "La versione latina," 135; Gleede,

the translation so early is its choice of Latin glosses for Greek terms. For example, ἔθνη is translated as *ethnici* rather than *gentes* (16.2). Likewise, σῴζω is translated variously as *sanare* or *liberare* rather than *saluare* (e.g., 5.10; 12.3). These are generally the marks of earlier Latin translations.[31] A unique feature of the Latin version of *Barnabas* is that it contains only 1.1—17.2. 18.1—21.9 is not contained in the manuscript.[32] The translation attests a shortened text at other points within 1.1—17.2, but the translation otherwise seems to have been made word by word.[33] It thus provides an important witness for textual criticism of the Epistle of Barnabas.

Syriac Translation (sy)

Fragments of a Syriac translation have been found in Codex Cantab. Univ. Add. 2023. The manuscript dates from the thirteenth century, was copied by two scribes, and preserves portions of the Epistle of Barnabas on folio 61^v.[34] The folio contains 19.1-2, 8; 20.1, but the entire fragment consists of only forty-nine words. The translation has been dated to the turn of the sixth century (ca. 500 CE). It may offer evidence for a separate transmission of the Two Ways Tradition in *Barnabas*.[35] However, the fragmentary nature of the material requires caution when characterizing the translation and the transmission.

A Coptic Translation?

Hans-Martin Schenke draws attention to a citation of *Barnabas* in the so-called "Coptic Book" that is otherwise known as P.Berol. 20915. The

---

Parabiblica Latina, 200; Heer, "Lateinische Barnabasbrief und die Bibel," 224; Prigent and Kraft, *Épître de Barnabé*, 53; Prostmeier, *Barnabasbrief*, 32.

31. For further examples, see Gleede, *Parabiblica Latina*, 199.

32. Gleede (*Parabiblica Latina*, 200–203) follows Heer (*Versio Latina*, lxix) in finding an anti-Jewish tendency in the translation. He then posits that Barn. 18–21 is missing from the Latin translation because it did not fit the translator's anti-Jewish purposes.

33. Gleede, *Parabiblica Latina*, 201, 203. One exception to this word-by-word translation technique arises when the translator introduces scriptural quotations, on which, see Dentesano, "La versione latina," 140–41.

34. The whole manuscript has been published in Wright, *Catalogue*, 2.600-628. The text of the Epistle of Barnabas is found in Wright, *Catalogue* 2.611–12; Baumstark, "Barnabasbrief," 236 n 2. Baumstark (Review, 209) referred to this manuscript in 1902 in his review of Wright's work.

35. See further Batovici and Verheyden, "Digitizing," 105–6; Prostmeier, *Barnabasbrief*, 32–34; Prostmeier, "Einleitung," 25–26.

papyrus may date as early as the second or third century, but Schenke dates the papyrus to the fourth century.[36] The text quotes Barn. 6.11–13, 17–18 in support of its understanding of creation. Schenke maintains that it is more likely for the author to have translated a Greek text of *Barnabas* as needed.[37] If so, P.Berol 20915 is evidence not for a lost Coptic translation but rather for an *ad hoc* translation of a few verses.

Indirect Witnesses and the Question of Canon

The Epistle of Barnabas was quoted and mentioned by early Christian authors in the centuries after it was written. This section will highlight a few of the most important authors and texts to mention Barnabas or his letter. Some of these authors grant a high level of authority to the Epistle of Barnabas, raising questions about the degree of authority that *Barnabas* had in early centuries. This section will thus conclude by reflecting on the letter's place in the canon and arguing that a more nuanced understanding of authority is required than the simple question of whether a text is in or out of the canon allows.

Indirect Witnesses

Clement of Alexandria

Writing around the end of the second century or start of the third century,[38] Clement of Alexandria makes the most use of the Epistle of Barnabas of any single early Christian author whose writings are extant.[39] Clement echoes the record of Barnabas found in Paul's letters and Acts by connecting Barnabas to Paul. Clement identifies Barnabas as Paul's co-worker (συνεργὸς τοῦ Παύλου; *Strom.* 2.116.3 [20]).[40] Barnabas is also referred

---

36. Schenke, "Barnabasbrief," 911. The papyrus has been published and translated into German in Schenke Robinson, Schenke, and Plisch, *Berliner "Koptische Buch"* and is dated to the second or third century by the editors.

37. Schenke, "Barnabasbrief," 932–33.

38. For a helpful account of the relationships between the various writings attributed to Clement, see Osborn, *Clement*, 5–15.

39. Windisch (*Barnabasbrief*, 301, 328–29) finds earlier readers in Justin (e.g., 1 *Apol.* 31–33; 52; 63–64), Marcus (see Irenaeus, *Haer.* 1.15.2), and Irenaeus (4.20.4). However, it is difficult to ascertain whether these references are directly to *Barnabas*. They will thus not be included in the discussion here.

40. All quotations from Clement's *Stromateis* come from Stählin, *Stromata Buch I-VI*.

to as an apostle in his own right. This occurs in both nominal form (ὁ ἀπόστολος Βαρνάβας; *Strom*. 2.31.3 [6]; Βαρνάβας ὁ ἀπόστολος; 2.35.5 [7]) and through the use of an adjective (ἀποστολικός; *Strom*. 2.116.3 [20]).[41] Although Clement highlights Barnabas's apostolic credentials as Paul's collaborator, he also ties Barnabas to the ministry of the historical Jesus.[42] While introducing a quotation from Barn. 16, Clement declares that Barnabas was one of the seventy (ὃ δὲ τῶν ἑβδομήκοντα ἦν; *Strom*. 2.116.3 [20]) who are mentioned in Luke 10.[43]

Clement is important not only because his writings indicate how the Epistle of Barnabas may have been used and interpreted by at least some of his earliest readers but also because some of the lengthy quotations of the Epistle of Barnabas may shed some light on the text of the letter around the end of the second century.[44] His citations of the Epistle of Barnabas center around *Barnabas's* quotations of scripture.[45] For example, Clement's citation of Isa 58:4–7 in *Paed*. 3.90.1–2 (12) is strikingly similar both to the text and interpretation in Barn. 3.1–3.[46] Clement employs *Barnabas* as a model for some of his allegorical interpretations. This is clearest with regards to the ethical interpretation of the Levitical food laws in Barn. 10.[47] However, Clement does not feel obliged to follow *Barnabas's* interpretation at every point. Although Clement finds some value in the literal interpretation of the kosher laws (*Paed*. 2.17.1 [1]; *Strom*. 2.105.1–3 [20]),[48] he rejects the

41. In referring to Barnabas as an apostle, Clement may implicitly reflect his awareness of 1 Cor 9:6. When writing to the Corinthians, Paul places Barnabas alongside himself as an example of apostolic figures who have given up marriage in the service of the gospel. For further accounts of the way in which Paul and Barnabas worked together, see especially Acts 13:1—14:28.

42. For more on Clement's introductions of Barnabas, see Ruwet, "Clément," 391.

43. Öhler (*Barnabas: Der Mann in der Mitte*, 158–60) helpfully outlines the way in which Clement of Alexandria, Pseudo-Clementine literature, and others in early Christianity discuss Barnabas as a disciple of Jesus. On the textual problem in Luke 10:1 regarding the number seventy or seventy-two, see Cole, "P45 and the Problem of the 'Seventy(-two),'" 203–21; Metzger, "Seventy or Seventy-Two Disciples," 299–306; Wolter, *Lukasevangelium*, 376–77. Clement provides evidence for the reading "seventy" from late in the second century.

44. For further evaluation of Clement's value for textual criticism on the Epistle of Barnabas, see Prostmeier, *Barnabasbrief*, 45–46; Prostmeier, "Einleitung," 27–29.

45. Van den Hoek, "Clement," 97; van den Hoek, "Techniques," 235.

46. All quotations from Clement's *Paedagogus* come from Stählin, *Protrepticus und Paedagogus*.

47. *Paed*. 3.75.3–76.1 (10); *Strom*. 5.51.2–52.1 (8). See Barn. 10.3–4, 11

48. Clement's allowance of both a literal and figurative understanding of the law mirrors his understanding of both an old and new covenant (e.g., *Paed*. 1.59.1 [7]). On Clement of Alexandria and the Epistle of Barnabas, see further Carleton Paget, *The Epistle of Barnabas*, 244–45.

interpretation of the hyena in Barn. 10.7 and suggests that there is a confusion between nature and passion in the Barnabean interpretation (*Paed.* 2.83.4–5 [10]).[49] While Clement regards the Epistle of Barnabas as an authoritative text and cites it regularly in the *Paedagogus* and *Stromateis*, he feels free to interject, supplement, and occasionally disagree with the interpretations of scripture that *Barnabas* records.[50]

Other Witnesses

Origen, Didymus, Eusebius, and Jerome likewise employ the Epistle of Barnabas in their works. Writing a few decades after Clement, Origen likewise cites the Epistle of Barnabas. In *Princ.* 3.2.4, he refers to the authority of angels over the two ways from Barn. 18.1.[51] Later in Origen's career, he claims that Celsus took the teaching that the apostles were infamous from Barn. 5.9 (*Cels.* 1.63).[52] Origen introduces the initial citation by referring to what Barnabas declares in his letter (*Barnabas in epistola sua declarat*; *Princ.* 3.2.4), while the second mention of the Epistle of Barnabas describes what is found "in Barnabas's catholic letter" (ἐν τῇ Βαρνάβα καθολικῇ ἐπιστολῇ; *Cels.* 1.63). Didymus the Blind follows Origen and Clement by referring to the letter as if Barnabas wrote it. He highlights Barnabas's relationship with Paul in their work on behalf of the uncircumcised in a citation of Barn. 1.1 (*Zach.* 259), while Didymus twice mentions the connection that *Barnabas* makes between blackness and the devil (*Zach.* 234; 355).[53] Like Clement, Eusebius knew of a tradition in which Barnabas was reported to have been

---

49. Ruwet, "Clément," 392. Clement likewise shows himself to be both indebted to and independent from the interpretation of the food laws in Barn. 10 when he prefers other interpretations of Ps 1:1 than the explanation offered in Barn. 10.10 (*Strom.* 2.67.1–69.4 [15]). On these passages, see Brooks, "Clement of Alexandria," 46; van den Hoek, "Clement," 97.

50. On the authority that the Epistle of Barnabas had for Clement, see Brooks, "Clement," 47; Cosaert, *Text of the Gospels*, 22 n 8. For lists of citations from the Epistle of Barnabas in the writings of Clement, see van den Hoek, "Clement," 97 n 20; Prigent and Kraft, *Épître de Barnabé*, 54; Prostmeier, *Barnabasbrief*, 36–44.

51. All quotations from Origen's *De principiis* can be found in Behr, *On First Principles*. This work can be dated around 230 CE (Behr, *On First Principles*, 1.xvii).

52. All quotations from Origen's *Contra Celsum* come from Borret, *Contre Celse*. *Contra Celsum* likely dates to a time not long before the Decian persecution, perhaps around 246–248 (Chadwick, *Contra Celsum*, xiv–xv).

53. On the blackness of the devil and its connections to the Epistle of Barnabas, see Rothschild, "Ethiopianising the Devil," 236. All quotations of Didymus's *Commentary on Zechariah* come from Doutreleau, *Didyme*. Didymus links the Epistle of Barnabas with the Shepherd of Hermas in the latter two passages and may have a passage like Herm. *Sim.* 9.19.1 (96.1) in mind (Ehrman, "New Testament Canon," 12–13).

included among the seventy (*Hist. eccl.* 1.12.1). It is thus not hard to see how Eusebius can describe Barnabas as an apostle (*Hist. eccl.* 2.1.4).[54] However, he makes a clearer distinction between the Epistle of Barnabas and other books that have canonical authority (*Hist. eccl.* 3.25.4) than Clement, Origen, or Didymus.[55] Jerome similarly attributes one letter to Barnabas. He views it as "suitable for the encouragement of the church" (*ad aedificationem ecclesiae pertinentem*) but notes that "it is collected among the apocryphal writings" (*inter apocryphas scripturas legitur*; *Vir.* 6).[56] Like Eusebius, Jerome separates the Epistle of Barnabas from other writings that had greater authority in the ecclesial communities of his day.

Such clear third- and fourth-century attestation is intriguing to read alongside a canon list found in Codex Claromontanus.[57] The catalogue is unusual because it omits Philippians, Hebrews, and the Thessalonian letters. However, it includes the Epistle of Barnabas, the Shepherd of Hermas, the Acts of Paul, and the Apocalypse of Peter. Since Hebrews is omitted from the catalogue and there was a tradition that Barnabas wrote Hebrews (Tertullian, *Pud.* 20.2; Jerome, *Vir.* 6), some have understood the reference to *Epistula Barnabae* in the list of books as another name for *Epistula ad Hebraeos*.[58] However, since the catalogue was inserted into the codex later, it is unclear whether *Epistula Barnabae* refers to Hebrews or to the Epistle of Barnabas that is now included in collections of the Apostolic

---

54. While Eusebius associates Barnabas with Jesus's ministry, Tertullian emphasizes his links to Paul by quoting 1 Cor 9:6. Tertullian concludes from this that Barnabas was "a man fully authorized by God" (*a Deo satis auctoritati uiri*; *Pud.* 20.2). All quotations from Tertullian's *De pudicitia* come from Micaelli, *Tertullien: La pudicite*.

55. All quotations from Eusebius's *Hist. eccl.* come from Bardy, *Histoire ecclésiastique*.

56. All quotations from Jerome's *De viris illustribus* come from Richardson, *Hieronymus, Liber de viris illustribus*.

57. For the text, see Tischendorf, *Codex Claromontanus*, 468–69; Westcott *A General Survey*, 555–57. Codex Claromontanus (BnF gr. 107) can be viewed online at https://gallica.bnf.fr/ark:/12148/btv1b84683111 (accessed December 2, 2020). The catalogue is found on folios 467v, 468r, and 468v. This codex contains a dual-language edition of the Pauline epistles and has been dated from the fifth to the seventh centuries. On the date of the codex, see Aland, Hannick, and Junack, "Bibelhandschriften II," 123; Houghton, *Latin New Testament*, 243; Parker, *Introduction*, 259–60. The codex is dated to the second half of the fifth century on the website of the Bibliothèque Nationale de France, where the manuscript is housed (https://archivesetmanuscrits.bnf.fr/ark:/12148/cc21107b; accessed 2 December 2020). It is unclear when the catalogue was composed and incorporated into the codex.

58. Westcott, *A General Survey*, 557 n 1; Kraft, *Barnabas*, 41; De Boer, "Tertullian on Barnabas's Letter to the Hebrews," 252.

Fathers. On balance, it seems better to understand Codex Claromontanus as referring to the Epistle of Barnabas.[59]

Authority and the Question of Canon

The high regard with which the Epistle of Barnabas was held can thus be traced in several pieces of evidence from the centuries after it was composed, while others attempted to differentiate the place of the letter from the writings included in the New Testament.[60] Clement exposits Barn. 16.7–9 (*Strom.* 2.116.3–2.117.4 [20]) not long after a citation of Matt 7:7 and without any distinction of authority between the two texts (*Strom.* 2.116.2 [20]).[61] Didymus justifies his understanding of Zechariah with reference to 1 Corinthians, Galatians, 1 Peter, and the Epistle of Barnabas (*Zach.* 259). Since Didymus does not distinguish between the authority of Paul, Peter, or Barnabas, Ehrman argues that Didymus's New Testament canon extended to include the Epistle of Barnabas.[62] On the other hand, Eusebius differentiates the Epistle of Barnabas from canonical writings when he places *Barnabas* in the category of ἀντιλεγούμενα (*Hist. eccl.* 3.25.6).[63] Jerome specifies that the Epistle of Barnabas is included among the apocryphal writings, and its authority is thus regarded in different terms from texts included in the New Testament (*Vir.* 6). *Barnabas*'s place within manuscripts is also noteworthy in such discussions. The inclusion of the Epistle of Barnabas in S as well as the catalogue in Codex Claromontanus has been thought to provide evidence for its inclusion within at least some canons held by early Christians.[64] If the texts in H were placed together for

---

59. See further Tischendorf, *Codex Claromontanus*, 468–69; Westcott, *A General Survey*, 555–57.

60. For more on this topic as well as additional information about the Epistle of Barnabas's reception history, see Harnack, *Geschichte*, 1.58–62; Öhler, *Barnabas: Der Mann in der Mitte*, 156–58.

61. One may recall, however, that Clement disagrees with the Epistle of Barnabas, even though he attributed a great deal of authority to the text (*Paed.* 2.83.4–5 [10]; *Strom.* 2.67.1–69.4 [15]). Gwatkin (*Early Church History*, 1.105) includes Origen alongside Clement as early writers who viewed the Epistle of Barnabas as scripture.

62. Ehrman, "New Testament Canon," 14.

63. It may also be worth noting that the Epistle of Barnabas is not mentioned in Origen's list of New Testament books in *Hom. Jes. Nav.* 7.1. See further Carleton Paget, *Epistle of Barnabas*, 250–51. All quotations from Origen's *Hom. Jes. Nav.* come from Jaubert, *Homélies*.

64. However, Batovici ("The Apostolic Fathers," 599–605) has argued that the separation in S of the Epistle of Barnabas and the Shepherd of Hermas from texts of a similar genre may indicate that the texts are to be understood differently from the canonical texts in the manuscript.

a reason, the grouping of these texts may indicate that they are different in some ways from the texts included in the New Testament.[65]

The initially confusing data regarding the authority of the Epistle of Barnabas suggest the need for further nuance than a simple bifurcated choice might allow. Rather than asking whether *Barnabas* was or was not canonical for a particular author, it may be better to conceive of some sort of intermediate class of writings.[66] Such distinctions are necessary when looking at the history of early Christianity because certain books seem to have floated near the fringes of the canon. However, this choice of words keeps the discussion limited to terms of canon. Since canon suggests a fixed list of authoritative books, the evidence of the second and third centuries may be better served by reflecting on authority rather than canonicity.[67]

The Epistle of Barnabas maintained a great deal of authority for its readers in the centuries following its composition. This authority was of a different order, however, from the letters of Paul or the four Gospels. The relative difference in the weight given to the Epistle of Barnabas is illustrated in the fact that it is cited less often and less regularly even by some of the most well-read early Christians like Origen, Eusebius, and Jerome.[68] Lesser authority is also evident in Clement's willingness to prefer another interpretation of the food laws than what is evinced in Barn. 10. The Epistle of Barnabas thus fits well in what François Bovon usefully termed "books useful to the soul."[69] Such terminology honors the position given to the Epistle of Barnabas by some of its earliest readers while acknowledging that this authority was of a different order from at least some of the texts that were later included in the New Testament.

---

65. Prostmeier, *Barnabasbrief*, 58; Prostmeier, "Einleitung," 33.

66. Ruwet ("Les apocryphes," 334) similarly refers to "une classe de livres intermédiaire" (an intermediate class of writings) that exists in Origen's writings. For other attempts to distinguish levels of authority among early Christian writings, see McDonald, *Forgotten Scriptures*, 25; Sanders, *Torah and Canon*, 91; Sheppard, "Canon," 3.62–69; Sundberg, "Canon Muratori," 35; van Unnik, "De la règle," 1–36.

67. Carleton Paget's (*Epistle of Barnabas*, 248–58) use of the word "venerated" also fits the evidence well. For helpful discussion of issues surrounding the borders of the New Testament canon, see Gallagher and Meade, *Biblical Canon Lists*, 52–56.

68. Prostmeier (*Barnabasbrief*, 58–62; "Einleitung," 33–35) likewise points out that the Epistle of Barnabas is mentioned in only five canon lists from antiquity.

69. Bovon, "Canonical, Rejected, and Useful Books," 318–22; Bovon, "Beyond," 125–37; Bovon, "'Useful for the Soul,'" 185–95.

Date and Provenance

With a firm grasp of the ways in which the Epistle of Barnabas is attested in early manuscripts and quoted by some if its early readers, the next matter to turn to concerns the origins of the text. What evidence can be produced to clarify when and where this text originated? Both questions are difficult to answer with respect to the Epistle of Barnabas. However, this section turns to the place of origin first because it is slightly less complicated than the document's murky temporal origins.

Provenance

Three regions are suggested most often as possible places of origin for the Epistle of Barnabas: Alexandria, Asia Minor, and Syria/Palestine.[70]

Alexandria has been the most widely selected city chosen by those who have conducted research on the Epistle of Barnabas.[71] Four arguments are most commonly made in favor of Alexandrian origin. First, Alexandrian authors and manuscripts cite *Barnabas* earliest and most regularly. Clement of Alexandria, Origen, and Didymus the Blind all have Alexandrian connections and make use of *Barnabas*. The text in S may also have Egyptian connections, and the availability of the Epistle of Barnabas in Egypt suggests Alexandrian, or at least Egyptian, origins. Although the acceptance of *Barnabas* in a location does not necessitate that it originated there, its popularity among Alexandrian writers strongly suggests that its origins are Egyptian. Second, *Barnabas* makes heavy use of figural exegesis. Such modes of exegesis are widely attested at Alexandria in writers such as Philo, Clement of Alexandria, and Origen.[72] Third, Barnabas's

---

70. Greece and Rome are occasionally mentioned, but these options are rarely defended at length. For example, Lindemann and Paulsen (*Die apostolischen Väter*, 24) mention Greece as a possible origin for the Epistle of Barnabas, but they likewise do not expand on this suggestion. Prostmeier (*Barnabasbrief*, 119–20; "Barnabasbrief," 45–46; "Einleitung," 57; "Epistle of Barnabas," 33) mentions Greece and Rome in his discussions of Barnabean origins but does not expand upon why these options might be attractive.

71. Carleton Paget, *Epistle of Barnabas*, 36–42; Gunther, "Association," 21–29; Jefford, *Apostolic Fathers and the New Testament*, 31–33; Lightfoot, *Apostolic Fathers*, 1.2.504–5; Norris, "Apostolic and Sub-Apostolic Writings," 15; Pearson, "Earliest Christianity in Egypt: Some Observations," 150–51; Pearson, "Earliest Christianity in Egypt: Further Observations," 100–103; Pearson, "Egypt," 332; Prostmeier, *Barnabasbrief*, 119–30; Streeter, *Primitive Church*, 242–44;

72. For further discussion, see Funk, *Patres apostolici*, 1.xxv; Martín, "L'interpretatione allegorica," 173–83; Niehoff, *Jewish Exegesis*, 133–85; Runia, *Philo*, 92–93.

anti-cultic interpretations of scripture are reminiscent of Hellenistic Jewish groups that were known to Philo (*Migr.* 89–93).⁷³ Fourth, the Epistle of Barnabas refers to the practice of circumcision among Syrians, Arabs, pagan priests, and Egyptians (Barn. 9.6). Circumcision may have been widespread in Egypt, but it is not well-known in Syria. It is possible, then, that the author has extended what he found in his own Egyptian situation and considered it to be true of other regions.

Klaus Wengst has argued instead that Asia Minor would provide a suitable environment in which to envision the origins of the Epistle of Barnabas.⁷⁴ The primary piece of evidence that Wengst uses comes from the letters of Ignatius of Antioch. When writing to the Philadelphians, Ignatius refers to a group that insists on using the archives, which are best understood as a reference to Jewish scripture, as the basis for believing in the gospel (Ign. *Phld.* 8.2).⁷⁵ Wengst suggests that the similarities between the Epistle of Barnabas and Ignatius's Philadelphian opponents provide a provenance in which to read the Epistle of Barnabas.⁷⁶ Pierre Prigent argues that the Epistle of Barnabas was most likely written in Syria/Palestine.⁷⁷ He calls attention to soteriological, ethical, and eschatological similarities between *Barnabas* and some of the Qumran scrolls.⁷⁸ He also appeals to similarities between the Epistle of Barnabas and elements of Rabbinic tradition. Finally, he argues that common motifs in both the

---

73. Unless otherwise noted, all quotations of Philo come from Cohn and Wendland, *Philonis Alexandrini opera*, vols. 1–6.

74. Wengst, *Didache*, 115–18; Wengst, *Tradition und Theologie*, 113–18.

75. On Ignatius's opponents in Philadelphia, see Nicklas, *Jews and Christians*, 128; Paulsen, *Studien*, 57; Schoedel, "Ignatius and the Archives," 97–101; Speigl, "Ignatius in Philadelphia," 364; von der Goltz, *Ignatius von Antiochien*, 80; Zetterholm, *Formation of Christianity*, 209. On the Philadelphian incident, see further Hartog, "Good News," 105–21; Lookadoo, "Ignatius of Antioch and Scripture," 204–8.

76. "Der Phld zeigt eine Gemeindesituation, in die der Barn als Propagandaschreiben gut hineinpassen würde" ("*Philadelphians* exhibits a community situation in which *Barnabas* would fit well as a propaganda letter;" Wengst, *Tradition und Theologie* 118). Although Wengst prefers an Asian provenance for the Epistle of Barnabas, he indicates a willingness to leave the matter open in his *TRE* article. See Wengst, "Barnabasbrief," 239.

77. Prigent also argues against an Alexandrian origin by noting that the Epistle of Barnabas does not have a Logos Christology and maintains an eschatological focus, two things which he regards as unusual if *Barnabas* is indeed Alexandrian (Prigent and Kraft, *Épître de Barnabé*, 21).

78. Shukster and Richardson ("Temple and *Bet Ha-midrash*, 17–20) likewise point to the eschatological interest in *Barnabas* as evidence for a Syrian or Palestinian provenance.

Epistle of Barnabas and Justin's *Dialogue with Trypho* stem from their common origins around Syria/Palestine.⁷⁹

Although Prigent and Wengst point out that arguments for an Alexandrian origin are not decisive, the arguments for Alexandria continue to be the strongest. Clement's early and consistent citations of *Barnabas* suggest that the letter was known in Alexandria from an early time, and this is easiest to explain if the author wrote in or around the city. While Alexandria by no means had a monopoly on figurative exegesis, it was a popular mode of interpretation in some Alexandrian authors during the first three centuries CE. Such arguments cannot definitively decide the matter but tip the scales in favor of Alexandria as the place from which the Epistle of Barnabas originated.⁸⁰

Date

Although the *terminus post quem* and *terminus ante quem* can be decided with relative ease for the Epistle of Barnabas, more specific determination of when the letter was written has proved more difficult to decide. The destruction of the temple in Jerusalem is mentioned in Barn. 16.3–4. In light of this, the letter must have been written after 70 CE. The earliest citations of the letter provide the *terminus ante quem*. Clement of Alexandria employs *Barnabas* in his writings at the end of the second century. The Epistle of Barnabas can thus be securely dated to the years between 70 and 200 CE.⁸¹ Two additional pieces of evidence have been brought forward to help date the Epistle of Barnabas.⁸² The first is the references to the

---

79. Prigent and Kraft, *Épître de Barnabé*, 22–24. See also Murray, *Playing a Jewish Game*, 47–48. Justin reports that he was born in Flavia Neapolis (*1 Apol.* 1.1). All citations from Justin's *Apologies* come from Minns and Parvis, *Justin*. On Justin's biography, see further Barnard, *Justin*, 5; Minns and Parvis, *Justin*, 32.

80. Reidar Hvalvik (*Struggle for Scripture and Covenant*, 41–42) has argued that the Epistle of Barnabas cannot be located to a particular city or region, opting instead to say only that the text originated in the eastern part of the Mediterranean world, likely in dialogue with Diaspora Judaism.

81. Hvalvik, *Struggle for Scripture and Covenant*, 17; Prostmeier, *Barnabasbrief*, 111; Prostmeier, "Einleitung," 56; Williams, "Date," 337–38.

82. See also Barnard, "Date," 101; Carleton Paget, *Epistle of Barnabas*, 9; Carleton Paget, "*Epistle of Barnabas*," 74–75; Hvalvik, *Struggle for Scripture and Covenant*, 17; Jefford, *Apostolic Fathers and the New Testament*, 33–34; Lightfoot, *Apostolic Fathers*, 1.2.506; Prigent and Kraft, *Épître de Barnabé*, 26; Prinzivalli and Simonetti, *Seguendo Gesù*, 2.78; Richardson and Shukster, "Barnabas," 32; Wengst, "Barnabasbrief," 238; Wengst, *Didache*, 114; Williams, "Date," 337–46.

kingdoms, beasts, and horns in 4.3-5, while the second concerns reports of a rebuilding project in 16.3-4.

Barnabas 4.3-5

The author of the Epistle of Barnabas offers a series of ethical and eschatological warnings in Barn. 4.1-5 before turning to the question of covenantal possession in Barn. 4.6-10.[83] In Barn. 4.3, the author says that the final stumbling block has drawn near (τὸ τέλειον σκάνδαλον ἤγγικεν). This should motivate the people to act rightly and turn away from works of lawlessness. The author then writes:

> ⁴ λέγει δὲ οὕτως καὶ ὁ προφήτης· βασιλεῖαι[84] δέκα ἐπὶ τῆς γῆς βασιλεύσουσιν καὶ ἐξαναστήσεται ὄπισθεν αὐτῶν[85] μικρὸς βασιλεύς, ὃς ταπεινώσει τρεῖς ὑφ᾽ ἓν τῶν βασιλειῶν.[86] ⁵ ὁμοίως περὶ τοῦ αὐτοῦ λέγει Δανιήλ· καὶ εἶδον τὸ τέταρτον θηρίον πονηρὸν καὶ ἰσχυρὸν καὶ χαλεπώτερον παρὰ πάντα τὰ θηρία τῆς θαλάσσης[87] καὶ ὡς ἐξ αὐτοῦ ἀνέτειλεν δέκα κέρατα καὶ ἐξ αὐτῶν μικρὸν κέρας παραφυάδιον καὶ ὡς ἐταπείνωσεν ὑφ᾽ ἓν τρία τῶν μεγάλων κεράτων.

> ⁴ And so also the prophet says, "Ten kings will rule over the earth, and a small king will arise after them who will humiliate three of the kings at once." ⁵ Daniel likewise says about this, "And I saw the fourth beast, evil and strong and worse than all of the beasts of the sea, and how ten horns rose up from it, and a small horn from them—an offshoot—and how it humbled three of the great horns at once." (Barn. 4.4-5)

---

83. For a more detailed, although slightly different, outline, see Rhodes, *Epistle of Barnabas*, 44-45. Hilgenfeld (*Barnabae Epistula: Integram graece iterum edidit*, 9) moved Barn. 4.3-5 after Barn. 4.9 in the second edition of his text of the Epistle of Barnabas. He did not make this move in the first edition of his text (Hilgenfeld, *Barnabae Epistula: Integram graece primum edidit*, 8). Since there is no manuscript evidence for this move and little to justify such an alteration, there is no reason to seriously consider his emendation of the text.

84 This reading follows S and L, which read βασιλεῖαι and *regna*, respectively. However, H reads βασιλεῖς, which could be translated as "kingdoms."

85. The pronoun αὐτῶν is not found in H and L. At this point, the text used for this commentary follows S.

86 This reading again follows L, which contains *de regnis* and could provide evidence for a Vorlage of βασιλειῶν. On the other hand, S and H both read βασιλέων.

87. This reading follows H and L, which read θαλάσσης and *marinis*, respectively. S contains a different reading, namely, γῆς.

The quotations come from Dan 7:24 (Barn. 4.4) and 7:7–8 (Barn. 4.5). Certain elements of the quotations parallel the other. The ten kings in Barn. 4.4 mirror the ten horns in Barn. 4.5. The small king in Barn. 4.4 is set alongside the small horn in Barn. 4.5. The small king and small horn work to humiliate three of their betters. Moreover, they both succeed in humiliating their predecessors "at once" (ὑφ' ἕν).[88] The fourth beast that is more evil than the beasts of the sea represents Rome.[89] The ten kings and ten horns should thus be understood as Roman kings, while the smaller entity that follows likely refers to yet another Caesar.

With this interpretive background in place, the question now becomes one of identifying which king is in view. Two difficulties arise with regard to the ten kings. First, with whom should one begin counting?[90] Second, how should one count the kings who ruled for only very brief periods of time?[91] In answering these questions, authors have identified the small king as any of the Caesars from Vespasian (69–79 CE) to Hadrian (117–138 CE).[92] The most likely solutions to the riddle are Vespasian, Nerva (96–98 CE), and either Hadrian or a Nero redivivus figure at the time of Hadrian.

---

88. Some translate these words along the lines of "under one," thereby emphasizing the domination of the small king and horn over the three that precede it (e.g., Lake, *Apostolic Fathers*, 1.349, 351). Cunningham (*Dissertation*, 15) calls "under one" the "natural and obvious sense" of ὑφ' ἕν. For a defense of this interpretation, see Richardson and Shukster, "Barnabas," 39–40. However, such a translation would be more appropriate if the text contained the masculine number, i.e., ὑφ' ἕνα. With the neuter ἕν in Barn. 4.4–5, the prepositional phrase is employed temporally and emphasizes the way in which the three kings or three horns fell suddenly and collectively. See the translations in Holmes, *Apostolic Fathers*, 387, 389; Lindemann and Paulsen, *Apostolischen Väter*, 33; Prigent and Kraft, *Épître de Barnabé*, 95; Prinzivalli and Simonetti, *Seguendo Gesù*, 2.121; Wengst, *Didache*, 145. Defenses of the latter interpretation can be found in Barnard, "Date," 104; Carleton Paget, *Epistle of Barnabas*, 11; Hvalvik, *Struggle for Scripture and Covenant*, 27; Williams, "Date," 343.

89. A similar identification of Rome and the fourth beast can be found in Rev 17:7–14; *Sib. Or.* 3.388–400; 4 Ezra 11.36–46; 12.10–13. For discussion of the fourth beast's identity in Barn. 4.5, see Barnard, "Date," 103.

90. For example, does the author include Julius Caesar? Or is it best to begin with Augustus?

91. For example, how does one account for the place of Galba, Otho, and Vitellius during the Year of the Four Emperors? Should they be counted at all, collectively, or individually? Are any kings skipped and, if so, which ones? An additional problem comes when identifying the humiliated kings. Which three kings does the author mean and how does the author regard them as humiliated? Finally, who is the small king? Is this a real emperor who ruled in Rome? Or is the small king a symbolic figure?

92. Prigent writes that the enumeration in Barn. 4.4–5 "is open to several interpretations" ("est susceptible de plusieurs interprétations"; Prigent and Kraft, *Épître de Barnabé*, 26). For a convenient chart laying out the options with references to earlier scholarly discussion, see Hvalvik, *Struggle for Scripture and Covenant*, 29.

Barnard argues for the last option by numbering the ten kings beginning with Augustus rather than Julius and omitting the three short-lived emperors of 69.[93] He identifies these three kings with the Flavian emperors: Vespasian, Titus, and Domitian.[94] While such an interpretation of 4.5 is intriguing, the assertion that the three horns that are crushed by the small horn can refer to any three horns in the sequence seems strained.[95] Working backward in Roman chronology from Barnard's suggestion of Hadrian, Nerva provides the next option that has been considered. If one begins counting at Augustus and omits one of the three emperors who briefly followed Nero, Nerva is the eleventh Caesar and may thus be identified as the offshoot.[96] As a relatively small king in terms of his power, Nerva is a good fit to the riddle of the small horn.[97] That his ascension to the throne resulted in the downfall of the three Flavian emperors provides an additional point in his favor.[98] While Nerva is a fitting candidate for the small horn, Vespasian provides the easiest solution to the imperial scheme of ten emperors. For Vespasian to count as the final emperor in the ten, one must begin counting

---

93. He thus ends up with the following list: (1) Augustus, (2) Tiberius, (3) Gaius Caligula, (4) Tiberius, (5) Nero, (6) Vespasian, (7) Titus, (8) Domitian, (9) Nerva, and (10) Trajan (Barnard, "Date," 104).

94. Barnard ("Date," 107) concludes that Nero redivivus will arise during the time of Hadrian, but one could use the same enumerations to identify Hadrian as the small horn.

95. Even accepting Barnard's claim that the three once great horns can come from anywhere along the line, it is difficult to see how the Flavian emperors were humiliated at once (ὑφ' ἕν). See Hvalvik, *Struggle for Scripture and Covenant*, 30–31.

96. This would lead to a list of (1) Augustus, (2) Tiberius, (3) Gaius Caligula, (4) Tiberius, (5) Nero, (6 and 7) two out of Galba, Otho, and Vitellius, (8) Vespasian, (9) Titus, (10) Domitian, (11) Nerva. Hilgenfeld (*Barnabae Epistula: Integram graece iterum edidit*, xxxvi–xxxvii) argued that Vitellius was not acclaimed emperor in Egypt and, if an Egyptian provenance is assumed for the Epistle of Barnabas, that the author did not include Vitellius in the imperial numbers. Alternatively, Richardson and Shukster ("Barnabas," 38–41) downplay the significance of the ten horns and instead focused on the identity of the small horn and three humiliated kings.

97. As an old and childless appointee of the Senate, he was not at first blush an obvious candidate for emperor with particularly strong military connections.

98. See the following for variant arguments and proposals in favor of Nerva: Bartlet, *Apostolic Age*, 521; Ewald, *Geschichte*, 7.157–58; Jefford, *Apostolic Fathers and the New Testament*, 33–34; Murray, *Playing a Jewish Game*, 44–47; Ramsay, *Church in the Roman Empire*, 307–9. Nevertheless, this identification is not without problems. For example, one may object that their humiliation did not occur ὑφ' ἕν. Vespasian died in 79 CE, while his son Titus followed him not long after in 81 CE. Domitian's assassination in 96 CE leaves a period of seventeen years between the death of the father and the fall of the second son—not immediately a period that one living at that time might refer to as happening at once. On this objection, see Hvalvik, *Struggle for Scripture and Covenant*, 30–31.

at Julius Caesar, whose self-acclamation as *imperator* famously led to his assassination. Every emperor after Julius can be enumerated without any further complications.[99] Alternatively, one may think that Vespasian is the tenth but argue that the offshoot is a reference to Nero redivivus.[100] In either case, the chronology with Vespasian is relatively neat.[101]

Either Vespasian (69-79 CE) or Nerva (96-98 CE) provides the most plausible identification of the small king and small horn in 4.4-5. The choice of Hadrian may owe some of its attractiveness to interpretations of the temple in 16.3-4. It is to this passage that we turn next.

Barnabas 16.3-4

The author transitions to a discussion of the temple in 16.1 and asserts that the Jews mistakenly placed their hope in a building rather than the God who created them. He insists that this is idolatrous and analogous to the gentiles (16.2). Jewish hopes in their temple have come to naught. This may allude to the destruction of the temple in 70 CE, but the author states this more clearly in 16.3-4.

³ πέρας γέ τοι πάλιν λέγει· ἰδού, οἱ καθελόντες τὸν ναὸν τοῦτον αὐτοὶ αὐτὸν οἰκοδομήσουσιν. ⁴ γίνεται·[102] διὰ γὰρ τὸ πολεμεῖν

---

99. This would thus run as follows: (1) Julius, (2) Augustus, (3) Tiberius, (4) Gaius Caligula, (5) Tiberius, (6) Nero, (7) Galba, (8) Otho, (9) Vitellius, and (10) Vespasian. Vespasian's place as the small horn would then come "from (among) them" (ἐξ αὐτῶν; Barn. 4.5), since he is included in the list of the ten and is also the offshoot. See Funk, *Patres apostolici*, 1.xxiv–xxv; Gwatkin, *Early Church History*, 1.105; Hvalvik, *Struggle for Scripture and Covenant*, 27–32.

100. The count would thus run as follows: (1) Julius, (2) Augustus, (3) Tiberius, (4) Gaius Caligula, (5) Tiberius, (6) Nero, (7) Galba, (8) Otho, (9) Vitellius, (10) Vespasian, and (11) Nero redivivus. Lightfoot, *Apostolic Fathers*, 1.2.510–12.

101. Difficulties associated with this view include whether Julius is an appropriate starting point for counting the horns and whether or not Vespasian can plausibly be said to have destroyed his three predecessors. For further discussion, see Carleton Paget, *Epistle of Barnabas*, 14–15.

102. The inclusion of γίνεται is one of the most difficult and interpretively significant variants in the Epistle of Barnabas. It is found only in G and L, which reads *et fiet*. However, it is missing in S and H. The tensions in the verb tenses that result from including γίνεται make it the more difficult reading. It is difficult to see why it should be added to a text that did not already include it, while it is easier to imagine the deletion of a difficult word for the sake of the readability of the text.

αὐτοὺς καθῃρέθη ὑπὸ τῶν ἐχθρῶν. νῦν καὶ αὐτοὶ[103] οἱ τῶν ἐχθρῶν ὑπηρέται ἀνοικοδομήσουσιν[104] αὐτόν.

³ Moreover, he says again, "Behold, those who tore down this temple will rebuild it." ⁴ It is happening. For because they went to war, it was torn down by the enemies. And now those who are servants of the enemies will rebuild it.

The most difficult question to answer with regard to 16.3–4 concerns the temple that is going to be rebuilt. The claim that the rebuilding "is happening" accentuates both the difficulty and the promise of answering this question.

Three options present themselves, and arguments for and against each of them will be given in more detail when the commentary comes to 16.3–4. In short, the temple that will be rebuilt could be spiritual, the temple to Jupiter in Aelia Capitolina, or a third Jewish temple. A spiritual temple is unlikely to be in view in 16.4 because it would interrupt the flow of the author's argument.[105] While Barnabas articulates the significance of a spiritual temple in 16.6–10, a physical temple is more likely to be in view in 16.4. Both Dio Cassius (*Hist.* 69.12.1–2) and Eusebius (*Hist. eccl.* 4.6.4) know of plans to rebuild a temple to Jupiter on the Temple Mount in Jerusalem.[106] Yet it is difficult to make sense of the grammar of 16.4 if a

---

103. S includes an additional καί after αὐτοί (i.e. νῦν καὶ αὐτοὶ καὶ οἱ τῶν ἐχθρῶν ὑπηρέται). If accepted, this would result in a two-part subject for the end of Barn. 16.4: "And now they and the servants of their enemies." Cunningham (*Dissertation*, 72–73) follows S. The text for this commentary follows H, G, and L (*nunc et ipsi inimicorum ministri*) on the supposition that these three collectively present the stronger manuscript basis. For this text, see Wengst, *Didache*, 184.

104. The text here follows the future indicative verb found in H and G. S includes the aorist subjunctive ἀνοικοδομήσωσιν. L reads *ab initio aedificant*, containing a present tense verb along with an additional temporal phrase. L brings the latter half of Barn. 16.4 into harmony with the claim that the rebuilding is happening (*et fiet*). If G and L are followed regarding the presence of γίνεται, then the future tense verb in G and, in this case, H provides the more difficult reading. The present-tense claim that the rebuilding is happening contrasts with the author's claim that the temple will be rebuilt. The future tense should thus be retained as the more difficult reading in the text.

105. For arguments in favor of a spiritual temple in 16.4, see Gunther, "Epistle of Barnabas," 151. Other proponents of this view include Prigent and Kraft, *Épître de Barnabé*, 190–91; Williams, "Date," 340–43. For arguments in favor of a temple to Jupiter, see Hvalvik, *Struggle for Scripture and Covenant*, 23; Lipsius, "Barnabasbrief," 371–72; Prostmeier, *Barnabasbrief*, 117–19; Prostmeier, "Einleitung," 56; Schwartz, "On Barnabas," 147–53. For arguments in favor of a rebuilt Jewish temple, see Shukster and Richardson, "Temple and *Bet Ha-midrash*," 21–23, 24–27; Smallwood, *Jews under Roman Rule*, 435.

106. All quotations from Dio Cassius's *Historia romana* come from Cary, *Dio Cassius*.

temple to Jupiter is in view. When Barnabas insists that the servants of the enemies will rebuild "it" (αὐτόν; 16.4), the most natural antecedent is the Jerusalem temple that Barnabas mentioned in 16.3. This objection is not fatal, but it leads on to another option for identifying the rebuilt temple in 16.4, namely, hopes for a rebuilt Jewish temple. A third Jewish temple was never rebuilt, and if plans for such a temple were ever made, there is no record of the planning advancing very far during the first third of the second century. Nevertheless, understanding 16.4 to refer to a Jewish temple makes sense of the grammar, and Barnabas may know of rumors of a third temple. While a definitive decision may not be possible, it seems best to view the hopes for a rebuilt temple in 16.3-4 to refer to a physical building—either an ironic remark about a temple to Jupiter or anticipation for a possible third Jewish temple.[107]

Bringing the Evidence Together

The considerations of 4.3-5 and 16.3-4 have explored what these passages may tell readers about when the Epistle of Barnabas was written. The commentary will say more about the function of these passages within the argument of *Barnabas*. For now, it is worth noting that the author's use of Daniel most likely refers to either Vespasian or Nerva. Two options have been identified with regard to the temple that is to be rebuilt in 16.3-4. If the author refers to the temple of Jupiter, then these verses could be dated quite certainly to the time of Hadrian—most likely just prior to the Bar Kokhba War, though a time just after cannot be absolutely ruled out. If the author refers to a Jewish temple, the pronouns in 16.3-4 read smoothly but it is difficult to choose a single emperor where there is strong evidence that concrete hopes for a third temple existed.[108] Yet perhaps the strongest hopes for a Jewish temple would have arisen in the years preceding the Bar Kokhba revolt.[109] If so, dating the Epistle of Barnabas to the time of

---

107. For additional evidence and scholarly literature, see the discussion of 16.3-4 in the commentary.

108. Richardson and Shukster ("Barnabas," 53-55) argue that these hopes arose during Nerva's reign. Nerva's reputation as an emperor who was more friendly to Jewish people than his Flavian predecessors might incline one to put Jewish hopes for rebuilding a temple in his reign. Alternatively, it is possible to think that Jews would have desired to rebuild the temple immediately after its destruction in 70, but Vespasian's punitive policies following his experiences in Judea make it unlikely that this hope was anywhere near being realized.

109. The years under Bar Kokhba revealed hope for independence among some Jews, and the nationalistic fervor that resulted demonstrated itself in the minting of

Hadrian (117–138 CE) would thus be the most plausible way of dating the final form of the letter.

How, then, should one make sense of the apparently contradictory evidence of 4.3–5 and 16.3–4? The Hadrianic date for 16.3–4 is difficult to reconcile with the arguments that Vespasian or Nerva best fit the small king and small horn of 4.3–5. While it may be possible to argue that Hadrian is also in view in 4.3–5,[110] this is unlikely to have been the earliest interpretation of 4.3–5. The best way to account for this evidence is to argue that the author here relies on an earlier source that could have been made in the first century.[111] The source of the tradition may thus have had either Vespasian or Nerva in view when interpreting Dan 7:7–8, 24.[112] However, the primary function of Barn. 4.3–5 does not necessarily need to be the identification of a particular king but rather the evocation of a quickly approaching eschaton. The function of 4.3–5 and 16.3–4 in the argument of the letter will be the primary focus of the commentary on these verses. For now, it is sufficient to say that the evidence collectively points to a Hadrianic date for the final text of the Epistle of Barnabas, most likely in 130–32 CE during the immediate lead-up to the Second Jewish Revolt.[113]

---

coins and references to Bar Kokhba as the "prince" (נשיא). This title can be found in the letter from Simeon ben Mattaniah to Bar Kokhba (Bar Kosiba; XHev/Se 30; Cotton and Yardeni, *Aramaic*, 103–4). For more on the title of נשיא as applied to Bar Kokhba, see Horbury, *Jewish War*, 355–62; Mor, *Second Jewish Revolt*, 420–29. While there is no evidence for an actual rebuilding of the temple, coins minted under Bar Kokhba include images of a reconstructed temple (Madden, *Coins*, 239, 244; Meshorer, *Jewish Coins*, nos. 179–81, 199–201). For more on the coins of the Bar Kokhba revolt, see Mor, *Second Jewish Revolt*, 414–18; Vinzent, *Writing*, 216–28. Reports and rumors of such hopes for a new temple appear to be the best background against which to envision Barnabas claiming that the rebuilding "is happening" (γίνεται; Barn. 16.4).

110. So Barnard, "Date," 104–7.

111. This source could be envisioned as a written source or a source that was otherwise firmly implanted within the memories and practices of Barnabas and his community.

112. Barnabas overtook this source material and may have intended for readers to understand that Hadrian was the small horn and small king.

113. For similar and more concise attempts to date the Epistle of Barnabas just before or after the Second Jewish revolt during the time of Hadrian, see Hvalvik, "*Epistle of Barnabas*," 272–74; Moreschini and Norelli, *Manuale*, 60; Öhler, *Barnabas: Der Mann in der Mitte*, 155–56; Vielhauer, *Geschichte*, 611.

Authorship and Attribution

Although the title, Epistle of Barnabas (Ἐπιστολὴ Βαρναβᾶ), appears in manuscripts, Barnabas's name does not appear in the text of the letter.[114] The reference to the temple's destruction (Barn. 16.1–5) and corresponding date after 70 CE mean that the Barnabas to whom Paul refers when narrating the so-called Antioch incident (Gal 2:11–14) would have been quite an aged author if he wrote *Barnabas*.[115] Viewing Barnabas as the author becomes increasingly difficult the further that the date is moved after 70 so that, if the letter was written during the time of Hadrian, it is virtually impossible to uphold Barnabean authorship. In addition, *Barnabas* contains teachings that contradict elements that are known from Pauline reports about Barnabas. For example, although Paul recounts Barnabas's choice to eat with Jewish believers in Antioch (Gal 2:13), *Barnabas* asserts that God's commandments have nothing to do with eating, claims that Moses spoke spiritually, and thereby allegorizes the food laws (Barn. 10.1–12). While Barnabean authorship is occasionally still defended, it has become extremely rare to find arguments for an authentically Barnabean letter.[116] This commentary follows the *communis opinio* in understanding *Barnabas* as either an anonymous or pseudepigraphic text.[117]

If *Barnabas* is an anonymous or pseudepigraphic text, however, why was it attributed to Barnabas? Two factors may be mentioned that help to explain why this text was thought to originate from Barnabas. First, the letter would likely accumulate more authority if Barnabas was thought to

---

114. In addition to references in Clement's writings, the title "Epistle of Barnabas" is found at the start of the text in S and H. It is unclear precisely when the title was connected to this text. The latest possible date for the Epistle of Barnabas to be linked to Barnabas is the end of the second century. Clement of Alexandria introduced quotations of the letter in ways that recognized Barnabean authorship (e.g., *Strom.* 2.31.2 [6]; 5.63.1 [10]). Of course, it is possible that the text was thought to have been written by Barnabas at an earlier time.

115. Unless otherwise noted, all translations of Scripture are my own.

116. However, Simon Tugwell (*Apostolic Fathers*, 44) has cautiously defended this position. See also Burger, "L'Énigme de Barnabas," 180–93.

117. As I use the terms here, an anonymous text would be a text that was written without an explicit statement of authorship. The title "Epistle of Barnabas" would then be added by another person at a later time. If *Barnabas* is a pseudonymous text, some indication would have been given by the pseudonymous author that it was supposedly penned by Barnabas. For similar positions in scholarship, see Barnard, "'Epistle of Barnabas' and Its Contemporary Setting," 172; Carleton Paget, *Epistle of Barnabas*, 3–9; Carleton Paget, "*Epistle of Barnabas*," 73–74; Hvalvik, "*Epistle of Barnabas*," 269; Hvalvik, *Struggle for Scripture and Covenant*, 43–44; Kayser, *Ueber den sogenannten Barnabas-Brief*, 53–85; Prigent and Kraft, *Épître de Barnabé*, 27–28; Vielhauer, *Geschichte*, 610–11.

have written it than if a lesser-known second-century figure authored the text.[118] Barnabas's Pauline connections and importance among early believers would likely ensure that he was a well-remembered figure in the second century. This leads to the second factor that helps to explain Barnabean attribution, namely, the way in which Barnabas was styled, described, and remembered as evidenced elsewhere in early Christian literature.[119] The attention that the letter devotes to Israel and Israel's scriptures demands an author that would be well-acquainted with both matters. Barnabas's Jewishness made him a prime candidate to discuss such matters (e.g., Gal 2:11–14; Acts 4:36; Pseudo-Clementine, *Hom.* 1.9.1; *Rec.* 1.7.7).[120] However, due to the letter's figurative interpretation of scripture and refusal to accept traditional Jewish practices, Barnabas's Pauline associations provide another ground for ascribing the letter to him (Acts 9:26–30; 13:1–12; 14:8–20; Gal 2:1–14; 1 Cor 9:6).[121] In addition, Barnabas was remembered in connection with texts elsewhere in early Christianity as both an author (Tertullian, *Pud.* 20.2; Origen, *Cels.* 1.63; Jerome, *Vir.* 6),[122] collector (Acts Barn. 24, 26),[123] and object of literature.[124]

---

118. One may think, for example, of Petrine texts from the second century like the Acts of Peter, Apocalypse of Peter, and *Kerygma Petri*; of Pauline texts like the Acts of Paul; or of Johannine texts like the Acts of John.

119. A more detailed account of this second factor can be found in Lookadoo, "Barnabas in History and Memory," 1121–62.

120. All quotations from the Pseudo-Clementine *Homilies* come from Rehm and Strecker, *Pseudoklementinen I*. Quotations from the Pseudo-Clementine *Recognitions* come from Rehm and Strecker, *Pseudoklementinen II*.

121. On Barnabas and Paul, see Bauckham, "Barnabas," 61–70; Breytenbach, *Paulus und Barnabas*, 3–97; Breytenbach, "Zeus und der lebendige Gott: Anmerkungen zu Apostelgeschichte 14,11–17," 396–413; Breytenbach and Zimmermann, *Early Christianity*, 62–73; Dods, "Barnabas," 334–46; Dunn, *Beginning*, 566; Gallaher Branch, "Barnabas," 307–17; Kollmann, *Joseph Barnabas*, 34–62; Öhler, *Barnabas: Die historische Person*, 4–86, 188–454; Öhler, *Barnabas: Der Mann in der Mitte*, 50–148; Schnelle, *Ersten Jahre*, 125–26. Additional literature on Barnabas and Paul can be found in commentaries on Acts, 1 Corinthians, and Colossians (e.g., Gaventa, *Acts*, 191–92; Schrage, *Erste Brief an die Korinther*, 2.295; Foster, *Colossians*, 98). For other connections between Barnabas and Paul elsewhere in early Christian literature, see Clement of Alexandria, *Strom.* 2.116.3 (20); Didymus the Blind, *Comm. Zach.* 259; Jerome, *Vir.* 5–6; Gregory of Nazianzus, *Or.* 43.32.3. All citations from Gregory of Nazianzus's funeral orations come from Boulenger, *Grégoire de Nazianze*.

122. On Tertullian, *Pud.* 20.2, see De Boer, "Tertullian on Barnabas's Letter to the Hebrews," 247–50.

123. After Barnabas's death in the Acts of Barnabas, John Mark preserves Barnabas's ashes and the Matthean documents that were in Barnabas's possession (Acts Barn. 24, 26).

124. The fifth-century Acts of Barnabas narrates Barnabas's work with Paul in

While the historical Barnabas acted differently from what one would expect in reading *Barnabas*, there are legitimate reasons to attribute the letter to Barnabas. However, it is too facile to say that the Epistle of Barnabas was linked to Barnabas simply because his name might grant the text an air of general authority or a chronological place early in the history of the Jesus movement. The memory of Barnabas's Jewish heritage, Pauline connections, and textual activity make Barnabas a suitable figure to which to ascribe this letter, regardless of whether that ascription was done by a pseudepigrapher or by later readers.

Outline and Integrity

The Epistle of Barnabas has a clear opening and clear ending. The text begins with an epistolary greeting, a commendation of the audience, and a statement of the purpose of writing (1.1–8). It concludes with a final paraenesis urging readers to walk in the Lord's requirements and a wish that the addressees would be well (21.1–9). In the middle, something that approaches a conclusion can be found in 17.1–2. Barnabas hopes that he has not left out anything and writes, "So much for these things" (ταῦτα μὲν οὕτως; 17.2). The Latin translation has a longer ending and does not include 18.1—21.9. This creates two distinct body sections in the letter. The first section begins in Barn. 2 and closes with the discussion of the temple in Barn. 16. The second section contains the Two Ways Tradition in 18.1—20.2.

The possible presence of two endings within the same text has raised questions about the integrity of the letter.[125] Wengst points to the conclusions in 17.1–2 and 21.9 early in his argument that Barnabas was dependent upon sources before proceeding in further study of the specific sources that were utilized by the author.[126] The similarity of the Two Ways Tradition in Barn. 18–20 and Did. 1–6 could add support to arguments for viewing the

---

Antioch and his journey to Cyprus. Alexander the Monk wrote a sixth-century exhortatory account of Barnabas's life that has come to be known as *Laudatio Barnabae*. On this text, see Kollmann and Deuse, *Alexander Monachus*. In addition, the *Decretum Gelasianum* indicates that there was a Gospel of Barnabas that circulated among late-antique apocryphal books. On the reception history of the figure of Barnabas, see Kollmann, *Joseph Barnabas*, 63–71; Öhler, *Barnabas: Der Mann in der Mitte*, 149–96.

125. In reflecting on how the letter may be outlined, one could also add that the way in which the author appears to skip from topic to topic suggests either the presence of multiple interpolations or the heavy use of sources. Robillard ("Épître de Barnabé," 184–209) argues for three redactors with different theologies who wrote at different times. On the use of sources, see the discussions in Wengst, *Tradition und Theologie*, 5–70; Koester, *Introduction*, 281; Wilhite, *One of Life*, 118–26.

126. Wengst, *Tradition und Theologie*, 9–14.

letter as a compilation without internal integrity. One might also point to the way in which the author moves from topic to topic, at times with apparently little regard for the way in which the issues might connect. The author separates the discussions of Jewish practices such as sacrifices and fasts (2.4—3.6) from reflections on circumcision and kosher laws (9.1—10.12) as well as Sabbath and temple (15.1—16.10). The author's analysis of the covenant and true people of God are also divided (4.6-8; 13.1—14.9). If these arguments are accepted, one may suppose that the Epistle of Barnabas is best read as a compilation with limited coherence. Put differently, the letter could be seen as a composite document whose compiler had varying levels of success in sewing sections of the text together.

Despite these difficulties in accounting for the arrangement of the text, the letter is better understood as a whole. The motif of diverging paths may be most prominent in 18.1—20.2, but it is not limited to the end of the letter. The author refers to the way of righteousness, the righteous, and the righteous way (1.4; 5.4; 11.7; 12.4). This path is contrasted with an evil way (4.10), the way of darkness (5.4), and the way of sinners or the ungodly (10.10; 11.7).[127] The presence of a strong contrast between "us" (4.7; 3.6; 8.7; 9.1, 3; 10.12) and "them" (4.7; 9.6; 14.1, 2) complements the sense of contrast in the Two Ways Tradition found at the end of the letter. It may be an overstatement to say that "the letter is constructed, in its general outline, according to an intelligible and fairly logical plan,"[128] but there is at least good reason to understand the letter as a unified whole. Thematic connections between the various topics with which the author deals in 2.1—16.10 and the Two Ways Tradition of 18.1—20.2 provide reasons not only for viewing 1.1—17.2 as a unity but also for reading 1.1—21.9 as a single document that articulates how the people of God can know and understand the covenant that God has given to them and thereby set themselves apart from those who misunderstand scripture.

Regardless of how the author compiled sources or wrote the letter, this commentary will approach the Epistle of Barnabas as a whole composition from 1.1—21.9. With this in mind, it may be helpful at this point to offer an integrated outline of the letter.

I. Greetings and Introduction (1.1-8)

I.1. Greeting (1.1)

---

127. See further Hvalvik, *Struggle for Scripture and Covenant*, 63–65. For a fuller discussion of outlining *Barnabas*, see Hvalvik, *Struggle for Scripture and Covenant*, 205–11.

128. Muilenburg, "Literary Relations," 50. On Muilenburg's understanding of the letter into haggada and halakha, see "Literary Relations," 50–53.

I.2. Commendation (1.2-4)

I.3. Purpose of Writing (1.5-8)

II. Revealing Knowledge in Scripture: First Body Section (2.1—16.10)

    II.1. Introduction: Alert and Seeking the Lord's Requirements in Evil Days (2.1-3)

    II.2. The Lord's Requirements (2.4—3.6)

        II.2.a. Sacrifices (2.4-10)

        II.2.b. Fasts (3.1-6)

    II.3. Scandals and Salvation (4.1-14)

        II.3.a. The Perfect Scandal and Salvific Inquiries (4.1-6a)

        II.3.b. Our Covenant (4.6b-9a)

        II.3.c. The Eschatological Life (4.9b-14)

    II.4. The Suffering of the Lord and Son of God (5.1—8.7)

        II.4.a. The Endurance, Suffering, and Resurrection of the Son (5.1—6.7)

        II.4.b. The Land Flowing with Milk and Honey (6.8-19)

        II.4.c. The Sacrifice and Scapegoat (7.1-11)

        II.4.d. The Red Heifer (8.1-7)

    II.5. Circumcision and Kosher Laws (9.1—10.12)

        II.5.a. Obedience and the Meaning of Circumcision (9.1-9)

        II.5.b. Right Living and Kosher Laws (10.1-12)

    II.6. The Water and the Cross (11.1—12.11)

        II.6.a. Water and Baptism (11.1-11)

        II.6.b. The Cross and the Son (12.1-11)

    II.7. The People, the Inheritance, and the Covenant (13.1—14.9)

        II.7.a. The Two Peoples and the Inheritance (13.1-7)

        II.7.b. The Covenant: Given and Sought (14.1-9)

    II.8. ἔτι καί: On Additional Matters (15.1—16.10)

        II.8.a. The Sabbath (15.1-9)

        II.8.b. The Temple (16.1-10)

III. Transition (17.1-2)

IV. Two Ways: Second Body Section (18.1—20.2)
    IV.1. Introduction (18.1-2)
    IV.2. The Way of Light (19.1-12)
    IV.3. The Way of the Black One (20.1-2)
V. Closing (21.1-9)
    V.1. Transition from Two Ways (21.1)
    V.2. Concluding Paraenesis (21.2-8)
    V.3. Letter Closing (21.9)

2

The Epistle of Barnabas and Scripture

THE EPISTLE OF BARNABAS relies heavily upon scripture and exegesis as a primary means of communication. More specifically, Barnabas employs biblical lines of reasoning to counter possible opponents and to encourage the audience to view scripture in the same way as the author. Scriptural arguments are particularly prevalent throughout 2.4—16.10 as Barnabas attempts to establish the significance of circumcision, sacrifice, and Sabbath. Scripture is a key way in which God reveals God's identity, desires, and actions for the people of God. Because Barnabas and his audience belong to God's people, they have received a special capacity to hear and understand how God has spoken through the prophets. *Barnabas* does not contain a definitive statement of what scripture is or how it functions. Nor does the author include a hint of which books might belong in a canonical list. Readers of the letter are left to determine the answers to these and other questions based upon what the letter says. This chapter takes up questions about the nature and function of scripture within the letter before turning to consider the books that Barnabas cites.

The Nature and Function of Scripture in *Barnabas*

Scripture is revelatory and closely tied to the prophets for Barnabas. Only those who belong to the people of God can understand scripture properly because right understanding reveals and is revealed by God. The way in which one interprets scripture is thus closely tied to one's place within God's people, and this covenant inheritance comes only through the Son of God. Scripture functions as a means by which to understand God and to interpret how what God has said in the past impacts the present. Scripture also defines right forms of community and provides a frame for how believers should live alongside one another.

The Nature of Scripture in *Barnabas*

Scripture is closely connected to the way in which God reveals Godself and to how believers are instructed in their knowledge.[1] Revelation and knowledge are oft-repeated themes within the Epistle of Barnabas. When Barnabas informs his audience that he writes so that he can add knowledge to their faith (1.5), he supplements this statement by reminding readers that God revealed the past, the present, and a taste of the future "through the prophets" (διὰ τῶν προφητῶν; 1.7). The prophets, who are experienced by Barnabas and his audience by means of their writings, are instruments by which God revealed the significance of events that occur in time.[2] God grants the knowledge that is required in order to interpret scripture. When Barnabas takes up the command to enter into the land flowing with milk and honey, it is knowledge that enables him to interpret entry into the land in terms of hope in Jesus (6.9).[3] The Lord has given wisdom and understanding of his secrets so that Barnabas and his audience can rightly understand what the prophet says about the Lord (6.10). Knowledge to understand scripture rightly is thus implanted in the audience by God (9.9).[4]

God's revelation comes through scripture, but scripture is not the only way in which God reveals Godself. The Son's incarnation is also a means of God's self-revelation. Jesus revealed himself to be the Son of God by calling sinful apostles to preach the gospel (5.9). Although the Son taught Israel and performed signs and wonders (5.8), Barnabas accuses them of rejecting Jesus just as they had previously persecuted the prophets (5.11). When Barnabas speaks of Jesus, he makes consistent reference to scriptural citations.[5] According to the author, the prophets spoke about Jesus because

---

1. The word *Godself* is utilized in this book as a gender-neutral reflexive pronoun that refers uniquely to God. The reflexive expression *God reveals Godself* is a way of describing God's self-revelation. Grammatically, the term is employed on a grammatical analogy with *himself* or *herself*. If *Sally reveals herself*, she is making a self-revelation, the content of which would require further definition. In the Epistle of Barnabas, scripture provides one means by which God reveals Godself.

2. "Alle Auslegungsmethoden werden sachlich dadurch zusammengehalten, daß die Schrift ihrem Wesen nach Vorausoffenbarung ist" (Wengst, *Didache*, 130).

3. The larger discussion occurs in Barn. 6.8–19. The focal point of this discussion concerns the command to enter into the land flowing with milk and honey. It draws on scriptural language from Exod 33:1–3; Lev 20:24; Deut 1:25.

4. After quoting Isa 53:5, 7 in Barn. 5.2, Barnabas urges the audience to give thanks to the Lord who has made known the past, made them wise in the present, and provided for them not to be foolish in the future (Barn. 5.3). A scriptural quotation is given by God for the sake of knowledge and wisdom.

5. Allowing for some difference in forms of citation, see e.g., Barn. 5.2 (Isa 53:5, 7), 5 (Gen 1:1), 12 (Zech 13:7), 13 (Ps 21:21 [22:21 MT]), 14 (Isa 50:6, 7); 6.1–2 (Isa

they received grace from the Lord (5.6). The prophets are vitally important for Barnabas, but the scriptural writings point forward to greater realities. Scripture ultimately bears witness to the Son of God, who revealed God in ways that make it possible for people to be saved by looking to him coming in the flesh, enduring suffering, and rising again.

While scripture is not the only or the most important means of revelation in the letter, the writings to which Barnabas appeals are authoritative because they are true revelations. The authority that scripture holds in a believer's life is assumed throughout the letter, but it is most evident in the degree to which Barnabas relies upon scripture to make his argument. Barnabas employs scriptural practices as the focal point of his exegetical work. These practices are paired with one another in the letter. After beginning with sacrifice (2.4–10), he discusses the significance of fasting (3.1–6). He turns to circumcision and food laws later in the letter (9.1—10.12) before interpreting the meaning of Sabbath instructions and the temple (15.1—16.10). The revelation of Jesus through scriptural motifs and sacrificial instructions plays a prominent role in the letter (5.1—8.7; 11.1—12.11). Finally, the right understanding of inheritance and covenant along with the two ways in which people can walk play an animating role in *Barnabas* (4.1–14; 13.1—14.9; 18.1—20.2).

Barnabas's reliance upon scripture can be illustrated by the sheer number of citations that are included in the letter.[6] While precise counts may vary from scholar to scholar depending on the criteria that each person uses to determine a citation, two examples may illustrate the ways in which scriptural citations populate the letter.[7] When Barnabas introduces the letter with an interpretation of the meaning of sacrifice and fasting (2.4—3.6), he begins by employing three citations and interspersing brief exegetical remarks about the significance of sacrifice.[8] Scripture is even more prominent in the discussion of fasting, taking up the entirety of 3.1–5 with the exception of small

---

50:8–9), 2–3 (Isa 28:16), 3 (Isa 50:7), 4 (Ps 117:22, 24 [118:22, 24 MT]); 6 (Ps 21:17, 19 [22:16, 18]; 117:12 [118:12 MT]); 7:6–7 (Lev 16:7–9); 8:1–7 (Num 19); 12.2 (Exod 17:8–13), 5–7 (Num 21:4–8), 10 (Ps 109:1 [110:1 MT]), 11 (Isa 45:1).

6. Without wanting to discount the creativity of Barnabas, Menken ("Old Testament Quotations," 295) rightly notes that in 1.1—17.2 "the document consists mainly of the presentation and explanation of passages from the OT."

7. Carleton Paget (*Epistle of Barnabas*, 86) counts a total of ninety-eight Old Testament quotations in the letter. For lists of citations in the Epistle of Barnabas, see Hvalvik, *Struggle for Scripture and Covenant*, 333–41; Kraft, *Barnabas*, 179–87; Prinzivalli and Simonetti, *Seguendo Gesù*, 509n17. On the variety of terminology that can be employed within discussions of scriptural citations in early Christian literature, see Osburn, "Methodology," 313–43.

8. The citations are found in 2.5, 7–8, 10. On the passages cited and the textual form in which the citations appear, see the commentary on 2.4–10.

remarks designating certain parts of Isa 58 "to them" and "to us." A second example illustrates how Barnabas depends on a variety of scriptural citations even when his focus is on a single statement in scripture. Barnabas's discussion of what it means to enter into the land is focused on an introductory statement from scripture (6.8–19, esp. 6.8). On the way, however, Barnabas also makes reference to Gen 1:26, 28 (6.12, 18), a prophetic promise of new creation (6.13), a promise of fleshly hearts that resembles Ezek 11:19; 36:26 (6.14), and a psalmic discussion utilizing language from Pss 21:23; 41:3; 107:4 (22:22; 42:2; 108:4 MT; Barn. 6.16). Scriptural citations occur routinely and scriptural motifs provide the basis for the interpretive comments that are contained within the Epistle of Barnabas.

When Barnabas refers to scripture, he understands scripture not only as revelation from God and an authority on which to rely but also in thoroughly prophetic terms. The prophets are a means of revelation through whom God speaks. Barnabas introduces his exegetical reflections on sacrifice by noting that God has revealed that sacrifices are unnecessary "through the prophets" (διὰ τῶν προφητῶν) (2.4).[9] Barnabas introduces other citations that are found in a prophet (6.14; 7.4; 9.1; 12.1, 4) or in a prophecy (13.4).[10] "The prophet" (ὁ προφήτης) is used fifteen times in introductory formulae.[11] A participle (ὁ προφητεύων) is similarly employed at 5.13. God prophecies directly to the community that he indwells (16.9). Barnabas depicts Moses and David participating in prophetic action by introducing citations from the Torah and the Psalter (6.8; 12.10). Barnabas does not conceive of scripture in exclusively prophetic terms, but the prophetic nature of scripture is enhanced by introductory formulae that describe scripture speaking.[12] Citations are introduced with the word λέγω more than seventy times.[13] On the other hand, a form of the word γράφω is utilized approximately eight times in *formulae citandi*.[14] Since Barnabas's primary way of understanding and depicting scripture is in terms of speech, his citations

---

9. See also 1.7.

10. Barnabas highlights the divine origins of these prophetic statements in 7.4; 9.1; 12.1, 4. See also Carleton Paget, "Old Testament in the Apostolic Fathers," 454.

11. 4.4; 6.2, 4, 6, 7, 8, 10, 13; 11.2, 4, 9; 14.2, 7, 8, 9.

12. The general term γραφή is utilized in 4.7, 11; 5.4; 6.12; 13.2; 16.5, while the priests play a revelatory role with regard to Jesus's crucifixion in 7.3.

13. See 2.4, 7, 10; 3.1, 3; 4.3, 4, 5, 7, 8, 11; 5.2, 4, 12, 13, 14; 6.1, 2, 3 (2x), 4 (2x), 6, 7, 8, 9, 10, 12, 13, 14, 16 (2x); 7.4; 9.1 (2x), 2, 3 (3x), 5 (2x), 8; 10.2, 9, 11; 11.2, 4, 6, 8 (2x), 9, 10; 12.2, 4, 8, 9, 11; 13.2, 4, 5, 7; 14.2, 7, 8, 9; 15.2, 3, 4, 6, 8; 16.2, 3, 5. Based on these counts, a form of λέγω is employed in citation formulae seventy-three times. The number has been left more open in the main text in order to allow for textual uncertainty.

14. See 4.3, 14; 5.2; 7.3; 11.1; 14.6; 15.1; 16.6.

of scripture enhance the prophetic overtones that the scriptural word has within the letter.[15] The prophetic nature of scripture provides the central lens through which Barnabas views scripture because the prophets were given grace from God in order to prophecy about the Son (5.6).

Yet the prophetic nature of scripture alone does not result in right understanding of scripture. After all, despite Israel's hearing of the prophetic words, they stand accused by the author of persecuting God's prophets and putting them to death (5.11). The interpreters of scripture thus have a vital role to play within the Barnabean hermeneutic. Two sets of interpretive communities are juxtaposed against one another in the Epistle of Barnabas.

The group that stands outside of Barnabas and his audience are referred to most often as "they" (ἐκεῖνοι) and are unable to read scripture rightly. They have been deceived (2.9) and thus have a law that is to be differentiated from the readers of the letter (3.6). While the significance of what scripture says is clear to Barnabas and his audience, the significance of scripture remains "dark" (σκοτεινός) because they have not listened to the Lord's voice (8.7). Barnabas puts this difference most vividly in his discussion of circumcision.[16] When reflecting on the meaning of circumcision, the opponents have failed to understand that the Lord was not describing a circumcision of the flesh. Nevertheless, they have gone astray "because an evil angel made them wise" (ὅτι ἄγγελος πονηρὸς ἐσόφιζεν αὐτούς; 9.4). Attributing their practice of physical circumcision to demonic deceit is a strident way of depicting the differences between the author and his opponents. Yet it demonstrates the stark difference that Barnabas perceives between himself and his opponents, thereby allowing Barnabas to further his anti-Jewish polemic through his scriptural exegesis.[17] It also fits with the Two Ways Tradition at the end of the document, in which the way of darkness is inhabited by the angels of Satan and the ruler of this age (18.1–2). On account of their deception, the opponents misconstrue scripture, practice what it says in faulty ways, and fail to see what is clear to Barnabas and his audience because their sight is occluded.

The second interpretive community in the letter includes the author and readers of the letter. This community is most often designated as "we" (ἡμεῖς).[18] The ability to understand scripture rightly comes from a

15. On the importance of terms of speech in Barnabean introductory formulae, see Prinzivalli and Simonetti, *Seguendo Gesù*, 2.87, 509n17.

16. Yuh, "Do as I Say," 273–95.

17. Carleton Paget, "Old Testament in the Apostolic Fathers," 467–68.

18. E.g., 3.6; 5.3; 7.1; 8.7; 10.12; 14.5. Barnabas thus employs pronouns to differentiate his audience from his opponents. On the near/far distinction, see Runge, *Discourse Grammar*, 365–84 and, with particular reference to its usage in John 1:1–18, Tovey,

privileged relationship with the God who is revealed through its words. Barnabas reminds his readers that they have received God's gracious gift through the Spirit that is implanted in them (1.2–3). The author likewise partakes in a unique relationship with God because God travels together with him (1.4). God's gift of teaching has thus been implanted in Barnabas and his community (9.9). Whereas Israel rejected God's revelation at Sinai in favor of worshipping idols, the covenant of Jesus has been inscribed directly into the heart of Barnabas's audience (4.8). Israel and believers thus form models between which Barnabas's readers are challenged to choose. Because of their spiritual gift, they are heirs of the covenant and can therefore rightly understand what scripture says (13.1–14.9). The reception of the covenant and the knowledge of scripture that comes along with covenant inclusion originate from outside of believers but enable them to construe God's revelation in scripture properly.

A key by which one may recognize the privileged relationship of the Barnabean interpretive community concerns the ability to divide between words that are spoken "to us" and "to them" (2.7–10; 3.1–5; 5.2; 8.7). Thanks to the gracious gift that they have received in order to read scripture rightly, Barnabas and his audience are able to establish the referent of the scriptural text with clarity.[19] When scripture is rightly understood with regard to its intended audience of "us" or "them," Barnabas views scripture as pointing to the incarnation of the Son and to the right actions of the community. The christocentric nature of scripture enables Barnabas to show that the Son's suffering, death, and resurrection were revealed long ago (5.1—8.7; 11.1—12.11).[20] The community is thus charged not to misunderstand the significance of cultic actions like sacrifices, fasts, circumcision, food laws, Sabbath practices, and temple worship.[21]

The right way to understand scripture's requirements does not pertain to literal practice. This is the way in which Barnabas's opponents understand scripture. Rather, Barnabas utilizes a largely figurative hermeneutic

---

"Narrative Structure," 158–60.

19. Contrasting *Barnabas* with the letters of Ignatius, Hurtado (*Lord Jesus Christ*, 567) writes, "citations of the Old Testament in the *Epistle of Barnabas* are mainly used as part of the author's concern to assert the superiority of the church and a particular understanding of the Old Testament commandments, over against Judaism."

20. On the christocentric nature of Barnabas's exegesis, see Carleton Paget, "Old Testament in the Apostolic Fathers," 466–67.

21. The interpretation of scripture thus plays a role in Barnabas's construction of the social identity of the community that he addresses while simultaneously demarcating them from others who would understand scripture differently. On social identity theory, see Hogg and Abrams, *Social Identifications*, 1–27; Trebilco, *Outsider Designations*, 9–13; Tucker and Baker, *T. & T. Clark Handbook to Social Identity*, passim.

in order to make sense of what God has revealed in scripture. While some may differentiate between allegorical, typological, and other forms of figurative readings,[22] Barnabas does not distinguish sharply between various forms of figurative interpretation.[23] Scripture is interpreted as a revelatory sign that points beyond itself, whether to the Son or to the true meaning of how one should live in accordance with the instructions given to Israel. The temple refers not to a building but to God's indwelling of believers (4.11; 6.15; 16.1–10). The rituals associated with the Day of Atonement are not about lambs that are slaughtered or sent away. Rather, these rituals were placed in scripture so that readers may know Jesus as the suffering and atoning sacrifice (7.3–11). To believe that circumcision had anything to do with a physical act misses the true teaching of circumcision that has to do with one's ability to listen to God (9.1–9). Even in instances where Barnabas acknowledges some truth in a historical, literal reading of scripture—as he does when examining the story of Abraham circumcising his household—the importance of the story has to do with the way that the number of men circumcised reveals Jesus on the cross (9.7–8). Barnabas's hermeneutical distinction between scriptural passages that speak to "us" and "them" is aided by his deployment of a consistent figurative interpretations throughout much of the letter.

The complex way in which Barnabas understands and utilizes scripture can be usefully compared to the ways in which scripture is discussed in two other early Christian texts: Ptolemy's *Letter to Flora* and Justin's *Dialogue with Trypho*.[24] Both Barnabas and Ptolemy maintain that a relationship with the God from whom scripture originated is required in order to understand scriptural words properly. This conviction grounds Barnabas's belief that he

---

22. E.g., Kannengiesser (*Handbook*, 1.423) describes the scriptural interpretation in *Barnabas* as allegorical and compares it to Ariston of Pella. Hurtado (*Lord Jesus Christ*, 572), on the other hand, cites examples of "Christian typological exegesis" and argues against seeing Barnabas as an allegorical interpreter. For further discussion, see Dawson, *Allegorical Readers*, 15–17; Dawson, *Christian Figural Reading*, 12–13; Rothschild, "Epistle of Barnabas," 191–201.

23. Johnson ("Interpretive Hierarchies," 702–6) puts forward an intriguing comparison of the hermeneutic implicit in *Barnabas* and that used by Origen. However, the hermeneutic in *Barnabas* is less nuanced and is better described in broad terms. I have thus opted to characterize the hermeneutic in the letter in broad terms such as "figurative."

24. Ptolemy's letter is known from its inclusion within Epiphanius's fourth-century *Panarion*. Citations from Ptolemy's *Letter to Flora* come from Quispel, *Ptolémée, Lettre à Flora* and are numbered in accordance with the relevant section in Epiphanius's *Panarion*. Citations from Justin's *Dialogue* are found in Marcovich, *Iustini Martyris*. For a study of Barnabas's use of scripture alongside other second-century texts, see Dunn, *Neither Jew nor Greek*, 550–69.

and his readers rightly interpret scripture, since they are the heirs of the covenant (4.6–8; 8.7; 13.1—14.9). Ptolemy reports that many have misunderstood the law of Moses because they failed to recognize the law's true founder (*Flor.* 33.3.1). Like Barnabas, Ptolemy finds that he and Flora are in a privileged position when it comes to interpreting scripture (*Flor.* 33.3.8).[25] Reading the law well should result in right behaviors (*Flor.* 33.4.7; 33.7.10). It is not enough simply to receive the law and remain unchanged. Although this is not the only way in which Ptolemy recommends that Flora should interpret the law, a proper reading of the law allows for a symbolic (τυπικός) component in Ptolemy's hermeneutic (*Flor.* 33.5.2). A figurative interpretation of the law is demanded for commands about offerings, circumcision, the Sabbath, fasting, and Jewish festivals (*Flor.* 33.5.8–15).[26]

Yet Ptolemy's hermeneutic differs from the Barnabean interpretation of scripture at key points. For example, Ptolemy's letter focuses on the law (*Flor.* 33.3.1), whereas Barnabas maintains a thoroughgoing emphasis on the prophetic nature of scripture. The most significant difference, however, is the tripartite division of the law by Ptolemy. Ptolemy argues that the Pentateuch was not written by a single author but by three: God, Moses, and the elders (*Flor.* 33.4.1–2). The tripartite apportionment of various laws corresponds to a threefold understanding of the ultimate ruler over each legal category. Ptolemy's opponents argue that the law was established either by God the Father or by the devil (*Flor.* 33.3.2–5). Ptolemy argues instead that the divine law contained within the Pentateuch originated from the creator of the world, whom Ptolemy perceives as a craftsman who is subservient to the perfect God (*Flor.* 33.7.2–7). The god of the Ptolemaic law is thus both "begotten and unbegotten" (καὶ γεννητὸς ὢν καὶ οὐκ ἀγέννητος; *Flor.* 33.7.6), whereas begottenness is not a quality that is appropriate to God the Father.[27] Whereas Ptolemy finds three understandings of divine beings, Barnabas insists that there are only two. The intermediary being described by Ptolemy is absent in *Barnabas*, where readers must choose between the rulers of light or darkness (Barn. 1.7; 18.2).[28] There is no alternative in the Barnabean hermeneutic.

25. On the polemic in *Flor.* 33.3.7–8, see Standhartinger, "Ptolemaeus und Justin," 137.

26. Barnabas likewise offers figurative interpretations of offerings (2.4–10), circumcision (9.1–9), the Sabbath (15.1–9), fasts (3.1–6), and specific sacrifices in the Jewish cult like the Day of Atonement (7.3–11) and the red heifer (8.1–7).

27. Ignatius uses the same opposing adjectives (γεννητὸς; ἀγέννητος) to describe Jesus with a view to Jesus's birth and evident humanity, on the one hand (γεννητὸς), and his origins with the Father and divinity, on the other (ἀγέννητος; Ign. *Eph.* 7.2).

28. Ptolemy here imbibes the contemporary middle Platonism of the second

Three matters are of interest when examining Justin's *Dialogue* alongside the Epistle of Barnabas. First, the *Dialogue* shares a heavy reliance upon prophetic writings with Barnabas's letter.[29] The prophets provide interpretive keys to demonstrate that the new law brings with it a new covenant (*Dial.* 11–47), Jesus the Messiah (*Dial.* 48–107), and a new people (*Dial.* 108–41).[30] Second, although Justin's *Dialogue* was likely written within three decades of the Epistle of Barnabas,[31] Justin allows for more differentiation in Christian practice than Barnabas. Indeed, those who obey the law can even be saved as long as they do not attempt to convince others to keep the law (*Dial.* 47.2–5).[32] Barnabas, however, regards physical interpretations of the commandments to be a result of Jewish deceit or disobedience (Barn. 4.6–8; 9.7–8; 14.1–5). Finally, Justin's citations of specific scriptural texts sometimes bear striking similarities to those found in the Epistle of Barnabas. Since Justin shows little awareness of *Barnabas*, one way in which this has been accounted for is to suggest that both Barnabas and Justin had access to similar testimony sources.[33] For example, Justin cites Jer 4:3–4 and 9:24–25 in a way that is similar to Barn. 9.4–5 (Justin, *Dial.* 28.2–3).[34] Although questions about the transmission of scripture in early Christianity lie outside the bounds of this essay, comparison of scriptural citations in *Barnabas* and other early Christian literature is an important topic that is likely to reward continued study.[35]

---

century. On this, see Löhr, "La doctrine de dieu," 184–89; Markschies, "New Research," 239–46; Markschies, "Valentinische Gnosis," 165–67.

29. For additional comparison of scripture in *Barnabas* and the works of Justin, see Engelhardt, *Christenthum*, 375–94; Osborn, *Justin Martyr*, 160–61; Shotwell, *Biblical Exegesis of Justin Martyr*, 65–66; Skarsaune, *Proof from Prophecy*, 110–13. On Justin's understanding of the Old Testament more generally, see also Aune, "Justin Martyr's Use of the Old Testament," 179–97; Barnard, "Old Testament," 395–406; Bobichon, *Justin Martyr*, 1.109–28; Wendel, *Scriptural Interpretation*, 81–277.

30. Skarsaune, *Proof from Prophecy*, 165–227. All citations from Justin's *Dialogue with Trypho* come from Marcovich, *Iustini Martyris apologiae*.

31. On the date of Justin's *Dialogue*, see Barnard, *Justin Martyr*, 23–24; Horbury, "Jewish-Christian Relations," 319; Horbury, *Jews and Christians*, 131; Wendel, *Scriptural Interpretation*, 11–12.

32. Horbury, "Jewish-Christian Relations," 338–39; Horbury, *Jews and Christians*, 153. Justin likewise allows that saints who lived prior to Jesus and obeyed the law would be saved (*Dial.* 45.4). On Justin's understanding of the law, see Henne, "Justin, la Loi, et les Juifs," 450–62.

33. On the rise and fall of the testimony hypothesis with regard to Paul's letters, see Lincicum, "Paul and the *Testimonia*," 297–308.

34. Kraft, "Epistle of Barnabas," 191.

35. For further discussion, see Norelli, "Il dibattito," 199–233.

The Function of Scripture in *Barnabas*

It will be helpful now to consolidate and expand what the exploration of the nature of scripture in *Barnabas* indicates about its function in the letter. In theological terms, scripture originates from God and reveals who God is. Barnabas understands scripture to point forward to the revelation of the Son in the flesh while also indicating how particular cultic activities in scripture are meant to define orthopraxy for Jesus-followers. God's chosen instrument to reveal his word was the prophets, and Barnabas makes liberal use of their writings. The prophetic texts can be correctly interpreted by those who already are rightly related to God, that is, Barnabas and his community.

Barnabas's understanding of the nature of scripture opens a fresh means of discourse by which the author communicates with readers. God speaks to people through the words of scripture, but the number of those who are able to hear God's Word is limited to those who have been chosen as heirs. The freshness in the Barnabean hermeneutic does not come in alternative forms of interpretation. Barnabas shares an interest in the Torah and prophets with other early Jewish and early Christian authors.[36] The newness in what Barnabas writes comes in the openness by which God can communicate with the covenant heirs. Barnabas's mode of interpreting scripture is not a report on what is in the text or an inquiry into what the text may have meant to previous generations of readers. For example, the discussion of the red heifer in 8.1–7 is not interested in the regulations regarding purification from corpses that provided the ritual's rationale in Num 19. Nor is Barnabas concerned with anything like the detailed legal questions posed in m. Parah. Rather, Barnabas's hermeneutic opens a way of discoursing about scripture that points to the reality of Jesus's incarnation and suffering that simultaneously asserts that the requirements of the law were always meant to be accepted in figurative ways.[37] Barnabas's Jewish opponents are thus mistaken in their desire to interpret the law with a view to physical actions. The key to understanding their mistake is to recognize their actions as idolatrous (4.6–8; 14.1–5). Barnabas, on the other hand, sets himself apart as a faithful interpreter of scripture because he has been enabled to hear God rightly (1.4; 9.9).

The scriptural discourse in *Barnabas* functions as a social identity marker by which Barnabas separates his audience from his opponents. As

---

36. On the interplay between legalistic and antinomian interpretations of Torah within early Judaism and Christianity, see Lincicum, Sheridan, and Stang, "Introduction," 1–8.

37. Chandler, "Rite of the Red Heifer," 99–114.

a result of their understanding of scripture, Barnabas and his readers are set apart from other mistaken readers of the Jewish scriptures as a distinct community of covenantal heirs. Whereas Israel went astray at Sinai, persecuted the prophets, and were responsible for the death of the Son, Barnabas and his readers are able to worship God rightly and to understand the significance of cultic activities on the Christian life. God has revealed Godself in the flesh by the person of the Son (5.1, 5–6, 11–14). Even the events at Sinai occurred so that the covenant of Jesus might be inscribed on the hearts of believers like those addressed in the letter (4.8; 14.5). Because Jesus indwells the community, Barnabas urges his readers to celebrate the cult rightly. Whereas Israel misunderstood the requirements of the law as physical sacrifices, circumcision, and temple worship, Barnabas and his readers are able to understand that a true sacrifice is a broken heart, the commands about circumcision were about right hearing, and temple worship occurs within the believers and the community whom the Lord indwells (2.4–10; 9.1–9; 16.1–10). Due to God's revelation through scripture, the community is able to walk along the path of life. While this path has ethical requirements that are evident in one's physical life (3.3–5; 10.11; 19.1–12), they are not the mistaken practices that Israel established but stem instead from the proper functioning of God's revelation within the life of the community.

Just as Barnabas and his community are set apart on account of their understanding of scripture, so the author defines his opponents as a mistaken social group on account of their faulty way of interpreting scripture. Israel's act of idolatry at Sinai plays a paradigmatic role in the argument because it represents the time when they rejected the covenant and forfeited any claims to inheritance (4.6–8; 14.1–5). As a result of the fundamental role that this event plays in the letter, Barnabas accuses his opponents of setting up other cultic actions as idolatrous mishandlings of the scriptural word (11.2; 16.1; 20.1). Their idolatry made them open to enlightenment from evil angels rather than from the true God (9.4). The physical acts of sacrifice are thus rejected because they were never required (2.4–10), while the food laws were designed to illustrate what lifestyles were appropriate and which ways of living should be avoided rather than to regulate dietary intake (10.1–12). If Barnabas and his community have a privileged understanding of scripture due to their status as heirs and temples in which the Lord dwells, Barnabas's opponents have a faulty and mistaken understanding of scripture because they stand accused of idolatry.

The Contents of Scripture

I now consider the question of the scriptural books that are utilized in *Barnabas* insofar as these can be ascertained from the citations in the letter. Some statements about Barnabas's use of scripture quickly become apparent while reading the letter. For example, the author makes regular use of Isaiah, Genesis, and the Psalter. However, it is not easy to draw clear boundaries around the precise books that Barnabas considers authoritative because of the way in which lines from different sources can be combined. An example will again be helpful. When setting out the instruction for the people to enter into the good land flowing with milk and honey (Barn. 6.8), Barnabas employs language that is closest to Exod 33:1, 3. However, his language may also have been influenced by Lev 20:24; Deut 1:25. Should Barn. 6.8 count as a citation of Exodus, all three Pentateuchal books, or none of them on the supposition that Barnabas is employing another Pentateuchal tradition? Rather than entering into the minutiae of how to determine precisely where a Barnabean citation may have originated, this section outlines the books that Barnabas makes most regular use of while also examining the blurry boundaries of books that Barnabas may or may not have cited. The organization of this section moves broadly from more certain to less certain.[38]

Authoritative Texts

Barnabas's use of Jewish scripture may be surprising in a document that contains anti-Jewish arguments, but these books were among the most regularly cited in early Christian literature. He utilizes Isaiah regularly in the letter. Words from the prophet are employed in arguments about the right understanding of cultic practices (Barn. 2.5 [Isa 1:11–13]; 16.2–3 [Isa 40:12; 49:17; 66:1]). The discussion of fasting is largely comprised of a citation from Isa 58:4–10 that Barnabas interprets as partly addressed to his opponents and partly to his readers (Barn. 3.1–5). Isaiah's words also enable Barnabas to understand Jesus's suffering and endurance (Barn. 5.2, 14 [Isa 50:6–7; 53:5, 7]), his place as a rock on which to hope (Barn. 6.2–3

---

38. Research into citation methodology has expanded in recent years and provides a reminder of some of the difficulties that arise when determining ancient references. While there are some references in *Barnabas* that may be difficult to classify as a "quotation," "citation," or "allusion," the biggest difficulty for interpreters of *Barnabas* has to do with the source of the citations. For further literature on citation methodology in ancient and particularly early Christian literature, see Gregory and Tuckett, "Reflections on Method," 61–82; Hill, "'In These Very Words,'" 261–81; van den Hoek, "Techniques of Quotation," 223–43; Whittaker, "Value of Indirect Tradition," 63–95.

[Isa 28:16; 50:7]), and the redemption that the Father charged him to bring (Barn. 14.7–9 [Isa 42:6–7; 49:6–7; 61:1–2]). Barnabas variously employs the Psalter throughout the argument. Without recounting composite quotations or influence from multiple psalms within a single citation there are at least nine distinct references to the Psalter: Barn. 2.10; 5.13; 6.4, 6, 16; 10.10; 11.6–8; 12.10; 15.4.[39] The varied ways in which Barnabas utilizes the Psalms are on full display in Barn. 6 as he employs psalmic quotations as part of a larger christological argument (6.4), uses a composite citation to summarize a significant theme in 5.1—6.7 (6.6), and cites the Psalter as the words of Jesus while considering what it means to enter into the land (6.16).[40] Genesis is likewise a book that Barnabas employs at several points throughout the argument, including in the christological discussions of Barn. 5–6 (5.5; 6.12, 18 [Gen 1:26–28]), the reflections on inheritance in Barn. 13 (13.2 [Gen 25:21–23]; 13.4 [Gen 48:9, 11]), and the exegesis of Sabbath practice in Barn. 15 (15.3 [Gen 2:2–3]).

While citations from Isaiah, Psalms, and Genesis comprise some of the central scriptural citations in *Barnabas*, they are by no means exhaustive. As may be expected from an author who gives such prominence to the prophetic nature of scripture, Barnabas appeals regularly to other words from the prophets. Imagery from Ezekiel about replacing stony hearts with fleshly hearts is found in Barn. 6.14 (Ezek 11:19; 36:26). Barnabas calls upon Jeremiah to further his definition of circumcision as an act of hearing (Barn. 9.5 [Jer 4.3–4]) and combines words found in Jeremiah with Isaiah and Zechariah (Barn. 2.7–8 [Jer 7:22–23; Zech 7:9–10; 8:17]; 11.1 [Jer 2:12–13; Isa 16:1–2]). Zechariah's prophetic words about striking the shepherd are cited in Barn. 5.12 (Zech 13:7).[41] The horns, beasts, and kingdoms from Daniel's apocalyptic visions are brought to the fore

39. A list of references to specific psalms in *Barnabas* should include Ps 1:1 (Barn. 10.10); 1:3 (Barn. 11.6–8); 21:17 (22:16 MT; Barn. 6.7); 21:19 (22:18 MT; Barn. 6.7); 21:21 (22:20 MT; Barn. 5.13); 21:23 (22:22 MT; Barn. 6.16); 41:3 (41:2 MT; Barn. 6.16); 50:19 (51:19 MT; Barn. 2.10); 89:4 (90:4 MT; Barn. 15.4); 109:1 (110:1 MT Barn. 12.10); 117:12 (118:12 MT Barn. 6.7); 117:22 (118:22 MT Barn. 6.4); 117:24 (118:24 MT Barn. 6.4); 118:120 (119:120 MT Barn. 5.13). The list in this note includes influence and amalgamations from different psalms (e.g., Ps 21:23 [22:22 MT]; 107:4 [108:4 MT] in Barn. 6.16) but does not appeal to allusions to increase the numbers. For more on the Psalter in *Barnabas*, see Vesco, "La lecture," 5–37.

40. See further Lookadoo, "Form and Function," 211–46.

41. References to Zech 13:7 can also be found in Matt 26:31; Irenaeus, *Epid.* 76; Origen, *Comm. Jo.* 32.61; Tertullian, *Fug.* 11.3. Citations from Irenaeus's *Epideixis* can be found in Rousseau, *Démonstration*. See also the English translation in Behr, *On the Apostolic Preaching*. References to Tertullian's *De Fuga* are taken from Bulhart and Borleffs, *Tertullianus: Ad matryras*, while the text of Origen's *Commentarium in evangelium Joannis* are from Preuschen, *Johanneskommentar*.

in Barn. 4.4–5 (Dan 7:7-8, 24). Barnabas makes further reference to a proverbial saying in Barn. 5.4 (Prov 1:17).

A Breadth of Scriptural Usage

Alongside words from the prophets, references to the Pentateuch make up the other significant source of scriptural material in *Barnabas*. Barnabas twice makes reference to God's speech to Moses on Sinai using language similar to Exod 31:18; 32:7; 34:28 (Barn. 4.7-8; 14.2-3). He appeals to language that may come from the same narrative in Barn. 6.8, noting that the people were commanded to enter into the good land that is flowing with milk and honey (Exod 33:1, 3). However, Barnabas's citation also resonates with Pentateuchal language found in other passages so that it is difficult to locate this passage with certainty.[42] Barnabas's discussion of the food laws in Barn. 10.3-8 bears some similarities to the instructions found in Lev 11 and Deut 14. Finally, if one moves beyond the level of strict citation, Barnabas's discussion of the Day of Atonement, red heifer ritual, circumcision, food laws, and Sabbath contain not only references to passages from the Pentateuch but also topics that assume knowledge of the texts and traditions therein.

The breadth of Barnabean scriptural usage can be found when one recalls the extensive use of imagery and the various citation formulae that name scriptural writers in the letter. Cultic imagery, portrayals of dual pathways, and allusions to the coming of Jesus are strongly bound by Barnabas to scripture. He enhances these scriptural connections by introducing citations as coming from particular scriptural figures. Moses speaks the words of scripture to Israel and to Barnabas's audience (6.8; 10.1-2, 9, 11; 12.6, 8) and models Jesus in advance by raising his hands when Israel was attacked (12.2-4). Barnabas appeals to David as a scriptural author (10.10; 12.11), while Isaiah (12.11), Daniel (4.5), and Enoch (4.3) are likewise voices that speak in scripture. Outside of citation formulae, Barnabas also mentions Adam (6.9), Abraham (6.8; 9.7-8; 13.7), the patriarchs (8.4; 13.2-7), Israel (4.14; 5.2, 8; 6.7; 8.1, 3; 9.2; 12.2, 5; 16.5), and the Ten Words (15.1), while certain instructions in the way of light sound similar to imperatives given in the Ten Words.[43] The Epistle of Barnabas is thus saturated in scripture from beginning to end.

---

42. E.g., Lev 20:24; Deut 1:25.

43. E.g., Barn. 19.4 (Exod 20:14; Deut 5:18), 5 (Exod 20:7; Deut 5:11), 6 (Exod 20:17; Deut 5:21).

Blurry Borders

Yet the reference to Enoch points to another matter that must be considered when examining Barnabas's use of scripture, namely, the uncertainty of the precise borders surrounding his understanding of scripture. The blurriness of the edges around Barnabas's list of authoritative writings can be illustrated in three ways. First, the reference to Enoch as a speaker is not differentiated from other introductory formulae so that Enoch appears to have an equally authoritative voice (4.3). Enochic tradition may lie behind the citation from scripture (γραφή) in 16.5. While discussing the temple, Barnabas notes that the Lord will hand the sheep, sheepfold, and tower to destruction. These words appear to come from the Enochic *Animal Apocalypse* (1 En. 89.56, 66) or from a similar text.

Second, Barnabas also quotes texts that are difficult to pinpoint with certainty, suggesting that he may have had access to texts or versions other than those that remain extant. The citation in 12.1 serves as a good example.[44] It is a two-part quotation attributed to an unnamed prophet who asks when these things will be completed. The question is answered with a citation that appears to be from the same text. Things will be completed whenever two qualifications are met. First, the tree will be laid down and raised up. Second, blood will drip from the tree. The origin of these words is unclear. On the one hand, the text appears similar to words that are found in 4 Ezra 4.33 and 5.5.[45] In addition, Barnabas's language is at least thematically analogous to the signs of the eschaton that are listed in more detail in 4 Ezra 5.4–9 and 6.21–24.[46] Menahem Kister has argued differently about the origins of Barnabas's citation, proposing instead that Barnabas appeals here to an Ezekiel apocryphon. Drawing upon questions about when the Lord's word will be fulfilled and images of a tree standing up in 4Q385 2, Kister posits that Barnabas is drawing upon a similar Ezekiel tradition in Barn. 12.1.[47] Kister's argument is strengthened by the presence of imagery

---

44. "Again, likewise, he declares about the cross in another prophet who says, 'And when will these things be completed? The Lord says, Whenever the tree is laid down and raised up and whenever blood drips from the tree.' Again you have something about the cross and the one who was about to be crucified" (Barn. 12.1).

45. 4 Ezra 4.33: "And I answered and said, 'How and when will these things be? Why are our years few and evil?'" (*et respondit et dixi: Quo et quando haec? Quare modici et mali anni nostri?*). 4 Ezra 5.5: "And blood will drip from the wood, and the stone will express its voice. And the peoples will be in commotion, and the goings of the stars will change" (*et de ligno sanguis stillabit, et lapis dabit uocem suam; et populi commouebuntur, et gressus commutabuntur*).

46. Carleton Paget, *Epistle of Barnabas*, 157–58.

47. Kister, "Barnabas 12:1," 63–67.

in Barn. 11.9-11 that is reminiscent of Ezek 40-48 and may come from an Ezekiel apocryphon. Whether Barn. 12.1 stems from 4 Ezra, an Ezekiel apocryphon, or another source, the edges around which writings are authoritative prove difficult to outline with clarity.

The answer to the question posed in Barn. 12.1 is introduced as something that the Lord says, and this illustrates a third way in which the borders of the texts that Barnabas regards as authoritative are blurry. Barnabas appeals to Jesus's words as authoritative, but it is not always clear where these words have come from. Although 12.1 finds Jesus's words within another prophetic word,[48] Barn. 7.11 quotes Jesus's words directly.[49] At the end of his discussion of the Day of Atonement, Barnabas appeals to an otherwise unknown saying of Jesus: "'Thus,' he says, 'those who want to see me and touch my kingdom ought to receive me by being oppressed and suffering.'" This saying from Jesus is not attested in this form elsewhere in early Christian literature. Although James Hardy Ropes argued that 7.11 should not be construed as a reference to Jesus's words,[50] the formula with which Barnabas introduces this reference strongly suggests that Barnabas appeals to something that Jesus purportedly said in order to strengthen his arguments.[51] One may rightly question the historical value of Barnabas's citation of Jesus's words, but 7.11 should nonetheless be recognized as a citation of Jesus's words from the second century.

Early Christian Texts

Allusions to Enoch, unknown prophetic traditions, and otherwise unattested words of Jesus witness to a blurriness around the edges of the authoritative books in *Barnabas*. It will now be helpful to say a final word about citations of the New Testament or other early Christian literature in the document.[52] If one dates the Epistle of Barnabas to the time of Hadrian, it is not necessary to follow Prostmeier's conclusion that all attempts to demonstrate the use of New Testament literature may be considered a failure,

---

48. Scriptural words are also placed in Jesus's mouth in 6.16.

49. For other studies and collections of agrapha in early Christian literature, see Charlesworth and Evans, "Jesus in the Agrapha," 479-95; Dunn, *Jesus Remembered*, 172; Ehrman and Pleše, "Agrapha," 351-69; Elliott, *Apocryphal New Testament*, 26-30; Hofius, "Versprengte Herrenworte," 1.76-79; Jeremias, *Unknown Sayings of Jesus*.

50. Hardy Ropes, *Sprüche Jesu*, 17-18.

51. Ehrman and Pleše, "Agrapha," 358-59.

52. See further Carleton Paget, "Barnabas' Anti-Jewish Use," 91-112; Carleton Paget, "*Epistle of Barnabas* and the Writings that Later Formed the New Testament," 229-49.

particularly if one allows for the uses of the New Testament that extend beyond verbatim citations alone.[53] Yet it is difficult to adduce clear examples of New Testament quotations within the Epistle of Barnabas. Barnabas introduces one saying that is similar to Matt 22:14 in Barn. 4.14 when he urges his readers to be careful "lest we be found, as it is written, 'many are called, but few are chosen.'" It is possible that Barnabas is citing a Jewish apocalyptic text or Jesus tradition similar to 4 Ezra 8.3; 9.15. Others have argued that Barnabas knew Matthew directly.[54] Given the small amount of possible Matthean or Synoptic materials elsewhere in the letter, it is difficult to argue with certainty about Barnabas's source in Barn. 4.14. One may note instead a point of contact between Barnabas, Jesus tradition, and other Jewish materials and comment on the use to which Barnabas puts this traditional aphorism. Barnabas comes close to Matthean language again in Barn. 5.9 when he describes Jesus's call as targeted at the sinners rather than the righteous (Matt 9:13).[55] Barnabas shares with John 3:14–15 a christological interpretation of the bronze serpent raised on a pole (Barn. 12.5–7). Yet it is difficult to argue with a high degree of certainty for a literary relationship between Barnabas and the canonical Gospels.

Barnabas's interpretation of the Abraham narrative (Barn. 13.7; see Rom 4:11), the appearance of justification language in Barn. 4.10, and his reflections on the law in Barn. 2.6; 3.6 suggest that Barnabas had some knowledge of Paul's teachings.[56] The attribution of the letter to Barnabas, Paul's close associate, may provide secondary evidence for Pauline connections. However, it is not possible to determine which, if any, Pauline letters the pseudepigraphal author might have known. Barnabas shares a prominent citation of Ps 109:1 (110:1 MT) with Hebrews (Barn. 12.10; Heb 1:3, 13; 8:1; 10:12) and depicts an eschatological Sabbath (Barn. 15.1–9; Heb 4:1–11), but there is no clear way to argue that Barnabas had a literary knowledge of Hebrews. Rather, it is better to say that Barnabas and the author of Hebrews operated in similar milieus with a shared focus on interpreting scripture in light of Christ. Barnabas's reference to vinegar and gall at Jesus's crucifixion (Barn. 7.5) is reminiscent of Gos. Pet. 5.16, while

---

53. "Alle Versuche, im Barn die Verwendung neutestamentlicher Literatur nachzuweisen, dürfen gescheitert gelten" (Prostmeier, *Barnabasbrief*, 97).

54. For further discussion, see Bartlet, "Barnabas," 18–19; Franco, "Une citation," 231–45; Jefford, *Apostolic Fathers and the New Testament*, 109–10.

55. Edwards, *Gospel*, 92–99; Jefford, *Apostolic Fathers and the New Testament*, 110.

56. Carleton Paget, "*Epistle of Barnabas* and the Writings that Later Formed the New Testament," 239–45; Carleton Paget, "Paul and the Epistle of Barnabas," 359–81; Carleton Paget, "Paul and the *Epistle of Barnabas*," 79–100. See also the discussions in Bartlet, "Barnabas," 3–16; Edwards, *Gospel*, 90–92.

the reference to Jesus being spit upon (Barn. 7.9) shares vocabulary with Gos. Pet. 3.9.[57] The closest parallels between Barnabas and any individual early Christian text should likely be drawn between Barn. 18.1—20.2 and Did. 1.1—6.2. Similarities between the Two Ways Traditions in each text are discussed in more detail in the commentary. However, it is again difficult to determine with certainty whether Barnabas used the Didache, the Didache used Barnabas, or whether both were dependent on a shared tradition. The hypothesis of shared traditions dominates current scholarship and appears to be the safest choice unless further evidence presents itself.

Summary and Conclusion

The exact borders of the texts that Barnabas used or found authoritative are thus difficult to outline with any high degree of certainty. Both the edges of what Barnabas understood as God's prophetic word and the means by which Barnabas received these texts remain unclear. The center of the Barnabean scriptural understanding is easier to highlight. Barnabas regularly cites from Isaiah, Genesis, and the Psalter. Other prophetic writings are referred to often, while other statements and traditions can be found from Proverbs and the Torah.

At the center of Barnabas's understanding of scripture lie three beliefs. First, scripture is spoken by God and reveals God's identity and actions. It is thus *a revelatory word*. Second, scripture comes through the prophets who received grace to understand how God would act. It is thus *a prophetic word*. Finally, scripture cannot be properly read by just anyone. Rather, a correct interpretation is a result of having insight that stems from a proper relationship with God. Scripture is thus *a word in need of interpretation*. Accordingly, Barnabas's scriptural citations function to make known who God is, to open a proper form of discourse about God's actions, and to form the community of believers by teaching them how they should recognize God, the ways in which they should worship, and the path along which they are called to walk.

---

57. References to the Gospel of Peter can be found in Kraus and Nicklas, *Petrusevangelium*.

3

Toward a Theology of the Epistle of Barnabas

THE EPISTLE OF BARNABAS is not a systematic theological tome nor is it simply a treatise in epistolary form. Although the letter contains detailed exegesis and stringent argument, it was written to communicate from one author to a larger audience within a particular historical situation. The historical circumstances surrounding the text are not easy to reconstruct in their entirety, but the situatedness of the text should not be ignored. Barnabas has much to say on some theological topoi, such as the significance of Jesus's suffering. On the other hand, it is difficult to find any information about the order of ecclesial communities. Nor is Barnabas's logic always linear. For example, rather than discussing Jewish symbols in one sustained series, Barnabas divides his reflections across 2.4—3.6; 9.1—10.12; and 15.1—16.10. Nevertheless, the apparently scattered comments coalesce into three groups of paired discussions about cultic activities. Care is required to adduce a Barnabean theology within a letter that was never meant to be organized into theological categories but rather to be read and studied from beginning to end.

With this caution set at the beginning, this chapter nevertheless hopes to provide a guide to some major lines of theological thought within the Epistle of Barnabas. It concentrates on what Barnabas has to say about God; the gracious and revelatory actions of God toward human beings; the two paths between which the audience must choose; the significance of the requirements, commandments, and law; the relationship between the Barnabean community and Israel; and finally the role of eschatology within Barnabas's letter.

Understanding God

Barnabas identifies God and God's activities with a variety of images and terminology throughout the letter. An overarching concern in the letter is the proper way in which to worship and obey God. Barnabas's figurative exegesis sets out the proper way in which God has made Godself known to the people of God and how the people of God are to act in response.

The common Greek word θεός, which is typically translated "God," appears approximately forty-one times in Barnabas.[1] One of the striking things about Barnabas's description of God is the extent to which God is active. God has given requirements (1.2). God is appealed to as a source of wisdom and is thus thought by Barnabas to be capable of granting it (21.5). Barnabas's readers can thus become people who are taught by God (θεοδίδακτοι; 21.6). Perhaps most importantly in Barnabas, God speaks (5.5, 12; 6.8; 9.2, 5; 19.2, 4).[2] God's speech in creation (5.5) leads to another identifying activity of God, namely, that God is creator (16.1). God created the world in six days (15.3), which Barnabas understands as a signal that God's charge over history will be complete in 6,000 years (15.4). Barnabas can thus refer to God as "the master" (ὁ δεσπότης; 1.7; 4.3). God is a ruling figure, and Barnabas can refer to "the kingdom of God" (ἡ βασιλεία τοῦ θεοῦ) as a future reward for those who walk along the path of light (21.1). Because God reigns as king, God is worthy of worship. Questions about music, sacramental practices, and other precise ways in which God should be worshipped within the community are not addressed within the letter. However, evidence for Israel's failure to worship God is found in their construction of a temple for God and their failure to recognize that God's true temple is formed as God indwells the community (16.1–2, 6–8). Idolatry and a lack of fear for God are thus characteristics of those who walk along the way of darkness (20.1).[3]

---

1. This count does not include compound words such as θεοδίδακτος (21.6). An approximate count is given here in order to allow for ambiguities due to textual critical issues in the manuscript tradition.

2. Barnabas's general outlook about God's speech may mirror in important ways statements by contemporary theologians. For example, "The God who has spoken in the past continues to speak in the present, but his message is the same now as it has always been. The forms change over time and new developments occur in the way that the truth is expressed, but its substance remains unaltered" (Bray, *God Has Spoken*, 21). "While other modes of divine communicative action were serviceable in the past, the Son is the supreme instance of God's self-communication. There is but one divine speaker, and the Son is the summit and summation of his speech" (Vanhoozer, *Remythologizing Theology*, 51). Barnabas's insistence on the singular way in which God has spoken overrules any allowance in the letter that changes may have occurred in the form of delivery, but Barnabas would gladly assent to the continuity of God's speech.

3. Construction language is intriguing to read in conjunction with Barnabas's abhorrence of idolatry. "The builders" (οἱ οἰκοδομοῦντες) who rejected the chief cornerstone are best identified as the Jews, whom Barnabas blames for Jesus's crucifixion in 5.1—6.4 (6.4; see Ps 117:22 [118:22 MT]). Similarly, Israel is said to have "built for

On the other hand, God is the Lord (κύριος) of the way of light (18.2). This leads to another challenge in articulating precisely who God is in the Epistle of Barnabas. Barnabas employs the term κύριος to refer to both the Father and the Son.[4] The Father is referred to as Lord in 2.1, 5, where the Lord's requirements are mentioned both in general and with regard to sacrifice. The Son is identified as Lord in 5.1 when Barnabas discusses his suffering in the flesh. Although this shared title can create instances of ambiguity when trying to determine whether κύριος refers to the Father or Son in certain instances,[5] this ambiguity is theologically significant because it represents a shared essential identity. Both Jesus and God are fully and robustly divine. In other words, both can be defined as God, and Barnabas employs a shared κύριος terminology in order to emphasize this point. Another way in which Barnabas illustrates the equality between God and Jesus is by illustrating that both were active in the creation of the world (5.5). Since both God and Jesus were involved in creation, they stand opposite human beings on the creator-creation divide. Nevertheless, they are not to be understood as identical. When Barnabas recounts what was said in the creation narrative, he differentiates between the Father (πατήρ) and the Son (υἱός; 5.5). Both the Father and Son were involved in creation "from the foundation of the world" (ἀπὸ καταβολῆς κόσμου; 5.5).[6] Father-Son terminology is used to identify God and Jesus elsewhere in the letter. The Father likewise speaks to the Son in 14.6 and has revealed who the Son is in Mosaic traditions (12.8).[7] The word υἱός is employed more often to identify Jesus, appearing approximately ten times.[8] By setting Jesus apart as the Son of God (12.10), Barnabas closely links Jesus with the Father while simultaneously distinguishing two persons.

While Jesus is uniquely linked with the Father as Son of God, Barnabas urges his readers to reckon with Jesus's suffering and incarnation. Jesus's suffering is emphasized particularly in 5.1—8.7.[9] The suffering occurs in Jesus's

---

themselves" (ἑαυτοῖς οἰκοδομήσουσιν; 11.1) something that stands against the water that God has given in baptism.

4. Edwards, "Identifying the Lord," 51.

5. For example, Edwards ("Identifying the Lord," 52) thinks that the references to the Lord in 1.3 and 4 are uncertain. Korn (*Die Nachwirkung der Christusmystik*, 40) thinks that κύριος most often designates the Father.

6. See also 6.12.

7. The word πατήρ is also used of God in 2.9.

8. E.g., 5.9, 11; 6.12; 7.2 (2x), 9; 12.8, 9, 10; 15.5.

9. E.g., 5.5, 13; 6.7, 9; 7.2, 5, 10–11. Jesus's suffering was also anticipated by Moses's act of raising his hands when Israel was at war and raising a bronze serpent when Israel fell victim to snakes (12.2–7).

flesh, and Jesus's coming in the flesh is thus a vital theme in this section of the letter (e.g., 5.1, 6, 10–13; 6.7; 7.5). His actions are described by Barnabas in terms of endurance (5.1, 5–6; 14.4). Barnabas's choice of language may encourage the audience to follow Jesus's example by enduring in their own lives (2.2).[10] The interpretation of the Day of Atonement and red heifer rituals are designed to shed further light on how Jesus's suffering was told beforehand while also pointing to what it achieved (7.3—8.7).[11] Because of Jesus's death and resurrection, Jesus is able to redeem Barnabas and his audience from darkness (14.5–9). He has inscribed his covenant on the hearts of believers in a way that Israel rejected and failed to recognize (4.8). All of this has been revealed to Barnabas and his audience in scripture. While Israel misunderstood the prophetic words that God addressed about Jesus, Barnabas and his audience rightly recognize that Jesus is the unique Son and Lord who has come from God and suffered in the flesh.

Barnabas's use of the word spirit (πνεῦμα) does not always designate the Holy Spirit. Indeed, the adjective holy (ἅγιος) is not used in conjunction with the word spirit within the letter. The audience is addressed with regard to their spirits on four occasions (1.2, 5; 19.2; 21.9). References to human spirits may also be in view in 7.3 and 11.9. When discussing why the Lord was given vinegar and gall to drink, part of Barnabas's reason is that he was about to offer "the vessel of the spirit" (τὸ σκεῦος τοῦ πνεύματος; 7.3). The same phrase is utilized in 11.9 to describe the land of Jacob. It is difficult to ascertain with certainty whether "the vessel of the spirit" contains a reference to the Holy Spirit who indwells Jesus and believers or if it refers instead to a human spirit, that is, the life within their vessels. Barnabas's use of the adjective spiritual (πνευματικός) directly ties the noun that it modifies to God. Thus, a spiritual gift is a gift that comes from God (1.2), spiritual people are people who fear the Lord and keep his commandments (4.11), and the spiritual temple is the body of believers that is being built up to the Lord (16.10).

These ambiguous references to the spirit do not, however, mean that *Barnabas* contains no references to the Holy Spirit. One reason for the author's joy is that the Spirit has been poured out on believers (1.3). The Spirit

---

10. If Barnabas's expectation that believers are living during the time of the final stumbling block is to be understood with reference to sufferings that believers will have to undergo, Barnabas's emphasis on the endurance of both Jesus and believers takes on a more significant nuance. For comparisons of *Barnabas* and other Egyptian messianic literature, see Carleton Paget, "Egypt," 192.

11. On the significance of narrative elements in Barnabas's portrayal of Jesus, see Ayres, "Continuity and Change," 111; Edwards, "Epistle of Barnabas," 30–31; Svigel, *Center and the Source*, 286–94.

has agency as Barnabas depicts the Spirit speaking directly to Moses's heart regarding the need to model the cross by raising his hands when Israel was attacked by foreign tribes (12.2). Likewise, the Spirit prepares believers who place their hope in God. The Spirit's preparation provides a rationale for Barnabas's command that masters treat their slaves without bitterness (19.7). The Spirit's agency comes from the way in which the Spirit is closely and uniquely related to God. This bond, however, is not described in ontological terms. Another indication of how the Spirit interacts with believers can be found in Barnabas's repetition of the phrase "in the Spirit" (ἐν πνεύματι).[12] Interpretations of events or words that come from Abraham, Moses, and another prophet are given "in the Spirit" (9.7; 10.2, 9; 11.11). When God wrote the Ten Words on Sinai, these words were inscribed by the finger of God's hand "in the Spirit" (14.2).[13] The phrase suggests either the Spirit's mediatorial agency in the revelatory act or perhaps the realm in which Barnabas and his audience can understand what God has said.

Barnabas's beliefs about God are largely assumed in the letter and thus not explicated at length. God is active and has revealed Godself in the world. One exception to Barnabas's largely assumed discussion of God has to do with God's revelation in the person of Jesus. Jesus was a human being who revealed himself to Israel (5.7–10). Israel's rejection of Jesus led to the suffering that he endured (5.2, 7, 11–14). However, Barnabas emphasizes that Jesus was with the Father at creation (5.5; 6.12). The Father and the Son are thus to be understood as God within the Epistle of Barnabas. The Spirit also functions as an extension of God's person in a way that marks the Spirit out from the creation. Moreover, the Spirit has agency and is able to speak to people (12.2). While little reflection is given to the Triune nature of God in *Barnabas*, the author nevertheless articulates a functional Trinitarianism by which God has revealed Godself to the world. The Father, the Son, and the Spirit are at work in the world in order to redeem Barnabas and his audience from the way of death.

God's Revelation and Redemption

After recognizing that Barnabas's beliefs about God are articulated primarily in functional and economic terms, one must then wrestle with how God acts on behalf of the believers whom Barnabas addresses. Barnabas's depiction of

---

12. See also 13.5 where Barnabas employs the dative τῷ πνεύματι without the preposition. Although the preposition is missing, the dative noun functions in the same way.

13. On 14.2, see the intriguing comments in Svigel, "Trinitarianism," 29.

God emphasizes God's active revelation of Godself by which it is possible for Barnabas and his audience to have knowledge of God. Barnabas's purpose in writing the letter is for his audience to have complete knowledge (1.5). Knowledge is something that is given by God (19.1), and Barnabas prays near the end of the letter that God will give knowledge and understanding of the Lord's requirements to the audience (21.5). God has made known the significance of past, present, and some future actions through the prophets (1.7). Scripture is thus a central means by which God reveals Godself.[14] The prophets received special grace in order to speak about who Jesus was and to reveal his death and resurrection ahead of time (5.6). The Son of God is the center of the divine revelation as he brings salvation to all who look to him. If the Son did not come in the flesh, it would be impossible for believers to have a full understanding of God (5.10). As a result, believers are called to look to the God who has been revealed in Jesus the Son rather than trying to construct their own means of salvation (16.10).

God's salvation of believers is thus a significant theme in the letter as Barnabas outlines the benefits of God's self-revelation.[15] Indeed, salvation motivates Barnabas's continued interactions with his readers in the first place (1.3).[16] Salvation is not an activity that takes place in isolation, but Barnabas's salvation is enhanced by his relation to his audience. Salvation is found in the God who indwells the temple of believers, and Barnabas does not depict any salvation outside of that initiated by God's own action (16.10). God's rescue of believers is intimately connected to the incarnation and cross of Jesus. People would not be able to be saved without the Son's incarnation because only in this event was it possible for people to see God (5.10). The life that comes in the cross was prefigured by Moses's act of making a bronze serpent. Just as those in the wilderness found life through a dead serpent on a wooden pole, so Barnabas and his audience have found life through Jesus through his death on the cross (12.7; Num 21:8–9). A similar conclusion is reached when Barnabas interprets Moses's act of raising his hands over Israel's battle so that Israel and readers of Israel's story may learn that they cannot be saved unless they place their hope in Jesus

14. See similarly 4.1; 5.3; 17.2.

15. Prostmeier ("Einleitung," 63) emphatically draws attention to the important role of soteriology: "Die Soteriologie (*Barn.* 4–8) ist das theologische Thema des Barnabasbriefes; die christologischen, ekklesiologischen und eschatologischen Themen sind ihr funktional zugeordnet und gewinnen ihre Konturen in der Sicherung der Soteriologie."

16. Barnabas ends his letter with a possible pun on the important theme in which he begins when he writes, "Farewell (σῴζεσθε), children of love and peace" (21.9). Although σῴζεσθε should be understood primarily as a parting phrase, the remains of its salvific connotations when the word is utilized elsewhere in the letter may not have disappeared entirely.

(12.2-3). Hope is thus closely linked with salvation in the Son, and Barnabas urges hope in Jesus, the name, and the cross as central to salvation.[17] The hope that Barnabas holds out to believers may give some insight into his instructions to be careful regarding salvation (2.10) or to seek the things that are able to save (4.1). Although God's actions are consistently faithful, believers must endure along the way of light in the same way that Jesus endured through his suffering on the cross.

Yet before considering the two alternatives that Barnabas sets out in his letter, it will be helpful to examine briefly what believers are saved from and what imagery Barnabas employs to enhance his descriptions of salvation. Jesus's death brought the power of death to naught (5.6). Rather than dying and staying within death's clutches, it was necessary for Jesus to suffer in order to show the resurrection of the dead. Jesus's death and resurrection are thus indicators that believers have been rescued from death and brought to life. Believers are likewise saved from sin because Jesus's death has purified their sin. The Lord endured the corruption of his flesh so that he could purify believers in the forgiveness of sins (5.1). This is the meaning of the red heifer ritual by which Barnabas interprets Jesus's death (8.1, 3). Barnabas describes believers as restored and made new because they are forgiven of their sin (6.11). Salvation thus results in new life by bringing forgiveness of sins. Finally, believers are rescued from the power of the evil one when they are saved. Satan continues to have power, but Jesus's actions have liberated believers so that they can walk in the way of the Lord and avoid the traps set out by the devil (2.10; 4.9, 13; 18.2).[18] The day in which the evil one will be utterly destroyed is thus approaching (21.3).

Alongside Barnabas's use of revelatory and soteriological language, he selectively employs redemptive and heliacal imagery in the letter. Redemptive terminology is used suggestively in 19.2 as believers are called to glorify the one who redeemed them from death.[19] Such language takes a focal place in the letter in 14.5-9. Jesus's work is set over and against Israel's sin at Sinai so that believers are redeemed from darkness even though their hearts had already been handed over to the lawlessness of deceit (14.5). Jesus received the command to redeem Barnabas and his audience from the Father (14.6), and the imagery of light and darkness plays an important role not only in Barnabean redemptive language but also in the Isaianic

---

17. E.g., 6.9; 8.5; 11.8, 11; 12.2; 16.8. See further Kraft, *Barnabas*, 30.

18. Instructions to flee from Satan and his works make little sense unless it is a possibility. Jesus's death makes Barnabas's imperative possible.

19. Barnabas also instructs his audience to work with their hands "for a ransom for your sins" (εἰς λύτρον ἁμαρτιῶν σου; 19.10).

citations that follow (14.6–8).²⁰ The image of the sun is employed to explain the significance of the Son's incarnation. The inability to gaze directly into the sun, which is a perishable entity in God's creation, forms an analogy with which Barnabas explains that salvation would not have been possible unless the Son came in the flesh (5.10). Since no one can see God in all of God's glory, the Son came in the flesh, performed wonders and signs, and called sinful apostles to proclaim the good news (5.8–9). Because the Son has made God known and rescued believers from darkness through his act of redemption, the audience is called to live in the way of light.

The Two Paths

Two paths thus characterize the Barnabean understanding of how one may live. On the one hand, Barnabas calls his readers to live in the way of light that God has already revealed to them in scripture and over which the Lord of eternity rules. This path is described as the way of light. On the other hand, Barnabas outlines a way of darkness that runs contrary to what God has said and is overseen by the ruler of the present time of lawlessness (18.1–2). The fullest and best-known form of this plank of Barnabean theology can be found in 18.1—20.2. Barnabas sets out the two ways that believers can choose near the end of his letter in a similar arrangement to what is found in other early Jewish and early Christian literature.²¹ The Community Rule that was discovered at Qumran contains a description of life that is divided among two paths and two angels (1QS III, 13–IV, 26). Asher is purported to have utilized a Two Ways Tradition in his last words to his children in the Testament of Asher (T. Ash. 1.3—6.8). The nearest parallels with the Two Ways Tradition that Barnabas employs can be found in Did. 1.1—6.2.²² While the arrangement of the material differs between the Didache and *Barnabas*, a close connection between these portions of the texts is evident. The imagery of alternate paths may be found elsewhere

---

20. Barnabas quotes from Isa 42:6–7; 49:6–7; 61:1–2.

21. The two-ways pattern can also be found in other Hellenistic literature (Xenophon, *Mem.* 2.1.21–39; Hesiod, *Op.* 287–92). For the text of Xenophon's *Memorabilia*, see Hude, *Xenophontos Apomnēmoneumata*. For the text of Hesiod's *Opera et dies*, see West, *Hesiod: Works and Days*. See the extensive list of texts in Wilhite, *One of Life*, 285–314.

22. The terminology and orthography utilized when referring to the Two Ways Tradition is far from standard. I have opted to use "Two Ways Tradition" when attempting to focus on literary collections of the two ways, including the one in the Epistle of Barnabas. References to "two ways" are an attempt to refer to the metaphorical paths set out and described in such literary traditions. See further Wilhite, *One of Life*, 54–74.

in early Christian literature. The Shepherd of Hermas speaks of opposing ways and angels in order to outline different ways of living (Herm. *Mand.* 6.2.1-10 [36.1-10]; *Sim.* 6.2.1—6.5.7 [62.1—65.7]).[23] Even in the fourth century, the Two Ways Tradition continues to be utilized by the author of the *Apostolic Constitutions* (*Const. apost.* 7.1.1-19).[24]

Barnabas's characterization of life in terms of sharply contrasting paths thus has a lengthy history in other early Jewish and early Christian traditions. For Barnabas, these divergent ways have been made clear by the suffering and death of Jesus Christ, by the interpretation of scripture, and by the way in which believers live. Jesus's suffering enabled Barnabas and his audience to receive the covenant and to seal it in the hearts of believers (4.8; 14.4-5).[25] His suffering took place "on account of us" (δι' ἡμᾶς; 7.2).[26] Barnabas and his audience are thus placed in hermeneutically privileged positions because they are able to understand rightly what God has revealed through the prophets. Some things in scripture are said to Israel, while others are directed to Barnabas and his audience (5.2). Since they rightly understand what God has done, Barnabas and his audience are able to understand scripture better than Barnabas's opponents.[27] Believers' places along the way of light result in a life that recognizes God's place as creator and redeemer (19.2) while also giving to their neighbor (19.8-9). On the other hand, those on the way of darkness are idolatrous and have no mercy for the poor (20.1-2).

The placement of the most systemic outline of the difference between the Two Ways Tradition at the end of the letter suggests that these through roads may also be the outcome of what God has done in Christ and revealed beforehand in scripture.[28] Barnabas places the Two Ways Tradition at the end of his letter (18.1—20.2) after he has articulated how God has revealed Jesus in scripture in 2.4—16.10. The way in which believers are called to live is a result of God's revelatory and salvific action for believers. Barnabas's description of what God has done for believers also utilizes way imagery.[29]

---

23. On the use of opposing pathways in the *Shepherd*, see Lookadoo, *Shepherd of Hermas*, 125-26, 142-43.

24. References to the *Apostolic Constitutions* can be found in Metzger, *Les constitutions apostoliques*, 3 vols.

25. Hvalvik, *Struggle for Scripture and Covenant*, 145.

26. See also 5.5; 14.4.

27. See also 2.7-10; 3.1-5.

28. Draper ("Barnabas," 89–113) accounts for the placement of the Two Ways Tradition at the end of *Barnabas* by arguing that the author depicts the two ways of knowledge as an advanced form of knowledge (γνῶσις) for the elite.

29. Jefford, *Apostolic Fathers and the New Testament*, 102.

When Barnabas cites Isa 65:2, he refers to God's act of stretching out God's hands to a people that oppose the righteous way (12.4). Barnabas's opponents oppose God's acts. After outlining Israel's failure and the covenant of Jesus that is on believers' hearts (4.6–8), Barnabas warns his readers about the evil way (4.10). People who have knowledge of the way of righteousness but become ensnared on the way of darkness are said to deserve destruction (5.4). On the other hand, Barnabas lists the Lord's accompaniment of him along the way of righteousness as part of his reason for writing in the first place (1.4). When these connections are examined alongside the overall shape of the letter, there is good reason to believe that there is a revelatory link between the Two Ways Tradition and God's actions in Jesus.

Requirements, Commandments, and Law

In order to aid his audience as they walk along the way of light, Barnabas urges them to pay attention to the requirements and commandments that the Lord has given. These terms suggest that the audience must actively engage with what God has revealed and accomplished on their behalf. Understanding God's revelation and walking along the way of light is not a passive disposition within the Epistle of Barnabas.

A central term by which to understand how Barnabas conceives of what the audience should do can be found by exploring the repeated use of the term "requirements" (δικαιώματα). A δικαίωμα can refer to a legal requirement, such as an ordinance, regulation, or precept. The emphasis falls on something that God has set forth for human beings to do in response to God's revelatory action. The author employs the term eight times in the letter, and it is significant that the term is included in the opening *captatio beneuolentiae* (1.2) and twice in the conclusion (21.1, 5).[30] By bracketing the letter with references to what is required of the audience, Barnabas urges his readers to act in response to what he has written. In 1.2, the author makes clear that the origins of the requirements are not from Barnabas but instead from God. The origins of these requirements are emphasized throughout the letter.[31] The emphasis on the origins of the requirements links the commendation near the beginning of the letter 1.2 and the concluding paraenesis in 21.5. Human mediation of the requirements is possible, but it is mentioned as a possibility only in 10.2 where Moses serves as a conduit of the Lord's requirements.[32]

30. 1.2; 2.1; 4.11; 10.2, 11; 16.9; 21.1, 5.
31. E.g., 2.1; 4.11; 10.11; 16.9; 21.1, 5.
32. See, e.g., Deut 4:1, 5.

TOWARD A THEOLOGY OF THE EPISTLE OF BARNABAS 61

The audience is instructed to rejoice in and to speak (4.11; 10.11) God's requirements to one another. The requirements are a good thing and are worthy of the audience's joy. They must also seek and keep (2.1; 10.11; 21.1) God's requirements. There is a responsibility to pursue and obey the statutes that God has established for walking on the way of light. The Lord's requirements are linked to knowledge (γνῶσις), since both knowledge and requirements are given by God (21.5).[33] Knowledge is likewise not far from the first reference to the requirements in Barn. 1. The requirements are mentioned in 1.2, while the first mention of knowledge occurs in 1.5. References to the requirements also occur in transition statements from the letter opening (2.1) and to the epistolary closing (21.1).[34] God's δικαιώματα are thus placed at key places in the letter, come from God, and provide a path in which the audience should seek to walk.

The requirements set forth by God are closely connected to God's commandments (ἐντολαί; 4.11; 10.2, 11; 16.9). "The wisdom of the requirements" (τῶν δικαιωμάτων) and "the commandments (αἱ ἐντολαί) of the teaching" are ways in which the Lord indwells the temple that he is constructing (16.9). The commandments find their origin in the God who gives them (4.11; 6.1; 19.2).[35] Effort must be expended in order to keep the commandments. Barnabas urges the audience to exert themselves in order to keep the commandments (4.11). Those on the way of light should not leave behind the Lord's commandments (19.2). The commandments come from God and may be associated with divine revelation, but a passive reception of the commandments is not in view in *Barnabas*. Instead, believers should fulfill every commandment because the commandments are "worthy" (ἄξια; 21.8). The divine origin of the commandments marks them out as worthy of obedience. By keeping the commandments to circumcise their hearts, the audience will be able to understand what God says (9.5). However, Barnabas employs the term commandment broadly, and it does not always apply directly to the moral effort of the audience. Barnabas cites a command that the Father gives to the Son as he undertakes his redemptive actions (14.5), while the Lord's command offers insight into the nature of Jesus's sacrifice (7.6). The commandment is applied to Jesus's suffering, and the word is utilized with regard to a citation from Isa 50:8–9 (6.1). Likewise, the commandment refers to instructions that were given about the Day of Atonement by which readers of scripture should recognize Jesus's suffering (7.3).

33. The requirements are also associated with wisdom in 16.9.

34. On the cohesion provided by the word δικαιώματα in 1.2 and 2.1, see Prinzivalli and Simonetti, *Seguendo Gesù*, 2.59.

35. The genitive that modifies "commandments" (ἐντολαί) in 4.11 and 19.2 should be interpreted as either a subjective or a possessive genitive.

The commandments that God gave regarding sacrifice when Israel came out of Egypt (2.7–8) occur near to another closely related term but less frequent term in the Epistle of Barnabas, namely, the law (ὁ νόμος; 2.6). Within the letter, the law is not a negative entity from which believers should distance themselves. Moses was a good lawgiver (10.11), and his reception of the covenant at Sinai is upheld as valid even though Israel rejected it (4.7–8; 14.1–5). Readers are called to follow in Moses's footsteps by being good lawgivers for one another (21.4). Yet Barnabas finds dangers in "their law" (ὁ ἐκείνων νόμος) and warns readers not to become shipwrecked as proselytes (3.6). The reference to "their law" is best understood not as a law that is different from what believers are called to obey. Nor is Barnabas's reference to be interpreted flatly as the Torah. Rather, "their law" is a way of highlighting Israel's *interpretation* of the law that fails to recognize that the Torah was given in the Spirit. By referring to "their law," Barnabas warns the audience not to accept his opponents' flawed, non-figurative interpretations of the Torah's cultic regulations.[36] Rather, Barnabas's audience is called to observe "the new law of our Lord Jesus Christ" (ὁ καινὸς νόμος τοῦ κυρίου Ἰησοῦ Χριστοῦ; 2.6).[37] The new law is not a new entity or set of commandments. Rather, the law that Barnabas follows and about which he writes is the law that comes from Jesus Christ and is interpreted in terms of God's self-revelation in the person of Jesus.

The Covenant, Inheritance, and Israel

The discussion of the law leads naturally to the key polemical topic in the letter. Barnabas's vehement opposition to non-figurative understandings of the law stems from his interpretation of the covenant and the way in which he places himself and his audience within the covenant. Although he recognizes that others may claim that they have inherited God's covenant at Sinai, there is only one people of the covenant for Barnabas.[38] The true people includes Barnabas and his audience, who have been marked

---

36. Lincicum ("Against the Law," 116–19) correctly categorizes the approach to the law in *Barnabas* as "hermeneutical."

37. For an interpretation of Barn. 2.6 alongside Gal 6:2 and Ign. *Magn.* 2, see Cho, "ὁ νόμος τοῦ Χριστοῦ," 263–94.

38. Knut Backhaus ("Bundesmotiv," 165) rightly observes, "The question of God's covenant and its legitimate 'owner' is a battleground that is clunkily distributed across the text and discussed precisely in those passages that are shaped by searing controversy" ("Die Frage nach dem Gottesbund und seinem rechtmäsigen 'Besitzer' ist ein Reizthema, blockartig über das Schreiben verteilt und gerade in solchen Passagen diskutiert, die von schneidender Kontroverse geprägt sind").

out by Jesus Christ. Israel lost the covenant "completely" (εἰς τέλος) when they rejected the commandments given by God at Sinai and instead acted lawlessly (4.7–8).[39] Moses's act of smashing the tablets that were written by God's finger symbolizes the fracture of the covenant. When Barnabas retells this story later in the letter (14.1–5), he specifies that Israel's lawless act was idolatry as they made molten images for themselves (14.3).[40] Israel's rejection by God thus has some basis in history and is grounded in the letter upon an action that occurred in space and time. Yet the importance of this action for Barnabas's audience is not the historical thatness of Israel's misplaced worship but rather its figurative bearing upon Barnabas's audience.[41] Barnabas confronts his readers with a choice. Either they can become like Israel by rejecting the way of light that God has revealed in the Son and scripture, or they can become the people of God on whose hearts God has transcribed the covenant of Jesus.[42]

The significance of the Sinai event thus has to do with the identity of the people whom Barnabas addresses. The addressees are warned not to be like some "saying that the covenant remains ours" (λέγοντας ὅτι ἡ διαθήκη ἡμῶν μένει; 4.6).[43] Barnabas refers to his opponents who, in his mind, falsely assert that the covenant remains theirs. Rather, Barnabas aligns himself and his readers as those who are members of the covenant over and against his

---

39. Barnabas polemicizes throughout the letter against Judaism. This has led to a significant amount of scholarly study regarding who Barnabas's opponents are. Were they non-Jesus-following Jews, ethnically Jewish Jesus-followers, or ethnic gentile Jesus-followers who were attracted to Jewish customs? In addition, one may wonder how or whether Jewish proselytism lies in the background of the letter. While these discussions are important and worthy of further study, the present commentator has nothing new to say on the matter. For further discussion of the Judaism and anti-Jewish polemic in and around the Epistle of Barnabas, see Alexander, "Jews and Judaism," 42–48; Barnard, "Background of Christianity and Judaism in Egypt," 27–51; Barnard, "The Epistle of Barnabas in Its Jewish Setting," 52–106; Barnard, *Studies in the Apostolic Fathers*, 41–55; Carleton Paget, "Jewish Proselytism," 65–103; Carleton Paget, "Antijudaism," 195–225; Carleton Paget, "Jews and Christians in Ancient Alexandria," 123–47; Edwards, *Gospel*, 48–51; Horbury, "Jewish-Christian Relations," 321–36; Kok, "Ethnic Reasoning," 81–97; Lincicum, "Against the Law," 117–21; Lieu, "Self-Definition," 214–29, esp. 220; Lowy, "Confutation of Judaism," 1–33; Murray, *Playing a Jewish Game*, 44–59; Prostmeier, "Antijudaismus," 38–59; Shukster and Richardson, "Temple and Bet Ha-midrash," 17–31; Taylor, *Anti-Judaism*, 132–38; Verheyden, "Israel's Fate," 237–62.

40. Lieu, *Christian Identity*, 80.

41. Rothschild, "Epistle of Barnabas," 191–212.

42. "Christians are no different from their Jewish predecessors apart from the fact that they have the benefit of learning from the past (which they need as 'newcomers,' 3:6). The allegorical interpretation of Barnabas is intended to encourage Christian readers of the letter" (Rothschild, "Epistle of Barnabas," 211).

43. On the textual critical issues in this phrase, see the commentary.

Jewish opponents who likewise lay claim to the covenant. A key way in which Barnabas accomplishes this is by the use of pronominal deictic markers.[44] Barnabas creates an us/them or near/far dynamic that permeates the letter and forces readers to choose with which side they will align.[45] God has made it possible for "us" to understand scripture, while things remain obscure to "them" (8.7). Certain things in scripture are said to "them" (3.1), while other words are addressed to "us" (3.3). Barnabas defines the pronouns in 5.2 by clarifying that he means Israel when he writes "them." Barnabas employs the near demonstrative "this" in ways that are parallel to "us," while the "first" people should be understood with respect to Israel (13.1). By utilizing pronouns in this way, Barnabas simultaneously includes his audience alongside himself while also forcing a choice. The audience must either agree with him or risk being alienated like "them."

Yet Barnabas's understanding of the two peoples is not a purely rhetorical construct. He finds a basis for his rationale in scripture.[46] The promises made to the patriarchs provide a rich source of material for the author. Although Barnabas allows that Israel has a longer historical track record, he points out that the younger son is given prominence in the narratives of Isaac and Jacob (13.2–6). Nor is one's genealogy the primary matter for Barnabas. Abraham was called as the father of gentiles (13.7). Since Israel forfeited their right to be part of God's covenant people at Sinai, Barnabas argues that they have no place within the people of God (4.6–8; 14.1–5).[47] This argument is grounded upon a belief that the covenant is singular. There are neither two parallel covenants for Israel and followers of Jesus nor two historical covenants, only one of which remains valid. Rather, Barnabas's letter is predicated on the assumption that there is only one covenant, that it has been made known through God's revelatory act, that Israel has rejected it paradigmatically at Sinai but also in their violence toward the prophets and the Son of God, and that Jesus has inscribed the covenant onto the hearts of believers in a way that Israel never experienced.[48] By demarcating his opponents in this way and associating his opponents with the way of darkness, Barnabas's understanding

---

44. For further discussion of this phenomenon in New Testament Greek, see Runge, *Discourse Grammar*, 365–84. A similar phenomenon can be found to differentiate Jesus from John in John 1:1–18, on which see Tovey, "Narrative Structure," 158–60.

45. Dodson, "Rejection and Redemption," 53–54.

46. On the relation between Barnabas's scriptural arguments and their relation to Judaism, see Jefford, *Apostolic Fathers and the New Testament*, 169–72.

47. Moreschini and Norelli, *Manuale*, 59–60.

48. See similarly Johnson, "Interpretive Hierarchies," 702; Kok, "Ethnic Reasoning," 90; Lieu, "Jewish Matrix," 220; Murray, *Playing a Jewish Game*, 50–54.

of Israel functions paraenetically to urge his audience to accept his understanding of Jesus, scripture, and the covenant.

Eschatology

Barnabas's consistent eschatological emphasis adds a sense of urgency to what he asks his audience to do, believe, and understand. Barnabas and his audience must act rightly in order to maintain their position within the covenant people of God. Awareness of the shortness of the remaining time should motivate the audience to live in accordance with what Barnabas outlines. They must hurry to perform the works to which they are called (19.1), just as Barnabas has hurried to communicate what he knows (1.5; 4.9). Barnabas and the audience find themselves living in climactically evil days that will precede God's final eschatological action (2.1).[49] The destruction of the Jerusalem temple is understood as an event connected to the last days which makes clear that the true temple is being constructed by God in and among believers (16.5–6). Although Barnabas allows that the present days are in some sense the kingdom of Jesus in which evil things may yet occur (8.5–6), he simultaneously refers to the time that he and his audience inhabit as a time of deception and lawlessness (4.1, 9; 18.2). Barnabas's use of the τελ-lexeme enhances the sense of urgency, approaching finality, and the corresponding desire for completion. As the world experiences the final stumbling block (4.3), so also believers should flee completely from evil works as they seek to complete their knowledge as part of God's temple (1.5; 4.1, 11).[50]

When Barnabas's eschatological emphasis is read alongside his understanding that God has revealed knowledge that is otherwise unknowable and wants to make all things new, it is possible to read the Epistle of

---

49. Pearson, "Earliest Christianity in Egypt: Further Observations," 100–101; Shukster and Richards, "Temple and *Bet Ha-midrash*," 23.

50. The noun τέλος is employed several times through the letter along with its verbal, adverbial, and adjectival cognates. The meaning of the term does not map easily on to any single English word, which makes the translation of such an important concept in *Barnabas* a challenge. The term suggests a goal toward which something is oriented and may accordingly carry connotations of fulfillment, perfection, completion, and conclusion. Barnabas employs the noun in his purpose statement when he tells the audience that the reason for his writing is because he wants to add perfect (τελείαν) knowledge to their faith (1.5). As Barnabas nears the end of his teaching on the food laws, he informs the audience that they now have his instructions about food "completely" (τελείως; 10.10). Although these uses are not particularly eschatological, the use of this root alongside other statements that emphasize the near completion of time adds to the urgent sense that all things will soon draw to a close.

Barnabas as a letter that has been informed by apocalyptic motifs. Light and darkness are strongly contrasted with one another. On account of what God has revealed to believers in the Son and scripture,[51] correct belief and understanding will aid them to walk in the way of light and to maintain their difference from what the author sees as Israel's misguided interpretations of scripture (18.1—19.12). There is a great difference (διαφορὰ πολλή) from the way of darkness (18.1). In addition to being characterized by many of the opposite actions as the way of light (5.4; 20.1–2), darkness is the realm from which Barnabas's audience has been redeemed (14.5–7). In order to strengthen the contrast between the alternate lifestyles, Barnabas reminds the audience that the way of darkness is overseen by the supreme evil figure. This figure is variously characterized as Satan (18.1), the Black One (4.10; 20.1), and the Evil One (2.10),[52] and the Lawless One (15.5).[53] Barnabas understands the world to be populated by angels associated with light and with Satan (18.1). Yet the supreme God who created and rules over all things has been revealed in Jesus and in the words of the prophets. This God seeks to make all things new (6.13), and a new creation motif can be found sprinkled across the letter. There is hope for a new world when the Son comes on the eschatological Sabbath (15.4–5). God's Spirit promises to replace the audience's stony hearts with fleshly hearts (6.14), and God will indwell the audience like a temple (4.11; 6.14–15; 16.6–10). New creation imagery, revelatory language, and a world influenced by the work of God, Satan, and their angels collectively suggest that Barnabas has imbibed motifs that can be broadly characterized as apocalyptic.

God's judgement provides additional motivation for believers to act with eschatological urgency as well as further evidence for Barnabas's assumption of certain apocalyptic motifs into his letter. Barnabas portrays judgement in financial terms. The good wage that God holds out at the

51. Barnabas employs Isaianic language to refer to light breaking in when fasting is rightly practiced (3.4; Isa 58:8) and the Son's redemptive work in rescuing believers out of darkness (14.7–8; Isa 42:6; 49:6).

52. If the reference to "evil" (τῷ πονηρῷ) in 21.3 is understood to refer to a personified being, one could add another reference to the Evil One in 21.3.

53. The text of 15.5 is uncertain and difficult to decipher at this point. The words τοῦ ἀνόμου are found in H but do not appear in S. Rather, S indicates that the Son will bring the time to naught but does not include a genitive further characterizing the age. Since L reads *iniquititatis*, it is possible that the translator's underlying Vorlage was τῆς ἀνομίας. The majority of the manuscripts in G contain αὐτοῦ, using the same pronoun that modifies the Son and apparently understanding the time to belong to God. Wengst (*Didache*, 180) follows L and reads τῆς ἀνομίας. However, τοῦ ἀνόμου is the reading found in Prigent and Kraft, *Épître de Barnabé*, 184; Prinzivalli and Simonetti, *Seguendo Gesù*, 2.160; Prostmeier and Lona, *Epistola Barnabae*, 122. The masculine adjective is here understood as a personified reference to Satan.

end of all things should lead believers to give without hesitation or grumbling (19.11). The approach of the Lord and his motivation are explicitly cited as motivation for those in high position to do good (21.3), while resurrection is the time during which the wage will be dispensed (21.1). Remembrance of God's forthcoming judgement is thus a key motivator for believers (19.10; 21.6), and Barnabas adds to this by insisting that believers have not yet been justified but will be in the future (4.11; 15.7). While God has revealed Godself to believers in unique ways, time will tell whether their salvation is complete.

In view of Barnabas's focus on future judgement and justification, he draws close lines between hope and salvation.[54] Barnabas interprets the command to enter into the promised land as an instruction to hope in Jesus's flesh (6.9). Those who place their hope on the cross of Jesus will live forever (8.5). Those who hope in the cross will receive their wage in its time (11.8), and they bear fruit in the present insofar as their lives are characterized by hope and fear (11.11). Shared hope in God is the basis upon which Barnabas grounds his instruction for masters not to be harsh to their slaves (19.7). While readers of Paul may expect more references to faith in these circumstances, Barnabas's eschatological orientation pushes him to link hope in Jesus's cross to the time when believers' salvation will be finally revealed. Nevertheless, faith is not entirely absent from Barnabas's letter and appears in conjunction with hope. Barnabas's readers have experienced a time before they believed God (16.7), but they will take their place in the temple as they place their hope in God (16.8). The one who is faithful to Jesus, the stone, will live eternally because Jesus's flesh is the ground of believers' hope (6.3). When Barnabas highlights the Lord's three teachings (1.6), he highlights hope as the beginning and end of faith. Although hope is emphasized by the author alongside his eschatological orientation, hope and faith cannot be easily separated in the Epistle of Barnabas.

By orienting his letter around an eschatological sense of urgency, Barnabas ties together his understanding of God, God's revelatory actions in the Son and scripture, his dismay that his audience may be influenced by practices that he regards as Jewish, and the need for right action in the present. Hope in what God has done is thus the antidote that enables believers to live rightly, to interpret scripture clearly, and to understand all that God has said and done.

---

54. Torrance, *Doctrine of Grace*, 104; Windisch, *Barnabasbrief*, 341–42. Korn (*Die Nackwirkungen der Christusmystik*, 41–42) finds Barnabas's conception of faith to be thoroughly other than Paul but understands his use of temple imagery (4.11; 6.15; 16.6–10) to follow Paul closely.

Part II

Commentary

I

Barnabas 1.1–8

Greetings and Introduction

I.1 Greeting (Barn. 1.1)

THE MOST COMMON FORMULA for opening an ancient Greek letter involved three components: sender in the nominative, addressee in the dative, and greeting.¹ These three things are found, for example, in Acts 23:26: "Claudius Lysias, to his Excellency, the Governor Felix, greetings."² Many early Christian letters attest to a willingness among their authors to follow this guide even while modifying it to suit their purposes. It was not unusual for early Christian authors to expand the epistolary inscription to include further descriptions of the sender, kinder words about the addressees, or more fulsome greetings.³ These greetings are given most often with an infinitive (χαίρειν) or a nominative phrase (e.g., χάρις καὶ εἰρήνη).

The Epistle of Barnabas opens somewhat differently. It starts with a greeting in the form of an imperative, does not mention the sender, and refers generally to the addressees in the vocative: "Greetings in peace, sons and daughters, in the name of the Lord who loved us" (χαίρετε, υἱοὶ καὶ θυγατέρες, ἐν ὀνόματι κυρίου τοῦ ἀγαπήσαντος ἡμᾶς ἐν εἰρήνῃ; Barn. 1.1). The difference in the form of the greeting along with other peculiarities in this letter have led some interpreters to question whether *Barnabas* is a genuine letter.⁴

---

1. Bauer, *Paulus und die kaiserzeitliche Epistolographie*, 45–46; Klauck, *Ancient Letters*, 17–18; Roller, *Formular*, 57–62; Trapp, *Greek and Latin Letters*, 34–35.

2. Κλαύδιος Λυσίας τῷ κρατίστῳ ἡγεμόνι Φήλικι χαίρειν (Acts 23:26).

3. E.g., Rom 1:1–7; 2 Cor 1:1; 1 Pet 1:1; 2 John 1; 1 Clem. 1.1; Ign. *Rom.* inscr.; Pol. *Phil.* inscr. See further Bauer, *Paulus und die kaiserzeitliche Epistolographie*, 79–83; Klauck, *Ancient Letters*, 20; Schnider and Stenger, *Studien*, 3–41; Tite, "How to Begin," 98; White, "Ancient Greek Letters," 98.

4. E.g., Barnard, "Epistle of Barnabas—A Paschal Homily?" 8–22; Vielhauer, *Geschichte*, 601–2; Wengst, *Didache*, 111–12; Wengst, *Tradition und Theologie*, 103–4;

However, comparison with other letters from the Roman period may shed some light on the admittedly unusual letter opening in Barn. 1.1.

Not all letters contain a reference to the sender.[5] P.Oxy. 7.1063 contains a letter from a parent to their son, whose name is Amois. The letter opens, "Greetings my son, Amois."[6] Because there is a parent-child relationship between the sender and addressee, it appears that the parent felt no need to identify themselves explicitly. The Epistle of Barnabas likewise indicates a metaphorical parent-child relationship between the sender and addressees by referring to the audience as "sons and daughters" (Barn. 1.1).[7] It was not always necessary to identify the sender by name. The intended reader in P.Fay. 129 is designated "most honored lord." While the letter does not mention the name of the addressee in the dative alongside the greetings, the papyrus contains instructions on the opposite side to "deliver to Serenus."[8] The address thus comes on the other side of the main letter, and the letter would presumably have been folded and sealed for delivery in a way that allowed these instructions to remain visible.[9]

Whereas the infinitive χαίρειν might be more common in a letter,[10] Barnabas's χαίρετε would be appropriate in direct speech such as one might use when greeting someone on the street.[11] Yet papyri letters illustrate that

---

Windisch, *Barnabasbrief*, 411–12.

5. This was pointed out early in the twentieth century by E. J. Goodspeed ("The Salutation," 162–65).

6. χαίροις, τέκνον Ἀμόι (P.Oxy. 7.1063). The *editio princeps* is found in Hunt, *Oxyrhynchus Papyri*, 7.217–18.

7. For further examples of the omission of the sender, see P. Rein 48 (second century; Reinach, *Papyrus grecs*, 149–50); P.Flor. 3.345 (third century; Vitelli, *Papiri Greco-Egizii*, 76); P.Fay. 129 (third century; Greenfell, Hunt, and Hogarth, *Fayum Towns*, 285–86). Like P.Fay. 129, both of these letters greet a master (κύριος), but the recipients' names are included in these texts. See further Hvalvik, *Struggle for Scripture and Covenant*, 72–73; Roller, *Formular*, 428–30 n 240.

8. Σερήνῳ ἐπί[δος]. The last three letters of the instructions are in brackets in Grenfell, Hunt, and Hogarth, *Fayum Towns*, 286. They have been replicated here.

9. Additional examples of this phenomenon can be found in P.Oxy. 7.1061 (first century BCE; Hunt, *Oxyrhynchus Papyri*, 7.214–15); P.Oxy. 6.929 (second or third century CE; Grenfell and Hunt, *Oxyrhynchus Papyri*, 6.294–95); P.Oxy. 6.931 (second-century CE; Grenfell and Hunt, *Oxyrhynchus Papyri*, 6.296–97). The verso of P.Oxy. 8.1157 contains both the recipient and the sender's names: "Give to Dionysia, from Pathermouthis" (ἀπόδος Διονυσίᾳ, παρὰ Παθερμούθιος; Hunt, *Oxyrhynchus Papyri*, 8.259–60). For further discussion, see Hvalvik, *Struggle for Scripture and Covenant*, 73–74.

10. E.g., 1 Esd 6.8; 8.9; 1 Macc 10.18, 25; 11.30, 32; 12.6, 20; 13.36; 14.20; 15.2, 16; 2 Macc 1.1, 10; 9.19; 11.16, 22, 27, 34; 3 Macc 3.12; 7.1; Acts 15:23; 23:26; Jas 1:1.

11. Roller, *Formular*, 449 n 267. See also Matt 26:49; 28:9; Luke 1:28; 2 John 10–11; Herm. Vis. 1.1.4 (1.4); 1.2.2 (2.2); 4.2.2 (23.2); Dio Cassius, *Hist.* 69.18.3.

χαίρω could be used to open letters in either the optative or imperative. P.Fay. 129 again provides a good example of this phenomenon. The first word in the letter is χαῖρε. The singular imperative is employed because the addressee is singular.[12] The plural imperative is found in Barn. 1.1, since *Barnabas* is directed to a community of believers. When this recognition is combined with the observation that the sender's name is not found in some letters and that the addressee could be referred to briefly in some letters, there is good reason to accept Goodspeed's claim that the Epistle of Barnabas, despite its epistolary oddities, "is genuinely and demonstrably epistolary."[13]

While χαίρω is commonly used as a greeting both in oral and epistolary settings, it is worth noting that the verb means to be glad or to rejoice.[14] The function of the word as a greeting takes clear priority in 1.1. However, the word contributes, at least aurally, to the expressions of joy in 1.2-3 (ὑπερευφραίνομαι; συγχαίρω). By doing this, Barnabas seeks to ingratiate himself with the audience, although this tactic does not exclude the possibility that the author feels real joy when reflecting on the audience. The greeting formula in 1.1 is completed by the adverbial phrase ἐν εἰρήνῃ. Although it may be possible to understand ἐν εἰρήνῃ with reference to the one who loved us (τοῦ ἀγαπήσαντος), it is better to interpret the prepositional phrase to modify χαίρετε because this resembles the Pauline greeting (e.g., 1 Thess 1:1) and because the author closes the letter by referring to the audience as children of love and peace (εἰρήνης; Barn. 21.9).[15] Both the greeting and the farewell are given with reference to peace.[16]

---

12. The same greeting is found in a fourth-century Christian letter where Peter is greeted as a beloved brother with a greeting that is shorter than but similar to Barn. 1.1: "Greetings in the Lord" (χαῖρε ἐν κ[υρί]ῳ; PSI 208). For the text of PSI 208, see Vitelli and Norsa, *Papiri greci e latini*, 3.69-70.

13. Goodspeed, "Salutation," 165. So also Hvalvik, *Struggle for Scripture and Covenant*, 75; Muilenburg, "Literary Relations," 48; Rhodes, "Two Ways Tradition," 804 n 18. See also the more cautious conclusions of Carleton Paget, *Epistle of Barnabas*, 44-45; Carleton Paget, "Epistle of Barnabas," 75-76.

14. E.g., Matt 18:13; Luke 6:23; John 3:29; Acts 5:41; Rom 12:12; Phil 4:4; 1 Pet 4:13; Rev 19:7; Herm. Vis. 3.3.2 (11.2); Clement of Alexandria, *Paed.* 3.1. See further BDAG, s.v; LSJ, s.v. I-II; PGL, s.v. 1.

15. On the similarities to the Pauline greeting formula in Barn. 1.1, see Hvalvik, *Struggle for Scripture and Covenant*, 75. When reflecting on the promise to restore Judah and Joseph (*Zach* 259), Didymus the Blind likewise refers to Barn. 1.1 alongside references to the audience as children in Paul's letters and in 1 Peter (1 Cor 4:15; Gal 4:19; 1 Pet 1:14). See further Berger, "Apostelbrief," 204; Carleton Paget, *Epistle of Barnabas*, 253; Prinzivalli and Simonetti, *Seguendo Gesù*, 2.506 n 1; Prostmeier, *Barnabasbrief*, 148-49.

16. Prostmeier adds an additional lens through which to consider the greeting when he writes, "The greeting χαίρετε in 1.1 is a medium ἐν εἰρήνῃ of messianic blessing and

The reference to the audience as "sons and daughters" further specifies the relationship that the author seeks to represent between himself and the audience. By calling the audience υἱοὶ καὶ θυγατέρες, Barnabas participates in the early Christian practice of employing family language with reference to other believers. There are both horizontal and vertical elements to the use of such language. If they are sons and daughters of the author, they are brothers and sisters of one another.[17] "Sons and daughters" thus strengthens horizontal social bonds in 1.1. Yet Barnabas also legitimates his position of authority as a father-figure to his sons and daughters. The close relationship between the author and addressees may provide a reason why the author does not include his name in the greeting, but the paternal relation simultaneously creates an authoritative role that the author seeks to fill.

The author characterizes the greeting to the brothers and sisters not only in terms of peace but also "in the name of the Lord who loved us" (ἐν ὀνόματι κυρίου τοῦ ἀγαπήσαντος ἡμᾶς; 1.1).[18] The word κύριος can be used to refer to both the Father and the Son, and the author gives no further specification about who is in view in 1.1.[19] Nevertheless, there are at least two reasons to incline toward identifying Jesus as the Lord in 1.1. First, 16.6–8 repeats a similar prepositional phrase with reference to Jesus, indicating that the construction of God's house takes place "in the name of the Lord" (ἐπὶ τῷ ὀνόματι κυρίου; 16.6) and that construction occurs after believers have "placed their hope in the name" (ἐλπίσαντες ἐπὶ τὸ ὄνομα; 16.8).[20] The emphasis on the name (ὄνομα) of Jesus (Joshua) in 12.8–9

---

messianic proclamation" (Der Gruß χαίρετε in 1,1 ist also vermittels ἐν εἰρήνῃ messianischer Segen und messianische Proklamation; *Barnabasbrief*, 145).

17. In this way, the term may function similarly to the use of other fraternal and sororal language that is used in early Christian literature as a way of talking about believers (e.g., Rom 7:1; 12:1; 1 Cor 1:10; 10:1; 2 Cor 8:1; Gal 4:28; 1 Thess 4:10; 2 Thess 3:13; Heb 3:12; Jas 3:1; 2 Pet 3:10; 1 John 3:13; 1 Clem. 4.7; 13.1; 2 Clem. 1.1; 13.1; Ign. Phld. 3.3; Herm. Vis. 3.1.4 [9.4]). See further Aasgaard, "Brothers and Sisters," 285–316; Harland, "Familial Dimensions," 491–513; Horrell, "From ἀδελφοί to οἶκος θεοῦ," 293–311; Horrell, *Making of Christian Morality*, 75–96; Punt, "He is Heavy," 153–71; Trebilco, *Self-Designations*, 16–67; Venter, "Implicit Obligations," 283–302.

18. While S and H both contain the first-person pronoun ἡμᾶς, L provides evidence for the second-person pronoun (*uos*; ὑμᾶς). S and H collectively provide the stronger manuscript evidence over against L. So also in Wengst, *Didache*, 138; Prostmeier and Lona, *Epistola Barnabae*, 72.

19. Indeed, Ménard (*Sancti Barnabae*, 1.81) appears to feel no need to discuss this identification but simply uses the term *Dominus* (Lord) and *Deus* (God) interchangeably at this point in his notes. On the ambiguity of κύριος in the Epistle of Barnabas, see Edwards, "Identifying the Lord," 51; Hvalvik, *Struggle for Scripture and Covenant*, 110; Rhodes, *Epistle of Barnabas*, 8 n 18.

20. This prepositional phrase can be used with reference to Jesus elsewhere in early

provides additional support for understanding the name of the Lord with reference to Jesus in 1.1.[21] Second, the Latin translation expands the Greek phrase "in the name of the Lord" (ἐν ὀνόματι κυρίου) and reads "in the name of our Lord Jesus Christ" (*in nomine domini nostri Iesu Christi*). Although the longer text is more likely to be a later expansion and should thus be rejected as the earliest reading for text-critical purposes, L shows how at least one early reader of Barn. 1.1 understood the word κύριος in 1.1.[22] For the translator, the Lord is a reference to Jesus Christ.[23]

The author thus establishes fictive kinship relations by greeting the audience warmly. Although there is an implicit power dynamic built into the familial language of 1.1,[24] the peaceful and joyous greeting suggests authority because it is given in a way that is reminiscent of other apostolic greetings. Authority is further established because Barnabas's greeting is given in the name of the Lord. This christological reference authorizes everything that follows in the letter with the stamp of the Lord's approval.

I.2 Commendation (Barn. 1.2-4)

As in many ancient letters, Barnabas seeks to endear himself to his readers following the greeting with a *captatio beneuolentiae* in 1.2-4. The purpose of this section is to create an ethos of trust and credibility between author and audience. The author admires the audience and rejoices over what has been given to them (1.2). He finds joy and hope for salvation because of the Spirit that has been poured over them. For this reason, he longs to see them (1.3). The author also speaks of his authority and locates its origins in the Lord who has walked with him. He thus finds himself compelled to love because of the faith and love that indwell them (1.4).

Barnabas opens by stating the reason for his joy. The genitive absolute that opens 1.2 describes God's requirements as great (μεγάλων) and rich

---

Christian literature. E.g., Acts 16:18; 1 Cor 5:4; Eph 5:20; Col 3:17; 2 Thess 3:6; 1 Pet 4:14. See similarly Edwards, "Identifying the Lord," 52.

21. Edwards, "Identifying the Lord," 52; Prinzivalli and Simonetti, *Seguendo Gesù*, 2.506n2.

22. It is difficult to explain how "Jesus Christ" would fall out of the textual tradition in S and H. However, Hilgenfeld (*Barnabae Epistula: Integram graece primum edidit*, 2) accepted L and incorporated this reading into the Greek text of his first edition (κυρίου ἡμῶν Ἰησοῦ χριστοῦ). He accepted the shorter reading (κυρίου) when he revised the text eleven years later (Hilgenfeld, *Barnabae Epistula: Integram graece iterum edidit*, 3).

23. Edwards, "Identifying the Lord," 52.

24. For more on the language that the author uses to address the audience and the sort of authority that the author claims, see Prostmeier, *Barnabasbrief*, 146-50.

(πλουσίων).²⁵ However, the word "requirements" (δικαιωμάτων) is the key word in this genitive absolute, and the author also employs the word in important ways throughout the letter. In 1.2, the origins of the requirements are found in God; the author refers to τῶν τοῦ θεοῦ δικαιωμάτων. These requirements provide a reason for Barnabas's joy because God's requirements are great and rich on behalf of the audience.

The author continues to express the reason for his joy at the end of 1.2. The object of the author's joy is his audience, which Barnabas describes by referring to their "blessed and glorious spirits" (ἐπὶ τοῖς μακαρίοις καὶ ἐνδόξοις ὑμῶν πνεύμασιν; 1.2). Placed just after the greeting, this effusive description contributes to the *captatio beneuolentiae* that runs throughout 1.2–4. The audience is linked with the Holy Spirit's activity through this term. The connection is emphasized in the following clause when Barnabas notes that the audience has received "the implanted grace of the spiritual gift" (ἔμφυτον τῆς δωρεᾶς πνευματικῆς χάριν; 1.2).²⁶ The gift that the audience has received comes from the Spirit and is thus properly described as spiritual. The origins of grace lie outside of the audience, but Barnabas's readers have received what the Spirit has given. By referring to the audience as "spirits" (πνεύματα), the author enhances the links between the audience and the Spirit.²⁷

The reason for Barnabas's joy receives further attention in 1.3. While the reasons for the author's joy are related to God's actions toward the audience (1.2), this does not preclude his own benefit from God's actions. The author rejoices while hoping to be saved (1.3). Although the grace that comes to the audience is given by the Spirit, one reason that the author hopes for salvation comes from experience with the readers. The author's hope comes "because I truly see in you the Spirit that has been poured out on you from the wealth of the Lord's spring" (1.3).²⁸ The Spirit is again the

25. I thus understand the genitive absolute (ὄντων . . . δικαιωμάτων) to be in a causal relationship to the main verb (ὑπερευφραίνομαι).

26. The author again refers to an implanted gift (ἡ ἔμφυτον δωρεά) in 9.9.

27. See further Prigent and Kraft, *Épître de Barnabé*, 33–34; Prinzivalli and Simonetti, *Seguendo Gesù*, 2.506n4.

28. The Greek text that has been followed in this translation is ὅτι ἀληθῶς βλέπω ἐν ὑμῖν ἐκκεχυμένον ἀπὸ τοῦ πλουσίου τῆς πηγῆς κυρίου πνεῦμα ἐφ' ὑμᾶς. Apart from some slight spelling differences, this text is found in Ehrman, *Apostolic Fathers*, 2.12; Holmes, *Apostolic Fathers*, 380; Prigent and Kraft, *Épître de Barnabé*, 72–74; Lindemann and Paulsen, *Apostolischen Väter*, 26; Prinzivalli and Simonetti, *Seguendo Gesù*, 2.112; Prostmeier and Lona, *Epistola Barnabae*, 72. The earliest text of 1.3 to which textual critics can return is not, however, easy to reconstruct with certainty. Two variants are worth observing in this phrase, and both relate to "the Lord's spring" (τῆς πηγῆς κυρίου). The first variant concerns the differences between L and the Greek manuscripts. Whereas S

one who comes to the audience in order to give richly. The Spirit has been poured out on to the audience and thus becomes available to them. Moreover, the Spirit is poured out of divine wealth (πλούσιος). As in the case of describing the audience as spirits, so also this divine wealth forms a connection with the audience, which was described in 1.2 as "rich" (πλούσιος). The wealth from which the Spirit is poured metaphorically flows from the Lord like a spring of water. It is not clear whether κύριος in 1.3 is a reference to the Father or the Son, but the Spirit's divine origins are emphasized in either case.[29] Yet the author's emphasis lies on his experience of this reality in the audience. The result of the experience of joy that the author has had with the audience is introduced with the word "thus" (οὕτω; 1.3),[30] and the consequence of all that the author has said so far leads him to feel overwhelmed by his desire to see his readers.[31]

Barnabas next turns to another important matter to establish early in a letter: the trustworthiness of the author (1.4). The author asserts that he can be trusted for two reasons. First, since the author knows the Lord travels with him and knows the audience well, one can expect that this letter comes from a source that speaks truly.[32] Second, Barnabas is trustworthy because he is compelled to love the audience. This relationship is

---

and H both read ἀπὸ τοῦ πλουσίου so that the Spirit is poured "from the wealth" of the Lord's spring, L reads *ab honesto fonte dei* (from the eminent spring of God). What is important in this variant is the change of case. L clearly indicates that *honesto* modifies *fonte* because both words are in the ablative case. Windisch (*Barnabasbrief*, 304) follows L or a modified version of L because he regards it as the simplest and most natural text. Yet since S and H agree in reading πλουσίου and since L may be understood as a clarification of a difficult Greek text, I have followed S and H at this point. A second variant that should be mentioned concerns whether the author speaks about the Lord's spring (τῆς πηγῆς κυρίου) or the Lord's love (τῆς ἀγάπης κυρίου). I have translated "the Lord's spring" following H and L. However, S reads "the Lord's love," and this text is followed by Cunningham, *Dissertation*, 4; Wengst, *Didache*, 138. The difference between these manuscripts can be explained best if πηγῆς is assumed to be the earlier reading. The word then made its way into the manuscript tradition due to the similarity in the endings (πης), the influence of the language of Rom 5:5, or some combination of the two. On the text of 1.3, see further Prostmeier, *Barnabasbrief*, 136–37; Windisch, *Barnabasbrief*, 304.

29. For further discussion of this issue, see Edwards, "Identifying the Lord," 52; Prinzivalli and Simonetti, *Seguendo Gesù*, 2.506n4.

30. Prostmeier (*Barnabasbrief*, 141) thus rightly notes that οὕτω(ς) is connected to the author's statement of joy in 1.3 rather than to the addressees' reception of the Spirit.

31. L omits this sentence. However, it is present with slight variations in S and H. I have here followed S along with Prostmeier and Lona, *Epistola Barnabae*, 72.

32. The word τοῦτο, translated this in the phrase "I have been convinced of this" (πεπεισμένος οὖν τοῦτο; 1.4), is best understood as pointing forward to the statements that follow in 1.4 rather than pointing backward to what has already been said in 1.2–3.

born out of the audience's experience with the faith, love, and hope of life that come from God.

A few additional matters should likewise be noted when examining 1.4. First, the author suggests that he is known in the community.[33] He claims that he has said many things (λαλήσας πολλά) to the audience, and his knowledge of the addressees is thus based in part on personal experience.[34] Second, 1.4 contains the first mention of the "way of righteousness" (ὅδος δικαιοσύνης). While the Two Ways Tradition in 18.1—20.2 shows remarkable similarities to other Two Ways Traditions in early Judaism and early Christianity and will be explored in further detail when looking at 18.1—20.2, this tradition is not slapped at the end of *Barnabas* in a hackneyed fashion. Rather, the reference both to a way and to righteousness will be repeated throughout the letter.[35] Although references to the ways of light and darkness come to a booming crescendo as *Barnabas* draws to a close, the pathways along which one can walk are a significant motif throughout the epistle.[36] Third, the author depicts himself as particularly devoted to the audience. He loves them more than his own soul (ὑπὲρ τὴν ψυχήν μου; 1.4). Barnabas speaks here in terms that are reminiscent of declarations made by other speakers. Nevertheless, his expressions can be understood as genuine and are consistent with what he writes elsewhere in the letter.[37] Finally, a key reason for the author's love comes "because great faith and love indwell you in the hope of his life" (μεγάλη πίστις καὶ ἀγάπη ἐγκατοικεῖ ἐν ὑμῖν ἐλπίδι ζωῆς αὐτοῦ). As has already been noted briefly, the author provides verbal links throughout 1.2-8, and faith, love, and the hope of life will be mentioned again in 1.6. Since the statement in 1.6 gives more information about this list, full comment may await that portion of the commentary. Yet it is worth noting now that faith and love come from outside the community and now indwell the community. Moreover,

---

33. Prostmeier, *Barnabasbrief*, 143.

34. While the author's speech and experience among the addressees provides a reason for the author's confidence in 1.4, the translation has left the syntactic relationship open in order to imitate the more open ways in which people with shared experiences can recall memories. If 1.4 is meant to recall a remembered experience—whether real or fictive—a more open-ended way of speaking seems appropriate. See further Prostmeier, *Barnabasbrief*, 143; Windisch, *Barnabasbrief*, 304.

35. On the variations in vocabulary by which the Epistle of Barnabas can allude to these pathways, see Hvalvik, *Struggle for Scripture and Covenant*, 63-65; Rhodes, "Two Ways Tradition," 803.

36. Hvalvik, *Struggle for Scripture and Covenant*, 63-65; Rhodes, "Two Ways Tradition," 797-816; Smith, "*Epistle of Barnabas*," 472-84.

37. The author similarly proclaims his love for the audience in 4.6. For further characterization of the author, see 1.8; 4.9; 6.5; 9.9.

the hope of life is not a hope for their own life but rather a hope that is somehow grounded in the Lord's life.[38]

I.3 Purpose of Writing (Barn. 1.5-8)

Barnabas begins to articulate the reason why this letter has been written in 1.5-8. He continues to cultivate a reliable authorial ethos by appealing to his desire to receive a reward for his service to them (1.5) and by insisting that he is not a teacher but instead "one of you" (εἷς ἐξ ὑμῶν; 1.8). He has thus written briefly to offer the audience knowledge to accompany their faith (1.5). Closely connected with this knowledge are three teachings of the Lord: the hope of life, righteousness, and the love of gladness and exultation (1.6). Barnabas reflects on what the Master has made known through the prophets and on how God's people should approach in response (1.7), and he hopes that his writing will result in the audience's joy (1.8). While 1.5, 8 continue to outline the author's reliability, this section also moves the rhetoric forward by outlining the purpose of the letter in terms of knowledge, teachings about hope, righteousness, and love, as well as revelation through the prophets.

The thrice-repeated use of logical connectors suggests that the author understands 1.5-8 to be tied together as a unit and closely linked to what precedes it.[39] The author does not always show the logical connections between the statements in 1.5-8 clearly but employs such conjunctions in ways that allow them to resonate next to one another. A key way by which the author allows these statements to resonate with one another is by reiterating certain lexemes across 1.5-8.[40] In these verses, the repetition of words with the γνω- root play an important role.[41] Barnabas says that he is writing to his audience so that they may have "perfect knowledge" (τελείαν τὴν γνῶσιν) with their faith (1.5). The purpose of the letter thus has to do in some way with increasing what the audience knows. God "made known" (ἐγνώρισεν) things that the audience should know about the past, present, and future (1.7). Both the author and God take part in revealing knowledge to readers of this letter.[42]

---

38. The antecedent of αὐτοῦ is κύριος.
39. The word οὖν is used in 1.5, 6, while γάρ appears in 1.7.
40. Rhodes, *Epistle of Barnabas*, 35-36.
41. Hvalvik, *Struggle for Scripture and Covenant*, 168.
42. In addition to vocabulary links, 1.5-8 are also held together by an interest in temporal connections. Each of the three teachings of the Lord are the beginning and the end of something (1.6). While the author has in view the start and culmination of

Before telling the audience the reason for his haste in writing, Barnabas links the description of the purpose back to the earlier discussion of the author's person. He tells the audience that he wrote when he reckoned that he would receive a reward for ministering to his readers.[43] Yet his decision to write is not a completely altruistic act of service. Instead, the author looks forward to the reward (μισθός) that he will receive. From a twenty-first-century Western perspective, the line between payment and rewards or gifts could sometimes be blurred in antiquity.[44] The author looks forward to receiving some divine recompense for caring about the audience enough to pass on a portion of what he received. Just as the author earlier referred to the Lord walking with him in the way (1.4), so also the reference to what the author has received in 1.5 suggests that the author has been divinely approved and is thus worth hearing.

After ensconcing the decision to write in a self-recommendation and praise of the audience, the author turns to the purpose of the letter. The purpose is given in language that is typical of ancient letters. The author has hurried "to send a short piece" (κατὰ μικρὸν ὑμῖν πέμπειν; 1.5).[45] While divergences may be found between an ideal and its practice, Barnabas locates his letter alongside ancient models of concise writing.[46] He then tells the audience the reason for which he writes: "so that you might have perfect knowledge with your faith" (1.5).[47] The author introduces this topic without

things in 1.6, 1.7 notes that God has made known the past and the present through the prophets. Yet the prophets also give a glimpse into things that will come. Even at the opening of the letter, the author's view of time is telic and oriented toward the end.

43. In addition to saying something about the author, 1.5 again refers to readers as "spirits" (πνεύμασιν). The noun "spirit" (πνεῦμα) and the adjective "spiritual" (πνευματικός) were already used in 1.2–3.

44. For more on gift-giving, rewards, and wages in early Christianity and the ancient world, see Barclay, *Paul and the Gift*, 11–65; Downs, *Alms*, 11–25.

45. Similar claims to write briefly occur in other early Christian letters (e.g., Heb 13:22; 1 Pet 5:12; Ign. *Rom.* 8.2), while Demetrius insists that the length of a letter must be as carefully regulated as its style (*Eloc.* 228). All quotations from Demetrius's *De elocutione* come from Roberts, *Demetrius On Style*.

46. Hvalvik, *Struggle for Scripture and Covenant*, 80.

47. The Greek text on which this translation is based is ἵνα μετὰ τῆς πίστεως ὑμῶν τελείαν ἔχητε τὴν γνῶσιν. I have followed S and H in this reading. L reads *ut fidem uestram consummatam habeatis et scientiam* (in order that you may have your faith and perfect knowledge). The word *et* (καί) is unattested in S or H, but Clement of Alexandria may have known this reading. He quotes Barn. 1.5 in *Strom.* 2.31.2 (6). The portion that is under consideration runs as follows in Clement's citation: ἵνα μετὰ τῆς πίστεως ὑμῶν τελείαν ἔχητε καὶ τὴν γνῶσιν (in order that you may also have perfect knowledge with your faith). If so, a text including the word καί circulated in Alexandria by the end of the second century. The longer text is followed by Prigent and Kraft, *Épître de Barnabé*, 76. Despite its early attestation, the longer reading likely strengthens the sense

precisely defining the contents of knowledge. At least three things that can be said about knowledge based on 1.5. First, knowledge provides a fundamental ground for which the author desires to write this letter. Second, knowledge is intimately connected with faith. Knowledge does not oppose faith.[48] Third, knowledge can be perfected. In other words, knowledge is designed to grow telically until it reaches its fullest extent.

After introducing the perfection of the audience's knowledge as the epistolary goal, the author immediately introduces three doctrines that come from the Lord. These doctrines (δόγματα) modify what the author means by knowledge and refer to teachings or precepts that govern how believers should conduct their lives.[49] Knowledge in *Barnabas* is not primarily esoteric but will have an impact on how the audience acts and believes. Moreover, these teachings come from the Lord.[50]

---

of the shorter reading and is thus likely to be secondary. The shorter reading is preferred by Ehrman, *Apostolic Fathers*, 2.14; Holmes, *Apostolic Fathers*, 380; Lindemann and Paulsen, *Apostolischen Väter*, 26; Prinzivalli and Simonetti, *Seguendo Gesù*, 2.112; Prostmeier and Lona, *Epistola Barnabae*, 72; Wengst, *Didache*, 138.

48. The close connection between knowledge and faith make it difficult to define γνῶσις in the Epistle of Barnabas in "proto-gnostic" terms. As 1.6–7 will clarify, knowledge is something that is given from God and something that has been revealed. Thus, "knowledge does not have an abstract epistemological valence in *Barnabas*, but it is at the same time understanding of the revelation given by God mediated through scripture and a life lived in conformity with God's will, that is with his δικαιώματα" ("la conoscenza non ha in Barn un'astratta valenza epistemologica, ma è insieme comprensione della rivelazione data da Dio mediante la Scrittura, e vita vissuta in conformità ai voleri di Dio, cioè ai suoi δικαιώματα;" Prinzivalli and Simonetti, *Seguendo Gesù*, 2.58).

49. It is not easy to translate δόγματα precisely in 1.6. Ehrman (*Apostolic Fathers*, 2.15) translates the word as "firm teachings," while Holmes (*Apostolic Fathers*, 381) and Kraft (*Barnabas*, 82) refer to "basic doctrines." Wake (*Genuine Epistles*, 262; italics and capitalization original) offers a more paraphrastic translation, "Three Sorts of things to be considered *in what relates* to the LORD," along with a more wooden translation in the margins, "constitutions of the Lord." Non-English translations include "Grundsätze," (Prostmeier and Lona, *Epistola Barnabae*, 73; Wengst, *Didache*, 141), "Satzungen" (Lindemann and Paulsen, *Apostolischen Väter*, 27; Windisch, *Barnabasbrief*, 305), "enseignements" (Prigent and Kraft, *Épître de Barnabé*, 77), and "insegnamenti" (Prinzivalli and Simonetti, *Seguendo Gesù*, 2.113–15), These translations offer a sense of the ways in which one may interpret the word. In 1.6, δόγματα are teachings and precepts that find their source in the Lord and that impact the audience's disposition as well as the way in which the audience should behave in certain circumstances. As is evident from their position in the midst of the author's discussion of the purpose of the letter, these three teachings should be foundational characteristics of believers. The word is likewise used with regard to how readers should act or think in certain circumstances in 3 Macc 1.3; 4 Macc 10.2; Philo, *Opif.* 172; *Spec.* 4.107; Did. 11.3; Diogn. 5.3; Ign. *Magn.* 13.1. For further definition of δόγμα, see Cunningham, *Dissertation*, 8; LSJ, s.v. 1; PGL, s.v. D.2.

50. Since the author will refer to "the Master" (ὁ δεσπότης) in 1.7 and there likely speaks of God, κύριος may likewise be understood with reference to God in 1.6

The three teachings that the Lord gives are the hope of life,[51] righteousness, and love of gladness and exultation.[52] Each of these dogmas are connected with the beginning and end of another virtuous disposition—the hope of life with faith; righteousness with judgement; love of gladness and exultation with a witness to works of righteousness.[53] The beginning and end are used as a merism to connect the first two teachings to their closely associated attitudes and actions.[54] By speaking in this way, the author creates a divinely sanctioned web of doctrine that defines and develops the knowledge that the author has mentioned in 1.5. The hope of life provides the beginning and end of "our faith" (πίστεως ἡμῶν; 1.6); hope for life is thus intimately affiliated with faithfulness.[55] Likewise, righteousness is the beginning and end of judgement so that just actions are closely linked to correct scrutiny of one's conduct. Finally, the love of gladness and exultation serve as a witness and bear testimony for works that are conducted in righteousness.[56]

(Edwards, "Identifying the Lord," 52–53). The only other reference to ὁ δεσπότης in *Barnabas* is found in a reference to 1 Enoch in Barn. 4.3. God is most likely in view in both 1.7 and 4.3.

51. It is possible that ζωῆς modifies κυρίου, which comes before, rather than ἐλπίς, which comes after. However, since ζωῆς was already used to modify ἐλπίς in 1.4, it is better to understand ζωῆς ἐλπίς to be the first member of the triad in 1.6.

52. Virtue lists can be found elsewhere in early Jewish and early Christian literature: e.g., Prov 1:7 (LXX); 2 Bar. 57.2; 1 Cor 13:13; Gal 5:22–23; Ign. *Eph.* 14.1; Pol. *Phil.* 3.3; Justin, *Dial.* 110.3; Acts John 109. All citations of the Acts of John can be found in Junod and Kaestli, *Acta Johannis*.

53. Although more linear in orientation, the progressive lists of virtues in Jas 1:2–5; 2 Pet 1:5–7; Herm. *Vis.* 3.8.2–8 (16.2–8); *Sim.* 9.15.2 (92.2) function similarly by creating close links between the dispositions that believers are called to embody. For further discussion, see Dibelius, *Hirt*, 623.

54. Ignatius likewise speaks about the beginning and end (ἀρχὴ καὶ τέλος) with regard to ethical activity (Ign. *Eph.* 14.1; *Magn.* 13.1). He refers to faith and love as "everything" (τὸ ὅλον; Ign. *Smyrn.* 6.1). See further Schoedel, *Ignatius*, 24–26; Zañartu, "Concepts," 329–30. An additional point of comparison between knowledge in Barn. 1.5 and the list in 1.6 can be found when Clement of Alexandria links knowledge to faith and love as the beginning and end (*Strom.* 7.55.6 [10]). Citations from Clement of Alexandria *Strom.* 7 can be found in Stählin, *Stromata Buch VII und VIII*.

55. Prostmeier (*Barnabasbrief*, 157) notes that hope in 1.6 should be understood with reference to the resurrection. Hope for the resurrection is then "not only the indispensable kernel of Christian faith; it is the life principle of Christians" ("nicht nur der unverzichtbare Kern des christlichen Glaubens; sie ist das Lebensprinzip der Christen").

56. The continuation of lexemes that can be placed in the domain of joy continue a theme mentioned with regard to the audience in 1.2–3 but develop the earlier brief references by understanding gladness and exultation as part of the Lord's pedagogical curriculum, connecting joy to love, and forming a relationship between joy and

Although some have considered this verse to be a secondary addition,[57] 1.6 plays an important, if parenthetical, role in the flow of thought in 1.2–8.[58] The shared vocabulary between 1.4 and 6 link the author's self-commendation with the purpose of the author's writing. The author writes because of the audience's association with faith, love, and the hope of life (1.4), while the knowledge that Barnabas wants to share includes three teachings from the Lord that are comprised of or connected to faith, love, and the hope of life (1.6). This verse thus defines the content of the knowledge that was introduced in 1.5 and that the author aims to share in this epistle. It also connects this knowledge to God by highlighting that these three teachings that are associated with knowledge ultimately find their origin in God. Rather than considering 1.6 to be secondary, it may be better to view this sentence as both epexegetical, with reference to 1.5, and preparatory, with reference to 1.7.[59]

The author next turns to God's revelation in 1.7 in ways that recall what he has already said about himself in 1.4–5. The author specifies a key way in which knowledge is revealed: the Master (ὁ δεσπότης) made things known through the prophets (διὰ τῶν προφητῶν). What the Master has made known (ἐγνώρισεν; 1.7) provides the basis upon which the author hopes that the audience will have knowledge (γνῶσις; 1.5). The author highlights three things that the Master has revealed: the past, present, and future.[60] As will become increasingly clear throughout the Epistle of Barnabas, the prophets are frequently appealed to as sources of divine revelation for all that has happened. Barnabas trusts that the Master is the ultimate source of prophetic revelation. Words that come from prophetic scriptures are thus to be understood as part of the Master's self-revelation. Barnabas also implies that he has properly interpreted the Master's revelation.

---

righteous works. On joy in early Christian literature with particular reference to Luke-Acts, see Harnack, *Acts*, 277–81.

57. Windisch (*Barnabasbrief*, 305) entertains the possibility that 1.6 is secondary but leaves open the possibility that it is original. Hvalvik (*Struggle for Scripture and Covenant*, 169–70) argues for the originality of 1.6.

58. Kraft (*Barnabas*, 82) emphasizes the parenthetical function of 1.6 within 1.5–8.

59. On the rhetorical function of 1.6, see further Prostmeier, *Barnabasbrief*, 144.

60. The translation made for this volume is based on the following Greek text in 1.7: τὰ παρεληλυθότα καὶ τὰ ἐνεστῶτα καὶ τῶν μελλόντων δοὺς ἀπαρχὰς ἡμῖν γεύσεως. This text follows L and the marginal note in S made by a later corrector. It is also the text used in Ehrman, *Apostolic Fathers*, 2.14; Holmes, *Apostolic Fathers*, 382; Prigent and Kraft, *Épître de Barnabé*, 78; Lindemann and Paulsen, *Apostolischen Väter*, 28; Prinzivalli and Simonetti, *Gesù*, 2.114; Prostmeier and Lona, *Epistola Barnabae*, 74. However, S and H omit the second καί. This text is followed by Wengst, *Didache*, 140.

The section is drawn to a close with a final statement in which Barnabas depicts himself as a reliable author (1.8). Having explained his purpose for writing, he again writes in the first person. His sentence can be discussed in three parts. First, he tells his readers that he will point out a few things to them. As in 1.5, the author includes language that underlines the brevity of the letter and that was typical in epistolary rhetoric. Second, he claims that he is writing not as a teacher but as a fellow-member of the audience. Barnabas's rhetorical approach emphasizes his solidarity with the audience, even if his authoritative position cannot be ignored. Finally, what the author will write will provide a means by which the audience should rejoice. Although the language is often stereotypical, 1.8 brings the opening of the letter to a fitting close by ending with a verb that is in the semantic domain of joy (εὐφραίνω), just as the typical greeting formula in 1.1 likewise used a verb from the same semantic domain (χαίρω).

II

Barnabas 2.1—16.10

Revealing Knowledge in Scripture:
First Body Section

AFTER PRAISING THE READERS, introducing himself, and outlining the purpose of the letter, Barnabas turns to an extended series of reflections on the way in which God has revealed knowledge about himself and his requirements (δικαιώματα) in scripture. This is a wide-ranging section that discusses the significance of covenant, cultic practices, identity markers, and interpretation of scripture. The themes in this section are united not so much by relations between the topics that are explored as by the exegetical means by which they are examined. Yet while hermeneutical concerns and interpretive explications reign supreme in this section, Barnabas is also consistently interested in the way in which believers act, how they understand their identity as the people of God, and what is happening during the times and seasons in which he and his audience are living. While the section is largely unified around God's revelation in scripture, the number of topics that are studied and the various hermeneutical methods that are employed create significant diversity throughout 2.1—16.10.

II.1. Introduction: Alert and Seeking the Lord's Requirements in Evil Days (Barn. 2.1–3)

Before starting a head-on topical exegesis, however, the author transitions from the introductory epistolary matters of 1.1–8 by combining two significant motifs in 2.1–3: an apocalyptic outlook and corresponding ethical concerns. The sentence opens with two genitive absolutes that highlight the evilness of the times and a mysterious figure who is working with authority. These two clauses are not expounded at any length. Instead, they are asserted as facts to which the author expects assent. Barnabas points to circumstances and realities that exist outside of believers themselves and calls attention to their influence. The evilness of the current times is a common theme in apocalyptic literature and in texts from other genres that are nevertheless influenced by apocalyptic themes.[1] The supreme evil figure is mentioned elsewhere in the letter and is further identified as Satan (18.1) or the Black One (4.9; 20.1).[2] Yet Barnabas does not outline these realities in any detail here. The primary reason for mentioning these realities to his audience is instead to connect believers' behavior to the wicked state of the world in which they live. Thus, the main clause in 2.1 calls readers' attention to how they should respond in light of who has authority in the present. Believers should seek the Lord's requirements.

Living rightly in response to evil times, in expectation of judgement, or in hope of God's final eschatological activity is a motif found in much Christian literature during the first two centuries. The author of 1 Peter reminds his audience that they will give account to the one who judges the living and the dead (1 Pet 4:5). Since the end of all things is near, they should be sober-minded in their prayers, love one another, and demonstrate hospitality (1 Pet 4:7–9). In Ephesians, believers are reminded that they once followed the ruler of this world (Eph 2:2), that they were then in darkness (Eph 5:8), and that the days are now evil (Eph 5:16). However, they have been raised with Christ and seated in the heavenly places (Eph 2:5–6), should live as children of the light (Eph 5:8–9), and should understand what the Lord's will is (Eph 2:17).[3] A change in behavior occurs in the midst of the evil that surrounds believers, is motivated by future judgement, and results from the change that occurs within them. Similarly, Barnabas urges his audience to be alert and seek the requirements of the Lord.

---

1. E.g., Acts 26:17–18; Gal 1:4; Eph 2:2; Mart. Ascen. Isa. 2.4; 4.2.; Ps.-Clem. *Hom.* 15.7.4. For further discussion and examples, see Prinzivalli and Simonetti, *Seguendo Gesù*, 2.508n14. All citations of the Martyrdom and Ascension of Isaiah come from Giambelluca Kossava et al., *Ascensio Isaiae*. All citations from the Pseudo-Clementine *Homilies* come from Rehm and Strecker, *Pseudoklementinen I*.

2. Satan is similarly said to have some authority in the present age in Mark 16:14 (W; the so-called Freer Logion); Luke 4:6; 12:5; John 14:30; Acts 26:18; Eph 2:2; 6:11; 2 Thess 2:7; Rev 13:2; Mart. Ascen. Isa. 4.1–3; Ign. *Eph.* 17.1; *Magn.* 1.2; *Rom.* 7.1; *Phld.* 6.2; Mart. Pol. 2.4–3.1; Herm. Mand. 4.3.4, 6 (31.4, 6); 12.5.1–12.6.5 (49.1–50.5). On Satan's authority in Barn. 2.1, see Burke, "Satan and Demons," 157; Farrar, "Intimate and Ultimate Adversary," 539; Kraft, *Barnabas*, 83; Prigent and Kraft, *Épître de Barnabé*, 79 n 7; Prinzivalli and Simonetti, *Seguendo Gesù*, 2.508 n 13; Prostmeier, *Barnabasbrief*, 163–64.

3. Timothy Gombis (*Drama*, 19–21) offers a concise account of the importance of viewing Ephesians in apocalyptic terms. On the spatial implications of soteriological language in Ephesians, see Hoselton, "'You Have Been Raised,'" 32–37.

Believers are not left alone in their quest to keep the Lord's requirements. Just as grace was implanted within them in conjunction with the requirements of 1.2, so also there is assistance for believers as they seek to keep the requirements in 2.1. Fear and endurance are designated aides (βοηθοί) of the faith that Barnabas and his readers represent, while patience and self-control serve as allies (συμμαχοῦντα; 2.2). These virtues are personified so that they appear to have an agency of their own that assists believers in seeking the Lord's requirements during such evil days. Right ethical dispositions aid believers as they seek the knowledge of God. When these virtues remain "in purity with regard to the Lord" (τὰ πρὸς κύριον ἁγνῶς), wisdom, understanding, intelligence, and knowledge join together in joy (2.3).[4] Right actions are associated with proper knowledge. Ethics and epistemology are thus connected in 2.2–3 as believers seek what the Lord requires in these evil times. Despite Barnabas's thoroughgoing interest in scriptural interpretation, knowledge (γνῶσις) and other terminology related to understanding cannot be limited to something that can be learned from study. Right behavior should result from the revelation and knowledge that are highlighted throughout 2.1–16.10.[5] These three verses introduce this section not simply by providing a bridge from the epistolary introduction of 1.1–8 but also by stressing both the eschatological realities in which Barnabas and his readers live as well as the ethical dispositions that assist them in living within those realities.[6]

II.2. The Lord's Requirements (Barn. 2.4–3.6)

The author turns next to demonstrate how God has revealed what is required through the prophets. The argument begins with a declaration that God revealed what is necessary about sacrifices, a citation from the prophets illustrating that God does not need burnt offerings, and a provisional conclusion showing that God destroyed physical sacrifices in favor of the new law

---

4. Barnabas's reference to the rejoicing (συνευφραίνονται; 2.3) of epistemic qualities is particularly appropriate because it joins the repetition of words in the semantic domain of joy in 1.1–8.

5. Wengst (*Didache* 141n20) makes a similar point when he says that the theoretical virtues only become effective when the practical virtues are maintained in service to the Lord. While the distinction between practical and theoretical virtues may not be the most helpful language with which to describe virtues in *Barnabas*, Wengst is correct insofar as knowledge is conceived of holistically in ways that affect one's behavior.

6. Prostmeier (*Barnabasbrief*, 164) rightly observes that when believers live as called in 2.1–3, they bear witness to the reality of what the author said about them in 1.1–8.

(2.4-6).⁷ The author employs the prophets to show that sacrifices were not even required by God in the exodus (2.7-8). Readers should notice instead that the Father defines sacrifice as a broken heart that glorifies its creator (2.9-10). Fasting is closely connected to the matter of sacrifice, and a similar argumentative structure carries into 3.1-6. The author cites a prophetic scripture about fasting in which God speaks "to them" (3.1-2) while elsewhere the prophets speak "to us" (3.3-5). God does not define fasting in terms of an abstention from food but rather as just actions. God has revealed these things beforehand so that readers can follow the law properly.⁸

II.2.a. Sacrifices (Barn. 2.4-10)

The author begins this section by claiming that what is necessary to offer God has been revealed "to us" (ἡμῖν) through the prophets (2.4).⁹ The use of the conjunction γάρ in 2.4 indicates that what follows is closely connected to what has come before. In addition, the reference to revelation through the prophets recalls the Master making the past, present, and future known "to us" (ἡμῖν) through the prophets (1.7).¹⁰ The combination of the divine revelatory act, the first-person plural recipients, and the prophetic mediators link the discussion of sacrifice closely to the epistolary purpose statement.¹¹ The author employs three words for sacrifices in 2.4: sacrifices (θυσίαι), whole burnt offerings (ὁλοκαυτώματα), and general offerings (προσφόρα). These three words are employed collectively to strengthen the sense of comprehensiveness in the following argument. The words also provide associative hinges by which the author can link scriptural quotations together. The first quotation of scripture comes from Isa 1:11-13 (2.5). The prophet records the words of the Lord as the Lord asserts that he is full of the people's burnt offerings (ὁλοκαυτώματα), incense, and new moon festivals. God has no need of the people's sacrifices of bulls or goats and thereby denies the efficacy of objects offered on the altar. Barnabas draws a preliminary conclusion based

---

7. There is a marginal note in H next to Barnabas's citation of Isa 1:11-13 (Barn. 2.5) that marks the citation as coming from Isaiah and includes the topical heading "That the Master of Isaiah requires nothing" (ὅτι οὐδενὸς χρῄζει ὁ δεσπότης Ἡσαίου).

8. For a slightly different outline, see Prostmeier, *Barnabasbrief*, 170-71.

9. On God's lack of need for sacrifices, see also 2 Macc 14.35; 3 Macc 2.9; Acts 17:25; 1 Clem. 52.1; Justin, *1 Apol.* 13.1; *Dial.* 23.2; Tatian, *Or. Graec.* 4.5. For additional references, see Windisch, *Barnabasbrief*, 310-11. Citations of Tatian's *Oratio ad Graecos* come from Nesselrath, *Gegen falsche Götter*.

10. Prostmeier, *Barnabasbrief*, 172.

11. Hvalvik, *Struggle for Scripture and Covenant*, 171; Rhodes, *Epistle of Barnabas*, 38-40.

on this citation in 2.6. God abolished these sacrifices so that the new law that is associated with Jesus Christ could have an offering.

The author extends this provisional conclusion in 2.7–8 in order to clear the path for a proper definition of sacrifice.[12] The author seeks to extend this argument through another citation from a prophet. This time Barnabas employs words that are similar to Jer 7:22–23; Zech 7:9–10; and 8:17. God again speaks through these words and denies that burnt offerings (ὁλοκαυτώματα) and sacrifices (θυσίαι) were part of the commandment when the people came out of Egypt. Instead, God's command focused on care for the neighbor: "Let none of you remember an evil deed in their heart against a neighbor, and do not love a false oath" (2.8). For Barnabas, sacrifice and burnt offering were not part of what God commanded when God led the people out of Egypt. The instruction was rather to live rightly and truly with one's neighbors. The scriptural arguments in 2.4–8 illustrate the way in which scripture and sacrifice have been misunderstood according to the author.[13] God does not need sacrifice (2.5). God never asked for burnt offerings after the exodus (2.7). Such offerings have been abolished to make way for the new law of Jesus Christ (2.6), and readers should recognize that God demanded a certain disposition toward the neighbor instead of sacrifice (2.8).[14]

The author next urges readers to know the Father's purpose (γνώμη) regarding what the audience should seek to bring as an offering (2.9).[15] As in earlier sections of the argument, Barnabas again appeals to scriptural language in order to define sacrifice rightly. Sacrifice should be understood in terms of a broken heart (2.10). Utilizing language that is similar to Ps 50:19 (51:17 MT), Barnabas refers to a broken heart as a sacrifice to God, while a heart that glorifies its maker is an aroma that pleases the Lord. On the basis of this understanding of sacrifice, Barnabas urges the audience to seek carefully what can be known about salvation. In light of the argument in 2.4–10, this search will involve knowledge and correct interpretation of scripture. Since

---

12. For another concise account of the shape of Barnabas's argument in 2.4–10, see Downs, *Alms*, 92–94.

13. Albl, "*Testimonia* Hypothesis," 192.

14. On the use of legal terminology for the purpose of self-definition in early Christianity, see Kühneweg, "Neue Gesetz," 129–36.

15. It is noteworthy that another word with a γνώ- stem is employed at this point in the argument. The word γνώμη refers here to the Father's purpose, that is, the intention toward which his mind was set in giving the commandments. For further remarks on γνώμη and examples from early Christian literature, see BDAG, s.v.; PGL, s.v.

the evil one is active in deceit (2.10),[16] readers must rightly know what God says in order to avoid being taken down the wrong path.[17]

The focus on scriptural argumentation, similarities to other early Christian texts, and possible tensions in the theology of 2.4–10 with other portions of the letter have led some to argue that he is borrowing from a source.[18] The way in which the author employs scripture can be usefully compared not only to other early Christian citations of similar phrases but also to the multiple tradents through which Greek Jewish scriptures were transmitted.[19] The citation of Isa 1:11–13 shows minimal changes from the critical edition of the Old Greek text of Isaiah.[20] There is a change in spelling, a change in word order, and an Isaianic reference to the "great day" that is not found in the letter.[21] The quotation in Barn. 2.7–8 may be best accounted for as a composite citation that brings together Jer 7:22–23 and language from Zech 7:9–10; 8:17.[22] Finally, the quotation in Barn. 2.10 recalls Ps 51:17 (50:19) but continues with terminology that is not found in the psalm in any known format.[23] The presence of similar strings of citations that include precisely

---

16. Similar language about the evil one was already employed in 2.1.

17. Prigent and Kraft, *Épître de Barnabé*, 89n1.

18. Kraft ("The Epistle of Barnabas," 115–16) raises the possibility that the quotations in Barn. 2–3 stem from a collection of first-century Hellenistic Jewish teachings. See also Carleton Paget, *Epistle of Barnabas*, 102–8; Prigent and Kraft, *Épître de Barnabé*, 83 n 1; Wengst, *Tradition und Theologie*, 18–20.

19. Other early Christian texts that cite Isa 1:11–13, for example, include Justin, *1 Apol.* 37.5–8; Irenaeus, *Haer.* 4.17.1; Clement of Alexandria, *Paed.* 3.90.3 (12); 5 Ezra 1.31. For additional references to early Christian literature, see Windisch, *Barnabasbrief*, 311. References to Irenaeus's *Adversus Haereses* come from Rousseau et al., *Irénée de Lyon*. Citations of 5 Ezra are found in Bergren, *Fifth Ezra*.

20. For the critical text of Old Greek Isaiah, see Ziegler, *Isaias*.

21. E.g., spelling change: νουμηνίας (Isa 1:13) / νεομηνίας (Barn. 2.5) ; word order: πατεῖν τὴν αὐλήν μου (Isa 1:12) / πατεῖν μου τὴν αὐλήν (Barn. 2.5). The reference to the "great day" (καὶ ἡμέραν μεγάλην) in Isa 1:13 is lacking in Barn. 2.5.

22. I use the definition of a composite citation put forward by Adams and Ehorn ("What Is a Composite Citation," 3–4). A composite citation (1) fuses together two or more texts, (2) does not include conjunctions that break the two texts, and (3) does not refer to a plurality of sources before or after the citation. For the critical text of Old Greek Jeremiah, see Ziegler, *Ieremias*. For the critical text of Old Greek Zechariah, see Ziegler, *Duodecim*. A marginal note in H identifies the quotation as coming from Jeremiah.

23. A marginal note in H (folio 39v) indicates that "a sweet fragrance before the Lord is a heart that glorifies the one who has formed it" (ὀσμὴ εὐωδίας τῷ κυρίῳ καρδία δοξάζουσα τὸν πεπλακότα αὐτήν) comes from the Apocalypse of Adam. The note beside the citation of Ps 51:17 (50:19) in H reads, "Psalm 50 and in the Apocalypse of Adam" (ψαλμ[ὸς] Ν' καὶ ἐν ἀποκαλύψει Ἀδάμ). On marginal notes in H, see Prostmeier, *Barnabasbrief*, 17n35, 179n31; Wengst, *Didache*, 143. However, this citation is

these passages strongly suggests that the author is engaged with traditions whose origins can no longer be traced with certainty.[24]

In addition to incorporating passages from scripture in forms that suggest that the author is participating in an interpretive tradition, Barnabas has employed the citations in 2.4–10 within a letter written for a particular purpose.[25] It is thus important to consider not just where these texts might have come from but how they are collectively used to advance the author's argument. The author's scriptural references work together to juxtapose two descriptions of sacrifice. One definition is faulty while another is accurate and finds its origins in God. Sacrifices involving altars, animals, and holocausts do not constitute genuine offerings, according to the author's interpretation of scripture. Rather, the critiques of the prophets point to a true definition of sacrifice that involves believers' broken hearts. When one observes that this way of understanding sacrifice is taken from scripture and that these passages were used in analogous arguments in early Jewish reflections on sacrifice, it is tempting to say that 2.4–10 is not anti-Jewish but anti-cultic.[26] If the letter is viewed as a general treatise written in conjunction with a school environment, this option becomes more plausible.[27] However, if the letter stems from a situation of genuine opposition and if, as seems likely, 16.3–5 point to a date around the time of the Second Jewish War (132–135 CE), it becomes increasingly difficult to view Barnabas's comments as anti-cultic in a way that is abstracted from Judaism.[28] A specific opponent is in view, and this opponent is characterized in terms that are anti-Jewish because they represent physical Israel.[29] Israel has misunderstood what the Lord requires in scripture, and the author is worried that at least some in or around the audience will desire to participate in animal sacrifices. Barnabas, in contrast, understands sacrifice as a broken heart and

---

not known from any extant manuscripts of the Apocalypse of Adam. Hatch (*Essays*, 181) lists the citation of Ps 51:17 (50:19) in 2.10 as an example of Psalm quotations that adopted Greek phraseology but were never included in the Greek Psalter. For the critical text of the Old Greek Psalms, see Rahlfs, *Psalmi*.

24. For example, these passages occur together, albeit in a different order, in Clement, *Paed.* 3.90.3–91.4 (12).

25. Carleton Paget, *Epistle of Barnabas*, 102–8.

26. Kraft, *Barnabas*, 84; Prigent and Kraft, *Épître de Barnabé*, 83n1.

27. On the effect of schools as social and theological institutions within early Christianity, see Markschies, *Christian Theology*, 31–91.

28. For a concise analysis about the purpose of *Barnabas*, see Hvalvik, "Epistle of Barnabas," 284–85.

29. This is true whether one conceives of the opponents as non-Jesus-following Jews, Jewish Christians, or gentile Christians who are attracted to traditionally Jewish practices.

urges the audience to reflect carefully on God's mind and salvation as they can be known in scripture (2.9-10).

A final interpretive point that will be important as the letter continues concerns how one understands καταργέω (I make ineffective) and the law in 2.6. Although the word can refer to the abrogation or nullification of something,[30] such a meaning is not typically how the author speaks most often about Torah. In 2.4-10, the author does not allow even a limited sense in which animal sacrifice may have been considered a correct interpretation of the law. On the author's view, Israel's own scriptures invalidate such an understanding. In 2.6, then, καταργέω (I make ineffective) is better understood in terms of destruction of something that was never legitimate.[31] Although sacrifice may have been an option, it has now been abolished. Writing in a post-70 context, Barnabas makes the most of the temple's destruction and alludes to the simultaneous elimination of sacrificial practice.[32] Yet the end of sacrifice is not in itself the point to which the author draws readers' attention. The purpose of God's rejection through the prophets' words is to clarify the type of offering that is prescribed under the new law of Jesus Christ.[33] The law is properly defined in conjunction with Jesus Christ, while the lack of compulsion (ἀνάγκη) indicates that

---

30. In early Christian literature, this meaning may be best illustrated from the Pauline corpus: Rom 3:3, 31; 4:14; 1 Cor 1:28; Gal 3:17; Eph 2:15. Windisch (*Barnabasbrief*, 311) notes that the use of this verb in Barn. 2.6 suggests that sacrificial offerings at one time had legitimacy.

31. This understanding of καταργέω is enhanced when one notices how the word is employed in 9.4 and 16.2. Circumcision of the flesh was destroyed (κατήργηται). Since the author attributes Jewish practice to deception by an evil angel, it is difficult to interpret the verb here in terms of a nullification of a previously accepted practice. The author's opponents were similarly deceived about the temple (16.1). Readers are thus encouraged to hear what the Lord said when he destroyed (καταργῶν) the temple (16.2). In light of the deception that the author finds among the opponents, it is again difficult to interpret καταργέω in terms of abrogation or cancellation of something that was accepted at an earlier salvation-historical stage. The word is used in the same way, though not with regard to Torah practices, in Barn. 5.6. See also Ezra 4:21; 5:5; 6:8.

32. Carleton Paget, *Epistle of Barnabas*, 105-7; Hvalvik, *Struggle for Scripture and Covenant*, 123-24; Prigent and Kraft, *Épître de Barnabé*, 84 n 1; Prinzivalli and Simonetti, *Seguendo Gesù*, 2.510 n 18; Prostmeier, *Barnabasbrief*, 174-75; Rhodes, *Epistle of Barnabas*, 40-41.

33. Similar phrases are also used in 1 Cor 9:21; Gal 6:2; Ign. *Magn.* 2, while the law is defined in terms of the Son in second-century texts including Herm. *Sim.* 8.3.2 (69.2); Ker. Petr. 1a (in Clement of Alexandria, *Strom.* 1.182.3 [29]); 1b (in Clement of Alexandria, *Strom.* 2.68.2 [15]); Justin, *Dial.* 11.2; 43.1; Clement of Alexandria, *Strom.* 7.16.5 (3). All quotations from Justin's *Dialogue with Trypho* come from Marcovich, *Iustini*. See further Brox, *Hirt des Hermas*, 361; Cho, "ὁ νόμος τοῦ Χριστοῦ," 263-94; Dobschütz, *Kerygma Petri*, 28-29; Hvalvik, "Christ Proclaiming His Law," 418-24; Klevinghaus, *Theologische Stellung*, 23-24.

the offerings associated with this law bring freedom. In addition, the offering associated with this law has not been made by human beings (μὴ ἀνθρωποποίητον).[34] The offerings associated with this law find their origin in God, while their contents are defined in 2.8, 10.[35] When these observations about the law of Jesus Christ in 2.6 are read alongside the reference to "their law" (ἐκείνων νόμος) in 3.6, the connection between freedom and proper christocentric interpretation of the law becomes clearer: the law of Jesus Christ was always meant to bring life by rightly understanding the Torah in the way that it was revealed in the prophets.

II.2.b. Fasts (Barn. 3.1–6)

The author transitions to incorporate the practice of fasting into the discussion of what God has revealed. While the topic has shifted, Barnabas's argument in 3.1 continues what has come before in 2.4–10. God continues to speak (λέγει), and the author links these words with both οὖν and πάλιν.[36] Moreover, God has spoken "about these things" (περὶ τούτων). The use of the demonstrative pronoun indicates that the subject is already known. The discussion of fasts in 3.1–6 is thus a continuation and a development of what the author has already said regarding sacrifice in 2.4–10.[37]

Barnabas makes the argument for a proper understanding of fasting based on the prophets. In 3.1–6, the passage under consideration comes from Isa 58. The author again makes use of a distinction between "us" and "them." When Barnabas cites Isa 58:4–5, he understands God to be speaking "to them" (3.1–2). Fasting does not consist in shouted prayers, sackcloth, or ashes because God did not choose this way of fasting.[38] God's speech "to us" indicates that a different way of fasting is in order (3.3).

34. Hvalvik, *Struggle for Scripture and Covenant*, 123–24, 171.

35. Cho, "ὁ νόμος τοῦ Χριστοῦ," 271–72.

36. The conjunction οὖν associates the following words to what has preceded, while πάλιν is an adverb which here notes that 3.1 continues and develops what has preceded

37. The discussion of sacrifices and fasts can thus be linked to the revelation of things that are past (τὰ παρεληλυθότα) in 1.7. Prostmeier (*Barnabasbrief*, 170–71) argues that sacrifices are regarded as things that are past (τὰ παρεληλυθότα), while fasting is an example of things that are present (τὰ ἐνεστῶτα). This outline follows what the Master has made known in 1.7, but it misses two things. First, the discussion of sacrifices and fasts are linked with few indications of a break in thought. Second, references to the present are picked up in 4.1 when the author urges the audience to investigate present matters (τὰ ἐνεστῶτα). 2.4—3.6 are thus best understood in light of 1.7 as examples of things that God revealed in the past.

38. Prostmeier (*Barnabasbrief*, 183) rightly observes that God's choice in 3.1 is closely related to God's command in 2.7.

Barnabas looks to what God says in Isa 58:6–10 to describe the fast that God has chosen. Such a fast involves breaking up violent contracts, liberating the oppressed, feeding the hungry, and housing the homeless (3.3). God promises that people who act in this way will be clothed by God's glory (3.4).[39] God will hear prayers when such just, liberating, and merciful actions characterize believers. Indeed, God will say, "Behold, I am here" (ἰδοὺ πάρειμι; 3.5). Following these quotations from Isa 58:4–10 in Barn. 3.1–5, God's revelatory capacity again comes to the fore in 3.6. The author concludes the argument by claiming that God revealed these things "to us," that is, to Barnabas and his audience who have interpreted scripture rightly. The purpose of this revelation is to differentiate "us" from "them." A proper understanding of fasting, like a right understanding of sacrifice, requires the audience to recognize what God has shown ahead of time through the prophets and to live differently from the author's opponents who seem to be attracted to the physical act of sacrifices and fasts.[40]

The citation in Barn. 3.1–5 is recognizably from an Isaianic text (Isa 58:4–10). It follows the old Greek version of Isa 58. Most of the clauses in the passage from Isaiah are accounted for in the Barnabean citation. However, a few differences between the two texts can be noted. First, Barn. 3.1 twice repeats "says the Lord" (λέγει κύριος). These clauses do not appear in Isa 58:4 and 5, although the same statement can be found in Isa 58:6 (quoted in Barn. 3.6). Second, the citation in the Epistle of Barnabas contains differences in singular and plural references from critical editions of the old Greek Isaiah. For example, the second-person plural verbs and pronouns in Barn. 3.2 are consistently second-person singular in Isa 58:5. Finally, there are changes in word order between *Barnabas* and Isaiah. The most significant change occurs in the way that the clauses are ordered in Barn. 3.3 and Isa 58:7. Both texts begin with a reference to feeding the

---

39. A textual variant is found at this point in manuscripts of Barn. 3.4. L reads *uestimentia*, while Clement of Alexandria reads ἱμάτια in his citation (Paed. 3.89.4–5 [12]). If this reading is accepted, clothing is in view at this point in the letter. However, H reads ἰάματα. S has a more complicated history. The original scribe seems to have written IMATA. Soon thereafter, the original scribe or another corrector appear to have changed this to IMATIA. A later corrector altered this word to read IAMATA. If this is the right reading, "healing" is discussed in 3.4. Old Greek manuscripts of Isaiah attest both readings. ἰάματα has been accepted by Cunningham, *Dissertation*, 12–13; Holmes, *Apostolic Fathers*, 386; Prigent and Kraft, *Épître de Barnabé*, 88. Due to its presence in a second-century quotation, its attestation in L, and its similarity to Justin, *Dial.* 15, the text that has been accepted for this commentary is ἱμάτια. This reading is also accepted by Ehrman, *Apostolic Fathers*, 2.18; Lindemann and Paulsen, *Apostolischen Väter*, 30; Prinzivalli and Simonetti *Seguendo Gesù*, 2.118; Wengst, *Didache*, 142.

40. Or, to put it more strongly in accordance with 3.6, "assimilation to Jewish praxis would have meant assimilation to Israel's fate" (Rhodes, *Epistle of Barnabas*, 43).

hungry and close by mentioning the need not to overlook close relations who are in need. However, the two clauses in the middle of Isa 58:7 are reversed in Barn. 3.3. While Isaiah speaks first of the homeless and then of those who are in need of clothes, Barnabas begins with those who are insufficiently clothed and then moves to the need for housing.[41] Nevertheless, it is clear that the author has provided an extensive quotation of Isa 58:4–10 when admonishing the audience about proper fasting.[42]

It is possible that Barnabas is again drawing from an early Christian tradition rather than, for example, a complete Greek manuscript of Isaiah.[43] Since he has placed this citation in a document written for a particular purpose, however, it is important to consider the function of this citation and the role of Barn. 3.1–6 in the argument of the letter. As with the matter of sacrifice in 2.4–10, the author is concerned with the proper definition and understanding of fasting in 3.1–6. Fasting does not consist in a particular way of praying or dressing but should instead be understood in terms of cultivating justice, liberating those who are imprisoned by unfair bonds, and promoting the wellbeing of the weakest members of society. This definition depends on an argument from Jewish scripture, but the author's argumentative style suggests that a right understanding of how the passage is necessary. God has spoken in one way "to them" (πρὸς αὐτούς; 3.1) and in another "to us" (πρὸς ἡμᾶς; 3.3). By framing the hermeneutical argument in these terms, the author demarcates clearly the community's social boundaries. Determining who is in the group and who is outside of the group can be determined by how one understands scripture. Although the author is the one setting up the argument in this way, the construction of the scriptural citations is designed to point to a greater authority. After all, it is the Lord who speaks these words to us and to them (3.1, 3).[44] The author thus situates the community within

---

41. The order in Isa 58:7 is as follows: "(1) Break your bread for the hungry, and (2) bring the impoverished homeless into your house. (3) If you see someone naked, clothe them, and (4) do not overlook the members of the household of your child." On the other hand, clauses 2 and 3 are reversed in Barn. 3.4: "(1) Break your bread for the hungry, and, (2) if you see someone naked, clothe that person. (3) Bring the homeless into your house, and, (4) if you see someone humiliated, do not overlook them—neither you nor anyone from the household of your child."

42. For further comparison of Isa 58:4–10 and Barn. 3.1–5, see Kraft, "Barnabas' Isaiah Text and the 'Testimony Book' Hypothesis," 342–43.

43. Such an early Christian tradition may have existed in written form, been passed along orally, or, more likely, been handed down by various means. Of course, it is also possible that the author knew Isa 58 from the study of Isaiah itself rather than traditions alone. These means of study need not be juxtaposed incompatibly.

44. Since κύριος is taken over in Barn. 3.3 from Isa 58:6 and is likely used in Barn. 3.1 in accordance with prophetic speech, it is best to understand κύριος as a reference to God. So also Edwards, "Identifying the Lord," 53.

the us-group in order to urge them to act justly when it comes to fasting and to read rightly when it comes to scripture.[45]

The conclusion of the argument in 3.6 heightens this interpretive emphasis and links back to the revelatory language that has been used so far in the letter. The people who "will believe in innocence" (ἐν ἀκεραιοσύνῃ πιστεύσει) refers to the audience that Barnabas addresses. They are distinguished from outsiders by a right understanding of what God has said in 3.1–5. They are set apart so that they will not be broken like proselytes "against their law" (τῷ ἐκείνων νόμῳ).[46] The reference to proselytes suggests that there is an awareness on the part of the author that some people in or around the audience may be interested in further participation in cultic activity that follows the Torah. Yet the author insists that God has revealed this understanding of sacrifice and fasting beforehand. Since God's speech was given to the prophets prior to the community's present, they can trust that God's revelation is trustworthy. It should thus be accepted and followed. God is described as patient (μακρόθυμος) because God spoke these words previously and awaited their fulfillment. The reference to God's prior revelation in 3.6 links the argument about fasting to the discussion of sacrifice (2.4), thereby uniting this two-part interpretive argument about fasting and sacrifices to show how the Master has made things known (1.7).

II.3. Scandals and Salvation (Barn. 4.1–14)

After addressing how God has revealed a right understanding of sacrifices and fasts through the prophets, Barnabas turns to the way in which the audience should live under the covenant. The author maintains an eschatological and teleological outlook throughout this section.[47] It begins by urging readers to live properly based on what God has already made known, but this section also clarifies the way in which Barnabas

---

45. On the difference between inclusive and exclusive first-person-plural pronouns from a cross-linguistic perspective, see Cysouw, *Paradigmatic Structure*, 66–98; Cysouw, "Inclusive/Exclusive Distinction," *passim*; Song, *Linguistic Typology*, 419–20.

46. While H and L read προσήλυτοι/*proselyti*, S reads ἐπήλυτοι. I have followed the reading of S in agreement with Prostmeier (*Barnabasbrief*, 169–70; see also Prostmeier and Lona, *Epistola Baranbae*, 78). However, the English translation has maintained the word *proselyte* because the difference in meaning between ἐπήλυτοι and προσήλυτοι is negligible and because *proselyte* is the better-known English term. For further discussion, see Prostmeier, *Barnabasbrief*, 185–88.

47. A teleological shape can also be found in the theology of Hebrews, on which see Lindars, *Theology of the Letter to the Hebrews*, 42–47; Luckritz Marquis, "Perfection Perfected," 187–205; Peterson, *Hebrews and Perfection*, 49–187; Ribbens, *Levitical Sacrifice*, 241–47.

understands time. The approach of the end of time provides motivation to understand God's ways (4.1-6a). The following verses outline how the covenant belongs to the author and the audience (we) and why the opponents (they) showed themselves undeserving.[48] In light of their relational place in the covenant and their temporal location in the last times, the audience is again urged to live in ways that befit their identity as the people of God (4.9b-14). Two stark options are put forward in 4.1-14, and the identity of the true people of God is thereby further clarified.

II.3.a. The Perfect Scandal and Salvific Inquiries (Barn. 4.1-6a)

Barnabas considers the comments in 4.1-2 to follow from the discussion of sacrifices and fasts in 2.4—3.6. The opening sentence is linked to the previous section with the logical conjunction οὖν. The audience ought (δεῖ) to seek (ἐκζητεῖν) the things that are able to bring salvation (4.1). The verb ἐκζητεῖν was also used in 2.1 with a different verb that expressed a sense of duty or compulsion (ὀφείλομεν). The repetition of similar verbal formulae provides cohesion to what follows in and after 4.1. In addition, the audience's search for what is able to save takes place by means of an extensive investigation of "present matters" (τῶν ἐνεστώτων). Whereas God already "has revealed" (πεφανέρωκεν) how to understand sacrifices and fasts already (2.4), the author is about to lead the audience in what should be sought out in the present. Such language in 2.4 and 4.1 should be understood in light of the timescale set out in 1.7 in which the author indicates that the Master has revealed things that are past (τὰ παρεληλυθότα) and present (τὰ ἐνεστῶτα) through the prophets.

Three exhortations follow the transitional admonition to seek what is able to save. Each cohortative is followed by a statement providing a warning or rationale for why the audience should obey. The audience is encouraged to flee from all works of lawlessness so that these works do not overtake them (4.1). Their flight from lawless deeds should be complete (τελείως), the first usage of the τελ-lexeme in Barn. 4.[49] The reference in the following exhortation to hating the deceit that characterizes the present age and loving the coming age places the author's admonitions

---

48. Hilgenfeld (*Barnabae Epistula: Integram graece iterum edidit*) found the discussion of Sinai to intrude upon the paraenetical remarks. He went so far as to reverse the order of 4.6-9a and 4.1-5.

49. The lexeme is repeated in 4.3, 7, 10, 11. It was also used in the purpose statement of 1.5, the three doctrines of 1.6, and will appear later in 5.11; 6.19; 7.3; 8.1; 10.5, 10; 13.7; 14.5; 19.11.

firmly in an apocalyptic understanding of time (4.1). The audience should likewise not give themselves license to consort with sinners so that they do not become like them (4.2).

The author roots these instructions in an apocalyptic eschatology. "The final stumbling block" (τὸ τέλειον σκάνδαλον) has come (4.3). The use of τέλειον to describe this stumbling block indicates that the author views their current moment as the culmination of the present age. Barnabas's statement is supported by three citations. The first comes from Enoch (4.3).[50] The quotation does not come verbatim from any extant Enochic text, but similar language about abbreviated days is found in 1 En. 89.61–64; 90.17–18. The next two quotations come from Dan 7, although Barnabas attributes the first to "the prophet" (4.4; Dan 7:24) and the second to "Daniel" (4.5; Dan 7:7–8).[51] The verses are not quoted in the order that they appear in the text of Daniel but may rather be quoted with regard to the length of the quotations.[52] The Lord's shortening of the times, the parallel references to ten kings and horns, as well as the reference to the fourth beast specify that the audience is living in the days of the final stumbling block.[53] They should thus understand (4.6).

II.3.b. Our Covenant (Barn. 4.6b–9a)

What readers are called to understand has proved to be a challenging interpretive hurdle in scholarship on *Barnabas*. Although it is clear that 4.6b–9a rehearses the story of Moses, the Israelites, and idolatry at Sinai, three issues repeatedly come to the fore regarding Barnabas's presentation. First, there is a significant textual issue in 4.6b that can affect interpretations of 4.6b–9a. Second, there are questions about the way in which the passage should be

---

50. Although L attributes the citation to Daniel, S and H are united in ascribing the quotation in 4.3 to Enoch.

51. Richardson and Shukster ("Barnabas," 39) argue that Barnabas may thereby attribute the quotations to two different authors. Carleton Paget (*Epistle of Barnabas*, 13) offers a salutary reminder that the author of the Epistle of Barnabas may have been aware that the author of both quotations was the same but simply designated the author differently. As often in the interpretation of ancient documents, researchers must speak in terms of probability rather than certainty on this point.

52. Because of the different introductory formulae and the quotation lengths, it may be that Barnabas cites from a source other than a manuscript of Dan 7. Prigent and Kraft, *Épître de Barnabé*, 26; Wengst, *Didache*, 114; Wengst, *Tradition und Theologie*, 21–22, 105. A testimony source is possible, although the effects of social memory and other communal factors cannot be ruled out.

53. On the identification of the kings and horns, see the comments and literature on 4.3–5 in the discussion of *Barnabas's* date within the introduction to this commentary.

interpreted and, concomitant with this decision, about the topic that the scriptural story is meant to address. Finally, one must also inquire about the fittingness of this passage within 4.1–14. Each of the three issues have implications for the interpretation of this passage and the entire letter.

Turning to the text of 4.6, each of the three witnesses record a different text in the quotation at the end of 4.6.[54] The author urges the audience not to be like some people, "saying that" (λέγοντας ὅτι), but the content of what they say is unclear. S contains the shortest reading: "The covenant is ours, though" (ἡ διαθήκη ἡμῶν μέν).[55] H is the other Greek witness to 4.6 and contains second-person pronouns: "Your covenant remains for you" (ἡ διαθήκη ὑμῶν ὑμῖν μένει). L contains the longest reading: "The covenant is theirs and ours. For it is ours" (*testamentum illorum et nostrum est. nostrum est autem*). The reading in L suggests a Greek text along the following lines: ἡ διαθήκη ἐκείνων καὶ ἡμῶν. ἡμῶν μέν. Since L is the reading that makes the most sense of the train of thought in 4.6b–9a, it is the reading that is most often adopted as the earliest text of the different readings that are attested in the manuscripts.[56]

Others have offered conjectures to explain the variation between the manuscripts.[57] Although such emendations to the text can be difficult to make with confidence due to the lack of manuscript evidence, the challenge of explaining the current manuscript evidence opens the possibility that a conjectural emendation may be necessary in 4.6. The reading in L makes sense of the author's argument, but to choose this reading as the earliest text goes against two tenets of textual criticism: that the more difficult reading is most often right and that the shorter reading is most often right. With these objections in view, James Rhodes has suggested that the saying of 4.6 be emended to "the covenant remains ours" (ἡ διαθήκη ἡμῶν μένει; 4.6).[58] This reading has the advantage of being short and thus fits the preference in textual criticism for short readings. It can also account for the readings in the

54. G is not extant at 4.6, so only S, H, and L witness to the text.

55. It is not easy to account for μέν at the end of the saying. It is not accompanied by δέ and is an unusual use of the word. The English word *though* has been utilized as a place-holder in the translation.

56. E.g., Carleton Paget, *Epistle of Barnabas*, 113–14; Cunningham, *Dissertation*, 16; Ehrman, *Apostolic Fathers*, 2.22; Hvalvik, *Struggle for Scripture and Covenant*, 90; Prostmeier and Lona, *Epistola Barnabae*, 80–82; Wengst, *Didache*, 144; Wengst, *Tradition und Theologie*, 82 n 35; Windisch, *Barnabasbrief*, 321.

57. Prigent and Kraft (*Épître de Barnabé*, 96) suggest ἡ διαθήκη ἡμῶν ἡμῖν μένει, which could be translated as "Our covenant remains valid for us."

58. Rhodes, "Barnabas 4.6b," 385–86. Rhodes has been followed by Edwards, *Gospel*, 10n25; Holmes, *Apostolic Fathers*, 388; Prinzivalli and Simonetti, *Seguendo Gesù*, 2.120, 2.513 n 36; Rothschild, "Epistle of Barnabas," 207.

other manuscripts. S seems to have lost the final two letters, H has confused the first-person pronoun (ἡμῶν) for the second-person pronoun (ὑμῶν), and, if L had a reading similar to S that was difficult to understand, the translator may have supplied the longer translation in order to make sense of the text. Given the explanatory power of Rhodes's emendation, ἡ διαθήκη ἡμῶν μένει has thus provided the base text on which the translation in this volume is based and will be assumed as the text of 4.6 going forward.

After establishing the text of 4.6, it is important to note what follows in 4.7–8. The author claims that "they" (ἐκεῖνοι) lost the covenant "completely" (εἰς τέλος; 4.7). Both of these words have been important in the opening chapters of the letter. The reference to "them" refers to Barnabas's opponents, while this is the third appearance of the τελ-lexeme in chapter 4.[59] The opponents have lost the covenant despite Moses's earlier reception of the covenant. Barnabas then appeals to the story of Moses at Sinai.[60] After Moses received the tablets of the covenant on the mountain (4.7), God informs him that the people have turned to idols and he must thus go down quickly (4.8). Moses understood and threw the tablets down with the result that they broke. Barnabas interprets the broken tablets as a break in the covenant so that the covenant of Jesus "might be sealed into our heart" (ἐνκατασφραγισθῇ εἰς τὴν καρδίαν ἡμῶν; 4.8).[61] In contrast to the broken covenant, Jesus's covenant is associated with "us."

When reflecting on the interpretation and use of this story in *Barnabas*, an important methodological decision must be made that draws together the textual problem of 4.6 and the rehearsal of Moses's story in 4.7–8. The decision has to do with Barnabas's interpretive *modus operandi* in 4.6–8. To put it roughly, is Barnabas interpreting the story through a salvation-historical lens, or does Barnabas's understanding of the story rely upon allegory? A salvation-historical reading of 4.6–8 would locate the problem in Israel's rejection of the covenant and would find hope in Jesus's covenant that has been sealed into the heart of Barnabas and his readers. Such a reading lends itself well to the polemical language that Barnabas uses against his opponents. Yet it is not clear how the eschatologically

---

59. In addition to the continuity provided by the repetition in Barn. 4, the significance of εἰς τέλος is that Israel's loss of the covenant was utter and final.

60. This story is told in the Pentateuchal narrative in Exod 32–34 and is rehearsed in Deut 9:7–21. Barnabas's language is similar to language found in Exod 31:18; 32:7; 34:28; and Deut 9:12, while the overall shape of the narrative in Barn. 4.7–8 may be most similar to Deut 9:9–17.

61. Barnabas describes Jesus as "the beloved" (ὁ ἠγαπημένος; 4.8), a term that is also used in Asc. Isa. 9.5, 13; 10.7–8. On "the beloved," see Hurtado, *Lord Jesus Christ*, 596.

oriented paraenesis in 4.1–6a, 9b–14 would fit with such an interpretation. An allegorical understanding of this story would understand Israel's rejection of the covenant and the sealing of the covenant into the hearts of believers to be two different ways of reacting to God's covenantal activity. The audience is thus urged to accept God's covenant and to turn away from any way of rejection.

These two ways of interpreting 4.6b–8 alert one to the importance of methodological awareness but simultaneously form a false dichotomy if an either/or choice is demanded. The author's use of figural exegesis again comes to the fore in these verses. The statement of "some" (τισιν; 4.6) that the covenant remains "ours" indicates a belief that the covenant will always belong to them, that is, to Barnabas's opponents.[62] The "some" group appears to be either near or within the walls of Barnabas's community. "Some" articulate a view of the covenant that is permanently in Israel's possession.[63] In response, Barnabas argues that Israel lost the covenant in the construction of the golden calf at Sinai. Barnabas puts forward two possible results of the covenant. When appealing to Israel, he indicates that the covenant can be lost even after it is possessed. Although Moses had already received the covenant tablets "written by the finger of the Lord's hand" (γεγραμμένας τῷ δακτύλῳ τῆς χειρὸς τοῦ κυρίου; 4.7), Israel failed to take up the covenant when they turned to idols. The covenant does not permanently remain with anyone simply because it was given to them once. Barnabas's readers can lose the covenant just like the Israelites did at Sinai. The response of Israel and the implied "us" are allegorically represented in Barnabas's interpretation. For this reason, they must be careful to live rightly (4.1–6a, 9b–14). By doing this, they will continue to enjoy the covenant of Jesus that has been sealed into their heart (4.8).[64]

Such an allegorical reading of the Mosaic covenant does not, however, remove the polemical overtones of Barnabas's argument. The letter appears to have been written for multiple purposes. It encourages covenantal faithfulness among believers, a purpose that is best served by an allegorical interpretation of 4.6b–8. Yet Barnabas also writes polemically against opponents and warns readers against accepting interpretive practices that are associated with Jewish customs. Although the salvation-historical

---

62. Rhodes, *Epistle of Barnabas*, 31.

63. "Il baricentro dell'argomentazione sta nell'invito a non coltivare false sicurezze, bensì a impegnarsi, in vista della prova escatologica che si avvicina" (The argument's center of gravity lies in the invitation not to cultivate false security but, in view of the eschatological trial that is approaching, to commit oneself; Prinzivall and Simonetti, *Seguendo Gesù*, 2.513n36).

64. Rothschild, "Epistle of Barnabas," 208.

connotations of 4.6b–8 are not primary, the allegorical interpretation relies upon knowledge of how God's covenantal actions in the past have been rejected by people and recorded in scripture.[65] For Barnabas, there is only one covenant.[66] It was offered to the people through Moses, but the people rejected this by turning to idols. The covenant that belongs to Jesus can be inscribed directly into the heart of Barnabas's readers. Interpreting the Barnabean explanation of Moses's story with some historical referent allows 4.6b–9a to take its place alongside other polemical passages in the letter, while the allegorical emphasis on Moses's encounter highlights the choice that readers are compelled to make and fits with the emphasis on two ways and two peoples found throughout the epistle.[67]

To demonstrate the coherence of this multi-pronged interpretation of 4.6b–8, it will be useful to consider the role of this passage within the larger context of 4.1–14. An allegorical reading of 4.6b–8 makes Barnabas's eschatological admonitions more urgent. Since the final stumbling block has now drawn near (4.3), this is no time for the readers to turn away to idols like the people of Israel. Instead, they must flee works of lawlessness, hate the deceit of the present time, and not allow themselves to relax by consorting with those who are deemed evil (4.1–2). They should maintain their covenant faithfulness because the covenant of Jesus has been inscribed into their hearts (4.8). This interpretation of 4.6b–8 likewise fits what follows in 4.9b–14 where the audience is reminded that they live in the last days, a lawless time, and an age of further stumbling blocks (4.9). They should thus run away from futility (4.10), not sleep in their sin (4.13), and be alert about themselves in light of what happened to Israel (4.14). The warning about the signs and wonders that were done in Israel in 4.14 and Israel's lack of faithfulness further fits the anti-Jewish polemic that rumbles throughout the letter. For Barnabas there is a sense in which the loss of the covenant at Sinai is historical, and it is for this reason that the community should become a temple to God (4.11). The covenantal narrative of 4.6b–8 may be a digression, but it is neither accidental nor misplaced. Readers are given two options, allowed to belong to one of two peoples, and urged

---

65. "Barnabas seems to presuppose a radicalized Christian version of the Deuteronomistic view of history" (Rhodes, *Epistle of Barnabas*, 31). Rhodes may emphasize the historical elements of this Deuteronomistic view more strongly than the present commentary, but his claim that there are historical elements at work in Barnabas's exegesis is correct.

66. Hvalvik, *Struggle for Scripture and Covenant*, 91–92; Lieu, "Jewish Matrix," 220.

67. See similarly Edwards (*Gospel*, 10), who writes, "While the language of 'their covenant' in 4.8 is in some sense historical—where 'their' refers to the Israelites at Sinai—it is also contemporary."

to continue faithfully in the covenant. Whereas Israel lost the covenant in their idolatrous actions at Sinai and the tablets were broken as a result, Barnabas urges his audience to continue "in the hope of his faithfulness" (ἐν ἐλπίδι τῆς πίστεως αὐτοῦ; 4.8).[68]

This focus on a key interpretive puzzle in 4.6b–8 has not only been important for scholarship on the Epistle of Barnabas but also affects one's interpretation of the rest of the letter. The interpretation of 4.6b–8 can almost serve as a test by which to consider the way in which allegory, history, and scriptural interpretation are overlaid in the letter. However, this emphasis on an interpretive controversy risks overlooking other noteworthy elements in this passage. The author's self-presentation in 4.6b–9a suggests that this passage is important but most likely to be accepted with a carefully cultivated ethos. Barnabas writes "as one of you, who loves you all more than my own life" (ὡς εἷς ἐξ ἡμῶν ὤν, ἰδίως δὲ καὶ πάντας ἀγαπῶν ὑπὲρ τὴν ψυχὴν μου; 4.6). He does not overtly appeal to his authority but seeks to make his point by lovingly identifying himself with his audience. Barnabas speaks in a similar way in 4.9 when he says that he wants to write "not as a teacher but as is fitting for someone who does not like to leave out anything that we have" (οὐχ ὡς διδάσκαλος ἀλλ' ὡς πρέπει ἀγαπῶντι ἀφ' ὧν ἔχομεν μὴ ἐλλείπειν; 4.9).[69] He again refuses to place himself above the audience rhetorically. The reflections on the covenantal actions at Sinai are placed in the letter in the hopes of completing his thought. Barnabas thus writes as their "devoted servant" (περίψημα; 4.9).[70]

The rehearsal of the covenant in 4.6b–9a comprises an important section early in the letter that contributes much to how readers understand Barnabas, themselves, and the relationship of their actions to their status as the people of God. The author cultivates an image that demonstrates that he

---

68. Schliesser ("Faith in Early Christianity," 44) suggests that the genitive in ἡ πίστις αὐτοῦ (4.8) should be understood as an objective genitive because 4.9 clearly refers to human faithfulness. While this argument provides continuity in understanding faith across 4.8–9, I have hesitantly translated the genitive in 4.8 as a subjective genitive because the verb ἐνκατασφραγισθῇ is passive, indicating that this is something that has happened to believers. On this reading, Barnabas interprets the inscription of the covenant on believers' hearts as a result of the Sinai event that occurs in the hope of Jesus's faithfulness. On account of this hope and Jesus's faithfulness (his willingness to endure will be described at length in 5.1–14), believers are called to act rightly because their faith may come to naught if they do not resist the stumbling blocks in the lawless age (4.9). For further discussions of genitives and πίστις in second-century literature, see Harrisville, "ΠΙΣΤΙΣ ΧΡΙΣΤΟΥ," 233–41; Whitenton, "After ΠΙΣΤΙΣ ΧΡΙΣΤΟΥ," 82–109.

69. These phrases connect with Barnabas's professed desire in 1.8 to write as one of the audience rather than as a teacher. See also Windisch, *Barnabasbrief*, 323.

70. The word περίψημα is missing in L but found in S and H. The word is also found in 1 Cor 4:13; Ign. *Eph.* 8.1; 18.1. See further Kirk, "Ignatius' Statements," 66–88.

is both a competent interpreter of scripture and a loving and devoted member of the group. The audience should thus follow his admonitions to remain faithful until the eschaton because they are members of the people of God. Although the covenant may not be permanently given in the case of idolatry, readers' actions identify them with the covenant of Jesus that is inscribed into their hearts and sets them apart from faithless Israel.

II.3.c. The Eschatological Life (Barn. 4.9b–14)

Barnabas's exegesis of the broken covenant tablets leads to another paraenetical section in which he urges the audience to live properly "in the last days" (ἐν ταῖς ἐσχάταις ἡμέραις; 4.9). As in 4.1-2, much of the section is animated by cohortative verbs and potential consequences. The paraenesis in 4.9–14 is not a tightly arranged unit, but the use of cohortatives provides a loose structure that the author employs to encourage the audience to live rightly. Readers are called to be on the alert (προσέχωμεν) at the beginning and end of the exhortations (4.9, 14). In the middle, the audience is twice encouraged to become (γενώμεθα) something (4.11). The repetition of these verbs indicates the dynamic state in which believers find themselves. They have not attained their final state, and they ought to play an active role that is given to believers in the last days. The author's warning about Israel's Sinaitic failure continues to resound in this passage. As the covenant has been inscribed into readers' hearts, so also they must act in step with the Lord's requirements. The audience that received God's gracious gift from the Spirit (1.2–3) is called to participate actively while being transformed into the people of God.

Barnabas urges the audience to live rightly, warns them about the wicked way, and employs these warnings as motivations to act according to God's commandments. The audience should be on the alert as a consequence of what the audience has just heard about Israel's unfaithfulness (4.9, 14). They ought to resist the coming stumbling blocks since they are in the last days (4.9). They are called to meet together and to seek what is beneficial to the common good (4.10).[71] Barnabas employs pneumatic language that harkens back to the repetition of similar language in 1.2–3. The audience should become spiritual (πνευματικοί; 4.11). Closely connected to this concept, the audience is to be a complete temple (ναὸς τέλειος) to God (4.11). When combined with the dynamic use of cohortatives, such

---

71. O'Neil, "Origins of Monasticism," 277–78. See similarly Ign. *Eph.* 3.2—4.1; *Magn.* 7.2; *Pol.* 6.1.

language invites readers into a larger and more perfect outlook of what their lives should be.

Warnings closely correspond to this positive view of an eschatological life that accords with what is required by God. The audience should resist imminent stumbling blocks so that the Black One does not have an opportunity to sneak in (4.9).[72] Readers are reminded that they must flee futility, that they should hate the works of the evil age, and that they should not live separately as if they are already justified (4.10). The author quotes Isa 5:21 as a warning against those who live separately (4.11) and counsels readers not to fall asleep in their sins (4.13). Barnabas's negative paraenesis serves as a warning to the audience so that they will walk faithfully in God's requirements. References to God's judgment function similarly in 4.9–14. God judges without favoritism, so good actions receive the Lord's righteousness, while wicked actions will receive a corresponding wage (4.12). The audience should be careful so that the time of their faith does not go without benefit by stumbling at the end (4.9).[73] Israel again provides the key example of such a failure. Thus the audience should be alert so that they do not fall prey to the proverbial saying, "many are called, but few are chosen" (πολλοὶ κλητοί, ὀλίγοι δὲ ἐκλεκτοί; 4.14).

The closing proverb in 4.9–14 bears striking similarities to the Jesus tradition, particularly in Matt 22:14. At the end of Jesus's parable in which a man's invitations to a wedding are rebuffed and the wedding is peopled with anyone who could be found, the Matthean Jesus concludes, "Many are called, but few are chosen" (πολλοὶ γάρ εἰσιν κλητοί, ὀλίγοι δὲ ἐκλεκτοί). The clear resonances between the two statements and the authority that a statement would have coming from Jesus's lips make it possible that Barnabas quotes from Matthew, but the inexact verbal parallels and the possible proverbial nature of the statement make it difficult to be

---

72. Clare Rothschild ("Ethiopianising the Devil," 223–45) argues that the reference to the supreme evil figure as "the Black One" (ὁ μέλας) in 4.9 should be understood as part of a larger use of anti-Egyptian rhetoric in the letter. A key example of anti-Egyptian rhetoric cited by Rothschild occurs when the author refers to Egyptians as circumcised (9.6). Barnabas regards circumcision as a matter for the heart and ears rather than the foreskin. The counter-divine Black One is described in stereotypical language that Didymus the Blind connects to Ethiopians (Didymus, *Zach.* 234; 355). Rothschild's arguments and comparison to other third and fourth-century texts associating blackness with sub-Saharan peoples ("Ethiopianising the Devil," 230–39) are strongly suggestive that Barnabas portrays the devil as a marauder and is employing a stereotype that was available from the surrounding world.

73. For similarities between Barn. 4.9 and Did. 16.2, see Prostmeier, *Barnabasbrief*, 218n119; Windisch, *Barnabasbrief*, 324.

certain.[74] Wherever Barnabas learned these words, he draws this section to a close with a powerful reminder to the audience that it is necessary to be faithful to the end.

The ethical call of 4.9–14 provides a fitting conclusion to the focus on scandals and salvation in 4.1–14. The audience is urged to be on the alert and to become a complete temple to God. They must flee futility and hate the works of the evil way. In 4.1–2, they are likewise told to flee from works of lawlessness and to hate the deceit that is characteristic of the present age. Barnabas's ethical exhortations are established within an eschatological understanding of the ages. He and the audience live in the transition from the present to the coming age. Since they are at the end of the age, Barnabas notes that the final stumbling block has come near but warns that other stumbling blocks may arise (4.3, 9). It is possible to turn away from God's salvific covenant just as Israel did at Sinai. Such a turning away is connected to the misunderstanding of sacrifice, fasting, and other Torah practices that were considered in 2.4—3.6.[75] The audience must therefore cling to the covenant of Jesus that has been inscribed on their hearts.

II.4. The Suffering of the Lord and Son of God (Barn. 5.1—8.7)

After the admonitions for the audience to continue to be faithful to the covenant, Barnabas turns to Jesus's willingness to endure suffering. If the Lord was willing to suffer, the audience should likewise be prepared to stay true to the end (5.1–14). Yet the Lord did not suffer only as an example of endurance. His suffering effected salvation and fulfilled prophecy. Barnabas's salvific interpretation of the Christ-event in terms of the prophets is consistent throughout 5.1—8.7. The suffering of the Son should not lead to despair, for his passion was completed by resurrection (6.1-4). The person of the Son thus provides the hope that grounds believers' lives and activities. This hope is likewise found in Barnabas's interpretation of the land flowing with milk and honey (6.8-19). Nevertheless, Jesus's actions on the cross remain in the foreground throughout 5.1—8.7. The Lord revealed his suffering beforehand, and these revelations imbue the cross with meaning.

---

74. One might compare Barn. 4.14 to 4 Ezra 5.5; 8.3; and 9.15. For a strong argument in favor of finding a citation of Matt 22:14 in Barn. 4.14, see Franco, "Une citation," 231–45. For further discussions of the tradition cited in 4.14, see Bartlet, "Barnabas," 18–19; Edwards, "Epistle of Barnabas," 37; Edwards, *Gospel*, 92–93; Jefford, *Apostolic Fathers and the New Testament*, 109–10.

75. Similar discussions occur later in the letter. See 9.1—10.12; 15.1—16.10.

Barnabas interprets both the consumption of sour wine and Jesus's death as actions that were made known in scripture (7.1–11), while Israel's experience with the red heifer likewise prefigured the significance of Jesus (8.1–7). In light of these things, the audience should hear and hold to the covenant that has been given to them.

Barnabas signals a rhetorical transition with the phrase, "For it was for this reason" (εἰς τοῦτο γάρ; 5.1). He uses εἰς τοῦτο eight times in the letter to indicate the reason for a scriptural revelation.[76] Three of these uses come in 5.1–14 (5.1, 11, 12), and two additional uses are found in the larger section 5.1—8.7 (6.13; 7.10). 5.1–14 is thus occupied with the reasons that the Lord had to endure suffering. Barnabas communicates his aim to readers with the repeated use of this prepositional phrase. Yet 5.1 is not the only significant transitional phrase near the beginning of this section. After introducing a new topic in 5.1, Barnabas includes a scriptural citation that is introduced by the formula, "For it is written about him" (γέγραπται γὰρ περὶ αὐτοῦ; 5.2). A citation verb followed by the preposition περί with a genitive is likewise used in transitions at 9.1; 11.1.[77] This may be regarded as a secondary transition marker.[78] The rhetoric in 5.1–2 marks a clear transition to a new stage from that which occupied Barnabas in 4.1–14.

II.4.a. The Endurance, Suffering, and Resurrection of the Son (Barn. 5.1—6.7)

The focus on the Lord's endurance in 5.1–14 is introduced in the opening statement of the section: "For it was for this reason that the Lord endured to give his flesh up to corruption" (5.1). The focus on endurance is maintained throughout the section by the fivefold repetition of ὑπομένω (5.1, 5 [2x], 6, 12).[79] The arguments that follow do not proceed in linear fashion but are gathered in response to the authorial focus on the Lord's endurance. Barnabas offers an initial reason for why the Son suffered along with a hermeneutical principle (5.1–4). Additional reasons for the Lord's suffering follow

---

76. See 3.6; 4.3; 5.1, 11, 12; 6.13; 7.10; 14.5. In 1.4, Barnabas also employs εἰς τοῦτο, but it serves a different purpose. Rather than indicating the reason or purpose for a previously introduced revelation, it marks what the author is compelled (ἀναγκάζομαι) to do.

77. Prostmeier, *Barnabasbrief*, 227. A similar use of περί with a genitive noun is employed more consistently as a transitional rhetorical marker in 1 Cor 7:1; 8:1; 12:1; 16:1.

78. A similar formula appears at 6.12 in the middle of a 6.8–19.

79. The repetition of πάσχω (5.5 [2x], 13 [2x]), φανερόω (5.6, 9), and σάρξ (5.1, 6, 10, 11, 12) give further clarification about the key themes in 5.1–14. See similarly Rhodes, *Epistle of Barnabas*, 52 n 60.

along with a reference to Jesus's earthly life (5.5-10). The next stage in the argument contains an explication of why Jesus had to suffer in the way that he did, namely, on the cross (5.11-14). The author turns to the resurrection of Jesus, whose flesh is described as a mighty stone (6.1-4), before recapitulating key themes from this multifaceted section in 6.5-7.

As Barnabas introduces this section on the Lord's suffering, the first reason that he articulates has to do with the forgiveness of sins experienced by his audience and him. The Lord endured "so that we might be cleansed by forgiveness of sins" (5.1). The means by which this act of purification takes place is further adumbrated by the following clause. Purification occurs "by the sprinkling of his blood" (5.1).[80] The author follows this statement with a quotation from Isa 53:5 and 7 that highlights the way in which the servant's bruises heal believers and how the servant behaved like a lamb prior to slaughter (5.2).[81] Before this citation, however, Barnabas articulates a hermeneutical principle that readers have already seen in action in 2.4—4.14. When Barnabas reads scripture, he understands some of the statements within scripture to be targeted at Israel while other matters are directed toward "us" (5.2). After justifying the Lord's suffering in terms of "our" purification, the author employs language similar to 1.7 in order to emphasize the need to be thankful to the Lord. Gratitude is owed because the Lord made known things about the past and present while not leaving believers completely without knowledge about the future (5.3). For this reason, believers should stay on the path of righteousness. If they commingle with the way of darkness, nets are fittingly stretched out to entrap them (5.4).[82]

Three things can be added to this attempt to trace the thought of 5.1-4. First, Barnabas's use of Isa 53:5, 7 maintains strong similarities to the Isaianic text found in critical editions of Old Greek Isaiah. Within the quotation of Isa 53:7 (Barn. 5.2), the reference to the lamb's silence before

---

80. The antecedent of the neuter relative pronoun, ὅ, should be understood in terms of the act of purification described in the preceding clause.

81. Citations from Isa 53 abound in early Christian literature. See e.g., Acts 8:32-33; 1 Pet 2:21-24; 1 Clem. 16.3-14; Justin, *1 Apol.* 50.5-10; *Dial.* 13.1-7; 73.2; 89.3; Melito, *Pasch.* 64. All quotations from 1 Clement come from Jaubert, *Clément de Rome*. All quotations from Melito's *On Pascha* come from Hall, *Melito of Sardis*.

82. Barnabas quotes Prov 1:17 (Barn. 5.4). Barnabas introduces the quotation by saying, "Now the scripture says" (λέγει δὲ ἡ γράφη). He then quotes the proverb as follows: "Nets are not unjustly spread out for birds" (οὐκ ἀδίκως ἐκτείνεται δίκτυα πτερωτοῖς). Only the beginning of the text reads slightly differently in Prov 1:17, since the translator employs a conjunction to connect the verse to what comes before: οὐ γὰρ ἀδίκως ἐκτείνεται δίκτυα πτερωτοῖς. All quotations of Old Greek Proverbs comes from Rahlfs and Hanhart, *Septuaginta*.

its shearers appears with slightly different word order between the two texts.⁸³ However, Barnabas is selective about which portions of the Isaianic text that he utilizes. He skips a phrase that appears in Isa 53:5 and does not quote from Isa 53:6–7a.⁸⁴ This choice may be due to an earlier source or tradition of quotation, or it may stem from the author. In any case, it enables Barnabas to bring out two elements of the prophetic word: the benefits of the Lord's death and the slaughter that he underwent. When the author's hermeneutical principle is considered (Barn. 5.2), the scriptural words "to us" refer to the statements about benefits, while the description of the shearers should, on Barnabas's view, be interpreted with regard to Israel.⁸⁵ The second matter concerns the consistent interest in purification and sacrifice in Barn. 5.1–4. The Lord allowed his flesh to become corrupted in order to purify Barnabas and his readers by the forgiveness of sins (5.1). The purification from the Lord became efficacious by the sprinkling of his blood.⁸⁶ The Isaianic description of why the Lord's suffering was necessary as well as the healing that resulted (5.2) contributes to the sacrificial motif that runs through these verses (Isa 53:5). Finally, the digression in 5.3–4 points to the intersection of interpretation, ethics, and Christology

83. Isa 53:7: ὡς ἀμνὸς ἐναντίον τοῦ κείροντος αὐτὸν ἄφωνος; Barn. 5.2: ὡς ἀμνὸς ἄφωνος ἐναντίον τοῦ κείραντος αὐτόν. The two words in question have been italicized in both texts. However, Melito, Pasch. 64 quotes Isa 53:7 in a form that is similar to Barn. 5.2. For further discussion, see Kraft, "Barnabas' Isaiah Text and Melito's Paschal Homily," 372–73.

84. The phrase that is left unquoted from Isa 53:5 is "the discipline of our peace was upon him." The intervening words in Isa 53:6–7a are "we all have gone astray like sheep; a person has gone astray in his own way. And the Lord has handed him over for our sins. And because he was mistreated, he does not open his mouth."

85. For a slightly different articulation of how Israel and "we" are in view in 5.2, see Verheyden, "Israel's Fate," 250. While the interpretation here differs slightly, Verheyden helpfully outlines the way in which Barnabas's hermeneutical division between "Israel" and "us" is worked out in the citation of Isa 53:5 and 7.

86. A textual variant occurs in the manuscript tradition at the end of 5.1. Although S reads "by the blood of his sprinkling" (ἐν τῷ αἵματι τοῦ ῥαντίσματος αὐτοῦ), H and L offer readings that reverse the nouns: "by the sprinkling of his blood" (ἐν τῷ ῥαντίσματι αὐτοῦ τοῦ αἵματος; sparsione sanguinis illius). The order of S bears some similarities to Heb 12:24, which emphasizes that the mediator of the new covenant and blood of sprinkling (αἵματι ῥαντίσματος) are better than what is said through Abel. On the other hand, the order in H and L is reminiscent of 1 Pet 1:2 where readers are greeted as those who have been called for obedience and for "sprinkling with the blood" (ῥαντισμὸν αἵματος) of Jesus Christ. I have followed the reading in S since it seems to be the marginally more difficult reading. See similarly Holmes (Apostolic Fathers, 392), Prostmeier and Lona (Epistola Barnabae, 84), However, Cunningham (Dissertation, 20) Ehrman (Apostolic Fathers, 2.26), Prigent and Kraft (Épître de Barnabé, 104), Lindemann and Paulsen (Die apostolischen Väter, 34), Prinzivalli and Simonetti (Seguendo Gesù, 2.122), and Wengst (Didache, 148) prefer the text of H and L.

that pervades not only 5.1—8.7 but the entire letter. Readers are called to give thanks for the revelation that comes through scripture, understand it rightly as an act befitting the way of righteousness, and not turn away from the Lord who endured corruption for their purification.

Barnabas continues the overarching interest in the Son's endurance of suffering, but the topic shifts slightly in 5.5–11. 5.5 begins with a transitional phrase and a vocative to bring readers back from the digression in 5.3-4. The phrase ἔτι δὲ καὶ τοῦτο may be collectively translated into English as "moreover," while the reference to "my brothers and sisters" aids the author in transitioning subjects.[87] The protasis that follows resumes the theme of 5.1-2: the Lord endured his suffering "for our soul" (περὶ τῆς ψυχῆς ἡμῶν; 5.5). The Lord's suffering for the benefit of believers was mentioned in 5.1-2 and supported with reference to Isa 53. Barnabas now raises another question about the Lord's endurance. The question follows from two premises that Barnabas lays out following the reference to suffering for believers. First, Jesus suffered "even though he was Lord of all creation." Second, Jesus is the one to whom God spoke when he was creating the world. Jesus was thus the audience of Gen 1:26: "Let us make human beings in our image and likeness" (5.5).[88] Given the Lord's authority, Barnabas inquires, "How then did he endure to suffer at the hand of people?" Put differently, one may wonder how the Creator suffers from actions committed by the creation.

The audience is brusquely instructed to "learn" (μάθετε) how this was the case (5.5). The answers that follow in 5.6–7 come from the prophets and are introduced by two ἵνα-clauses.[89] The Lord endured to make death ineffective and to exhibit resurrection from the dead (5.6). He also endured so that he could make good on the promise to the ancestors and to show that he will judge when he brings the resurrection to fruition (5.7). Jesus demonstrated these things even while he was preparing a new people for himself. Israel and Jesus's incarnate actions prior to his death are taken up in 5.8–9. Jesus preached and showed his love for Israel by teaching them

---

87. A similar transition is employed in 4.6 as the author shifts from ethical paraenesis in light of the final stumbling block to his consideration of Israel's actions at Sinai. In 4.6, the same transitional phrase is employed (ἔτι δὲ καὶ τοῦτο) without the vocative directly addressing the audience.

88. Skarsaune ("Jewish Christian Sources," 402–8) helpfully compares Barnabas's use of Gen 1:1 with other second-century discussions of Wisdom's role in creation. The author will turn again to a larger discussion of Gen 1:26 and 28 as part of the reflections on the land flowing with milk and honey in Barn. 6.8–19.

89. The prophets are able to set out these purposes because they received grace from God (5.6). Ignatius similarly claims that the prophets were able to live in accordance with Christ because they received grace (Ign. Magn. 8.2).

and doing signs and wonders (5.8).⁹⁰ Moreover, Jesus revealed himself to be God's Son when he chose his disciples. He selected sinful men in order to demonstrate that he did not come to call the righteous but the sinners (5.9). Barnabas contrasts Israel and the disciples as those who are righteous but not called by Jesus, on the one hand, and those who were sinful but called by the Son of God, on the other. He also hints at another reason for Jesus's endurance by raising the counterfactual possibility that Jesus's advent may not have occurred. If Jesus did not come in the flesh, human beings would have had no way to be saved (5.10). Salvation only came to human beings because they could see him.⁹¹ After all, human beings are not able to look

---

90. I thus take the participles διδάσκων and ποιῶν to indicate the means by which Jesus's proclamation and love were executed. It is also important to note that four quite different texts are attested in S, H, L, and G leading interpreters to struggle with what the earliest text is in 5.8. S reads "he was preaching and they loved him exceedingly" (ἐκήρυσσεν καὶ ὑπερηγάπησαν αὐτόν). On this reading, Jesus was preaching while he was incarnate, and the people of Israel loved him. H has a different text: "not because he was preaching and they loved him exceedingly" (οὐχ ὅτι ἐκήρυσσεν οὐδὲ ὑπερηγάπησαν αὐτόν). It is difficult to make sense of H at this point, but it seems to indicate that Jesus's teaching and signs did not occur because Jesus preached or because Israel loved him. L is again different when it says that "they (the Jews) neither believed nor loved him" (non crediderunt nec dilexerunt illum). Finally, G reads, "he preached and loved him (Israel) exceedingly" (ἐκήρυξε καὶ ὑπερηγάπησεν αὐτόν).

Although H and L are difficult to account for, they point to the difficulty in the textual tradition of 5.8. S is the lectio difficilior because the plural verb ὑπερηγάπησαν speaks positively of Israel's love for Jesus. In a letter that rarely portrays Israel in a positive light, this is surprising. It is possible that this reading could have been emended—consciously or unconsciously—in the textual tradition. A secondary difficulty in S is the unusual use of the imperfect tense to describe Jesus's preaching. However, G is a more likely indicator of the earlier text in 5.8. The singular verb ὑπερηγάπησεν keeps the focus on Jesus, where the focus lies throughout 5.6–9. The change to the plural verb may be explained by early scribal changes. It is difficult to know whether this was a conscious or unconscious change, but the presence of a plural verb in S, H, and L speak to the prevalence of this tradition. Nevertheless, Barnabas speaks here of Jesus's love for Israel (αὐτόν). Yet the question of the tense of κηρύσσω is more difficult to answer. I have accepted the aorist tense found in G because it offers manuscript support for the translation and interpretation (so also Prinzivalli and Simonetti, Seguendo Gesù, 2.124; Wengst, Didache, 150). However, the difficulty of the imperfect tense leads some to accept the imperfect tense from S (e.g., Cunningham, Dissertation, 24; Ehrman, Apostolic Fathers, 2.28; Holmes, Apostolic Fathers, 392; Prigent and Kraft, Épître de Barnabé, 110; Lindemann and Paulsen, Apostolischen Väter, 36; Prostmeier and Lona, Epistola Barnabae, 86). The difference in tense is intriguing, but it makes a negligible difference in the interpretation.

91. Barnabas's understanding of the incarnation's purpose is thus articulated not only in terms of forgiveness but also in terms of revelation. See further Svigel, Center and the Source, 291.

directly into the sun, which was created by God, so it would be *a fortiori* impossible for human beings to gaze directly upon God.[92]

Jesus and Israel both receive attention in 5.5–10 in ways that are unique within *Barnabas*. The author alludes particularly to additional details about Jesus's incarnation in 5.8–9. Jesus is portrayed as a teacher and wonder-worker who loved and preached to Israel. Although the covenant of Jesus was contrasted with the covenant given to Moses in 4.6–8, readers should not conclude that ethnic Israelites have no place within Barnabas's understanding of the people of God. Jesus used his time to teach Israel. However, he also came to call apostles who were "more lawless than all sin" (ὑπὲρ πᾶσαν ἁμαρτίαν ἀνομωτέρους; 5.9).[93] The apostles were called to imitate Jesus's proclamatory acts (5.8–9). Their undeserving and sinful status also shows that Jesus did not come to call the righteous but the sinners (5.9). It is through this choice that Jesus "revealed himself to be Son of God" (ἐφανέρωσεν ἑαυτὸν εἶναι υἱὸν θεοῦ; 5.9). By bringing Jesus's choice of sinners to the fore,[94] Barnabas highlights the Son's flesh, his willingness to endure throughout his earthly life, and his work in preparing a new people.[95]

The intertwining of figurative and salvation-historical uses of Israel in the letter also come into clearer focus in 5.5–10. Although the connections between these symbolic uses of Israel were evident in 4.6b–9a, the author now highlights the grace by which the prophets prophesied and the teaching, signs, and love that they received from Jesus (5.6, 8). The reality of these events in history is assumed.[96] Yet this passage cannot be read without the author's challenge to "Israel's" way of reading scripture and reaction to the covenant echoing through readers' minds.[97] While the prophets were graciously allowed to prophecy, Israel represents an implicit rejection of the love that Jesus showed toward them (5.8). The gifts that Israel received are mentioned in order to elevate the devastation of their rejection and to warn readers not to follow in their way of acting or interpreting scripture.

92. For similar arguments in other early Christian texts, see the extensive list of citations in Windisch, *Barnabasbrief*, 330–31.

93. According to Origen (*Cels*. 1.62–63), Celsus cited Jesus's choice of wicked followers as evidence for Jesus's own lacking moral character. Origen cites Barn. 5.9 and argues instead that Jesus's transformation of his followers from evil characters to morally pure individuals demonstrates the power of the gospel (*Cels*. 1.63).

94. On Jesus's relationship with sinners elsewhere in early Christian literature, see Matt 9:13; Mark 2:17; Luke 5:32; 2 Clem. 2.4; Justin, *1 Apol*. 15.7–8.

95. Prostmeier, *Barnabasbrief*, 247–48.

96. Hvalvik, *Struggle for Scripture and Covenant*, 140. Klevinghaus (*Die theologische Stellung*, 44) thus goes too far when he concludes that it is impossible for Barnabas to take salvation-history seriously.

97. See 2.4–3.6; 4.6b–9a; 5.2.

The repetition of οὐκοῦν in 5.11 and 12 plays a complex rhetorical role in the development of 5.1–14. On the one hand, the conjunctions extend the argument so that it moves beyond the excursive reflections on Israel and the apostles. On the other hand, it brings the reader back to the main argument by linking what follows not only to the Lord's suffering (5.5) but also to the larger theme of endurance that runs throughout 5.1–14. Barnabas begins by reprising what has been said in 5.5–10: the Son of God came in the flesh to complete the sins of those who persecuted the prophets (5.11).[98] Israel's actions are squarely in view. So also is the telic-motif that runs throughout the letter but was especially prevalent in Barn. 4. The sins associated with those who persecuted the prophets reached its end (τὸ τέλειον) as they were summarized (ἀνακεφαλαιώσῃ) in the actions Christ. Barnabas further charges that Israel is responsible for the wounds in Jesus's flesh. Although Jesus endured these blows, Barnabas quotes Zech 13:8 in order to show that God foretold this event. Yet he does not allow one to think that God made his Son suffer unwillingly. Indeed, he says that Jesus wanted to suffer specifically on the cross (5.13). In order to show this, Barnabas cites three verses from scripture as Jesus's own words. The Psalmist's prayer in Ps 21:21 (22:21 MT) petitions God to spare his life from the sword.[99] This verse is interpreted with reference not to death in general but to avoid a specific manner of death. Similarly, the second quotation from the Psalter forms a request for Jesus's flesh to be nailed.[100] The Son's final quotation comes in the words of Isa 50:6–7, where the prophet allows his back to be scourged but sets his face "like a solid rock" (ὡς στερεὰν πέτραν; 5.14).[101]

While Barnabas suggests a general hermeneutical principle with which Barnabas interprets scripture in 5.2, his words in 5.13–14 complicate any simplistic use of that statement within the argument of 5.1–14. Jesus is the speaker in 5.13–14, while God is identified as the speaker in Gen 1:26 (Barn. 5.5). The benefits that come from the servant's death in Isa 53:5 (Barn. 5.2) are addressed "to us," that is, to Barnabas and his audience.

---

98. Similar connections between Jesus's death and the summation of Jewish sin can also be found in Matt 27:25; Barn. 14.5; Diogn. 9.2; Didasc. 5.17; Gos. Pet. 5.17. The text of the Epistle to Diognetus can be found in Wengst, Didache. References to the Didascalia come from Vööbus, Didascalia.

99. While Barnabas employs the verb φεῖσαι, the critical edition of Ps 21:21 (22:21) contains ῥῦσαι.

100. The quotation appears to come from Ps 118:120 (119:120 MT). Foster (Gospel of Peter, 337–38) helpfully compares various statements about Jesus and nails in other early Christian texts (e.g., John 20:25; Gos. Pet. 6.21).

101. Barnabas's citation reads differently from the Old Greek of Isa 50:7. Moreover, the quotation that has been placed in Jesus's mouth contains no reference to the Lord's help in Isa 50:7.

Given the near proximity of Isa 53:5, 7 to the hermeneutical rule in Barn. 5.2, it is best to understand the references to the Lord's slaughter and silence as a reference to Israel's role in Jesus's death. Yet the scriptural prediction of those who killed Jesus only becomes clear in the citation of Zech 13:7 (5.12), where the implied third-person plural subject refers to those who persecuted the prophets (5.11). Jesus's psalmic words in 5.13-14 enable the author to transition to the next section of the argument.

As the consistent focus on Jesus's endurance and suffering shifts again in 6.1-4, Jesus continues speaking in 6.1-2 as in 5.13-14. Barnabas placed Isa 50:6-7 on Jesus's lips in Barn. 5.13-14, and Isa 50:8-9 follows in Barn. 6.1-2. Jesus's prophetic statement is supposed to have been made "then when he gave the commandment" (ὅτε οὖν ἐποίησεν τὴν ἐντολήν; 6.1). It is not immediately obvious what commandment is in view, but ἐντολή in 6.1 is best understood as a reference to what Jesus has already said in 5.13-14 for two reasons. First, since Jesus is the speaker throughout 5.13—6.2, the near context suggests that commandment most naturally refers to the words that Jesus has already said. Second, the broader use of ἐντολή throughout the letter refers regularly to scripture and its fulfillment. Jesus's consumption of sour wine and gall on the cross is understood with reference to the commandment (ἐντολή) in Lev 23:29-30 (7.3). Barnabas likewise finds a commandment when the people are taught not to sow among thorns (9.5). The reason for finding a commandment is closely connected to the scriptural claim that God is the one who is speaking. In the Epistle of Barnabas, commandment is thus not a purely ethical or imperatival figure of speech. Indeed, "the commandments of his teaching" (αἱ ἐντολαὶ τῆς διδαχῆς) are a means by which God indwells the people who comprise the temple (16.9).

The commandment in 6.1 is thus best understood with reference to Jesus's revelatory teaching in 5.13-14. 6.1 extends the Lord's words by taking up Isa 50:8-9. The Lord's speech provides a challenge to would-be opponents. The two rhetorical questions in 6.1 are answered by third-person imperatives that enjoin Jesus's adversaries to oppose him and make note of his status as the Lord's servant. His quotation continues with a warning. These opponents will pass away like a moth-eaten garment.[102] Since Barnabas's opponents are implicitly connected to those who stood against Jesus, they are simultaneously charged with standing on the side of those who were responsible for Jesus's death. Jesus's prophetic warnings against his opponents are brought to bear on Barnabas's own opponents.

---

102. Barnabas's quotation of Isa 50:9 mirrors the text of Isa 50:9 in Codex Sinaiticus and Codex Vaticanus in that it does not contain a second ὡς.

Whereas the opponents will be devoured, Barnabas points to Jesus's incorruption by highlighting stone imagery that is employed in scripture. The introduction of the quotations in 6.2–4 recalls 5.14: Jesus has been set "like a strong stone" (ὡς λίθος ἰσχυρός). Jesus the stone will lie in Zion's foundation as a "cornerstone that is costly, chosen, and precious."[103] This language is reminiscent of Isa 28:16, and the author picks up the consequence of God's choice stone in 6.3: "whoever hopes on him will live forever" (ὅς ἐλπίσει ἐπ' αὐτὸν ζήσεται εἰς τὸν αἰῶνα).[104] The author then seeks to clarify the meaning of these poetic words. It is not that believers' hope should be placed on a stone but rather that the Lord established his flesh in strength (6.3). As the Lord set his face like a rock when enduring the crucifixion, so also in the resurrection Jesus's flesh is formed like a solid rock (6.3; see also Barn. 5.14; Isa 50:7). Two further words are quoted from "the prophet," both of which come from Ps 117 (118 MT). Allusions to Jesus's suffering and vindication are found in the reference to the stone that was rejected by builders but was then used as the chief cornerstone (6.4; Ps 117:22 [118:22 MT]).[105] Moreover, Jesus's resurrection and the hope that is found in it are alluded to in the claim that this is the great and marvelous day that the Lord has made (6.4; Ps 117:24 [118:24 MT]).[106] Barnabas thus moves the argument in 6.1–4 from a focus on Jesus's flesh with reference to incarnation, endurance, and suffering (5.1–14) to include Jesus's resurrection in the flesh and the resultant hope that believers now have.

The series of arguments that runs from 5.1—6.7 begins to draw to a close in 6.5.[107] The author seeks in these verses to write "more simply" (ἁπλούστερον).[108] Such language suggests that what follows draws together

---

103. Barnabas participates in a broader early Christian tradition that understood Jesus as the cornerstone. See especially Rom 9:32–33; 1 Pet 2:4–10. For further discussion of Barnabas's stone imagery in the context of similar imagery elsewhere in the Septuagint and early Christian literature, see Derry, "One Stone on Another," 515–28.

104. The translation for this commentary follows the text of G in reading ὅς ἐλπίσει. S, H, and L read slightly differently: ὁ πιστεύων (*qui crediderit*). G has been followed at this point because it seems more likely that S, H, and L have inserted phraseology here that brings *Barnabas* into closer alignment with Pauline theology.

105. Barnabas quotes this phrase from the Psalms in the same form in which it appears in critical editions of the Old Greek Psalter. See further Rahlfs, *Psalmi*, 286.

106. The inclusion of the adjectives "great and marvelous" in the Greek manuscripts of *Barnabas* is not found in early manuscripts of the Old Greek Psalter. L may attest knowledge of this because L omits the adjectives in its quotation of Ps 117:24 (118:24). For further discussion of the textual form of the Psalter in Barn. 6.4, see Lookadoo, "Form and Function," 216–17.

107. L omits 6.5 and joins 6.4 directly to 6.6. However, 6.5 is included in all of the major Greek witnesses and has been accepted as the earlier text in this commentary.

108. Prinzivalli and Simonetti, *Seguendo Gesù*, 2.520n67.

the chief point that the author desires the audience to understand from what precedes.¹⁰⁹ Barnabas again refers to himself in the first-person at a transitional point in the letter. A similar move was made at the beginning and end of 4.6b–9a. Here the author refers to himself as "a devoted servant of your love" (περίψημα τῆς ἀγάπης ὑμῶν; 6.5). The author furthers a rhetorical tension between his authoritative status as a scriptural interpreter and a self-effacing attitude as a member of the audience who is devoted to caring for them. Barnabas again turns to scripture in order to summarize the argument of 5.1—6.7. He fuses Ps 21:17, 19 (22:17, 19 MT) as a prediction of what Jesus was to endure in his suffering.¹¹⁰ The prophet revealed ahead of time that "a synagogue of evildoers" (συναγωγὴ πονηρευομένων) would surround Jesus like bees around honeycomb. Likewise, they would cast lots for his clothing (6.6).¹¹¹ Although Barnabas's utilization of these words mimics early Christian usage elsewhere in the Gospels, he does not reflect at length on the experience of Jesus on the cross.¹¹² Instead, the point is that Jesus revealed these things beforehand through the prophets. The words were given just before Jesus was "about to be revealed and suffer" (μέλλοντος φανεροῦσθαι καὶ πάσχειν; 6.7). Barnabas then cites Isa 3:9–10 as words that the prophet spoke "to Israel" (ἐπὶ τὸν Ἰσραήλ). He employs this passage to indict the Israelites for putting Jesus to death by binding "the righteous one" (ὁ δίκαιος).¹¹³

The citations in 6.6–7 thus imitate the shape of Barnabas's hermeneutical principle in 5.2. The prophets said some things "to Israel" and other things "to us." Even before he came to earth, Jesus revealed his endurance, suffering, and actions in the flesh. His prior revelation becomes clear in Barnabas's reading of the prophets. Jesus endured suffering so that Barnabas and his audience can be purified by forgiveness of sins (5.1), for their souls (5.5), to make death ineffective (5.6), to demonstrate resurrection from the dead (5.6), to give the promise to the fathers (5.7), to

---

109. The purpose of 6.5–7 is thus for the audience to understand (ἵνα συνιῆτε; 6.5). On the relationship between understanding and knowledge in *Barnabas*, see Prostmeier (*Barnabasbrief*, 206–7), who points out that these concepts overlap and are at least partially synonymous in the letter.

110. Adams and Ehorn, "What is a Composite Citation?" 4–7.

111. Vesco, "La lecture," 10.

112. For example, the reference to Jesus's clothes in 6.6 sounds similar to Matt 27:35; Mark 15:24; Luke 23:34; John 19:24. See further Menken, "Old Testament Quotations," 302.

113. Isaiah 3:10 is cited by Melito, *Pasch.* 72, while Justin offers a fuller textual discussion of this verse in *Dial.* 137.3. See further Kraft, "Barnabas' Isaiah Text and Melito's Paschal Homily," 371–72. Dodson ("Rejection and Redemption," 56–57) observes similarities between the language in Barn. 6.7 and Wis 2.12.

reveal the new people that he is preparing (5.7), and to complete Israel's sin (5.11-12). The emphasis on Jesus's incarnation and death lead the author to consider further Jesus's love for Israel through his teaching and wonders as well as the sinfulness of the disciples who surrounded Jesus (5.8-9). Jesus's endurance, along with the hope that comes through the rejected and resurrected stone (6.1-4), provides the central source of hope for Barnabas and his audience, while these events provoke the author's warning for those who are associated with Israel.

II.4.b. The Land Flowing with Milk and Honey (Barn. 6.8-19)

After recapitulating the main points of the argument in 6.5-7, Barnabas introduces another scriptural quotation in 6.8. The key image in the quotation is the land flowing with milk and honey. The author's continued focus on a single image is the longest sustained reflection in the letter to this point. The length of this passage is comparable to the discussions of food laws (10.1-12), Sabbath (15.1-9), and temple (16.1-10). It has not been immediately obvious to interpreters of the letter how this section fits into 5.1—8.7 and the larger focus of the letter as a whole. For those who have focused on the sources that were employed in *Barnabas* and who identify this passage as coming from a different source from those used in 5.1—6.7 and 7.1—8.7, Barnabas's words in 6.8-19 can be interpreted independently of the context.[114] For those who have devoted attention to the letter as a whole, 6.8-19 is challenging to read within the flow of 5.1—8.7 and contains some motifs that appear to fit loosely with the rest of the letter.[115] Further discussion of the relation of 6.8-19 to the rest of the letter will follow in due course. Before that, though, it will be helpful to trace the argument that Barnabas makes within 6.8-19.

Barnabas identifies Moses as the speaker of the quotation that sparks the exegesis of 6.8-19. He is described as "another prophet" (ὁ ἄλλος προφήτης; 6.8) to distinguish him from the prophetic quotations of Isaiah and the Psalter in 5.13—6.7.[116] Although Moses is the prophetic mouthpiece, the quotation will clarify that the ultimate speaker is God and the

---

114. For views that see 6.8-19 as separate from the context of the letter, see Windisch, *Barnabasbrief*, 326; Wengst, *Tradition und Theologie*, 16, 29.

115. On the integration of 6.8-19 into the larger context of the letter, see Hvalvik, *Struggle for Scripture and Covenant*, 180-82.

116. The quotations in 5.13 (Ps 21:21 [22:21 MT]); 6.2 (Isa 28:16); 6.4 (Ps 117:22 [118:22 MT]); 6.6 (Ps 21:17, 19 [22:17, 19 MT]; 117:12 [118:12 MT]); and 6.7 (Isa 3:9-10) are all introduced as coming from the prophet (ὁ προφητεύων [5.13]; ὁ προφήτης [6.2, 4, 6, 7]). See further Prostmeier, *Barnabasbrief*, 262.

audience is "them" (αὐτοῖς). Moses's words were thus first directed to Israel. The quotation in 6.8 is not found within the Torah in precisely the form that Barnabas gives. It contains phrases that appear in Exod 33:1, 3; Lev 20:24; and Deut 1:25.[117] The imperative is to "enter into the good land that the Lord swore to Abraham, Isaac, and Jacob." God instructs hearers to inherit the land, and the land is further described as a "land flowing with milk and honey."[118]

Barnabas's interpretation of the land (γῆ) drives the discussion through 6.16. Yet although 6.9–16 holds together as an extended explanation of the land in Moses's words, Barnabas will end up offering two definitions of the land. The first account appears in 6.9 and defines the land christologically: the land is Jesus, who revealed himself and suffered in the flesh. The second definition is worked out in 6.14–16. It also interprets the command to enter the land with regard to Jesus, but the command is read with a view to the Son's recreative work in God's people.

Barnabas begins his exegesis by addressing the audience with a question and an imperative. "Now what does knowledge say? Learn" (τί δὲ λέγει ἡ γνῶσις; μάθετε; 6.9). The author then reinterprets the Mosaic command in terms of Jesus. Readers who have knowledge will recognize that Moses's words are an instruction to place their hope in "Jesus who is about to be revealed to you in the flesh" (τὸν ἐν σαρκὶ μέλλοντα φανεροῦσθαι ὑμῖν Ἰησοῦν). This interpretation highlights the place of Israel as the audience. Moses gave this instruction before Jesus's self-revelation as an incarnate and suffering Son. Barnabas justifies this interpretation by defining human beings in terms of the land. To be human is to be "suffering earth" (γῆ πάσχουσα) because Adam was created from the face of the earth (6.9). Barnabas relies on a Hebrew wordplay in the narrative of Gen 2:4–24 between Adam/human (אדם) and earth (אדמה).[119] Since Christ revealed himself in the incarnation, he likewise underwent suffering (5.1–14; 6.5–7).

Barnabas thus defines the land christologically in 6.9, but he exhibits a continued interest in the interpretation of the land in what follows. He praises the Lord because he has revealed his secrets (οἱ κρύφιοι αὐτοῦ) to Barnabas and his audience (6.10). This is evident due to a prophetic saying

---

117. Barnard, "A Note on *Barnabas* 6,8–17," 263.

118. Given the centrality of the quotation in 6.8 for what follows in 6.8–19, it may be helpful to include both the text and a translation here: "'Behold,' thus says the Lord God, 'enter into the good land that the Lord swore to Abraham, Isaac, and Jacob, and inherit it, a land flowing with milk and honey'" (ἰδού, τάδε λέγει κύριος ὁ θεός, εἰσέλθατε εἰς τὴν γῆν τὴν ἀγαθήν, ἣν ὤμοσεν κύριος τῷ Ἀβραὰμ καὶ Ἰσαὰκ καὶ Ἰακώβ, καὶ κατακληρονομήσατε αὐτήν, γῆν ῥέουσαν γάλα καὶ μέλι; 6.8).

119. Hegedus, "Midrash and the Letter of Barnabas," 22.

that only the wise, understanding, and loving can perceive what the Lord is doing.[120] Barnabas pursues a further interpretation of the Mosaic word because he and the audience are being recreated by God through the forgiveness of sins (6.11).[121] To legitimize this claim, the author notes two of God's speeches about creation.[122] First, the author cites Gen 1:26 and 28 to show that the creation of human beings was spoken by the Father while the Son was present and that human beings were created to rule over the land (6.12).[123] The Son's presence justifies the first-person plural verbs in the Genesis story and forms an analogy to the new creation anticipated in 6.11. This prefigurement is confirmed when the Lord says that he will make the last things like the first (6.13). Since human beings do not rule over the land and a second creation is also in view, Barnabas asserts that Moses has this second creation in mind when he tells the people to enter into the land.[124] The combination of citations in 6.12–13 works together in Barnabas's understanding of what it means to enter the land.

This interpretive understanding of God's creative statements leads the author back to a fresh understanding of the land. Barnabas and his audience are being recreated just as the Lord spoke when he promised to replace stony hearts with fleshly hearts (6.14). Barnabas borrows language found in Ezekiel, but the form of the text that he quotes does not appear in Ezekiel.[125] Nevertheless, Jesus can transform the hearts of the audience into fleshly hearts by entering into the hearts of his people in order to make them into a holy temple (6.15).[126] Believers become a holy temple as the Lord takes up residence in their newly restored fleshly hearts. In order to cement this interpretation, Barnabas again places the Psalter on Jesus's lips. A two-part quotation follows in which Jesus asks how he will appear before the Lord (Ps 41:3 [42:3 MT]) and answers it by quoting a text that resembles Ps 21:23

120. Although Barnabas identifies this saying as a "parable of the Lord" that comes from a "prophet," the pre-Barnabean provenance of this statement is unknown. Clement of Alexandria cites this parable twice (*Strom.* 5.63.1–6 [10]; 6.65.2 [8]).

121. Koch, "Taufinterpretationen," 835.

122. Hvalvik (*Struggle for Scripture and Covenant*, 112) rightly contrasts the "we" who are addressed in 6.12 with "Israel" in 6.7.

123. Appealing to Barnabas's quotation of Gen 1:26 among other passages, Korn puts Barnabas's understanding of the Son well: "Christus selber gehört völlig auf die Seite Gottes" (Korn, *Nachwirkungen der Christusmystik*, 39). Of course, Barnabas also highlights the incarnation, particularly in his insistence on the suffering of the Son in 5.1—6.7; and 7.1—8.7.

124. Dahl, "La terre," 66.

125. Derry, "One Stone on Another," 519. Note the similarities in language found in Ezek 11:19 and 36:26.

126. See also 4.11.

(22:23 MT).[127] Jesus will confess his Father "in the congregation of my brothers and sisters" (ἐν ἐκκλησίᾳ ἀδελφῶν μου) and promises to sing psalms "in the midst of the congregation of the saints" (ἀναμέσον ἐκκλησίας ἁγίων).[128] In the context of 6.14–16, the prepositions ἐν and ἀναμέσον in 6.16 suggest that Jesus will indwell believers, not merely be present among them. It is by means of this indwelling that believers are likewise brought into the good land. The good land is both Jesus's flesh (Barn. 6.9) and the believers in whom Jesus lives as a temple (Barn. 6.14–16).[129]

Barnabas's multifaceted explanation of what it means to enter the land has not yet answered what it means that the land flows with milk and honey. He turns to answer this question in 6.17–19. He notes that a child is made alive (ζωοποιεῖται) first by honey and then by milk (6.17). Believers are likewise made alive (ζωοποιούμενοι) by two things: the faith of the promise and the word. While milk and honey are thus equated with faith and the word, Barnabas links this interpretation of milk and honey back to the new creation themes that pervade 6.8–19. As believers are made alive, they will live "ruling over the earth" (κατακυριεύοντες τῆς γῆς). The author echoes the language found in God's speech in Gen 1:28, which he immediately quotes again (6.18).[130] Since human beings do not presently have authority over the beasts, fish, and birds, Barnabas urges the audience to understand what was said to them earlier (6.18; see 6.12–13). Barnabas and his audience will become heirs of the Lord's covenant when they are brought to completion (6.19). Although no imperative follows, the audience is implicitly urged to continue to live rightly as they seek to understand the secrets that God has revealed to them in order that they may be perfected and receive their inheritance from the covenant.[131]

127. However, the verbs in Barnabas's citation are found in Ps 107:4 (108:4 MT). Barn. 6.16 may be regarded as a composite text. See further Albl, "*Testimonia* Hypothesis," 194. Edwin Hatch (*Essays*, 180–81) suggested that the freedom to recombine phrases from the Psalter was a result of an existence within early Christianity that "breathed the Spirit."

128. This psalm is also cited as Jesus's words in Heb 2:12. On the text and usage of Ps 21:23 (22:23 MT) in Hebrews, see Steyn, *A Quest*, 148–58. See also Justin, *Dial.* 98.5; 106.2; Skarsaune, *Proof from Prophecy*, 126.

129. Lookadoo, "Form and Function," 225–26.

130. It is striking that Barnabas quotes Gen 1:28 in different forms in 6.12, 18. In 6.12, the author cites Gen 1:28 as follows: "increase and multiply and fill the earth" (αὐξάνεσθε καὶ πληθύνεσθε καὶ πληρώσατε τὴν γῆν; 6.12). The text is given in a variant form in 6.18: "and let them increase and be multiplied and rule over the fish" (καὶ αὐξανέσθωσαν καὶ πληθυνέσθωσαν καὶ ἀρχέτωσαν τῶν ἰχθύων; 6.18). The former is closer to the text of old Greek Gen 1:28. For further discussion of the translation of Old Greek Gen 1:28, see Wevers, *Notes on the Greek Text of Genesis*, 16.

131. In a larger study of the church in the Apostolic Fathers, Carleton Paget ("The

While the focus on land and creation hold 6.8–19 together, the passage has proved challenging to incorporate into the rest of the letter and to understand on its own merits. Windisch regards 6.8–19 as an interpolation (Einschaltung) that distracts from the otherwise consistent reflections on the incarnation and passion of Christ in 5.1—8.7.[132] Based on his account of Barnabas's sources, Wengst argues that Barnabas has worked the material now contained in 6.8–19 into another piece of tradition that is evident in 5.5–7, 11b—6.4; 7.2.[133] In support of their source theories, Wengst and Windisch both underline the oddity of 6.8–19 within the larger context. Others have attempted to locate the source or, more loosely stated, the tradition that Barnabas used in 6.8–19 in second-century baptismal or catechetical practices.[134] If so, Barnabas may provide second-century evidence for the use of milk and honey in baptismal rites.[135] However, "there is nothing in the text itself that demands, or even strongly suggests, this interpretation," that is, an interpretation in terms of baptism.[136]

Questions about the origins of the tradition underlying 6.8–19 are important, but for the purposes of this commentary it is more significant to consider the function of the passage within *Barnabas*. 6.8–19 forms a distinct unit, but it is connected to the rest of the letter by means of rhetorical links and creation themes. The most obvious rhetorical link when reading through 5.1—8.7 is the description of Moses as "another" (ἄλλος) prophet (6.8), thereby distinguishing Moses's words from the psalmic and Isaianic prophetic quotations in 6.6–7. Barnabas blesses "our Lord" (ὁ κύριος ἡμῶν) for granting knowledge "to us" (ἐν ἡμῖν) in order to understand God's secrets (6.10), and the first-person language fits with the

---

Vision of the Church," 205) encapsulates the point well: "Salvation was not brought about solely by entry into the Church (*Barn.* 4.14; 6.17f), and once baptized, the call was to persevere in the face of a final judgement (*1 Clem.* 35.4; *2 Clem.* 7.1; *Barn.* 4.11)."

132. Windisch, *Barnabasbrief*, 326.

133. Wengst, *Tradition und Theologie*, 29. Elsewhere Wengst (*Tradition und Theologie*, 16) classifies 6.11–19 as an "Ad-hoc-Bildung" (ad-hoc formation).

134. Barnard, "A Note on *Barnabas* 6,8–17," 263–67; Dahl, "La terre," 70; Schille, "Zur urchristlichen Tauflehre," 31–52; Koch, "Taufinterpretationen," 834–37.

135. The imagery of entering into the new land, the language of new creation, and the allusions to milk and honey provide evidence in favor of this interpretation. See *Trad. ap.* 21.28, 33–37; Tertullian, *Cor.* 3.3; *Marc.* 1.14.3; Jerome, *Lucif.* 4. Quotations from the *Traditio apostolica* come from the translation in Bradshaw, Johnson, and Phillips, *Apostolic Tradition*. Quotations from Tertullian's *De corona militis* come from Fontaine, *Tertullien, De corona*. Quotations from Tertullian's *Adversus Marcionem* come from Evans, *Tertullian: Adversus Marcionem*. Quotations from Jerome's *Altercatio Luciferiani et orthodoxi* come from Canellis, *Débat entre un luciférien et un orthodoxe*.

136. Kraft, *Barnabas*, 99.

interpretive principle set forth in 5.2. Some words are said to Israel, but the words of 6.8–19 belong to Barnabas and his audience. Creation language is also a motif that runs intermittently throughout 5.1—6.19. The quotations of Gen 1:26 and 28 in 6.12 recall the quotation of Gen 1:26 in 5.5.[137] Barnabas is clear in both places that the Father addresses these words to the Son.[138] His reflections in 6.8–19 come in response to the continued reflections on the Lord's suffering at the hands of human beings.[139] If the question in 5.5 centered on how the Lord could endure suffering at the hands of humans whom he created, the next citation of Gen 1:26 extends the topic of creation to include new creation (6.12–13) and makes the topic of direct relevance to the audience by appealing to their restoration (6.11, 14–16).[140] The third reference to material from Gen 1:26–28 points to the limitations of human authority over the natural world as an indication that the new creation is yet to be completed (Barn. 6.18). Although the argument in 6.8–19 appears in some ways to contain a unit on its own, this section fits rhetorically and thematically within the letter.[141]

How, then, should readers assess the flow and contribution of 6.8–19 within 5.1—8.7? The flow of 6.8–19 within the larger section may be best conceived of in terms of a digression. Since Barnabas maintains a consistent focus on the Lord's death and resurrection in 5.1—6.7 and 7.1—8.7, the discussion of entry into the land in terms of Jesus and new creation represents a departure from the main topic of 5.1—8.7. Nevertheless, the links between 6.8–19 and the rest of the letter strongly suggest that the digressive material can be situated within the flow of the argument. Since the argument in 5.1–14 underlines that Jesus's suffering occurred for the benefit of believers and due to Israel's violence while 6.1–4 continues the story to include Jesus's resurrection and vindication in the flesh, the digression in 6.8–19 can be read with a view to the recreation that the resurrected Lord promises to those who hope in him as a result of his suffering. Barnabas makes three contributions in 6.8–19. First, he continues to show the

---

137. Hanson, "Activity of the Pre-Existent Christ," 156.

138. Martín ("L'interpretazione allegorica," 175n11) points out, however, that the emphasis in the rest of the interpretation of 6.12 falls on the image in which human beings are created.

139. The definition of human beings as "suffering earth" (6.9) may also provide an additional link to the descriptions of the Lord's suffering in 5.5, 13; 6.7. See also Hvalvik, *Struggle for Scripture and Covenant*, 180.

140. "Urzeit und Endzeit gehören zusammen" (Lindeskog, "Schöpfer und Schöpfung," 635).

141. One could also note similarities between the temple language in 4.11; 6.15; 16.1–10 and between the creation language in 6.8–19; 15.1–9.

efficacy of his emphasis that the promises of scripture find their fulfillment when applied "to us." Second, Barnabas develops his focus on the suffering of Jesus by calling to mind the benefits of new creation that result from his death. Finally, he reminds readers in 6.18-19 that these promises are yet to be effected and will only become final when believers are completed (6.19). The reflections in 6.8-19 provide further motivation for the ethical comments in the rest of the letter.

Two additional matters should be considered before leaving 6.8-19 behind. First, the author quotes scripture often in 6.8-19.[142] Two of these quotations are repeated and prove to be the interpretive focal points of 6.8-19. The repetition of the command to enter into the land (Barn. 6.8, 10, 17) provides the passage with focus, while Gen 1:26 and 28 (Barn. 6.12, 18) indicate that the key to interpreting this passage rightly is found in creation themes. Moreover, several quotations are found in unusual forms. The instruction to enter into the good land in Barn. 6.8 is most like Exod 33:1, 3, although similar language is also found in Lev 20:24 and Deut 1:25. Barnabas also refers to a prophet who quotes a "parable of the Lord" (παραβολὴ κυρίου): "Who will understand except the one who is wise and understanding and loves their Lord?" (6.10). The prophetic origins of this proverb are unclear. The Lord's declaration, "I am making the last things like the first" (Barn. 6.13), likewise does not appear in scripture in its current form. Although it contains language similar to Isa 43:18-19 and 46.10, the precise way in which Barnabas came by this sentence remains unknown.

The oft-repeated references to scripture—along with the fact that the origins of some quotations can be difficult to pin down—leads to a second issue deserving of attention in 6.8-19, namely, the unusual role of "knowledge" (γνῶσις) in 6.9.[143] Knowledge is required in order to interpret the manifold scriptural quotations in 6.8-19. The personified presentation of γνῶσις results in Barnabas depicting knowledge as able to speak to readers in a way that enables them to learn. On this understanding, knowledge is not something to be possessed but something from which to learn. Knowledge is closely related to scriptural interpretation. Indeed, knowledge is what enables readers to understand how Barnabas interprets the command to

---

142. In addition to the passages cited in the remainder of the paragraph, see also Ezek 11:19; 36:26 (Barn. 6.14); Ps 41:3 (42:3 MT; Barn. 6.16); Isa 49:5 (Barn. 6.16); Ps 21:23 (22:23 MT; Barn. 6.16); 107:4 (108:4 MT; Barn. 6.16).

143. The use of knowledge in 6.9 has been widely discussed in studies of *Barnabas*. For example, Kraft (*Didache*, 24) appeals to 6.9 in order to show that Barnabas discusses "exegetical knowledge" over and against "ethical knowledge." Similarly, Edwards defines knowledge in *Barnabas* in terms of "the proper interpretation of scripture" (*Gospel*, 30n71).

enter into the good land (6.8–9). Yet knowledge is immediately connected to salvation.[144] The γνῶσις that Barnabas describes leads to active understanding, since it interprets the command to enter into the good land as an instruction to hope in Jesus. Knowledge thus provides the understanding that allows believers to perceive the scriptures correctly and to live in a right way as a result.[145] Knowledge should result in a right lifestyle that demonstrates salvation and enters into the flesh of the suffering Jesus while waiting for the perfection that will come about in the new creation.

II.4.c. The Sacrifice and Scapegoat (Barn. 7.1–11)

Following the digression about entering the land in 6.8–19, Barnabas clearly marks his return to the main line of argument. He uses the inferential conjunction οὐκοῦν along with the direct address of the audience as "children of gladness" (τέκνα εὐφροσύνης) to indicate a transition. The command to understand that the Lord revealed all things to us beforehand continues to separate the interpretations of Barnabas and his community from the interpretations of Barnabas's opponents. Yet understanding is not a purely intellectual or interpretive exercise. The purpose of the Lord's revelation was so that the audience would recognize to whom they should give thanks and praise (7.1). In order to move the letter away from the digression on new creation (6.8–19), the author sets up a contrast regarding the high status of the Son and his suffering. If the Son suffered even though he was Lord and judge of all, he suffered to bring life to Barnabas and his audience. The Son of God was unable to suffer "except on our account" (εἰ μὴ δι' ἡμᾶς; 7.2). In addition to setting up the discussion of Jesus's passion in what follows, the author also resumes here the discussion of suffering "for us" that occupied much of 5.1–14.

The extension of an earlier argument is enhanced by the conjunctions in 7.3.[146] The author's introduction of the crucifixion with "moreover" (ἀλλὰ καί) indicates that he is adding information about something that the audience already knows. The information regards Jesus's crucifixion and the sour wine and vinegar that were given to Jesus while he was on the cross. The specific nature of what Jesus endured was already under discussion in 5.13–14

---

144. Prostmeier and Lona, *Epistola Barnabae*, 64.

145. It is also important to observe that the use of γνῶσις is closely related to revelatory terminology. The word γνῶσις is thus closely associated with what can be known about scripture when it is interpreted in the correct way by Barnabas.

146. On 7.1—8.7 as an extension of "the passion apologetic" of the previous two chapters, see Rhodes, *Epistle of Barnabas*, 56.

with regard to the blows and flogging that Jesus endured. As in 5.13–14, the significant point that Barnabas wants to make in 7.3–5 is that Jesus's consumption of sour wine and vinegar was revealed beforehand. Moreover, the priests were the instrument that God used to reveal Jesus's drink. Barnabas goes on to cite the commandment that he has in mind: "Whoever does not keep the fast will certainly die." These words resemble instructions in Lev 23:29–30 that were given about self-humbling and works done on the Day of Atonement. The author brings these words to bear on the practice of fasting during the Day of Atonement and asserts that the Lord instructed this practice because he was coming to offer his spirit as a sacrifice for sin (7.3). By doing this, Jesus not only takes the place of the Yom Kippur sacrifice but also becomes a second Isaac on the altar.[147]

Barnabas turns to a word "in the prophet" (ἐν τῷ προφήτῃ) that is likewise concerned with practices on the Day of Atonement.[148] The command is to eat the goat that was offered during the fast. More specifically, "the priests alone" (οἱ ἱερεῖς μόνοι) should eat the intestines "with sour wine" (μετὰ ὄξους). The sour wine consumed by the priests when eating the sacrifice is then related to Jesus's own consumption of sour wine. Jesus speaks directly to the priests in 7.5 and provides the key to the argument. Since the priests were about to offer Jesus vinegar and sour wine to drink, they are instructed to drink it alone while the people fast. Jesus's interpretation of the priests' actions on Yom Kippur show that he must suffer because of the priests (7.5). His words thus give christological meaning to the scriptures about priestly rituals in 7.3–4.

Barnabas introduces a related discussion in 7.6–11. There is no logical marker or linking conjunction. The author simply instructs the audience to "pay attention to the things that were commanded" (7.6). The imperative marks a straightforward extension of the argument in 7.3–5. Sour wine and vinegar are no longer in view. Rather, the author is spurred by the reference to the goat in 7.4 and reflects in more detail on the goats that were utilized in the Yom Kippur rituals.

The audience's eyes are drawn to the scriptural instruction to take two goats and allow the priest to offer one goat as a whole burnt offering. Although the quotation is given in a way that suggests that Barnabas views these words as authoritative, the text differs markedly from what is said in Lev 16. Nevertheless, the command to take two goats and to offer one of them "for

---

147. On Isaac typology in the context of the Day of Atonement within early Jewish literature, see Prigent and Kraft, *Épître de Barnabé*, 131n2.

148. The passages that most resemble Barnabas's quotations come from Num 29:11 and Exod 29:32–33.

sins" (ὑπὲρ ἁμαρτιῶν; 7.6) is reminiscent of Lev 16:7 and 9.[149] The first goat to which Barnabas draws attention is the goat that should be offered as a whole burnt offering (7.6), but the second goat receives more detailed comments. The most significant description of this goat is that it is cursed (ἐπικατάρατος; 7.7). The ritual of what happens to the cursed goat is then outlined in some detail in 7.8. People are instructed to spit on the goat, to pierce it, and to wrap scarlet wool around its head. One person is charged to carry the goat into the desert. While in the desert, the one who has brought the goat should remove the scarlet wool and place it in a shrub known as Rachē.

Barnabas portrays each of the goats as a type of Jesus. The goat that is killed for the whole burnt offering is like Jesus because it is "for the altar" (ἐπὶ τὸ θυσιαστήριον; 7.9). The interpretation of the cursed goat is again described in more detail than the goat to be sacrificed. The cursed goat is like Jesus because it was crowned even while it was cursed. Barnabas understands this in terms of Jesus's vindication before those who had put him to death. Just as the scapegoat wore a red woolen crown, so Jesus will wear a scarlet robe around his flesh.[150] The people who cursed him will be amazed as they remember the person whom they crucified and who claimed to be the Son of God. Barnabas probes this matter further in 7.10 by simultaneously comparing Jesus to the goat that was cursed and the goat that was sacrificed. Jesus is like both goats because they are equally fine in form. Barnabas highlights the wonder that people will experience when they see him coming "then" (τότε), at a later time (7.10). This later time is not clearly defined in 7.9–10, but it refers to Jesus's second advent—a time when Jesus will return with a crown. Barnabas draws his christological interpretation of the goats from Yom Kippur to a close when he reinforces that these are a type of Jesus, "who is destined to suffer" (μέλλοντος πάσχειν; 7.10). On Barnabas's interpretation, Jesus's two appearances can not be neatly mapped onto the two goats.

Barnabas draws this section to a close by asking about another feature of the Yom Kippur ritual, namely, the scarlet wool that is placed in the thorns (7.11). He finds in this act a type of Jesus being set in the church. The logic for Barnabas's interpretation draws readers into becoming an

---

149. The goat is similarly to be offered "for sin" (περὶ ἁμαρτίας) in Lev 16:9. Although the subject matter is similar, the textual form of Barn. 7.6 differs markedly from Lev 16:7 and 9.

150. Red cloth is also utilized with reference to Jesus and Israel's scriptures in 1 Clem. 12 with regard to the story of Rahab's rescue from Jericho by means of a red cord (Josh 2:1–24; 6:17, 22–25). The red cord is interpreted by the author with reference to Jesus's blood and is understood as a sign of Rahab's faith and prophecy (1 Clem. 12.7–8). See further Carleton Paget, "Old Testament in the Apostolic Fathers," 465–66.

active part of the argumentative logic. Whoever wants to take up the wool must suffer because of the thorns. It is only by undergoing such affliction that believers can obtain the scarlet wool from out of the Rachē shrub. Just as the suffering of the Son has made Barnabas's audience alive (7.2), so also must believers experience suffering in order to take up Christ (7.11). To support this interpretation of Yom Kippur imagery, Barnabas quotes an otherwise unknown word of Jesus in which Jesus says that anyone who wants to touch his kingdom must receive him in affliction and suffering.[151] Barnabas's reflections on the Day of Atonement lead him to locate believers within the actions of that day.

In a passage that interprets the suffering of the Son "for us" with an eye to the Day of Atonement, it is striking that paraenetic elements are sprinkled throughout 7.1–11. Believers are urged to praise the Lord for revealing these things to us (7.1). They should believe that the Son of God suffered only for believers. No other reason is sufficient for his suffering (7.2). The praise and steadfast belief in 7.1–2 give way to instructions to join in his suffering when it comes (7.11). Barnabas does not give his closing paraenesis in the form of an imperative. Yet it is only in suffering that believers can truly take up Jesus as the scarlet wool. The paraenetic intentions become clear when one accounts for the language of necessity (δεῖ) and the target audience of those who want (ὅς ἐὰν θέλῃ) to take the red wool and who want (οἱ θέλοντες) to see Jesus and touch his kingdom. These instructions evoke an immediacy between readers and their encounter with scripture by placing them alongside Jesus and outlining the necessity that they join him in suffering.

Barnabas's argument relies heavily upon typology, a form of argument whose name derives from a Greek word (τύπος), which has to do with an impression or pattern made by a blow and is often defined with an eye toward continuity between Jewish scripture and early Christian fulfilment.[152] Yet this term cannot be defined quite so simply in the Epistle of Barnabas. Barnabas utilizes the word τύπος four times in Barn. 7 (7.3,

---

151. James Hardy Ropes argues that Barnabas is not quoting Jesus at this point in the letter (*Die Sprüche Jesu*, 17–18). However, it is difficult to avoid the conclusion that Barnabas has inserted a citation that he places in Jesus's mouth, even if the citation is somewhat formulaic in nature (Vielhauer, *Geschichte*, 618). In other words, the formula with which Barnabas closes this section of the letter is similar to that of a citation. While the words support Barnabas's argument and draw strongly upon the context of 5.1—7.11, it seems best to interpret 7.11 as an attempt to strengthen the argument by appealing directly to Jesus's words. Since these words are not known elsewhere, Ehrman and Pleše rightly place this verse in the collection of Agrapha—sayings attributed to Jesus that are otherwise unrecorded ("Agrapha," 358–59).

152. On Barnabas's hermeneutic, see Dawson, *Allegorical Readers*, 15–17; Dawson, *Christian Figural Reading*, 12–13; Hurtado, *Lord Jesus Christ*, 572; Johnson, "Interpretive Hierarchies," 702–6; Rothschild, "Epistle of Barnabas," 191–201.

7, 10, 11). Each of these usages indicate that something about Jesus was revealed beforehand, whether through Isaac (7.3), the scapegoat (7.7, 10), or the scarlet wool (7.11). The word is employed to similar effect elsewhere in the letter.[153] Yet the word is not always used with reference to prior revelation. The audience that is being renewed by the Son's work is described in 6.11. Barnabas claims there that Jesus "made us into a different model" (ἐποίησεν ἡμᾶς ἄλλον τύπον; 6.11). Fundamental to Barnabas's use of the word τύπος, then, is not a perceived connection between a prior scriptural sign and an event in the life of Jesus or his followers. Rather, Barnabas employs the word with an eye to a more basic meaning of the term by observing forms, models, and patterns that can be linked from Jewish scripture to the audience but which can also be drawn with broader reference to Jesus without emphasizing scriptural precedent.

While such language in Barn. 7 portrays Jesus as the true sign that was revealed by the model of Yom Kippur, the author redefines traditions surrounding the Day of Atonement in terms of Jesus. In so doing, he also bears witness to traditions associated with the Day of Atonement in other early Jewish and early Christian texts. Barnabas refers to fasting and quotes a commandment to the effect that anyone who does not fast will die. Harsh penalties for failing to keep the Day of Atonement properly are found in Lev 23:29–30, but these are in relation to working and not humbling oneself. Barnabas refers to the Day of Atonement with regard specifically to fasting. Philo and Josephus likewise refer to the Day of Atonement as a fast.[154] Barnabas's allusion to fasting on the Day of Atonement falls in line with traditions that are not found in Leviticus but are attested in Second Temple texts. When the author refers to eating the goat that has been offered, he again breaks with what is written in Lev 16:27, in which the goat that is offered on Yom Kippur is burned outside of the camp. Rather, Barnabas may have some knowledge of a tradition of eating the goat that is mentioned in m. Menaḥ. 11.7.[155]

---

153. See Barn. 8.1 (2x); 12.2, 5, 6; 13.5.

154. See Josephus, A.J. 17.165, 167; 18.94; Philo, Decal. 159; Mos. 2.23; a 1.168, 186; 2.41, 193, 194. See also 1QpHab XI, 7–8; LAB 13.6; Acts 27:9. All quotations from Josephus's works come from Niese, Flavii Iosephi opera. Quotations from 1QpHab are from Trever, Scrolls. Quotations from LAB are found in Jacobson, Commentary. On names for the Day of Atonement in early Jewish literature, see Stökl Ben Ezra, Impact of Yom Kippur, 15–17.

155. Hegedus, "Midrash and the Letter of Barnabas," 23; Stökl Ben Ezra, "Fasting," 174. References to the Mishnah come from Blackman, Mishnayoth. The tradition in m. Menaḥ. 11.7 may also be evident in Philo, Spec. leg. 1.190, although a textual issue in the Philonic manuscript tradition makes it difficult to say for certain.

While these verses bear witness to Yom Kippur practices found in early Jewish texts, the passage can also be fruitfully compared to passion traditions in early Christian literature.[156] The most obvious of these traditions concerns the offering of a drink to Jesus while on the cross. Although the meanings that the Evangelists ascribe to this action differ, Jesus receives something to drink in Matthew, Mark, Luke, and John (Matt 27:48; Mark 15:36; Luke 23:36–37; John 19:28–30). As in Barn. 7.3, Jesus is offered both sour wine and gall in Gos. Pet. 5.16. Whereas Gos. Pet. 5.17 indicates that those who carried out Jesus's death fulfilled all things (ἐπλήρωσαν πάντα), Barn. 7.3–5 is closer to the Evangelists' presentation in which Jesus is the subject of fulfillment. The New Testament accounts portray his drinking as a fulfillment of Ps 68:22 (69:22 MT). Although Barnabas demonstrates no explicit knowledge of Ps 68, he partakes in a larger tradition of interpreting Jesus's drinking on the cross in terms of scripture. For Barnabas, however, the scriptures are related not to the Psalms but to the Torah, especially traditions related to Yom Kippur. Jesus's words in Barn. 7.5 further the interpretation of the sour wine and gall in terms of the Day of Atonement while also contributing to the theme of prior revelation that was announced in 1.7.

Similarities between descriptions of the Day of Atonement in *Barnabas* and Lev 16 are closest in Barn. 7.6–8. The author's scriptural quotations instruct the people to take two goats and to allow the priest to kill one while releasing the other (Barn. 7.6–7). The scapegoat that is released should be sent into the desert (Barn. 7.8). Moses likewise told the Israelites to take two goats, to kill one, and to release the other. The method of choosing was to be by casting lots (Lev 16:7–10). The goat that was released was to be sent into the desert after Aaron confessed Israel's sins over it (Lev 16:21).[157] However, the similar appearances of the goats, the abuse of the goat, and the scarlet thread are nowhere to be found in Lev 16. Barnabas bears witness to one way of interpreting the Torah instructions regarding Yom Kippur in which the two goats had to be similar in appearance (m. Yoma 6.1; b. Yoma 62b).[158] His report about the scapegoat's abuse (Barn. 7.8) not only links well with the Isaianic description of Jesus (Barn. 5.14 [Isa 50:6–7]) but is also attested in a later Mishnaic text. The scapegoat in m. Yoma 6.4 was to have its hair pulled on the way out of Jerusalem. A similar tradition to the Barnabean scarlet thread around the scapegoat's head is likewise attested when describing the preparation of the scapegoat in m. Yoma 4.2.

156. Links between fasting and the Day of Atonement can also be found in early Christian literature, on which, see Stökl Ben Ezra, "Biblical Yom Kippur," 498–502.

157. Hurtado, *Lord Jesus Christ*, 572.

158. All translations of the Babylonian Talmud come from Neusner, *Babylonian Talmud*.

Atonement theology plays an important role in some early Christian texts,[159] and the author of the Epistle of Barnabas is not alone among second-century members of the Jesus-movement in mentioning extra-canonical traditions.[160] Justin also refers to the similarity of the goats in his christological interpretation of Yom Kippur (*Dial.* 40.4). A fragmentary commentary of Hippolytus on Prov 30:31 (LXX) describes Jesus as a goat crowned with scarlet wool.[161] Tertullian highlights the similar appearances of the goats while also mentioning that the scapegoat was to be spit upon and to have a scarlet thread tied around it (*Marc.* 3.7.7–8; *Jud.* 14.9–10).[162] Like Barnabas, Tertullian mentions that the scapegoat was to be cursed (ἐπικατάρατος; Barn. 7.7; *maledictus*; *Marc.* 3.7.7; *Jud.* 14.9). Although neither Tertullian nor Barnabas make explicit mention of why they use this word, they may participate in an early Christian exegetical tradition of Deut 21:23. Perhaps the best-known interpretation of Deut 21:23 along these lines comes from Gal 3:10–14, where Paul interprets Jesus's death on the cross as a curse of the Torah through which the blessings of Abraham are extended to gentiles. Despite the use of quotations whose origins in scripture are difficult to pinpoint with precision, Barn. 7.3–4 and 6–8 demonstrate an awareness of traditions related to Yom Kippur that are attested elsewhere in early Jewish and early Christian literature.

Barnabas is not writing to inform his audience about how to conduct the Yom Kippur ritual but instead to interpret Jesus's death in terms of the Day of Atonement.[163] The theological contribution of this passage should thus be regarded as preeminent when interpreting the letter, while some of the unique elements of the passage can be clarified alongside the previous comparison to other ancient texts. These verses further the anti-cultic interpretation of the Torah found throughout the letter as well as the blame of the Jews for Jesus's death. Although Barnabas shares a knowledge of traditions about the Day of Atonement that are found in other texts, the Great

---

159. For first-century statements of atonement theology, see e.g., John 1:29, 34; Rom 3:25–26; Heb 5:1–10:18; 1 Pet 2:22–24; 1 John 2:1–2; 4:10. For further discussions of atonement concepts in documents that are now included in the New Testament, see Eberhardt, *Kultmetaphorik und Christologie*; Hengel, *Atonement*; Hengel, "Stellvertretende Sühnetod Jesu," 1–25, 135–47; Stuhlmacher, *Reconciliation*.

160. For the possibility of a source underlying some or all of these citations, see the discussions in Prigent, *Testimonia*, 99–110; Skarsaune, *Proof from Prophecy*, 307–10; Wengst, *Tradition*, 30–33.

161. The text is found in Richard, "Fragments."

162. All quotations of Tertullian, *Adversus Judaeos* come from Tränkle, *Edition*.

163. Barnabas, like Aristides *Apol.* 14.4, offers a strictly figurative interpretation of Yom Kippur. For the text of Aristides's *Apology*, see Pouderon and Pierre, *Aristide, Apologie*.

Fast is interpreted by Barnabas solely with a view to Jesus and without any regard for its practice or validity prior to the incarnation.[164] For Barnabas, the Jews have misinterpreted these texts and prove to be the primary actors in putting Jesus to death. Justin and Tertullian employ their christological interpretations of Yom Kippur to similar effect.[165]

Barnabas differs, however, in the degree to which he distinguishes between the two goats. Justin interprets the scapegoat as a prefigurement of Jesus's first appearance, while the goat that is offered represents Jesus's second coming because all will recognize that Jesus was offered for sinners (*Dial.* 40.4). Tertullian similarly understands the scapegoat with reference to Jesus's first appearance. The goat that is offered as a burnt offering symbolizes Jesus's second appearance in which all will see him as an offering for sins and believers—the priests of the spiritual temple—will feast on the Lord's grace in Christ (*Marc.* 3.7.7). Barnabas, on the other hand, allows his references to Jesus's appearances to be assigned to both goats. The scapegoat is cursed, just as Jesus was on the cross. Yet people will ultimately see Jesus dressed in scarlet and recognize his true identity when he comes again (7.9). The goat that was sacrificed as a whole burnt offering receives less attention, but it complements Barnabas's emphasis on forgiveness of sin (7.6). Collectively, both goats demonstrate that Jesus was destined to suffer (7.11), but Barnabas's use of Yom Kippur imagery is not as distinguished as similar passages found in the writings of Justin or Tertullian.

The theological contribution of this passage within the Epistle of Barnabas is to enhance the interpretation of Jesus's suffering that has been ongoing since 5.1. Jesus's suffering is given meaning because it was revealed beforehand and occurred "on our account" (7.1-2). The reason that Jesus received vinegar and gall on the cross was to signify that he was the sacrifice whose offering could forgive sins (7.3-5). The goat that was offered as a whole burnt offering was thus offered on the cross (7.6). The scapegoat was cursed, abused, and rejected as an exile in order to take the sins of the community away. Jesus's suffering occurred for the same reason (7.7-10). Barnabas thus furthers the anti-Jewish interpretation of Jesus's death from 5.7-8 and 11-14, while also demonstrating that Jesus's crown only came about as a result of his curse (7.9). Since the promise of new creation lies immediately before this passage (6.8-19), the Yom Kippur interpretations also remind readers that they must suffer in order to see Jesus's kingdom (7.11).

---

164. In addition to what has already been said about 7.1-11 and other early Jewish traditions, see Skarsaune, "Development of Scriptural Interpretation," 387.

165. E.g., Justin, *Dial.* 40.4-5; Tertullian, *Jud.* 14.9. For other interpretations of Jesus's death with a view to Jewish blame, see Matt 27:25; Gos. Pet. 1.1-2; 3.6; 6.23; 7.25.

II.4.d. The Red Heifer (Barn. 8.1–7)

After interpreting the two goats offered at Yom Kippur with a view to their fulfillment in Jesus, Barnabas turns to another picture of sacrifice from the Torah. As in much of Barn. 5–8, the focus of his interpretation is on the way in which Jesus suffered, how Jesus's death should be interpreted, and the significance of Jesus's death for his readers. The relationship between the discussion of the red heifer is thus not far from the exegesis of Yom Kippur texts in the preceding section. Barnabas indicates this thematic nearness with his use of the conjunction δέ in 8.1. Along with the shift in topics, the conjunction indicates a transition in subject matter without drawing a contrast or finding a logical continuity between the topics.

The transition brings Barnabas to another type (τύπος) of Jesus's death (8.1). However, the scriptural passage that follows is not quoted directly. Instead, the author relies on indirect quotation, something that is unusual to this point in the letter. The indirect quotation that follows is closest to the ritual of the red heifer that is described in Num 19.[166] Barnabas reports that Israel should offer a heifer, slaughter it, and burn it. Children should then come to put the ash into a jar, to wrap scarlet wool and hyssop around a piece of wood, and to sprinkle the people individually. This should be done in order to purify the people—who have already been described as completely sinful—from their sins (8.1). Although Num 19 knows nothing of children acting in this way, the other elements of 8.1 can be found in Num 19.[167]

Barnabas then offers an allegory of this ritual so that the text is understood with regard to Jesus's death. He implores his audience to understand how "it is speaking to you" (λέγεται ὑμῖν; 8.2). The second-person pronoun removes the author from the audience of this interpretation, but

---

166. For a parallel synopsis of Num 19 and Barn. 8, see Chandler, "Rite of the Red Heifer," 101–3.

167. However, elements of the ritual in Num 19 are also omitted in Barn. 8.1. For example, Barnabas does not discuss the requirements of the heifer, the role of the priests, the link between the rite and the tabernacle/temple, cleansing of uncleanness brought on by contact with a corpse as the rite's *raison d'être*, the uncleanness that those who participate in the rite of the red heifer can contract, the location of the rite outside of the camp, or the process of mixing the water and ash. On Barnabas's omissions as a form of exegesis, see Chandler, "Rite of the Red Heifer," 103–4; Hegedus, "Midrash and the Letter of Barnabas," 24.

his statement and interpretation function similarly to the first-person references to "us" that are found throughout the letter. The way in which the passage speaks is described as "single-mindedly" (ἐν ἁπλότητι; 8.2). Barnabas highlights the simplicity with which the text addresses the audience. The interpretation that follows is correspondingly simple in outline, since it understands the passage as an allegory.[168] The calf that was offered, slaughtered, and burned stands for Jesus. Those who offered him are described as "sinful men" (ἄνδρες ἁμαρτωλοί; 8.2). Language about sin has been used with regard to Barnabas's Jewish opponents earlier in the letter (4.6; 5.11). In 8.2, "sinful men" should likewise be understood with regard to Jews, who are said to have crucified Jesus. These men and "the glory of sinners" (ἁμαρτωλῶν ἡ δόξα) fall away after killing Jesus (8.2), and Barnabas brings forward the children who sprinkled the people (8.3). The children are identified as those who brought the good news of forgiveness to Barnabas and his audience. As Barnabas goes on to clarify, the bearers of this good news are the apostles. They were given the authority to preach the gospel. The reason that twelve of them were called is to bear witness to the twelve tribes of Israel (8.3). Barnabas elevates three children from this group of twelve. They represent the patriarchs: Abraham, Isaac, and Jacob. "These were great before God" (οὗτοι μεγάλοι τῷ θεῷ; 8.4).

After identifying the people in the scripture (8.2–4), the discussion moves to the tools that the children used for sprinkling. The wool on the wood that was mentioned in 8.1 depicts Jesus's kingdom, which is located "on the wood" (ἐπὶ ξύλου; 8.5).[169] Those who place their hope in Jesus are promised life (8.5), just as Barnabas has already noted that Jesus suffered in order to bring people to life (7.2). The reason that hyssop is mixed with the wool is that the days when Barnabas and his audience will be saved are characterized as evil. Yet Jesus's suffering in the flesh was healing only by means of the hyssop. The hyssop is thus both therapeutic and associated with the filth of the times that Barnabas and his audience inhabit. Just as 5.2

---

168. It is worth noting, however, that the key to the allegory is held by the author because it has only been disclosed to his audience and him. This is made clear at the end of the interpretation in 8.7. See also 5.2; 9.9; 10.12.

169. It is possible that Barnabas is aware of a variant text in Ps 95:10 (96:10 MT) in which the Lord is said to have "reigned from the tree" (ὁ κύριος ἐβασίλευσεν ἀπὸ τοῦ ξύλου). Justin (1 Apol. 41.4; Dial. 73.1) and Tertullian (Marc. 3.19.1; Jud. 10.11) both knew Ps 95:10 in this form, increasing the plausibility that Barnabas may also have known the psalm in this way. However, since Barnabas does not quote this text in his discussion of the cross (Barn. 12), his knowledge of Ps 95:10 must remain conjectural. It may be instead that Barnabas is simply setting the table for his discussion of the cross in Barn. 12. For further discussion, see Kraft, Barnabas, 104; Skarsaune, Proof from Prophecy, 35–42, 443.

opened the christological section in Barn. 5–8 with an interpretive principle, so also 8.7 draws the allegory to a close with a hermeneutical statement: "The things that have happened have thus been revealed to us, but they are dark to them because they did not listen to the Lord's voice" (8.7). The author and audience are starkly juxtaposed against Barnabas's Jewish opponents. This happens not only through the author's choice in pronouns (us / them; ἡμῖν / ἐκείνοις) but also by means of hearing. Whereas Barnabas's opponents fail to understand scripture because they do not hear the Lord's voice, he and his audience can interpret the red heifer rite correctly because they have listened properly. This claim enables Barnabas to transition to 9.1.[170]

The reference to the ritual in Num 19 in Barn. 8.1 differs from many of the other citations in the letter because the author employs indirect quotation. By introducing the text in this way, Barnabas enables significant changes to be made to the ritual as it is known in Num 19 and as he employs it for his figurative interpretation. Situated within the pentateuchal narrative, the Lord offers extensive instructions to Moses and Aaron about how Eleazar the priest should offer the sacrifice of the red heifer. Moses and Aaron are told about the specifications of the heifer, the duties of the priest, the way in which the heifer's ashes should be mixed with water, and the placement of the ritual outside the camp. These aspects of the ritual are all missing in Barn. 8.1.[171] Whereas the cedar wood, hyssop, and scarlet wool are thrown into the fire in Num 19:6, these are combined to become the means by which the people are sprinkled (Barn. 8.1, 5, 6).[172] The ritual is also applied for alternative purposes in *Barnabas*. The point of the red heifer sacrifice in Num 19 has to do with purity after a member of the community has come into contact with a corpse (Num 19:11, 13, 16). Barnabas shifts the emphasis so that the reappropriated purpose is related to purification from sins that comes through christocentric forgiveness and results in pure hearts (Barn. 8.1, 3).[173]

Although Barnabas is selective in his use of Num 19, he again bears similarities to traditions about the red heifer ritual found in the Mishnah.[174] Children do not appear in the sprinkling described in Num 19, but

---

170. Kraft, *Barnabas*, 104.

171. On Barnabas's omissions as a form of exegesis, see Chandler, "Rite of the Red Heifer," 103–4.

172. Hegedus, "Midrash and the Letter of Barnabas," 24.

173. Hegedus, "Midrash and the Letter of Barnabas," 24. However, this difference should not be overemphasized, since the MT of Num 19:9 refers to purification from sin (נדה חטאה), while the Vulgate reasons that the heifer is burnt "for sin" (*pro peccato*).

174. For discussion of the red heifer in Barn. 8.1–7 and m. Parah, see Chandler, "Rite of the Red Heifer," 99–114. On Barn. 8.1–7 and additional Rabbinic comparisons, see Skarsaune, "Baptismal Typology," 221–28.

m. Parah 3.3–4 allude to children sprinkling ashes during the red heifer ritual.[175] The use of Num 19 in an alternative format allows him to highlight the role of the disciples in making Jesus's sacrifice known to Barnabas and his audience. Barnabas interprets the children with reference to those who proclaimed good news to the community about the forgiveness of sins and purity of their hearts. This potentially ambiguous reference to the evangelists is then specified so that the twelve disciples come into view (8.3). Barnabas understands the disciples as the genuine tribes of Israel so that Israel is constituted in terms of the disciples. Such an interpretation coheres with both his christological hermeneutic throughout Barn. 5–8 and his exegesis of traditional Jewish symbols, such as sacrifices and fasting in 2.4—3.6. More surprising, perhaps, is the way in which the children who sprinkle the ashes of the heifer are understood with reference to the patriarchs (8.4). In Barnabas's view, Abraham, Isaac, and Jacob were also involved in spreading the good news of Jesus's sacrifice.[176]

When Barnabas turns to the wood and scarlet wool (8.5), he refers to "those who hope on him [Jesus]" (οἱ ἐλπίζοντες ἐπ' αὐτόν). These receive eternal life through Jesus's kingdom that is found on the wood of the cross. Yet the way in which hope is employed in this saying may be surprising for readers who are more familiar with the Pauline formula that salvation and life come by faith.[177] Hope has been used elsewhere in the letter in contexts where it appears to play a salvific role. Barnabas clarifies that believers do not hope on a stone but in the Lord's flesh (6.3). Believers are thus to hope in the flesh that is revealed by Jesus (6.9). Moses stretched out his hands over the Israelites while they were at war in order that the people could know that salvation only comes through hope in the cross (12.2–3). The reference to those who hope on Jesus in 8.5 is part of an emphasis in the letter on the importance of hope in making the actions of Jesus in the flesh and on the cross efficacious for believers.

Barnabas thus utilizes the red heifer rite described in Num 19 as a representation (τύπος) of Jesus and the cross. The red heifer represents Jesus, who is sacrificially offered by sinners, whom Barnabas construes

---

175. According to m. Parah 3.4, a dispute arose between the views of R. Jose and R. Akiba. R. Jose argued that children needed to be sprinkled as well as sprinkling. R. Akiba, on the other hand, argues that children did not have to be sprinkled. The Mishnah appears to accept R. Akiba's view.

176. See similarly 9.8 and 13.2–7. That the patriarchs predated Moses and the Sinai event makes it easier for Barnabas to incorporate the patriarchs into his argument.

177. E.g., Rom 1:16–17; 3:21–26; 4:13–25; Gal 2:16–20; Eph 2:8–9; Phil 3:9. Of course, the question of whose faith is active in some of these passages has been heavily disputed. For recent coverage of this topic, see Morgan, *Roman Faith*, 262–306; Schliesser, "Faith in Early Christianity," 3–50.

as his Jewish opponents. The wood, hyssop, and scarlet wool in Num 19 are likewise interpreted in a thoroughly christological manner. Since the wood represents the cross, it is understood as the location of Jesus's kingdom (8.5), while the wool and hyssop provide the means by which the evil days in which Barnabas and his audience find themselves can be healed. Yet this healing only comes through suffering in the flesh, something that Jesus did programmatically as the red heifer but something in which the audience is implicitly invited to participate (8.6). Life comes about only as a result of hope in Jesus's suffering (8.5). Yet readers have reason to hope. They received the good news about forgiveness from the twelve disciples, the true Israel (8.3). Jesus's sacrifice was also revealed ahead of time to Abraham, Isaac, and Jacob (8.4).

The theological claims regarding Israel and the patriarchs illustrate the anti-Jewish contribution that this passage makes to the letter. Not only is the red heifer only rightly understood in terms of Jesus's sacrifice, but even the twelve tribes must be understood in terms of the twelve disciples. The opponents whom the author describes as sinful men are the ones who are responsible for killing Jesus. Their role in the story does not continue beyond Jesus's death, for they no longer exist (8.2). Barnabas insists that his interpretation of the red heifer remains dark to them "because they did not listen to the Lord's voice" (ὅτι οὐκ ἤκουσαν φωνῆς κυρίου; 8.7), while he and his audience rightly understand what has been revealed. The hermeneutical principle at 8.7 draws the christological reflections in 5.1—8.7 to a close by echoing the author's earlier statement that God addresses some things to Israel and others "to us" (5.2).[178] This section focuses on Jesus's suffering in the flesh while also highlighting how Israel misunderstood God's actions in Jesus and the life-producing benefits that hope in Jesus's suffering offers for believers. The reference to hearing the Lord's voice simultaneously paves the way for the discussion of circumcision that follows.

II.5. Circumcision and Kosher Laws (Barn. 9.1—10.12)

The motif of hearing God's voice rightly continues from 8.7 into 9.1—10.12 as the topic returns to figurative exegesis of two well-known Jewish practices: circumcision and kosher regulations. Language about hearing connects the discussion of Jesus's suffering in the flesh on our behalf (5.1—8.7) to Barnabas's reflections on circumcision and food laws. While Barnabas's

---

178. Barnabas indicates that only some can interpret God's revelatory word rightly (5.2; 8.7). While 5.2 suggests that this was God's intention, 8.7 finds that hearers bear some responsibility as well.

opponents have failed to hear the Lord's voice (8.7), the author now turns to consider more thoroughly what the Lord says "about the ears" (περὶ τῶν ὠτίων; 9.1). Barnabas relates right hearing of what God has said to the act of circumcision.[179] The discussion of hearing and circumcision extends throughout 9.1–9 and illustrates that right hermeneutical practices are closely connected to how Barnabas identifies the people of God. Yet the significance of right hearing does not fall away after the author turns to kosher laws. God's circumcision of the way in which Barnabas and his audience hear provides rhetorical closure to this section in 10.12. While the right interpretation of what should and should not be eaten occupies the author's attention throughout 10.1–11, the final verse returns to a hermeneutical statement by which the author asserts that his understanding of scripture is right because "our" hearing has been circumcised.

Between these rhetorical markers, Barnabas devotes much of his attention to compiling scriptural evidence to demonstrate that the correct practice of circumcision corresponds to hearing (9.1–3). Jews have misunderstood this circumcision in terms of the flesh because they were deceived by a demon. Barnabas points to the circumcision practices of other nations as evidence against interpreting physical circumcision as a uniquely Jewish sign of the covenant (9.4–6). He further reasons that even the first man to receive circumcision understood the rite christologically. Abraham's circumcision of 318 men is interpreted in terms of Jesus and the cross (9.7–9). In 10.1–12, the author takes up kosher laws as another Jewish practice that should be understood in terms of obedience rather than physical activity. Barnabas interprets the commands not to eat specific foods as an instruction not to associate with certain types of people (10.1–8). Prohibited foods are outlined in threes, and both Moses and David are said to agree with the Barnabean interpretation (10.9–10). The command to eat animals with cloven hooves is correspondingly understood as an instruction to develop relationships with particular kinds of people (10.11). Barnabas and his readers understand this rightly because their ears have been circumcised (10.12).

II.5.a. Obedience and the Meaning of Circumcision (Barn. 9.1–9)

As the Lord speaks about the ears in 9.1, Barnabas's use of the adverb "again" (πάλιν) alludes to the earlier reference to listening to God's voice in 8.7. The Lord speaks in order to show how he circumcised believers'

---

179. Yuh ("Do as I Say," 273–95) argues that the discussion of circumcision has significance for how one understands the entirety of *Barnabas* and thus goes beyond the limited discussion in 9.1–9.

hearts. Barnabas introduces three terms in the first sentence of this section that are key to the discussion throughout 9.1–9. First, he mentions the ears (ὦτα). The reference to the ears prepare the reader for the repetition of words related to hearing that will accumulate throughout this section.[180] Second, the author speaks about God's act of circumcising (περιτέμνω). Circumcision provides the guiding imagery by which to understand how one listens properly to God's voice and is interpreted as an objectionable practice when executed physically. Finally, the author mentions the heart (καρδία). Although cardiac language is employed less often than the other terms in 9.1–9, the heart is the location of true circumcision in Barnabas's understanding of the practice.[181]

Alongside these three terms are recurring statements that the Lord speaks. Introductory formulae using the verb λέγει are found throughout the letter, but they are especially numerous in 9.1–9, occurring twelve times.[182] The increased repetition of God's speech, particularly when compared to the relative dearth of such introductory speech formulae in 7.1—8.7,[183] enhances the emphasis on using the ears to hear rightly in 9.1–9. The Lord's speech comes by means of the prophets, and the first quotation draws attention to its origins by noting that the Lord spoke "by the prophet" (ἐν τῷ προφήτῃ; 9.1). The quotation is close to Ps 17:45 (18:45 MT) and lifts up the "hearing of the ear" (ἀκοὴν ὠτίου) by which people are called to obey God. The next citation is connected by means of the keyword ἀκοή. Quoting Isa 33:13, Barnabas reports that those who are far away "will surely hear" (ἀκοῇ ἀκούσονται) and make known what the Lord has done (9.1). Barnabas then quotes a command from the Lord to circumcise (περιτμήθητε) your hearts (τὰς καρδίας

---

180. Carleton Paget, *Epistle of Barnabas*, 144.

181. Ptolemy likewise locates true circumcision in the heart (*Flor.* 33.5.11). In Ptolemy's interpretation of the Torah, God does not desire circumcision of the foreskin but rather of the spiritual heart. Philo understands circumcision to have figurative meanings, including the excision of pleasure and the discarding of human arrogance (*Spec.* 1.8–10, 304–6; *QG* 3.46–47). However, Philo does not allow for a *solely* figurative understanding of circumcision (*Migr.* 92). For further discussion of Philo's view of circumcision, see Barclay, "Paul and Philo on Circumcision," 538–43. For additional connections between Philo and Ptolemy on the interpretation of the Torah, see Standhartinger, "Ptolemaeus und Justin," 140.

182. See 9.1 (4x), 2, 3 (3x), 5 (3x), and 8. L adds one more introductory formula prior to the final citation in 9.5 when it reads *dicit autem* (λέγει δέ) instead of λάβε πάλιν with H and the correctors of S. The number twelve that is employed for this commentary on *Barnabas* does not include the introductory formula in L and does not include every instance of the word λέγω in 9.1–9. The word λέγω is only counted when employed in an introductory formula in order to highlight how often God's speech is emphasized in this section.

183. Within 7.1—8.7, λέγω is only found in 7.4 and 8.2.

ὑμῶν; 9.1) before turning back to "surely listening" (ἀκοῇ ἀκουσάτω) to the Lord's servant as a qualification for living forever (9.2). Even heaven and earth are charged to listen (ἄκουε) and give ear (ἐνωτίζου) to what the Lord says (9.3). Rulers are likewise charged to listen (ἀκούσατε) to the word of the Lord, while the audience is addressed as children and charged to listen (ἀκούσατε) to the voice crying out in the desert. The conclusion that the author draws from this barrage of imperatives to listen in 9.1–3 is that the Lord circumcised "our hearing" (ἡμῶν τὰς ἀκοάς) in order that Barnabas and his audience would believe the word that they hear.[184]

Following this profusion of passages outlining the way in which hearing and circumcision are connected in the prophets, Barnabas addresses "the circumcision about which they are persuaded" (ἡ περιτομὴ ἐφ' ἧ πεποίθασιν; 9.4). This periphrastic phrase denotes the physical act of circumcision practiced by Barnabas's Jewish opponents. However, the author claims that it has been destroyed since the Lord was not speaking about the flesh. As the passages in 9.1–3 indicate, Barnabas understands circumcision to have always been about the right way of hearing God's voice. Turning again to the prophets, Barnabas asserts that Jews should be circumcised to the Lord rather than sowing among thorns (9.5; Jer 4:3–4). Circumcision should take place with reference to their hard hearts (Deut 10:16) and not with regard to the foreskin (9.5; Jer 9:26). Barnabas then addresses a potential Jewish objection by using a rhetorical question. Someone in the audience may object that the people were circumcised for a seal (εἰς σφραγίδα; 9.6). Barnabas twists the knife when addressing this question by pointing out that Syrians, Arabs, and priests to idols are likewise circumcised. Even Egyptians are circumcised and thus included "in the circumcision" (ἐν περιτομῇ).[185] Barnabas taunts this objection by asking whether these might also be included as members "of their covenant" (ἐκ τῆς διαθήκης αὐτῶν). Whether they may be included in their covenant, the clear implication is that physical circumcision does not signify membership in our covenant.

Barnabas's claim that the Jewish practice of circumcision was the result of an evil angel's deception sounds shockingly harsh. While other early Jewish and early Christian texts describe demons as dishonest and find fault in the law,[186] finding the origins of physical circumcision in demonic

---

184. Yuh, "Do as I Say," 282–83.

185. Philo (*Spec.* 1.2, 5) likewise mentions the Egyptian practice of circumcision.

186. On limitations or flaws in the law, see Ezek 20:25; Gal 3:19; Ptolemy, *Flor.* 33.3.2; Irenaeus, *Haer.* 4.15.1; Origen, *Cels.* 7.20; Ps.-Clem. *Hom.* 2.38–40; 3.42–51. For additional contextualization of 9.4 in wider early Jewish and early Christian literature, see Carleton Paget, "Barnabas 9.4," 243–48.

enlightenment is extreme.[187] After all, even the Pauline understanding that circumcision was unnecessary for salvation but could still be practiced by Jewish believers was controversial in the first century.[188] Philo offers a spiritualized interpretation of circumcision in which circumcision represents the excision of deluding pleasures and symbolizes the act of discarding of self-conceit in favor of self-knowledge (*Migr.* 92; *Spec.* 1.8–11). Yet Philo also finds benefit in the physical act of circumcision (*Spec.* 1.3–7), and he reprimands those who do not practice physical circumcision because of the symbolic significance (*Migr.* 89–90).[189] When Ptolemy teaches Flora about the Torah, he knows of some who contend that the law was established by the devil (*Flor.* 33.3.2).[190] Although Ptolemy holds such people to be in error (*Flor.* 33.3.3), his description differs slightly from Barnabas. Barnabas holds his opponents to be deceived by the devil regarding the interpretation of Torah, but he upholds the law of circumcision. Even so, Barn. 9.4 is surprising because it is harsher than what is found in other early Jewish and early Christian literature and because it is more severe than what Barnabas says about other Jewish customs elsewhere in the letter. The harshness of 9.4 suggests that the practice of circumcision may have continued to be a practice in and around the community that Barnabas was addressing.

Barnabas turns from contemporary circumcision practice to its origins in the Abraham narrative. He urges the audience to learn (μάθετε) and addresses them directly as "children of love" (τέκνα ἀγάπης; 9.7). Abraham was the first person to whom circumcision was given and the first to pass circumcision on to others, but Barnabas claims that Abraham looked ahead to Jesus in the Spirit as he performed the act of circumcision. Circumcision is thus christologically oriented. In order to teach about Abraham's reception "of the three letters" (τριῶν γραμμάτων; 9.7), Barnabas combines two elements of Abraham's story (9.8). In Gen 14, Abraham takes all the members of his household to liberate Lot from captivity. These men number 318 (Gen 14:14). He then circumcises everyone in his household as part of the covenant relationship with God in Gen 17:1–14, 23–27. Although no number is given when the narrator reports that all the men in Abraham's household

---

187. This charge thereby marks Barnabas's opponents out as others. See further Lieu, *Christian Identity*, 291.

188. E.g., Rom 2:25–3:2; 1 Cor 7:18–19; Col 4:11. Paul does, however, have harsh things to say about those who wield circumcision as a weapon by which to force people to be circumcised (Gal 5:11–12; Phil 3:2).

189. Kraft, "Epistle of Barnabas," 187.

190. Quispel, *Ptolémée*, 76. See also Rothschild, "Apostolic Mothers," 184.

are circumcised (Gen 17:23, 27), Barnabas connects the 318 men from Gen 14:14 with the report about circumcision in Gen 17:23 and 27.[191]

Barnabas works from this combination to illustrate how Abraham saw a symbol for Jesus in this action. Greek numerals could be written with Greek letters. In order to write 318, one could make use of a *tau* (T), which stood for the number 300. The letter *iōta* (I) represented ten, while eight is made with an *ēta* (H). Barnabas begins from the latter two letters (9.8). *Iōta* and *ēta* are the first two letters of Jesus's name (Ἰησοῦς). Thus they indicate that Abraham was pointing to Jesus when circumcised. More specifically, Abraham connected Jesus with the cross, because the shape of a *tau* resembles a cross and thus symbolizes the means of Jesus's death.[192] While Barnabas indicates that Abraham physically circumcised members of his household, the point for him was not that circumcision should be passed down to his descendants.[193] Rather, Abraham circumcised people in his household in order to point to Jesus and his death. Barnabas claims that God knows what he has said about Abraham (9.9).[194] God's knowledge grants Barnabas's interpretation credibility, and Barnabas can therefore assert that he has never taught a "more reliable" (γνησιώτερον) word.

Barnabas's interpretation of 318 offers a provocative way to understand the Abrahamic narrative. The use of gematria was not uncommon in ancient texts, and Barnabas's exegesis seems at first glance to coincide with rabbinic interpretations of Abraham's 318 men. Rabbi Ami bar Abba is reported to have interpreted the 318 men in Gen 14:14 as a reference to Eliezer (b. Ned. 32a).[195] This interpretation relies on gematria, since all the letters in Eliezer's name compute to 318. Barnabas does not use a strict form of gematria based on all the letters in one name, but his interpretation relies on a form of the practice that has been modified with reference to *nomina sacra* and Jesus's

---

191. Carleton Paget, *Epistle of Barnabas*, 147–48; Edwards, *Gospel*, 54.

192. Hurtado, *Lord Jesus Christ*, 572.

193. Carleton Paget, *Epistle of Barnabas*, 147; Edwards, *Gospel*, 55.

194. The description of God as "the one who set the implanted gift (τὴν ἔμφυτον δωρεάν) of his covenant within us" is reminiscent of the author's description of the audience as those who received "the implanted (ἔμφυτον) grace of the spiritual gift (δωρεᾶς)" (1.2).

195. The same interpretation can be found in Tg. Ps.-J. (Gen 14:14). John Bowker (*Targums and Rabbinic Literature*, 195) locates early Christian interpretation of Jesus and 318 alongside Jewish exegetical traditions that are evident in Rabbinic texts. All references to Targum Pseudo-Jonathan come from Ginsburger, *Pseudo-Jonathan*.

cross.[196] The precise origins of *nomina sacra* remain obscure.[197] The term refers to the early Christian practice of abbreviating certain words in a text, particularly words relating to the divine. While these are attested in ancient manuscripts, the author's exegesis is unusual because it creates an interpretation of the text based on what appears to be a *nomen sacrum* of Jesus's name: IH. The letter T indicates that Barnabas envisions a T-shaped cross and suggests that cross piety was alive and well by the time that Barnabas wrote in the second century.[198] If the use of *nomina sacra* or cross piety were relatively new in the second century, this may also indicate why Barnabas is so proud of what he has taught his readers (9.9).[199]

There is a tension between Barnabas's negative view of fleshly circumcision in 9.1–6 and his positive outlook on Abraham's physical act of circumcision in 9.7–8. Barnabas defines circumcision in terms of the ears and heart in 9.1–6 so that circumcision results in believers being able to hear God rightly. The physical act of circumcision is rejected as a lie that stems from an evil angel and a practice characteristic of other nations (9.4, 6). On the other hand, the author does not denigrate Abraham's act of circumcising his household in 9.7–8. While the 318 men who received circumcision are interpreted christologically, the physical action is simply observed as a fact. This tension led Windisch to suppose that 9.7–8 comes from a second edition.[200] This hypothesis is unnecessary, however.[201] Abraham's circumcision was valid despite its physical practice because it was done with a view toward Jesus. Thus the author locates the source of his figurative interpretation of 318 not solely in himself but in Abraham, who "looked ahead in the Spirit to Jesus" (ἐν πνεύματι προβλέψας εἰς τὸν

---

196. Bovon, "Names and Numbers," 277, 281–82; Blumell and Wayment, "'Number of the Beast,'" 128–29; Hegedus, "Midrash in the Letter of Barnabas," 334–35; Hvalvik, "Barnabas 9.7–9," 278–79. Such a method is presumed, for example, in Irenaeus's identification of the antichrist as the beast of the earth. Irenaeus suggests that 666 may be interpreted as Euanthas, Lateinos, and Teitan, all names whose letters add up to 666 (*Haer.* 5.30.3). See similarly Hippolytus, *Antichr.* 50. The text of Hippolytus's *De Christo et Antichristo* is found in Bonwetsch and Achelis, *Hippolytus Werke*.

197. For helpful studies of *nomina sacra*, see Hurtado, "Origin of the *Nomina Sacra*," 655–73; Hurtado, *Earliest Christian Artifacts*, 95–134.

198. The same isopsephy can be found in Clement of Alexandria, *Strom.* 6.84.2–3 (11).

199. On the geographical and temporal spread of cross symbolism prior to the fourth century, see Longenecker, *Cross before Constantine*, 163–68.

200. Windisch, *Barnabasbrief*, 357. Windisch asserts that 9.6–9 is an addendum to 9.1–5. Edmond Robillard understands 9.4–6 as an addition to 9.1–3 that was added later by another author ("Épître de Barnabé," 188 n 9).

201. For different arguments for reading 9.1–9 as a unified section of the letter, see Carleton Paget, "*Barnabas* 9.4," 249–50.

Ἰησοῦν; 9.7). Since Abraham passed on a christological understanding by acting in the Spirit, his physical act is acceptable. What is problematic in Barnabas' view is the mistaken practice of his opponents who see circumcision itself as the act that Abraham passed down.

The rhetorical and theological contributions of Barnabas's discussion of circumcision can now be assessed more directly. First, the deliberations on circumcision join the author's reflections on sacrifices and fasting (2.4—3.6) in offering a figurative interpretation of Jewish ritual practices. However, the allusions to and implicit warnings about the loss of covenant in 4.6-9 enable readers to see why Barnabas interprets scripture in this way. Barnabas and the audience are called to be different from the Jews by interpreting scripture rightly and acting in ways that demonstrate their place in the true covenant. By reflecting at length on Jesus's suffering and its implications (5.1—8.7), Barnabas outlines the underlying motivation for acting in accordance to scripture. The audience should thus hear and obey scripture with circumcised ears and hearts because scripture points to Jesus and his death on the cross. Second, the exegesis of the circumcision ritual joins other passages in the letter in underlining the importance of rightly interpreting scripture. Right interpretation only comes about by means of circumcised ears and hearts (9.1-5). God is the one who performs this act, and scripture demonstrates the need for understanding circumcision with regard to the ears and heart. As Abraham himself knew, circumcised ears enable one to see that scripture points to Jesus. Finally, the discussion of circumcision enhances the social solidarity of Barnabas and his audience. Since "we" have circumcised hearts and ears and thereby rightly understand scripture and "they" have been deceived by an evil angel, Barnabas employs 9.1-9 to outline more clearly the limits of who belongs to the audience while simultaneously aiming to increase the level of solidarity among those who are in the group. Collectively, they are enabled to listen to scripture aright with their circumcised ears and heart in order that they may obey what God has revealed to them in scripture.

II.5.b. Right Living and Kosher Laws (Barn. 10.1-12)

After defining circumcision with regard to the hearts and ears, Barnabas turns to consider the meaning of kosher laws in 10.1-12. The transition from circumcision to food is abrupt, but the thematic links may be justified since both circumcision and kosher practices were important social markers in the Torah and Second Temple Jewish praxis. As in the case of sacrifices, fasting, and circumcision, Barnabas regards it as a misinterpretation of scripture to physically follow *kashrut* (10.9, 12). Moses is instead said to have spoken spiritually (10.2, 9). Barnabas relies on the number three in 10.1–12. He notes that Moses received three teachings (10.1, 9). The interpretation of the animals divide into two groups of three (10.3–5, 6–8).[202] David likewise knew about the three doctrines (10.10). Barnabas's use of the number three enables him to discuss an initial set of three teachings from Moses (10.1–5), to consider a secondary set of three animals (10.6–8), to summarize the teachings in Moses and David (10.9–10), and to look to what people ought to eat in the Torah before bringing the section to a conclusion (10.11–12).

The passage begins with a quotation of scripture that draws on language from Lev 11 and Deut 14. Moses declared that pigs, eagles, hawks, crows, and fish without scales were forbidden (10.1). Despite the list of five animals, Barnabas states that Moses gave three teachings, apparently grouping the birds together. He follows this with an elaboration that he credits specifically to Deuteronomy.[203] Moses spoke spiritually about eating, but he also reports that God's covenant with the people is established through the requirements that God gives (10.2). The three doctrines are then elaborated in 10.3–5. The animals are interpreted spiritually with a view to the behaviors and characters of people. Not to eat pigs is to refuse to associate with people who forget the Lord when all is well but who cry out for the Lord when they are in need.[204] The rationale for this interpretation is that pigs cry out when they are hungry but do not know their master when they are full (10.3). Barnabas lists the individual types of birds and fish so that there are three categories of people to avoid when this list is added to the pigs. The birds on the list scavenge, and Barnabas connects this activity to those who take what others have earned by their own work (10.4).[205] Likewise, the sea eel, octopus, and cuttlefish are grouped together because they swim deep in the sea and hide in the mud. Such an activity is associated with utter wickedness and is thus to be avoided by Barnabas and his audience (10.5).

Barnabas adds three more items to the list of teachings in 10.1–5, and each of these is introduced with a conjunction that indicates addition (ἀλλὰ καί; 10.6, 8; ἀλλὰ οὐδέ 10.7). The manner of interpretation is similar to 10.1–5 in that a commandment is reported and then interpreted with a view to the behaviors of people. When the commands are read spiritually as Moses intended them (10.1, 9), the kosher laws thus

202. Prigent and Kraft, *Épître de Barnabé*, 149 n 2.

203. "In addition, he says to them in Deuteronomy" (πέρας γέ τοι λέγει αὐτοῖς ἐν τῷ Δευτερονομίῳ; 10.2).

204. Or, in the more vivid paraphrase of Hanson (*Allegory and Event*, 97): "The pig means careless, extravagant behaviour."

205. Barnabas lists vultures, hawks, kites, and crows.

instruct readers about the sorts of people they should become by offering negative examples that ought to be avoided. Readers should not eat the hare, which Barnabas understands as an instruction not to be a "child-corrupter" (παιδοφθόρος; 10.6).[206] The ancient belief that rabbits annually added a new anus provides the impetus for this command.[207] Neither the instruction nor the rationale is entirely clear, but in light of the interpretations of the animals in 10.7–8, the commandment is best read with a view to illicit sexual activity—whether pedophilia, homosexuality, or the abortion of unwanted children as a result of sexual activity.[208] The hyena is similarly forbidden based on the belief that hyenas were hermaphroditic and switched their sex from year to year. Barnabas's lesson is that people should not be adulterers or seducers (10.7). Finally, people are instructed to hate weasels (10.8). Weasels were purported to conceive their children through their mouth. Barnabas employs this imagery to warn his readers against committing lawlessness with their mouth.[209]

Barnabas relies upon beliefs about animal genitals and reproductive habits that were known elsewhere in Greco-Roman scientific literature in order to make the allegorical interpretations of 10.6–8. For example, Pliny the Elder (*Nat.* 8.81 [217–19]) and Varro (*Rust.* 3.12.4) both assert that the age of a rabbit can be determined with reference to its regular production of new holes while also describing the fecundity of rabbit procreation.[210] In his study of animals, Aelian reports that hyenas change

206. Similar references to the corruption of children can be found in Barn. 19.4; Did. 2.2; 5.2.

207. For further discussion of ancient beliefs about rabbits—as well as hyenas and weasels (10.7–8)—see the following paragraph.

208. Rothschild ("Down the Rabbit Hole," 412–15) notes that commentators have a tendency to opt for the "sexiest" interpretations of 10.6, that is, those interpretations that have to do with sexual, often homosexual, behavior. I hope not to have succumbed to this tendency but to have based this interpretation on the surrounding context in 10.7–8. Barnabas's references to the hyena and weasel address sexual matters more explicitly than the admittedly ambiguous description of child-corruption in 10.6. Although she may prove wiser in leaving the interpretation of 10.6 open (Rothschild, "Down the Rabbit Hole," 433–34), I have nevertheless opted to interpret the passage with a view to illicit sexual behavior.

209. Committing lawlessness with one's mouth is likely a reference to oral sex. When discussing this passage, Maurizio Bettini (*Women and Weasels*, 108–9) highlights women who do things with the mouth that are forbidden. While this interpretation takes into account the feminine participle in 10.8, the interpretation should not be restricted to women alone. Barnabas lists two groups in 10.8. Although the second is denoted with the feminine participle (ταῖς... ποιούσαις), the first group, "those who do lawless things with their mouth because of uncleanness," is designated with a masculine participle (ποιοῦντας).

210. On rabbit procreation, see also Aelian, *Nat an.* 13.15, though there are

their sex year by year (ἀνὰ ἔτος) and have characteristics of both male and female (*Nat. an.* 1.25).²¹¹ Ovid is aware of the hermaphroditic capacity of hyenas and incorporates it into a series of reflections on animals that can change rapidly (*Metam.* 15.408–10).²¹² Turning to weasels, Aristotle notes that Anaxagoras was among those who believed that weasels could bring forth young from their mouth. Aristotle asserts that this view is based on limited evidence and consideration, arguing instead that weasel embryos make their way from the uterus in the same way as other quadrupeds (*Gen. an.* 3.6 [756b]).²¹³ He attributes the legend that weasels give birth through their mouth to the fact that weasels often carry their young in their mouth (*Gen. an.* 3.6 [757a]). It is more likely that Barn. 10.8 refers to conception through the mouth, but his allegory may be based on a similar sort of scientific knowledge to that which Aristotle attributes to Anaxagoras.²¹⁴ Although Barnabas draws ethical allegories from each of the statements that he makes in 10.6–8, his statements are based on tradents of animal knowledge that are found elsewhere in Greco-Roman writers.

Having listed two sets of three teachings that Barnabas finds in the Torah and interpreting them spiritually as he thinks Moses gave them, Barnabas summarizes the Mosaic kosher laws in 10.9. Moses received three teachings (τρία δόγματα) about which he spoke "in the Spirit" (ἐν πνεύματι). Although Moses spoke in the Spirit and thus had in mind the types of people that one should avoid or not become, Moses's Israelite audience received these instructions as if they were really about food. As in the case of idolatry when Moses received the covenant (4.7–8), so also Barnabas finds Moses's audience guilty of misunderstanding the significance of his words in 10.9.²¹⁵ Barnabas brings

---

significant textual issues at this point in the manuscript tradition. All citations from Pliny the Elder's *Naturalis historia* come from Jones and Rackham, *Pliny: Natural History*. All citations from Varro's *De re rustica* come from Hooper and Ash, *Cato and Varro: On Agriculture*. All citations from Aelian's *De natura animalium* come from Scholfield, *Aelian: On the Characteristics of Animals*. Pliny the Elder and Varro both rely upon Archelaus of Chersonesus for their zoological analysis of the rabbit. See further Rothschild, "Down the Rabbit Hole," 418–31.

211. For further references in ancient literature as well as a helpful admonition for contemporary readers to read ancient texts sympathetically, see Pendergraft, "'Thou Shalt Not Eat the Hyena,'" 75–79.

212. All citations of Ovid's *Metamorphoses* come from Miller, *Ovid: Metamorphoses*. On the enduring effect of hyena hermaphroditism, see Rabassini, "L'ombra della iena," 87–104.

213. All citations of Aristotle's *De generatione anamalium* come from Peck, *Aristotle: Generation of Animals*.

214. See also Let. Aris. 165.

215. To borrow from Verheyden's ("Israel's Fate," 261–62) recent treatment of Israel, one may note, however, that Israel's voice is not heard in this trial.

David into the discussion as an ally because David received "knowledge of the three teachings" (τριῶν δογμάτων γνῶσις; 10.10). David's knowledge is evident in the opening declaration of the Psalter that righteous people are blessed for avoiding three types of unrighteous people (Ps 1:1). Those who follow the counsel of ungodly people are like fish who wander in the darkness at the bottom of the sea (see 10.5). Those who take the paths of sinners are compared to pigs who only appear to fear the Lord (see 10.3). Finally, those who sit in the seat of pestiferous people are like birds that sit waiting for plunder (see 10.4). By connecting David's words to the three teachings of Moses about kosher laws, Barnabas tells his audience that they have now received the things related to food "perfectly" (τελείως; 10.10).[216]

Yet there is one more thing that Barnabas turns to discuss in 10.11—the laws concerning what *should* be eaten. Moses instructed his hearers to eat anything that has a divided hoof and chews the cud. This group represents people who know the one who feeds them and who rejoice as a consequence. More specifically, Moses's commandment instructs people to associate with people who fear the Lord and meditate on what they have received from the Lord. Meditation is linked with chewing the cud and thereby ruminating on what one is given. The divided hoof symbolizes two timeframes: the present and the coming ages. A righteous person recognizes that they live in this world but are also looking forward to "the holy age" (ὁ ἅγιος αἰών; 10.11). This understanding of the Mosaic law escapes Barnabas's opponents—an assertion that he makes by asking how they could understand his interpretation (10.12).[217] He then links his understanding of the kosher laws with the discussion of circumcision in 9.1–9 by declaring that "we" are able to understand the commandments in the same way that the Lord spoke them because he circumcised "our" hearing and hearts (10.12).[218] It is thus by God's gracious act of circumcision that Barnabas and his audience are able to understand what Moses has said about food.

Barnabas categorizes Moses's teachings about food into three doctrines (10.1, 9). Yet Barnabas's initial citation from the Torah lists five animals before asserting that he received three teachings "in understanding" (ἐν τῇ συνέσει; 10.1). From the author's perspective, it is this understanding that enables him to properly comprehend Moses's teachings with reference to the number three. The initial list from 10.1 is taken up in 10.3–5 and divides roughly into animals that reside on the ground (pigs), in the air (birds),

216. This description brings the teaching on kosher laws into alignment with the author's overall purpose for the audience to have complete (τελεία) knowledge with their faith (1.5).

217. Klevinghaus, *Theologische Stellung*, 25–26.

218. Lincicum, "Against the Law," 119.

and in the water (fish). Barnabas's second set of three examines individual animals: the rabbit, hyena, and weasel (10.6–8). These threefold interpretations of kosher laws provide the organizing apparatus for 10.1–9. The citation from David in 10.10 privileges the first Mosaic triad, since the people whom the blessed person avoids in Ps 1:1 are interpreted with reference to fish, pigs, and birds. Barnabas's threefold organization is not limited to his interpretation of the food laws, however. The teachings of the three letters that were given to Abraham place the focus of circumcision on Jesus and the cross (9.7–8). Lists of triples were given to Abraham, Moses, and David, allowing Barnabas to unite these central figures. They are also linked to Jesus, who gave three teachings concerning the hope of life, righteousness, and love of gladness and exultation (1.6). By discovering three teachings (τρία δόγματα) in conjunction with central figures in God's revelatory scheme, Barnabas heightens his claim that God consistently makes Godself known to his people in the past, present, and future.

In keeping with the focus on dietary laws, the greatest emphasis is given to texts associated with Moses. The prohibitions cited by Barnabas are closest to words found in two of the largest discussions of kosher practices in the Torah: Lev 11 and Deut 14. Barnabas's use of "You will not eat" (οὐ φάγεσθε; Barn. 10.1) is repeated three times in Lev 11 and seven times in Deut 14.[219] The order in the first triad mirrors Lev 11 and Deut 14 in placing swine first among the animals that Barnabas discusses,[220] but Barnabas mentions birds prior to fish, whereas the Torah reverses this order.[221] Although Barnabas's citation in Barn. 10.1 lists animals in a similar order to what is found in Lev 11 and Deut 14, his reference to the hawk (ὀξύπτερος) is not found in either passage of the Torah.[222] Similarly in the second triad, the Torah makes reference to the hare (δασύπους; Lev 11:5; Deut 14:7; see Barn. 10.6), while consumption of the weasel (γαλῆ) is prohibited in Lev 11:29. However, no mention of hyenas (ὕαινα) can be found in the Torah.[223] Barnabas's citation in 10.1 is compressed and not found in this form in Lev 11 and Deut 14. Barnabas's second quotation is introduced from Deuteronomy and contains a reference to setting the requirements of the Lord before the people (Barn. 10.2). Barnabas again compresses language when his language is compared to the old Greek form of Deut 4:1, 5. Barnabas

---

219. See Lev 11:4, 8, 42; Deut 14:3, 7, 8, 10, 12, 19, 21.

220. The first specific animals prohibited in Lev 11 and Deut 14 are the camel, hare, and rabbit (Lev 11:4–6; Deut 14:7).

221. See Barn. 10.1, 4–5; Lev 11:12–19; Deut 14:10, 12–17.

222. References to the Old Greek of Leviticus come from Wevers, *Leviticus*. References to the Old Greek of Deuteronomy come from Wevers, *Deuteronomium*.

223. Outside of the Torah, see Jer 12:9; Sir 13.18.

draws upon Torah traditions and specifically names Deuteronomy, but it remains unclear precisely how he came to know these texts.

Although Jewish dietary practices were a distinct and widely recognized identity marker, symbolic understandings of the Torah may also be found in the Second Temple period. In Elieazar's high priestly apology for the Torah in the Letter of Aristeas, the food laws are given by God for "our enhancement" (τῆς συγχωρήσεως ἡμῖν; Let. Aris. 150).[224] The wild and carnivorous birds that are prohibited by the law are forbidden as a reminder that God's people should not be violent or rapacious (Let. Aris. 146–47). The weasel's conception through the mouth is likewise understood figuratively, not in sexual terms as in Barn. 10.8, but in terms of transmitting rumors and hearsay (Let. Aris. 165–66). Moses's commandments were made not out of regard for animals but "for the sake of righteousness" (δικαιοσύνης ἕνεκεν; Let. Aris. 144).[225] Philo similarly interprets the legal instructions about animals with reference to ethical teaching. Pork and fish without scales should not be eaten as an act of self-control due to the delicious taste of their meat (Philo, *Spec.* 4.101). Moses instead instructs followers of the law to eat herbivores because "he was considering what was fitting for our soul" (λογιζόμενος τὸ πρέπον ἡμέρῳ ψυχῇ; Philo, *Spec.* 4.103). In the act of eating animals that chew the cud, Moses offers a symbol to teachers and students to use their memory to recall what they have learned by constant exercises (*Spec.* 4.106–7). The split hoof represents an ability to distinguish the virtuous life from the vicious (*Spec.* 4.108).

Philo and the Letter of Aristeas share a figurative interpretation of the dietary laws with *Barnabas*. This symbolic understanding of animals was incorporated by other early Christians.[226] The clearest example may be found in the *Physiologus*, a collection that can be dated to the second or third century CE.[227] The text employs the sex-switching nature of the hyena to describe the double-minded (*Physio.* 38). The *Physiologus* reports that female weasels receive sperm through their mouth and give birth through their ears. This observation provokes a discussion of the need for the ear to rightly hear God's Word. However, the rich are like the weasel because they cast the Word away from the ears (*Physio.* 35). While the ear provides a different focal point from Barn. 10.8, *Barnabas* and the *Physiologus* share a

---

224. All citations from the Letter of Aristeas come from Pelletier, *Lettre d'Aristée*.

225. See similarly Let. Aris. 150, 168–69.

226. Rhodes, *Epistle of Barnabas*, 59–60.

227. On the date of the *Physiologus*, see Curley, *Physiologus*, xvii–xxi; Scott, "Date of the *Physiologus*," 430–41; Scully, "Redemption for the Serpent," 422–55; Schneider, "Einführung," 5–6; Treu, "Zur Datierung des *Physiologus*," 101–4. All references to the *Physiologus* come from Curley's translation.

figurative reading of the Levitical instruction not to eat the weasel.[228] Clement of Alexandria quotes *Barnabas* as he employs a figurative reading of the commands not to eat the vulture, hawk, kite, or crow. The vulture symbolizes robbery, while the hawk is allegorized in terms of injustice (Clement of Alexandria, *Strom.* 5.52.1–2 [8]). Clement adds that the raven is a figure of greed before closing with Theognis's poetic observation that people learn good things from what is good but destroy their minds by mixing with what is bad (Clement of Alexandria, *Strom.* 5.52.4 [8]).[229] The lines from Theognis support Clement's earlier reference to animals that chew the cud and have a divided hoof, showing that they belong to two ages (Clement of Alexandria, *Strom.* 5.51.4–5 [8]; see Barn. 10.11).

The attention to other early Jewish and early Christian sources demonstrates that *Barnabas* is not an unusual text simply because it interprets the Mosaic dietary regulations figuratively. The author joins Philo, the Letter of Aristeas, the *Physiologus*, and Clement of Alexandria in attributing allegorical meaning and ethical significance to the food laws. Moreover, Barnabas illustrates the multifaceted ways in which he can utilize scripture in order to make his arguments. Not only does he draw from the Torah and similar traditions, he finds the same teaching in an entirely different portion of scripture. By placing Ps 1:1 and the Torah together, Barnabas finds cohesion across scripture. Both Moses and David received the three teachings about the true meaning of the food laws. Even Abraham had earlier received teachings about three letters that, although they relate to a different topic, exhibit cohesiveness in scripture as the locus of God's revelation to God's people. Nevertheless, Barnabas is unusual insofar as he rejects any justification for the physical practice of kosher observance at any time. Philo and the Letter of Aristeas assume that the food laws are observed and understand the figurative teachings to be additive and learned while practicing. Early Christian authors vary in their precise response to the Torah's dietary requirements but regularly allow that these observances were valid for at least some people.[230] The unusual element of Barn. 10.1–12 is thus not the reading of Moses speaking "in the Spirit"

---

228. Differently from Barn. 10.4, the *Physiologus* takes the vulture as a positive example because the vulture is said to travel to India when pregnant and to give birth on the *eutocius* stone, which has an internal and external part. The external portion of the stone is said to be God-bearing, while the internal part of the stone represents the Savior (*Physio.* 33).

229. See Theognis, 1.35–36. All quotations from Theognis's poetry come from Young, *Thenogis Megarensis*.

230. E.g., Rom 14:1—15:13; 1 Cor 8:1—10:33; Justin, *Dial.* 20.3–4; Tertullian, *Marc.* 2.18.2–3. On early Christian responses to dietary laws, see Carleton Paget, *Epistle of Barnabas*, 152–53; König, *Saints and Symposiasts*, 127–28.

(10.2, 9). Barnabas is unusual in thinking that Moses spoke in the Spirit to the *exclusion* of any corporeal practice.

This interpretation of the legal instructions regarding food fits with Barnabas's understanding of sacrifice, fasting, and circumcision. In all cases, Jews have failed to grasp the true meaning of what God revealed through the prophets. Barnabas is more specific in his location of the interpretive error in the case of circumcision when he finds the flaw in Jewish practice to be in their enlightenment by an evil angel (9.4). Although Barnabas does not speak of an evil angel in 10.1–12, he finds the mistaken practices of his opponents to be just as flawed. He rhetorically asks how they could know or understand (νοῆσαι ἢ συνιέναι) his interpretation of the Torah (10.12). The implicit answer to this question is that they were not able. On the other hand, Barnabas and his readers know the commandments rightly (δικαίως νοήσαντες τὰς ἐντολάς) and can therefore understand (συνιῶμεν) these things (10.12). Barnabas makes a strong distinction between us and them, and he heightens this connection with the repetition of νοέω and συνίημι Failed understandings and full understanding fall along group lines. This distinction is related to the prior discussion of circumcision. Barnabas and his readers are able to understand the food laws rightly because the Lord circumcised their ears and their hearts (10.12). Barnabas links his analysis of the food laws to the discussion of circumcision and thereby draws 9.1—10.12 to a close.

II. 6. The Water and the Cross (Barn. 11.1–12.11)

Just as Barnabas draws a connection between 9.1—10.12 by returning to circumcision in 10.12, so he begins 11.1—12.11 by previewing the topics to come in 11.1. He and his audience are going to embark on a search to find whether the Lord has revealed anything "about the water and about the cross" (περὶ τοῦ ὕδατος καὶ περὶ τοῦ σταυροῦ; 11.1). Water is an image that is closely connected to baptism, while Barnabas expands the image of the cross to include other references to wood in scripture. Within 11.1—12.11, special attention is paid to instances where hydric and ligneous imagery overlap (11.6-8, 10–11; 12.1). In addition to the introduction of this twofold topic in 11.1, Barnabas transitions in 12.1 to the cross by saying, "Again, likewise" (ὁμοίως πάλιν). He cements the connection between the topics with these two adjectives. This section contains both some of the closest readings of scripture and some of the most intricate and challenging scriptural connections in the letter. Barnabas's accumulation of scriptural texts strengthens his understanding of the symbolism of water and wood within scripture, but it can be challenging to understand precisely how the various passages are meant to fit together within the argument. It is to this formidable task that the commentary now turns.

II.6.a. Water and Baptism (Barn. 11.1–11)

After the introduction to the new topics of water and the cross, the author turns to what scripture has to say "about the water" (περὶ μὲν τοῦ ὕδατος; 11.1). The use of the preposition περί introduces the subject that Barnabas will discuss first. He then offers a sort of thesis that hints at two ways of understanding the water. Israel's failure to accept the baptism that brings forgiveness was foretold in scripture. Instead, the written word indicated that they would construct something for themselves (11.1).[231] The object in 11.1 has to do with water and baptism, so one would think that the construction that Israel makes would likewise be related to water. Yet it is difficult to ascertain precisely what Barnabas may have in view. The precise rite remains unspecified, but the author's statement fits both with his consistent emphasis on the right interpretation of scripture and also his concern about worship and idolatry. Israel's rejection of baptism in favor of something they make for themselves is an idolatrous replacement of God.

In order to demonstrate the veracity of his thesis, Barnabas turns to scriptural citations that are largely drawn from the prophets.[232] Israel's replacement of the right understanding of the water with their own construction is what leads "the prophet" (ὁ προφήτης) to call the heavens and earth to marvel (11.2).[233] The link between idolatry and the water is now made explicit.[234] God speaks through the prophet to charge Israel with two crimes. First, they rejected God, who is further characterized as "the fountain of life" (πηγὴν ζωῆς; 11.2). Second, they dug for themselves a "pit of death" (βόθρον θανάτου). Borrowing imagery from Jer 2:13, Barnabas explicitly accuses Israel of idolatry. He links their misplaced veneration so that the rejection of God is a rejection of the fountain of life. Although Barnabas turns to a different prophetic text in 11.3 (Isa 16:1–2), God continues to speak through the prophet. He declares that his holy mountain, which

---

231. Verheyden, "Israel's Fate," 256.

232. In light of the connection between baptism and the cross in 11.1, Hanson (*Allegory and Event*, 70–72) argues that the baptismal rite in 11.1–11 is transformed by the cross.

233. The referent of "about this" (ἐπὶ τούτῳ) in 11.2 is thus the statement that Israel will construct something for themselves in 11.1.

234. Koch, "Taufinterpretationen," 840–41.

Barnabas identifies as Sinai, is not a "deserted rock" (πέτρα ἔρημος; 11.3).[235] The adjective ἔρημος fits the context in *Barnabas* well. It allows the author to defend God's life-giving power by suggesting both that Israel's abandonment of God has not left Sinai deserted (ἔρημος) and that Sinai is not a desert (ἔρημος) but instead has water flowing through it. Israel's position is precarious as they are described as birds who flutter weakly about when they are taken from the nest (11.3).

Another Isaianic citation is introduced in 11.4 and continues to employ mountain imagery. This time, however, the prophetic word speaks to the promise that believers find in scripture. God will go before his people to flatten mountains, break down bronze gates, and smash iron bars so that he can give them dark, hidden, unseen treasures. God's purpose in acting this way is so that others "may know that I am the Lord God" (γνῶσιν ὅτι ἐγὼ κύριος ὁ θεός; 11.4). God's actions bring revelatory knowledge of God's identity to the people. The prophetic word continues to offer promises of life to the people as it looks forward to a time when God's people will dwell in a cave made of solid rock (πέτρας ἰσχυρᾶς; 11.5). The water in that cave will continue to flow without failing.

Terms related to building and demolition occur throughout this section, and the description of Israel's construction in 11.1 is the first instance. Israel is accused of constructing something for themselves (ἑαυτοῖς οἰκοδομήσουσιν; 11.1). They are similarly purported to have "dug" (ὤρυξαν) a pit of death (11.2). On the other hand, God's work is destructive in 11.4–5. God will level mountains, crush bronze gates, and break iron bars. The people of God will instead be able to dwell in a cave made of strong rock (πέτρας ἰσχυρᾶς; 11.5). On Barnabas's view, Israel has built something for themselves that replaces the baptism that God has given. Instead of treating Sinai as the rock that God has chosen, they have replaced the source of life with a pit of death.[236] In response, God has revealed ahead of time in scripture that the true people will live in a cave comprised of strong rock. In order to make this happen, God's actions in

---

235. Carleton Paget, *Epistle of Barnabas*, 155. Barnabas refers to God's holy mountain as Sinai (Σινᾶ; 11.3). The prophet whose words he borrows speaks about God's holy mountain as Zion (Σιών; Isa 16:1).

236. Barnabas's understanding of the covenant centers on Sinai and is not related to Jerusalem. In 5 Erza, the book's namesake similarly receives his command from the Lord "on Mount Horeb" (*in monte Horeb*; 5 Ezra 2.33). Rhodes (*Epistle of Barnabas*, 170) raises the intriguing possibility that the reference to Horeb and Israel's rejection of the Lord's commandment in 5 Ezra 2.33–34 may place the moment of revelation and disobedience in the closest possible relationship. A similar motif may be in play in *Barnabas* with the references to Sinai.

11.4 are described in destructive terms that contrast with Israel's mistaken attempt to replace what God has given to them.[237]

While discussions of building materials have not been found in such high concentrations thus far in the letter, the references to rocks are reminiscent of 5.13—6.4. The "strong rock" (πέτρα ἰσχυρά) is of particular interest (11.5). Similar Isaianic terminology is placed in Jesus's mouth during Barnabas's account of the crucifixion in 5.14, while the references to Jesus as a stone include a proclamation that God has established the Son "like a solid rock" (ὡς στερεὰν πέτραν; 6.3). Stone imagery in 5.13-14 is more explicitly christological than what is found in 11.2-5. In the latter, however, Barnabas again employs a lithic metaphor drawn from prophetic texts in order to clarify the promise of God's actions on behalf of his people. The two stones in 11.3 and 5 distinguish the dual peoples and diverging ways with which Barnabas is concerned throughout the letter.

Barnabas turns to yet another prophet in 11.6 (ἐν ἄλλῳ προφήτῃ).[238] The citation comes from Ps 1:3-6 and stretches across 11.6-7. The image of a tree planted by streams of water provides the initial focus and represents the righteous person. This tree bears fruit in its season and has leaves that do not fail. On the other hand, the ungodly (οἱ ἀσεβεῖς) will be like chaff that is driven off the face of the earth by the wind. The ungodly will not be able to judge the righteous because "the Lord knows the way of the righteous, and the way of the ungodly will perish" (γινώσκει κύριος ὁδὸν δικαίων, καὶ ὁδὸς ἀσεβῶν ἀπολεῖται; 11.7). The Lord's knowledge clarifies the contrast between two ways and concisely recapitulates the citations that have been employed throughout 11.2-7. This leads Barnabas to an exposition of the citation from Ps 1. He points out that the water and the cross coexist in the prophetic word as the tree (τὸ ξύλον) is planted by outlets of water (τὰς διεξόδους τῶν ὑδάτων).[239] Barnabas interprets this imagery with an eye to his audience. Those who hope in the cross are blessed because they will receive their wage in its season (ἐν καιρῷ αὐτοῦ). God will be directly responsible for paying what is owed. The leaves that do not fail are understood by Barnabas with regard to how his audience should speak.[240] Everything that they say with faith and love will result in the conversion and hope of many. While the water and the tree exist together in the prophetic word (11.6-7; Ps 1:3-6), it is

---

237. For other connections between Barnabas's stone imagery and idolatry, see Derry, "One Stone on Another," 525.

238. Vesco, "La lecture," 14.

239. Svigel, *Center and the Source*, 292.

240. Vesco, "La lecture," 15.

Barnabas's interpretation of the imagery that demonstrates the implications that this imagery has for the lives of his hearers.

Barnabas continues to draw together hope and fruit in an interpretation of language that is reminiscent of Ezek 47:1–12 or an Ezekiel apocryphon. These comments likewise bring the text to bear on his audience. The praise of the land of Jacob represents God's glorification of the vessel in which his Spirit dwells (11.9). Barnabas highlights the image of a river with trees growing out of it from which people can eat and live forever (11.10; see Ezek 47:9). In addition to being similar to what was found in Ps 1, Barnabas adds that the river represents baptism. Believers descend into the water filthy and sinful, but they emerge bearing the fruit of fear and hope in Jesus. Barnabas adds more to the interpretation when it comes to those who eat of the fruit and live forever. Those who eat from the fruit that believers bear represent those who hear and believe. Barnabas again connects right hearing with the right interpretation of scripture (11.11).[241] People who hear scripture aright are able to live forever through the life that comes through baptism. Although Israel is not mentioned at the end of the passage, the imagery in the final verses contrasts with the idolatrous construction of something else in 11.1.

The two ways of understanding water are key to Barnabas's argument in 11.1–11. Israel's mistaken understanding of the water is not simply set forth as wrong. It signifies a rejection of the understanding of water that God has revealed through the prophets (11.1). Ultimately, Israel is viewed along with the ungodly whose way is outlined in Barnabas's quotation from Ps 1 (11.6–7). Their way is like chaff that is thrown "from the face of the earth" (ἀπὸ προσώπου τῆς γῆς). They will not rise in judgement or be associated with the righteous. Their way will ultimately be destroyed. In contrast to Israel's rejection, those who understand what the prophets say about baptism will flourish. They will dwell in a high cave (11.4), and they will be like trees planted near streams of water with thriving leaves that never fall (11.6). Such trees will bear fruit that will come in its season (11.6, 11). Barnabas utilizes baptism to further his contrast between two people, describing Israel's lack of understanding about water in idolatrous terms and offering prophetic images of ecological flourishing in response.[242]

A contemplative strain arises in Barnabas's reflections on scripture when he begins to consider baptism. In addition to enjoining the audience to seek (ζητέω) whether the Lord revealed anything about the water and urging the audience to perceive (αἰσθάνομαι) how the water and the cross

---

241. See also 8.7; 9.1–9; 10.12
242. Koch, "Taufinterpretationen," 844–45.

occur together in Ps 1, Barnabas's quotation of Isa 33:18 promises that those who are baptized "will meditate on the fear of the Lord" (μελετήσει φόβον κυρίου; 11.5). Although this phrase comes in a scriptural citation, it recalls Barnabas's earlier instruction to attend (μελετάω) to the fear of the Lord in the paraenesis that follows the interpretation of the Israelites' idolatry at Sinai (4.11). Meditation is a characteristic of the people represented by animals with a split hoof as they attend to the meaning of the word in their heart. Such attention (μελέτη) is a work of gladness (10.11). People who walk along the way of light are called to meditate (μελετάω) on saving lives by word (19.10), while Barnabas draws his letter to a close urging his audience to attend to what he has written (21.7). When μελετάω or its cognates is used, no consideration is given to the possibility that they may attend to something evil. Rather, meditation is a characteristic of those who walk along the path of light and separates them from those who are on the path of darkness. The overtones of the two ways may be clearest in 4.11 and 19.10, but the stark admonitions against Israel's construction of something to replace the forgiveness that comes through baptism suggest that the contemplation promised in 11.5 will separate those in the light from those in the dark.[243]

The imagery that Barnabas utilizes is drawn directly from his prophetic citations and is consistent with the figurative interpretation that he employs throughout the letter. Some of the figures are given a single meaning throughout 11.1-11. Water consistently represents baptism throughout the discussion (11.1, 2, 5, 6, 8, 11). The leaves drawn from Ps 1 likewise signify a single thing, namely, the words that believers utter and which lead to the repentance and hope of those who hear them (11.6, 8). However, Barnabas also attributes double meanings to certain prophetic pictures. The most surprising instance of this phenomenon is related to the tree (11.6-11). The tree in Ps 1 is identified as the cross and provides the source of hope by which believers enter into baptism (11.6, 8). This interpretation is consistent with the introductory question in 11.1 regarding the significance of the water and the cross. Since the discussion in 12.1-11 will continue to reflect on Jesus and the cross, it is not surprising that the arboreal metaphors in Ps 1 are interpreted with a view to the cross. What is more startling is the way in which the tree is interpreted with reference to believers in Barnabas's interpretation of Ezekiel. The prophet refers to beautiful trees rising out of a river (11.10). Instead of outlining the significance of this image with a view to the cross, Barnabas interprets the imagery with an eye to believers who have been baptized (11.11). Barnabas's hermeneutic allows him to portray arboreal imagery in multiple ways so that trees can signify either the cross or believers.

243. On Israel's construction and replacement of baptism, see 11.1-3.

Barnabas's figurative interpretation of the prophets in 11.1-11 follows from his belief that God has revealed all things beforehand (11.1; see also 1.7; 3.6). Baptism is closely associated with the removal of sins. It provides the means by which God has opted to bring forgiveness of sins to God's people (11.1). People enter into the water filthy and sinful but come out bearing fruit (11.11).[244] Hope is keenly associated with baptism. Hope in the cross provides a prerequisite for believers to enter the waters of baptism (11.8). The hope by which believers enter the water enables them to live when they exit the waters of baptism. Moreover, baptism is a communicative event. It not only brings forgiveness to believers but extends its influence to those whom believers meet. Those who have received baptism speak in ways that are faithful and loving and which, in turn, lead to hope and a turn toward God in those who hear them (11.8). Baptism thus enables believers to live forever (11.10), and those who listen to the baptized will likewise live eternally (11.11). Barnabas's rich baptismal imagery and interpretations contrast with the mistaken cultic actions on the part of his Jewish opponents. Barnabas replaces what he sees as the deceit of physical circumcision and kosher practices with an understanding of the prophets that focuses on baptism that brings forgiveness of sins.

II.6.b. The Cross and the Son (Barn. 12.1-11)

Barnabas's analysis of the water is only half of what he inquired about in 11.1. He continues in 12.1-11 to consider whether God has revealed anything beforehand about the cross. The revelation of the cross is primarily addressed in 12.1-7, while 12.8-11 uses the cross as a springboard from which to discuss prior disclosures of Jesus's identity.[245] Barnabas employs scriptural citations throughout his consideration of the cross, but Moses plays a particularly active role Barnabas's interpretations (12.2-3, 5-7). The reflections on Moses enable Barnabas to transition to his interpretation of Jesus's name and identity, for it is Moses's discussion with Joshua that prompts Barnabas's digression (12.8-9). The Greek name for Joshua is Jesus (Ἰησοῦς). The discussion moves from Jesus's name to Jesus's identity as messiah by appealing to David and Isaiah (12.10-11).

244. Entrance into the water is consistently described by Barnabas as a downward movement with the use of the word καταβαίνω in 11.8 and 11. This downward movement may stand in implicit opposition to Israel's choice to build something for themselves (11.1).

245. The close connections between water and cross in 11.1—12.7 lead Vielhauer (*Geschichte*, 601) to unify this passage as a section in his outline, separating 12.8-11 as a passage on Jesus as Son of God. See similarly Kraft, *Barnabas*, 118-22. For outlines that loosely hold 12.1-11 together, see Hvalvik, *Struggle for Scripture and Covenant*, 191-92; Prostmeier, *Barnabasbrief*, 83-85; Prostmeier, "Einleitung," 44-46.

Barnabas transitions from water to wood with the use of the phrase, "Again, likewise" (ὁμοίως πάλιν; 12.1). The subject of the verb "declare" (ὁρίζω) is left unstated but should likely be understood as the Lord to whom Barnabas referred in 11.1. The Lord's declaration marks something out about the cross to establish it clearly, and the means that the Lord employs is another prophet. The prophet asks when these things will be completed. The Lord answers that they will end "whenever the tree is laid down and raised up and whenever blood drips from the tree" (ὅταν ξύλον κλιθῇ καὶ ἀναστῇ καὶ ὅταν ἐκ ξύλου αἷμα στάξῃ; 12.1). The author understands the words with reference to the cross and the one who was about to be crucified. The decline and ascension of the wood metonymically portrays Jesus's death and resurrection. His death on the cross marks the teleological completion of God's work.

Barnabas turns to consider how Moses showed the cross to Israel. The author appeals to the story of Israel's war against the Amalekites in Exod 17:8–16. The Amalekites are not mentioned by Barnabas but are generalized as "foreign tribes" (οἱ ἀλλόφυλων; 12.2). As in 10.2 and 9, Moses is again accepted as someone who spoke and acted in the Spirit as Barnabas reports that the Spirit spoke to the heart of Moses.[246] Moses was charged to use his body to make a model (τύπος) of the cross and the one who would suffer. Whenever Moses stretched his hands out on the stack of weapons, Israel would begin to win their fight. They began to die whenever he lowered his hands. Barnabas argues that Israel was shown through this event that they must hope in the suffering Jesus for their salvation (12.2, 3).[247] Barnabas's brief narration of this story repeats words related to fighting and death so that Israel's death at the hands of their enemies seems to be tied to their rejection of Jesus. Barnabas then adds another prophetic word in which the speaker stretches out his hands to a disobedient and resistant people (12.4; see Isa 65:2).[248] The prophetic words are placed in the mouth of Jesus, who stretched out his hands on the cross.[249] Israel's failure is again highlighted.[250]

---

246. Prostmeier, *Barnabasbrief*, 436–37.

247. Longenecker, *Cross before Constantine*, 62–63.

248. See also Rom 10:20–21; Justin, *Dial.* 24.4. On the speaker of this verse in Barn. 12.4, see Bates, *Hermeneutics of Apostolic Proclamation*, 3–4.

249. Writing near the end of the second century, Irenaeus likewise reads Isa 65:2 as words that Jesus uttered from the cross (*Epid.* 79). In the process, Irenaeus quotes several phrases from Ps 21 (22 MT) including a mixed citation that combines words that are now found in Ps 21:21 (22:21 MT); 118:120 (119:120 MT); 21:17 (22:17 MT). For nearly identical psalmic quotations, see Barn. 6.6. For Isa 65:2 at other points in Irenaeus's writing, see *Epid.* 92; *Haer.* 2.6.1.

250. Nearing the conclusion of his analysis of Israel's fate within the Epistle of Barnabas, Verheyden ("Israel's Fate," 261) concludes, "Israel has continuously, and repeatedly, been misled and misguided, not by its leaders (see Moses and Joshua-Jesus in Barn. 12—no such leaders are mentioned for the disaster with the Temple) but by its own account—as a group or body, not as individuals. It is a harsh verdict, both because

Barnabas returns to Moses's symbolic actions in 12.5–7 and narrates how Moses hung a carved serpent on a tree so that Israel could be saved from a plague in the camp. Moses's actions provide a model of Jesus because Jesus had to suffer in order to make others alive (12.5).[251] The Israelite experience of death from serpent bites is linked to the coming of transgression into the garden through the serpent.[252] Their death at the time of Moses was also a prefigurement of the affliction that they would later experience because of their transgression.[253] Moses made the serpent and displayed it in a prominent place as a model of Jesus's suffering, despite his command that the Israelites should not make any molten or carved images as their god (12.6).[254] Moses's explanation of the serpent makes this clear (12.7). When the Israelites are bitten by a serpent, they should look at the serpent that Moses made in order to be healed. They should hope in the serpent, believing that it can restore life to them even though the serpent is dead. Barnabas urges his readers to understand scripture rightly and to see that all things are in Jesus and for him.[255]

Barnabas's quotation in 12.1 is teleologically oriented and fits with the eschatological emphasis throughout much of the letter. The prophetic word illustrates that the cross stands at the center of Barnabas's eschatological conception of time. Yet the prophetic quotation is not found in its current form anywhere in the Old Greek Bible. It is most similar to words that are found in 4 Ezra. After hearing Uriel's revelation about the grain of evil that comes from Adam's seed, Ezra asks, "How and when will these things be?" (*quo et quando haec*; 4 Ezra 4.33). Uriel later looks forward to the signs that will accompany the end. In addition to terror, unrighteousness, and desolation, Uriel points to cosmic abnormalities that will mark

---

of this sustained collective approach and of the indifference, to say the least, toward Israel's fate that speaks from it."

251. A similar tradition is also found in John 3:13–14. On *Barnabas* and John, see Braun, "La 'Lettre de Barnabé,'" 119–24; Carleton Paget, "Barnabas' Anti-Jewish Use," 108–9; Carleton Paget, *Epistle of Barnabas*, 225–30; Holtzmann, "Barnabas und Johannes," 336–51.

252. See Gen 3:1–7. For another attempt to link Num 21:8–9 with Gen 3, see Philo, *Leg.* 2.78–81; Martín, "L'interpretatione allegorica," 180–81.

253. The reference to the current experience of affliction is likely a reference to Jewish hostilities with the Romans, whether in the First Jewish War that ended with the destruction of the temple in 70 CE or in the lead up to the Second Jewish War in the 130s CE.

254. See Exod 20:4–5; Lev 26:1; Deut 5:8–9; 27:15.

255. Barnabas's statement that "all things are in him and for him" (ἐν αὐτῷ πάντα καὶ εἰς αὐτόν; 12.7) refers to Jesus and is similar to statements found in Paul's letters. See further Rom 11:36; 1 Cor 8:6; Col 1:16; Wengst, *Didache*, 175n196.

the eschaton. One of these signs is that "blood will drip from the tree" (*de ligno sanguis stillabit*; 4 Ezra 5.5). Barnabas employs language that was known to other apocalyptic authors, but Barn. 12.1 is longer than the lines from 4 Ezra and is implemented into the letter concurrently. The dissimilarities between Barn. 12.1 and other texts led Menahem Kister to argue that the Barnabean citation comes from an apocryphal Ezekiel text which is attested incompletely among the Qumran manuscripts.[256] Wherever the text comes from, Barnabas interprets it so that the tree is identified with the cross. The fall and rise of the tree represents Jesus's death and resurrection so that the blood that flows from the tree and the resurrection of the cross are read as symbols of Jesus.

Barnabas plays with terminology related to death and life in his description of Moses's symbolic actions in 12.2-3 and 5-7. Israel is "handed over to death" (παρεδόθησαν εἰς θάνατον) when they find themselves at war with other tribes. Similarly, Israel is "handed over to the distress of death because of their transgression" (διὰ τὴν παράβασιν αὐτῶν εἰς θλῖψιν θανάτου παραδοθήσονται; 12.5). Violent and pugilistic terminology is brought into conversation with necrotic language. Moses makes the sign of the cross with his body "when war was being waged against Israel by other tribes" (πολεμουμένου τοῦ Ἰσραὴλ ὑπὸ τῶν ἀλλοφύλων; 12.2). The word πολεμέω is repeated twice more in 12.2. Moses's symbolic action comes as a warning to "those who are being assaulted" (αὐτοὺς πολεμουμένους). Barnabas attributes the cause of the conflict that they are experiencing to their sins. By raising his arms as a sign of the cross, Moses demonstrates that Israel must place their hope in Jesus's cross. If they do not, "they will be at war forever" (εἰς τὸν αἰῶνα πολεμηθήσονται).[257] Although war is not in view in 12.5-7, Israel's experience of death is outlined in Moses's second symbolic action with similarly vivid imagery. His action comes as a sign (ἐν σημείῳ) "while Israel is falling" (πίπτοντος τοῦ Ἰσραήλ). Because the Lord caused every snake to

---

256. Kister, "Barnabas 12:1," 63-66. Kister's argument is helped by the presence of language similar to Ezek 40-48 in Barn. 11.9-11. Additionally, Kister suggests that the unknown citation in Barn. 4.3 may be a free rendering of an Ezekiel text similar to 4Q385 3 (Kister, "Barnabas 12:1," 66-67).

257. Barnabas appears to synergize the story of Israel at war in Exod 17:8-16 with the Roman-Jewish conflicts of the first two centuries CE. The war with Amalek during the time of Moses becomes a war with other tribes that extends forever. Given Barnabas's setting after the First Jewish War (66-70 CE) and most likely following the diaspora conflicts during the time of Trajan (115-17 CE), an eternal warning about war fits Barnabas's polemical circumstances well. If the letter was written during the lead-up to what would be the Second Jewish War (132-35 CE), the declaration of eternal war would suit Barnabas's purposes even better. For further discussion, see Edwards, *Gospel*, 61-62.

bite the Israelites, "they were dying" (ἀπέθνησκον; 12.5). Death is vividly described through war and unusual signs. Barnabas draws careful attention to the ways in which death was connected specifically with Israel.

The signs that Moses makes are also connected with fighting and death. Moses holds out his arms from a place above the battle while the fighting is ongoing. The Exodus narrative reports that Moses became fatigued from holding out his hands, so he sat on a stone while Aaron and Hur supported his hands (Exod 17:12). While Barnabas knows that Moses's hands required support, Moses stacks weapons on top of one another and stands with his hands outstretched on top of the armor (Barn. 12.2). The use of weaponry as a means to salvation provides another reminder of the military setting of Moses's salvific action. The lifeless state of the serpent is also emphasized. While living serpents are biting the Israelites and causing death, Moses fashions a bronze serpent even though he had instructed the people not to make images of God. Thus Moses "calls the people with a proclamation" (κηρύγματι καλεῖ τὸν λαόν) after placing the serpent in a public place (12.6). The serpent is made of bronze and is dead. Yet it is precisely this serpent that Moses instructs the people to look to when the people come to him seeking prayer for healing.

The serpent symbolism emphasizes mortality but also demonstrates the interplay between death and life in the models of Jesus's death that Barnabas finds enacted by Moses. Moses raises his hands while the Israelites fight against the other tribes who are assaulting them. When he does this, "Israel began to win again" (πάλιν ἐνίκα ὁ Ἰσραήλ). Conversely, when Moses put his hands down, "they began to die" (ἐθανατοῦντο; 12.2).[258] This happened because the Spirit told Moses to make "a model of the cross and of the one who is about to suffer" (τύπον σταυροῦ καὶ τοῦ μέλλοντος πάσχειν; 12.2).[259] Death and life come and go with the rise and fall of Moses's hands as a symbol of Jesus's death, which has been communicated by the Spirit.[260] The serpent likewise brings healing to the Israelites who will place their hope in what it represents. Healing is what the Israelites desire when they come to Moses asking for prayer (12.7). Moses responds that they will be saved (σωθήσεται) from their snakebites when they look to the serpent. Since the

---

258. I understand the imperfect tense to be inceptive and thereby to denote the start or, in this case, the restart of an action.

259. The Spirit is again connected to Moses's speech and actions. Moses spoke about the dietary laws "in the Spirit" (ἐν πνεύματι; 10.2, 9). Whereas Moses's agency is stressed in 10.2, 9 and the Spirit is the means by which he communicates, the Spirit is the subject who speaks in 12.2. Moses becomes the audience who hears and responds.

260. For similar uses of Moses's outstretched hands in the second century, see Justin, *Dial.* 91; 112; 131; Irenaeus, *Epid.* 46.

serpent is again a model of Jesus (τύπος τοῦ Ἰησοῦ), Barnabas's interpretation of the story in Num 21:4–9 is thoroughly christological. Jesus is the means to Israel's salvation even though they thought that he was destroyed (12.5). Barnabas insists again that Jesus had to suffer (δεῖ αὐτὸν παθεῖν). Jesus's suffering and the healing that comes through the dead serpent collectively illustrate that Jesus is likewise able bring life (αὐτὸς ζωοποιήσει) through his death (12.5). Both the Israelites who are directly addressed and Barnabas's readers who are implicitly in view are called to believe that "even though he was dead, he is able to make alive" (αὐτὸς ὢν νεκρὸς δύναται ζωοποιῆσαι; 12.7). The imagery of death and life enables Barnabas to show that Israel has failed to understand the narratives they find in the Torah, that Moses's actions reveal the suffering and death of Jesus beforehand, and that life must come by means of death.[261]

In addition to the interplay between death and life in Barnabas's Mosaic typology, there is also a tendency to generalize the narratives from what is found in the Pentateuch and to incorporate further pentateuchal traditions. The clearest example of generalizing occurs in 12.2, where Barnabas records that the Israelites were being assaulted "by other tribes" (ὑπὸ τῶν ἀλλοφύλων). Barnabas may know that the story of Moses raising his hands to give victory to Israel occurs when Israel is attacked by the Amalekites because he refers to the house of Amalek in a later citation (12.9). Yet the report about Moses raising his hands is generalized. The wrongdoing for which the Israelites are punished with snakes is also left unspecified in 12.5. The Israelites are handed over to death simply due to their transgressions. The undefined way in which Barnabas sets up the story is mirrored by his incorporation of other scriptural narratives into the serpent typology. The punishment of the Israelites' sin with snakes is fitting "since transgression came about in Eve through the serpent" (ἐπειδὴ ἡ παράβασις διὰ τοῦ ὄφεως ἐν Εὔα ἐγένετο; 12.5). Nor is the reference to the story of Eve's interactions with the serpent the only biblical tradition that Barnabas employs. He also makes reference to the Torah's teaching that images of God are unlawful. Barnabas's words correspond most closely to Lev 26:1 and Deut 27:15. Despite this, Moses makes an image that prefigures Jesus on the cross that is scripturally approved and reveals knowledge of God to Barnabas's readers (12.6). As Barnabas selectively appropriates the portions of the narratives that most clearly prefigure Jesus and discards particularizing details that do not aid his purpose, it is easier for him to weave further traditions from elsewhere in Israel's scripture into the story.

261. Jesus's glory is also found in these signs, "because all things are in him and for him" (ὅτι ἐν αὐτῷ πάντα καὶ εἰς αὐτόν; 12.7). See further Svigel, *Center and the Source*, 292.

Barnabas's focus on Moses's actions in the Pentateuch lead him to a digression that begins with Moses's interactions with Joshua. The points that follow in 12.8–9 assume readers know that the names Joshua and Jesus are identical in Greek: Ἰησοῦς.²⁶² Barnabas inquires why Moses instructed the people to listen only to Joshua. Joshua is further identified as a prophet, and Moses is said to have given Joshua his name (12.8).²⁶³ Barnabas makes reference to Joshua's work as a spy in the promised land (Num 13–14), but the quotation that he employs sounds most similar to what Moses told Joshua after his defeat of the Amalekites in Exod 17:14. Barnabas reports that the Son of God will cut down Amalek's house in the last days (12.9). Moses's words about Joshua point to Jesus, who is no son of man but rather the Son of God (12.10). Barnabas's extended reflections on Moses's work leads him to think further about a similar word attributed to David in response to the potential remark that the Messiah was to be the son of David. Barnabas appeals to Ps 109:1 (110:1 MT) and says that David prophecies (προφητεύει) about Jesus's true identity. David understood that some would be deceived and proclaims, "The Lord spoke to my lord" (εἶπεν ὁ κύριος τῷ κυρίῳ μου; 12.10). Barnabas moves immediately from this quotation to an Isaianic word where Isaiah similarly says, "The Lord spoke to Christ my lord" (εἶπεν ὁ κύριος τῷ Χριστῷ κυρίῳ μου; 12.11). In response to those who would see Jesus as the messianic son of David, Barnabas insists Jesus can only be Son of God because even David referred to him as Lord. Son of God and son of David are mutually exclusive titles in 12.10–11.

The discussion of Jesus's name and the links between Joshua and Jesus in 12.8–9 follows from Moses's prefiguring of the cross but also coincides with other early Christian texts that link Jesus to Joshua. Joshua and Jesus are connected in Heb 3:7—4:13 as the author argues that Sabbath rest is still to come even after Joshua's conquest of the land.²⁶⁴ In an argument that is more similar to Barnabas, Justin employs the destruction of Amalek in his reflections on Joshua's importance as a messianic precursor (*Dial.* 49.7–8). When Barnabas continues his digression to take up Ps 109:1 (110:1 MT), it is important that David refers to Jesus as his Lord

---

262. L maintains this wordplay even in translation. Both the Son of Nave and the Son of God are named *Iesus*. This contrasts, for example, with the Vulgate translation of Josh 1:1, which reads *Iosue*.

263. Moses is said to have changed Joshua's name in Num 13:16. In the Old Greek of Num 13:16, Joshua's name was Αὐσή until Moses changed it to Ἰησοῦς. The Masoretic Text reports that "Moses called Hoshea son of Nun Joshua" (ויקרא משה להושע בן-נון יהושע).

264. For further discussion of Joshua-Jesus typology in Hebrews, see Whitfield, *Joshua Traditions*, 205–65; Whitfield, "Pioneer and Perfecter," 80–87.

rather than his son.[265] The Barnabean discussion is thus thematically similar to the riddle that Jesus tells in the Synoptic Gospels (Matt 22:44; Mark 12:36; Luke 20:42–43).[266] Barnabas's point that Jesus is Son of God rather than a human son is furthered by his citation of Isa 45:1.[267] He makes use of a textual variant in the Isaianic text in which God speaks to Christ my "Lord" (κυρίῳ) rather than to Cyrus (Κύρῳ) my messiah. Barnabas's reflections on Jesus's name further specify how God has revealed knowledge beforehand and supports his larger reflections about the cross. Barnabas finds that scripture attests both to the cross as a means of God's work and to Jesus as the person who is to be crucified.

Barnabas does not offer a concluding reference to the water and cross in 12.11. He instead simply passes to the next section. Yet Barnabas's search for the Lord's prior revelation of the water and cross that began in 11.1 amply demonstrates that the author's initial search into whether the Lord revealed anything beforehand about the water and the cross must be answered affirmatively, at least from the author's perspective. In making his argument, he employs some of his most creative exegetical techniques and most fulsome analyses of scripture. The interpretations of Ps 1:3–6 (11.6–8), Ezekiel traditions (11.9–11), Exod 17:8–16 (12.2–3), and Num 21:4–9 (12.5–7) offer detailed, albeit selective, interpretations of scriptural passages to support the author's point. The understanding of the water and the cross that Barnabas urges his audience to undertake sets them apart from opponents who have built something for themselves and fail to recognize that the Spirit spoke through Moses. If the author's interpretations are accepted, Barnabas will have distinguished between two ways of reading scripture and between two peoples. The author thus returns to matters of covenant belonging and the true people of God in the next section.

---

265. Edwards, "Epistle of Barnabas," 36–37; Edwards, *Gospel*, 64–65.

266. Bockmuehl, "Son of David," 483. For other examples of how Ps 109:1 (110:1 MT) was used in literature of the first two centuries CE, see Acts 2:34; 1 Cor 15:25; Heb 1:13; 1 Clem. 36.5; Irenaeus, *Epid.* 48.

267. See similar usages of Isa 45:1 in Irenaeus, *Epid.* 49; Tertullian, *Jud.* 7.2; *Prax.* 11.8; 28.11. For additional references and further discussion of the textual form of Isa 45:1 in early Christian authors, see Kraft, "Barnabas' Isaiah Text and the 'Testimony Book' Hypothesis," 341–42. Citations of Tertullian's *Adversus Praxean* come from Evans, *Tertullianus*.

II.7. The People, the Inheritance, and the Covenant (Barn. 13.1—14.9)

References to "us" and "them," to dual ways of living, and to alternative interpretations have characterized much of *Barnabas* thus far. After the initial division outlined in terms of fasting and sacrifice and with a glance to the need for the audience to maintain their covenant membership in the eschatological context that they inhabit (2.4–4.14), the author turns to a discussion of Jesus's suffering and endurance (5.1–8.7) before returning to discuss circumcision, dietary laws, and God's scriptural revelation of the water and cross (9.1—12.11). Barnabas's fullest discussion of how he understands the two peoples occurs in 13.1—14.9. This passage sets out the author's view of the genuine people of God, that is, the people who inherit what was promised to the patriarchs and who are rightly identified as recipients of the covenant.

The passage begins with a cohortative verb that enjoins the audience to look with the author into the new topic: "let us see" (ἴδωμεν; 13.1). The author invites the audience to look with him at which of the two peoples inherit the covenant and to which people the covenant belongs. Barnabas turns first to the question of the people's identity and introduces the topic with a familiar prepositional phrase. His audience should listen to what scripture says "about the people" (περὶ τοῦ λαοῦ; 13.2).[268] What follows in 13.2-7 considers the people whom God sets apart as heirs in the patriarchal traditions. The lens shifts slightly in 14.1 as the author again calls the audience to look with him: "let us see" (ἴδωμεν; 14.1). Barnabas inquires whether the covenant was given and to whom it belongs. He considers whether the covenant was given to the Israelites on Sinai in 14.1-5, completing the earlier preview in 4.6b-9a. The section concludes by considering how the Father gave instructions for "us" to be redeemed and thus to become the people of God (14.6-9). The author thus offers a sustained argument in 13.1—14.9 that defines the true people of God, the genuine heirs to the patriarchal promises, and the real recipients of the covenant that God made.

II.7.a. The Two Peoples and the Inheritance (Barn. 13.1-7)

The transition from the discussion of the water and the cross (11.1—12.11) is marked with an exhortation for the author and audience to join together in looking. The formula is subjunctive verb + "now" (δέ) + "whether" (εἰ). It has already been used in 11.1. The same rhetorical marker will be

---

268. See similarly 9.1; 11.1; 12.1.

employed to mark transitions in 14.1 and 16.6. Barnabas introduces a twofold topic in 13.1. The first subject concerns whether "this people or the first will inherit" (οὗτος ὁ λαὸς κληρονομεῖ ἢ ὁ πρῶτος). No object is explicitly mentioned.[269] Based on what follows in 13.2–7, however, Barnabas seeks to determine the true heirs of the patriarchal promises. The second matter concerns whether "the covenant belongs to us or to them" (ἡ διαθήκη εἰς ἡμᾶς ἢ εἰς ἐκείνους; 13.1). This double theme comprises the focus of the closely defined exegetical argument in 13.1—14.9.

The topic of the argument continues to be narrowed as Barnabas instructs the audience to listen to what scripture says "about the people" (περὶ τοῦ λαοῦ; 13.2). It quickly becomes evident that the topic to consider is which people are in view when it comes to God's promise of inheritance. This discussion is part of a scriptural conversation in which Barnabas records and interprets what scripture says. The first passage to which Barnabas draws the audience's attention has to do with the children of Isaac and Rebecca. Quoting from Gen 25:21–23, Barnabas reports that Isaac and Rebekah were unable to have children, that Isaac prayed, and that Rebekah became pregnant. She then consults of the Lord and discovers that there are two peoples in her womb. According to Barnabas, "one people will rule over the other people, and the greater will serve the lesser" (13.2). After this quotation, Barnabas urges the audience to understand who Isaac and Rebekah represent. Unfortunately, he does not aid the audience in identifying Isaac and Rebekah. These characters remain unidentified in Barnabas's figurative interpretation. Yet the larger point for 13.2–7 is that "this people" (ὁ λαὸς οὗτος) is greater than "that" (ἐκεῖνος; 13.3).[270] The birth of Jacob and Esau are a figure of Barnabas's audience and his opponents. Barnabas identifies his Jewish opponents with Esau, while he and his Christ-following audience are categorized in terms of Jacob.

The next citation is found "in another prophecy" (ἐν ἄλλῃ προφητείᾳ) where Jacob speaks to his son (13.4). Barnabas's version of the story is a shortened form of the narrative in Gen 48:11–19.[271] Jacob celebrates that he has not been deprived of his son's presence and thus urges Joseph to

---

269. The lack of direct object makes κληρονομεῖ the more difficult reading. This reading is found in S and is followed by Ehrman, *Apostolic Fathers*, 2.60; Holmes, *Apostolic Fathers*, 422; Lindemann and Paulsen, *Apostolischen Väter*, 58; Prinzivalli and Simonetti, *Seguendo Gesù*, 2.154; Prostmeier and Lona, *Epistola Barnabae*, 114; Wengst, *Didache*, 176. However, H and G read κληρονόμος. This reading is accepted by Prigent and Kraft, *Épître de Barnabé*, 174. L reads *hereditatem capit*, a slightly different reading but one that places a direct object after the verb. The reading in S should be followed because it is the *lectio difficilior*.

270. Skarsaune, "Ethnic Discourse," 255–56.

271. Prigent and Kraft, *Épître de Barnabé*, 177 n 3.

bring Joseph's sons so that he can bless them. When Joseph returns to his father, he places Manasseh on Jacob's right so that he would be blessed more abundantly (13.5). The reason for this arrangement is that Manasseh is older and should receive a larger portion of the blessing. Barnabas, however, credits Jacob with seeing "in the Spirit a model of the coming people" (τύπον τῷ πνεύματι τοῦ λαοῦ τοῦ μεταξύ; 13.5). The coming people include Barnabas and his audience as those who hope in the Son of God. Upon seeing this model, Jacob switches his hands so that his right hand sits on Ephraim's head. When Joseph asks his father about this, Jacob answers in the same words that were said about him in 13.2: "the greater will serve the lesser" (13.5).[272] Ephraim will grow to be stronger than Manasseh. Barnabas urges the audience to notice which people was identified by the laying on of hands. The younger is privileged over the older, and Barnabas identifies his audience and himself with Jacob and Ephraim. They are the rightful "heir of the covenant" (τῆς διαθήκης κληρονόμον; 13.6). His Jewish opponents, on the other hand, are represented by Esau and Manasseh.

From the perspective of Barnabas's opponents, the readings in 13.2–6 represent radical redefinitions of who the people of God are.[273] Yet Barnabas's final example may be the most surprising. His appeal to Abraham begins with a premise. If the same thing that was found in the blessings given by Isaac and Jacob is also found in Abraham, "we receive the completion of our knowledge" (ἀπέχομεν τὸ τέλειον τῆς γνώσεως ἡμῶν; 13.7). The move backward in time from Abraham's descendants in 13.2–6 creates a chronological gap, but Abraham provides the summative point in the exegetical argument of 13.2–7. Abraham's significance for Barnabas's arguments comes in his relation to gentiles rather than Jews. Barnabas employs language that sounds similar to Gen 15:6 when he notes that Abraham only believed and "it was established for righteousness" (ἐτέθη εἰς δικαιοσύνην). God thus establishes Abraham as "the father of the gentiles who believe in God while uncircumcised" (πατὴρ ἐθνῶν τῶν πιστευόντων δι' ἀκροβυστίας τῷ θεῷ). The reference to Abraham as the father of nations is found in the Torah at Gen 17:4–5, but Barnabas's emphasis on the uncircumcised nature of the gentiles excludes Jews from the people of God.[274] Although it is not easy to specify precisely how δι' ἀκροβυστίας functions in 13.7,[275] Abraham's as-

272. Klevinghaus, *Theologsiche Stellung*, 16.
273. Kok, "Ethnic Reasoning," 90.
274. For another instance of fatherhood language applied to Abraham, see Rom 4:10–12.
275. See further Prostmeier and Lona, *Epistola Barnabae*, 117 n 9. It is difficult to see how uncircumcision could be the means of belief in God. I have thus opted for a temporal nuance to the phrase.

sociation solely with the uncircumcised and the concomitant omission of circumcised Jews represents a stark expansion of the Genesis narrative.[276] The completion of knowledge for Barnabas and his audience is to recognize that the people who are heirs of God's promises given in patriarchal narratives are uncircumcised gentiles alone.

Barnabas's exegesis supports his quest to determine which people is blessed and relies upon narratives in which the patriarchs are associated with the benediction of surprising recipients. In the examples of 13.2-6, the recipients of the blessing are the youngest children, which strengthens Barnabas's argument that the historically younger people (Christ-followers) are the true heirs over and against their elder and more established counterparts (Jews). The surprise in Isaac and Rebekah's blessing of Jacob and Esau occurs within the brothers' lifetime as Jacob acquires Esau's birthright (Gen 25:29-34) and tricks Esau out of his blessing (Gen 27:1-40). Since Jacob's name is changed to Israel (Gen 32:28), Jacob and Esau become eponymous representatives of the Israelites and Edomites, respectively.[277] Jacob continues to be identified with the Israelites in other early Jewish texts.[278] The use of the Jacob story among early Jesus-followers begins to shift the focus of its interpretation. Paul puts Jacob forward as an example of God's freedom to choose (Rom 9:10-13). Although Paul argues strongly for gentile inclusion throughout Rom 9-11, Israel will be saved and continues to be loved in accordance with God's choice (Rom 11:26-28).[279] The interpretation of two nations in the context of second-century Jewish-Christian discussion continues in the writings of Justin, Irenaeus, and Tertullian, with all three interpreting Jacob with reference to the church and Esau with reference to Jews.[280] Although these authors differ in precisely how they utilize the details of their interpretations, they share with Barnabas an interest in the two peoples symbolized by Jacob and Esau.

---

276. Yet it is interesting that knowledge of Abraham in the early centuries of the Common Era was not restricted to Jews and Christians, on which, see van der Horst, "Did the Gentiles Know," 61-75.

277. On Esau and Edom within the Genesis narrative, see Gen 25:30; 32:3; 36:1-43.

278. E.g., Jub. 19.15-31; Josephus, *A.J.* 1.18.1 (1.257-58). See also Dunn, "Tertullian and Rebekah," 123-24. Philo interprets Esau allegorically as wickedness or folly, while Jacob represents virtue (Philo, *Congr.* 129; *Sacr.* 4, 17). While Jacob is not strictly identified with Israel in these Philonic texts, a Jewish author interprets Jacob with regard to the virtue that should characterize the philosopher and thus the person of God.

279. Barclay, "'I Will Have Mercy,'" 82-106.

280. See Justin, *Dial.* 123.8; 134.6; Irenaeus, *Haer.* 4.21-23; Tertullian, *Adv. Jud.* 1.3-8. See further Dunn, "Tertullian and Rebekah," 119-45; Taylor, *Anti-Judaism*, 137-38.

Barnabas's interpretation assumes that readers will be able to identify the patriarchal characters figuratively (Barn. 13.3). Jacob is to be identified with "this people," while Esau stands for "that one." What is surprising is that Barnabas grants no chance for repentance to Esau and those whom he represents. Esau is a fixed type. Other elements of his interpretation remain unclear. Most importantly, he suggests that the audience should know who Isaac and Rebekah are, but he offers no hint in his scriptural citations (13.2–3). Barnabas's interpretation is thus selective. The selectivity becomes more evident in his use of the story of Ephraim and Manasseh. While Barnabas relays the story of how Jacob crossed his hands in order to privilege Ephraim in ways that are familiar from the Genesis narrative, he does not report about Jacob's blessing of Manasseh (Gen 48:8–20). This portion of the story is simply omitted by Barnabas or his source. By doing this, Barnabas places the focus on the people who are now "first" (πρῶτον), that is, primary in significance (13.6). He also excludes his Jewish opponents from inheriting the covenant. A similar phenomenon is found in Barnabas's use of Abraham as Abraham takes up a position as the father of gentiles (πατὴρ ἐθνῶν) in 13.7. Barnabas's Jewish opponents are excluded from belonging to Abraham. His application of paternal language to Abraham may draw from Pauline traditions. Paul refers to Abraham as "the father of all who believe while uncircumcised" (πατὴρ πάντων τῶν πιστευόντων δι' ἀκροβυστίας; Rom 4:11).[281] Yet for Paul Abraham is also the "father of circumcision" (πατὴρ περιτομῆς; Rom 4:12).[282] The use of Abraham is different in Barn. 13.7, however, as the author focuses on Abraham only insofar as he is the origin of non-Jewish believers. His selection thereby excludes Jews from claiming Abraham as their father.[283]

The exegesis of Abraham provides Barnabas with "the completion of our knowledge" (τὸ τέλειον τῆς γνώσεως ἡμῶν; 13.7). Both the telic nature of Barnabas's thought and the importance of knowledge have been discussed elsewhere in the letter.[284] Barnabas writes to his audience so that

---

281. Nickelsburg ("Abraham the Convert," 167–71) suggests that Paul's use of Abraham as a model of gentile conversion may draw upon Jewish traditions that portray Abraham as a pagan convert. E.g., Apoc. Ab. 1–8; Josephus, *A.J.* 1.154–57; Jub. 11–12.

282. Note also the similarity between Barn. 13.7 and Rom 4:17. For a convenient synopsis, see Ehorn, "Abraham in the Apostolic Fathers," 161. For additional discussion of Barn. 13.7 and Rom 4, see Edwards, *Gospel*, 90–91.

283. Barnabas's reading of the Abraham narrative in 13.6 fits well with his understanding of circumcision in 9.1–9. Circumcision is about hearing God rightly, while Abraham's act of circumcision points on to Jesus. Just so, Abraham is the father of the gentiles in 13.6 and not of circumcised Jews.

284. The τελ-lexeme is utilized in 1.5, 6 (2x); 4.1, 3, 7, 10, 11; 5.11; 6.19; 7.3; 8.1; 10.5, 10; 13.7; 14.5; 19.11. The word γνῶσις is found in 1.5; 2.3; 5.4; 6.9; 9.8; 10.10; 11.4;

they will flee lawless works completely (τελείως; 4.1) and looks forward to a time when all eschatological events will be completed (4.3; 6.19). Knowledge can be exegetically oriented and is personified so that it is capable of speaking for itself (6.9), while the key point for which Barnabas writes is to complete the knowledge of his audience (1.5). Abraham is an example of how the completion of knowledge works within the letter. The phrase is used to indicate that Abraham is the summative example from the exegetical discussion in 13.2–7. If even Abraham was called to be the father of the gentiles, Barnabas's opponents have no claim to the inheritance that was promised to the patriarchs.[285] Since Abraham is the capstone of the argument, this also explains Barnabas's chronological move backward from Isaac (13.2–3) and Jacob (13.4–6). The knowledge that is completed in 13.7 is again related to the interpretation of scripture, and the completion demonstrates itself by rightly understanding what scripture says about the inheritance that was promised to the patriarchs.

The question of which of the two peoples has the rightful claim to the inheritance promised by God is central to 13.1—14.9. It is one of the questions with which Barnabas begins the discussion in 13.1 as he seeks to discover whether "this people" (οὗτος ὁ λαός) or "the first" (ὁ πρῶτος) will be the lawful heirs. Although the patriarchal promises are the subject of Barnabas's exegesis in 13.1–7 and provide one way of understanding inheritance, Barnabas also speaks about the people as an "heir of the covenant" (τῆς διαθήκης κληρονόμον; 13.6). The inheritance involves a claim on the covenant and the relationship with God that corresponds to this covenant. Barnabas argues that he and his audience are included in the people of the inheritance (14.4). The examples in 13.1—14.9 make it clear that God has revealed the heirs beforehand. However, the inheritance is not yet complete (6.19). Nor is the offer of inheritance deserved by the people. Jesus is the heir, while Barnabas and his audience accept this status only by virtue of Jesus's inheritance (14.5). Previously, Barnabas remarked that the Lord has cut short the days in order that Jesus may come into his inheritance (4.3). Because Jesus has received his inheritance by enduring for Barnabas and his audience, they are likewise able to become heirs of the patriarchal promises in Christ.

The matter of who will inherit the promises can thus be answered before the inheritance becomes fully apparent, for Barnabas argues that he and his audience will receive this inheritance rather than the Jews, who claim

---

12.3; 13.7; 18.1; 19.1; 21.5.

285. Or, in the words of Ehorn ("Abraham in the Apostolic Fathers," 162), "Gentiles, then, are depicted as the true heirs of God's covenant and the promises to Abraham."

that they are the heirs.[286] Inheritance is exclusive in the letter. Only one of the two peoples are able to inherit, and Barnabas argues that "this people" alone are heirs. It is not possible to retain Israel's practices or Israel's understanding of scripture and to inherit the promises that were given to the forefathers. Yet one should note that the inheritance comes from outside of the people. The inheritance begins with something that was promised by God (13.2–7). It is given in God's time, which God has shortened in order to minimize the power of the final stumbling block (4.3). Barnabas and his audience receive this status only through the Son (14.5). Although it is possible to know who inherits the promises in the present, the inheritance will only finally be received in the future and thus remains something that the audience looks forward to when God's promises are completed.

Barnabas sets up the first stage of an argument in 13.1–7. The pericope is particularly focused on the question of which people are set apart as God's heirs. While the first (πρῶτος) people who are mentioned in 13.1 are older, Barnabas argues that the patriarchal narratives reveal that God works in surprising ways to bless the younger son. Moreover, Abraham was called to be the father of the nations and thus the gentiles. The patriarchal narratives affirm Barnabas's position that there is only one heir and people of God and that he and his audience are included in this people. They are rightly understood as the first (πρῶτος) people (13.6). Yet the question of inheritance on its own is insufficient. One may also ask what they are set to inherit and why the older people did not receive it. Barnabas turns to these matters in the second stage of the argument.

II.7.b. The Covenant: Given and Sought (Barn. 14.1–9)

Barnabas completes the first stage of his two-part argument with an affirmative exclamation: Yes (14.1).[287] The next stage is introduced with a bipartite exhortation to the audience to see (ἴδωμεν) and to seek (ζητῶμεν) something. The author and audience are going to explore whether the Lord really gave the covenant that he swore he would give to the people (14.1). The sentence is grammatically clunky with two verbs (ἴδωμεν; ζητῶμεν) and a twice-repeated particle (εἰ) indicating the objects that are sought. When combined with the affirmation that concludes the exegesis of 13.1–7, the opening of the second stage in 14.1 offers readers a chance

---

286. "Die Kirche aus den Heiden ist das Volk Gottes" (Klevinghaus, *Theologsiche Stellung*, 17).

287. I follow S and G in including the word ναί in 14.1. H and L do not contain this word.

to slow down. This opportunity, however, only lasts briefly as the author immediately answers the question for 14.1-9 in a single word: δέδωκεν (he has given it; 14.1). The Lord gave the covenant, but "they" (αὐτοί) were not worthy to receive the covenant because of their sins. While Barnabas will continue to explore the question that he has set in 14.1, the answer is given at the outset. Although the Lord gave the covenant, the Israelites' sinfulness made them unworthy to receive it.

The scriptural quotations in 14.2-3 illustrate both the Lord's bestowal of the covenant and the Israelites' unworthiness to receive it, while Barnabas further illuminates how this was the case in 14.4-5. The quotation in 14.2 is introduced as a prophetic word and is similar to the quotation from 4.7-8. The prophet narrates how Moses was fasting in order to take the covenant of the Lord "to the people" (πρὸς τὸν λαόν) on Sinai (14.2). Moses received the covenant on two stone tablets that were written with the Lord's finger.[288] When Moses received these tablets, he brought them "to the people" (πρὸς τὸν λαόν). However, God tells Moses that he should go quickly to the people because they have broken the law. At this point, Moses "understood" (συνῆκεν) that the people had made an image out of molten metal and threw the tablets down so that "the tablets of the Lord's covenant were broken" (συνετρίβησαν αἱ πλάκες τῆς διαθήκης κυρίου; 14.3). Barnabas concludes that Moses received the covenant, but the people were not worthy to receive the covenant because of their disobedience (14.4).[289]

Moses's reception of the covenant and understanding regarding the Israelites then gives way to the author's interpretation in 14.4-5. Barnabas is particularly interested in explaining how he and the audience received the covenant, and he again urges the audience to "learn" (μάθετε; 14.4).[290] The author makes a distinction between the way in which the covenant was revealed to Moses and to "us." Moses received the covenant while he was a servant (θεράπων ὤν), but the Lord himself (αὐτὸς δὲ ὁ κύριος) gave it to us.[291] The Lord's gift enables Barnabas and his audience to become the "people of inheritance" (λαὸν κληρονομίας). Moreover, the Lord even endured "on our account" (δι' ἡμᾶς) so that he could give the covenant and enable Barnabas and his audience to become the people of inheritance. The Lord was revealed for two purposes. To begin with, his revelation enabled the Israelites' sins to be completed. Simultaneously, the Lord's revelation allowed Barnabas and his audience to receive the covenant through its rightful heir,

---

288. Hanson, "Activity of the Pre-Existent Christ," 155.
289. Backhaus, "Bundesmotiv," 165.
290. The same imperative has already been used in 5.6; 6.9; 9.7, 8.
291. On Moses as God's servant, see also Heb 3:1-6; 1 Clem. 4.12; 51.3, 5.

the Lord Jesus. A lengthy relative clause follows in which Barnabas says more about why Jesus was prepared for these purposes. His revelation came when believers' hearts were already spent for death and handed over to the lawlessness of deceit. Yet Jesus redeemed believers' hearts from darkness and made the covenant "in us" (ἐν ἡμῖν) with his word (14.5).

The topic that Barnabas takes up in 14.1–5 is similar to what he discussed in 4.6–8 so that a comparison of these two passages may be enlightening. Barnabas's comments are more extensive in 14.1–5 and draw out themes that are only introduced in the earlier passage. The shorter comments in 4.6–8 are in keeping with the stereotyped language of abbreviation in 4.9. One reason for the variation in length may also have to do with the different contexts in which the exegeses of the golden calf episode are located. When readers first encounter the Sinai story, the author has just urged them to act rightly by fleeing lawlessness (4.1–2). Barnabas employs eschatological terminology that gives way to his belief that the final apocalyptic stumbling block has now appeared (4.3–5). The narrative of the Israelites' idolatry at Sinai is introduced as an implicit warning in the midst of Barnabas's paraenesis for his audience to act in ways befitting of their privileged place in God's revelatory scheme. 4.6–8 is thus characterized by a greater sense of urgency.

In 14.1–5, Barnabas returns to the idolatrous actions at Sinai in a position to offer a more contextualized account of his exegesis of the pentateuchal narrative. The reasons for this are twofold. First, Barnabas has demonstrated in more detail how scripture has enabled his audience to have confidence in God's revelation through the prophets. He has discussed how the prophets revealed why Jesus had to suffer, the significance of Jesus's endurance, and the importance of land inheritance, Yom Kippur sacrifices, and the red heifer (5.1–8.7). He has also shown that, when scripture is rightly interpreted, it speaks figuratively about circumcision and kosher laws while also pointing to the importance of baptism and the cross (9.1—12.11). When readers come to 14.1–5, they thus have a more complete grasp of why Jesus was revealed in the flesh and how the scriptures aid his revelation. Second, Barnabas has placed Israel's Sinaitic missteps in the context of a larger discussion of inheritance that began with the patriarchs (13.1–7). God's preferential choice of the younger son and Abraham's election as the father of the gentiles illustrates that Barnabas and his audience are the rightful heirs of the patriarchal promises. After setting out a larger context for his covenantal theology, Barnabas is able to make a fuller statement about the significance of the Sinai event in 14.1–5.

The citation of scripture is similar between 4.7–8 and 14.2–3, although subtle differences aid Barnabas in drawing out his chief points. Close comparison of the texts reveals small variations in word order, word choice, and verbal moods.[292] More significant variations can be explained by paying attention to the author's slightly different aims in 4.1–14 and 13.1—14.9. At the end of 14.2, Barnabas insists that Moses received the tablets "in the Spirit. And when Moses received them, he brought them down to give to the people" (ἐν πνεύματι. καὶ λαβὼν Μωϋσῆς κατέφερεν πρὸς τὸν λαὸν δοῦναι). This additional phrase has no exact counterpart at 4.7–8. Yet the phrase fits well in Barnabas's second exegesis of the Sinai covenant, since the author sets out to determine whether the covenant was ever given to the Israelites (14.1). Barnabas's addition ensures that readers do not miss the answer. The covenant was indeed offered to the Israelites. Another variation in the passages has to do with the people's idolatrous responses (4.8; 14.3). Barnabas first reports that the people lost the covenant when they turned to idols (4.8). Later he is more specific about what the people did: "they again made molten images for themselves" (14.3). The variation in how the Israelites' actions at Sinai are described conclude similarly, for Barnabas refers in both passages to the breaking of the law (ἀνομέω; 4.8; 14.3).

The difference in length, placement within the letter, and the precise citation of the biblical text leads on to a still more significant difference. Earlier in the letter, Barnabas locates the significance of the Israelites' idolatry in the space that it made for Jesus's covenant to be sealed into believers' hearts (4.8). The contrast between "us" and "them" is immediate and obvious as the Israelites lost the covenant through their idolatry while Jesus's faithfulness provides hope for Barnabas and his audience. The same contrast can be found in the explanation of 14.4–5, but its epistolary location allows Barnabas to say more about its importance. Although Israel had an opportunity to be included in the covenant, they were rejected based on their own actions because they were not worthy (14.4). Jesus's revelation further magnified the sinfulness of the Israelites (14.5). However, Barnabas moves on from this to explore the difference between Moses's reception of the covenant and the way in which he and his audience received it.[293] Although Moses received it as a servant (θεράπων), the Lord himself handed the covenant over to believers (14.4).[294] Jesus endured "on our account"

---

292. E.g., Moses takes the tablets from (ἀπό) the Lord in 4.7, while in 14.2 he takes the commandments from (παρά) the Lord with a different preposition. More substantively, Barnabas adds that God wrote on the stone tablets "in the Spirit" (ἐν πνεύματι; 14.2). This phrase is missing in 4.7. For additional comparison of 4.6–8; 14.1–5, see Klevinghaus, *Theologische Stellung*, 17–18.

293. Rothschild, "Epistle of Barnabas," 210.

294. Since Moses received the covenant, Barnabas's portrayal of Moses's servant status should not be understood as suggesting a lack of knowledge or awareness of

(δι' ἡμᾶς; 14.4), and believers receive the covenant through Jesus the heir (14.5). The language of endurance relies upon the christological discussion of 5.1—6.7, that is, upon intervening material between the discussions of the Sinaitic events. Since Barnabas has discussed Jesus's endurance on behalf of his people, he can say more about the significance of Sinai. The longer explanation in 14.4-5 is thus due in large part to its placement in the letter. Barnabas adds that Jesus was prepared for the purpose of redeeming believers' hearts from darkness, death, and lawlessness. Jesus's covenant is thus established in believers by his word (λόγῳ; 14.5).

These theological reflections on how the covenant was received by its rightful heirs give way to further reflections on the revelation of the redeemer in the prophets (14.6-9).[295] Barnabas asserts that the Father's command to redeem us from darkness is foretold (14.6). The prophetic citations that follow thus apply to Jesus and his instructions to prepare a holy people for the Father. God's speech in Isa 42:6-7 emphasizes that the Father has called Jesus to be "a light for the gentiles" (φῶς ἐθνῶν) and to bring out "those who sit in darkness" (καθημένους ἐν σκότει; 14.7). Barnabas concludes that he and his audience know from this verse how they were redeemed. Redemption is an act that was ordained by the Father and handed over to the Son for the benefit of God's people. God's people are here defined as gentiles and include Barnabas and his audience. The transference from light to dark continues in 14.8 as Barnabas quotes Isa 49:6-7 and again emphasizes that Jesus was called as "a light for the gentiles" (φῶς ἐθνῶν). The final quotation comes from Isa 61:1-2 and contains the same imagery now cited as the words of Jesus. He emphasizes that the Lord's Spirit resides on him and that his call includes proclaiming "recovery of sight for the blind" (τυφλοῖς ἀνάβλεψιν; 14.9). As Jesus speaks about his own redemptive mission, the recovery of sight complements the interplay between light and darkness in 14.5-8.

These statements further illustrate Barnabas's understanding of who Jesus is and who the people are called to be. The people of God are not associated with Israel at all. For Barnabas, God's activity was always for the nations. The prophet revealed beforehand that Jesus came to be a light for the gentiles (φῶς ἐθνῶν; 14.7, 8). The activity of the Son is set to open the eyes of the blind, thereby bringing healing to those who cannot see (14.7,

---

how God works. Hanson ("The Activity of the Pre-Existent Christ," 155) rightly states, "Moses was very fully informed about the Christian dispensation." Rather, the contrast between Moses's servanthood and the Lord's ability to grant inheritance is grounded upon their respective roles in the covenant economy.

295. Barnabas is particularly interested in Isaiah. In 14.7-9, Barnabas quotes Isa 42:6-7 (14.7); 49:6-7 (14.8); 61:1-2 (14.9).

9). His work of establishing a covenant for the peoples (διαθήκην γένους) is thus targeted at those who live in darkness (14.6, 7). Just as the covenant comes to the people from outside of themselves, so also Jesus was called by God and prepared ahead of time to set apart a holy people (14.6, 7, 9). Jesus's charge thus comes from outside of himself. Barnabas employs these prophetic words in order to demonstrate Jesus's work of redemption (14.6), and he observes from the prophets that Jesus is engaged in the same redemptive mission as the Father (14.8).

Such an interpretation supports Barnabas's portrayal of the Son's activity in 14.4-5. His Isaianic exegesis understands Jesus primarily in terms of redemption (14.5-6). In undertaking this mission, the Son is united with the Father in seeking to redeem a holy people (14.8). Yet this holy people is not connected with Israel. Israel showed themselves to be unworthy of the covenant when they rejected it by making molten images at Sinai.[296] By working as a light for the gentiles, the Son has incorporated the author and his audience into the people of God so that they are a holy people who have been set apart from Israel. The covenant was thus given, but only the author and his audience were able to receive it worthily. Moses received it, but he received it as a servant. Although the covenant was offered to Israel, they rejected it at Sinai because they were unworthy and sinful. The author and his audience find themselves in a privileged position because the covenant that they have received comes directly from the Lord who has already revealed his redemptive mission in the prophets.

The exegesis in 13.1—14.9 illustrates the close connections between the identity of the people of God, inheritance, and covenant. Yet while the covenant is described in various ways, it is never explicitly defined. While Barnabas focuses on Israel's rejection and the privileged place of himself and his audience, his discussion sheds further light on how the covenant was made effective. For Barnabas and his audience, the covenant comes through the Lord, who is also the true heir (14.5). More specifically, the covenant comes through Jesus's endurance on the cross (14.4). Covenant is tied to Jesus's actions as Son of God, right practices in life, and proper interpretation of scripture. The emphasis on redemption and the use of light-dark imagery in 14.5-9 point to a concept that is at the center of covenant in *Barnabas*, namely, forgiveness. There is only one covenant, and forgiveness is therefore found in only one person. The true people of God, on the other hand, recognize and receive the covenant that comes through Jesus's blood. Barnabas employs salvation-historical concepts in order to

---

296. Klevinghaus, *Theologische Stellung*, 19.

make his point, but his argument is not strictly historical in orientation.[297] While Israel and the people of God are symbolically set opposite each other, the borders between Israel and the people of God are traversable for individuals. One can enter the people of God through the Son. One can fall out of the people by rejecting the Son, most likely by misunderstanding what God has revealed in scripture.

The discussion of inheritance and the covenant in 13.1—14.9 thus functions as an implicit call to correct understanding, right action, and true identity within the true people of God. The repetition of the Sinai story from 4.6–8 indicates the importance of these themes for the author. Yet the fulsome discussion of the two peoples and the more complete definition of the people of God make 13.1—14.9 a central plank in the letter's ongoing argument. Barnabas defends the identity of the people of God by claiming the stories of the patriarchs for Jesus-followers and showing that Israel rejected God's covenant.[298] God's promises to redeem people from sin, death, darkness, and lawlessness do not come in sacrifices or molten images. Rather, God's covenant promises are revealed in the Son who is called to be a light to the gentiles and to give sight to the blind. The narratives and exegesis in 13.1—14.9 undergird the divergent interpretations and the two ways of living that are outlined in the rest of the letter. The treatment of Jesus's death in 5.1—8.7 in turn provides Barnabas with the means by which to articulate how the covenant was made effective in "us." Because Barnabas and his audience are the rightful heirs who have inherited the covenant through Christ, their interpretation of scripture is correct and their way of living is characterized by light.

II.8. ἔτι καί: On Additional Matters (Barn. 15.1—16.10)

Following the exegetical discussion of inheritance and covenant, Barnabas returns to an exegetical discussion of practices that set the two peoples apart. Barnabas has already discussed sacrifices, fasts, circumcision, and kosher practices (2.4—3.6; 9.1—10.12). He now turns to the topics of Sabbath (15.1–9) and temple (16.1–10). Each of these topics is introduced with the phrase ἔτι καί, which can be translated as something like "moreover." Yet this section does not form an appendix following the lengthy outline of the true people of God. Rather, Barnabas urges his readers to look afresh at two practices that characterized Jews during the Second Temple period and which the

---

297. Rothschild ("Epistle of Barnabas," 210–11) helpfully offers an allegorical reading of 14.4–5.
298. Hvalvik, *Struggle for Scripture and Covenant*, 92.

author argues that the Jews have also misunderstood. When God instructed Israel about Sabbath in the Torah, Barnabas claims that God had no intention of giving a weekly day of rest. Rather, God was revealing the mysteries of how time and resurrection are made known to the true people. Likewise, Barnabas argues that the construction of a physical temple was a mistake that resulted in people placing their hope in a building. The destruction of the temple by the Romans clarified the erroneous nature of Israel's choice. For Barnabas, the temple is instead defined in terms of believers in whom the Lord resides. The privileged place of Barnabas and his readers enables them to interpret scripture rightly and to understand the significance of the Sabbath and temple that God revealed beforehand.

II.8.a. The Sabbath (Barn. 15.1–9)

The introduction of new material with the conjunctive phrase, "Moreover, therefore" (ἔτι οὖν καί; 15.1) clearly indicates a break in thought as Barnabas introduces a new section. The topic is introduced with a prepositional phrase: "about the Sabbath" (περὶ τοῦ σαββάτου). Given the centrality of 13.1—14.9 to the theological thought of the letter and the introduction of 15.1 with a phrase that indicates additional matters, it is tempting to view the following discussion as an appendix. Yet two arguments suggest that 15.1–9 plays a more vital role in the letter than that of an appendix. First, Barnabas has employed similar transitional phrases elsewhere in the letter. He transitions to topics that play an important theological role in the letter in 4.6 and 5.5 with the conjunctions ἔτι δὲ καί.[299] The use of a similar transition in portions of the letter that are integral to the author's theological thought warns against viewing 15.1–9 as an appendix. Second, Barnabas links the discussion of the Sabbath to the Sinai narrative that plays a pivotal role in 4.6–8 and 14.1–5. The Sabbath command is found in the Ten Words (15.1),[300] which were written on the two tablets that Moses broke when he saw the Israelites' idolatry (4.7–8; 14.2–3).[301] God entrusted these words to Moses, who was able to receive the covenant despite the Israelites' failure (14.4; 15.1). Finally, the words were given at Sinai (15.1), which provides

---

299. The same phrase is utilized in 16.1.

300. Barnabas places the Sabbath within the Ten Words (οἱ δέκα λόγοι). Philo likewise makes reference to the Ten Words (οἱ δέκα λόγοι; e.g., *Decal.* 154; *Spec.* 1.1), while Ptolemy's *Letter to Flora* contains the earliest reference to the Decalogue (ἡ δεκάλογος; *Flor.* 33.5.3). See Standhartinger, "Ptolemaeus und Justin," 138n81.

301. On the tablets of the Ten Words, see also Philo, *Decal.* 50–51; *Her.* 168; *Opif.* 128.

the unstated setting for the events narrated in the previous section (14.1–5). The following considerations about Sabbath practice are thus to be viewed alongside what the author has previously written.

Barnabas lays out the scriptural basis for a right understanding of Sabbath in 15.1–3, and these verses will be the source from which the rest of the argument flows. God spoke to Moses face to face in order to tell the people that they should sanctify the Lord's Sabbath "with pure hands and pure hearts" (χερσὶν καθαραῖς καὶ καρδίᾳ καθαρᾷ; Barn. 15.1). The language of sanctification is found in Exod 20:8 and Deut 5:12, 15, but the verb appears as an infinitive complement rather than an imperative in Greek translations of the Torah.[302] The pure hands and heart that Barnabas lists as the means by which to sanctify the Sabbath are not listed in Exod 20 and Deut 5. Someone who is "innocent with regard to hands" (ἀθῷος χερσίν) and "pure with regard to heart" (καθαρὸς τῇ καρδίᾳ) is able to ascend the Lord's mountain in Ps 23:4 (24:4 MT).[303] Barnabas appears to employ a variation of the Sabbath commandment that is not found in the Torah. He also appeals to a promise from God that God's mercy will be upon those who keep the Sabbath (Barn. 15.2). Although the citation is introduced as a word from God to Moses, Barnabas employs language that comes from Exod 31:13–17; Jer 17:24–25. The words in the second quotation of this section are again not found in exactly this form in Greek Jewish scriptures. Barnabas locates the meaning of Sabbath in Genesis: God "speaks about Sabbath at the beginning of creation" (τὸ σάββατον λέγει ἐν ἀρχῇ τῆς κτίσεως; Barn. 15.3). God worked in six days, completed his work on the seventh, and rested on the seventh. Barnabas's citation comes from Gen 2:2–3.

Having established the scriptural basis for his discussion of the Sabbath, Barnabas turns to interpretation in 15.4–7. He begins by urging his audience to pay attention to specific lines regarding God's actions on the seventh day. As in the epistolary greeting (1.1), he refers to his audience as children (τέκνα), thereby drawing attention to his close relationship with the audience and to his authority over them (15.4). Barnabas interprets God's completion of creation in six days with reference to Ps 89:4 (90:4 MT). In order to do this, however, Barnabas rearranges the verbal phrases from (Gen 2:2–3 [Barn. 15.3]). The citation in Barn. 15.3 notes that God made (ἐποίησεν) the works of his hands in six days and finished (συνετέλεσεν) it on the seventh day. In the analysis of Barn. 15.4, Barnabas shuffles the verbs so that God finished (συνετέλεσεν) the work in six days. The work of creation is then extended to

---

302. Exod 20:8: μνήσθητι... ἁγιάζειν; Deut 5:12: φύλαξαι... ἁγιάζειν; Barn. 15.1: ἁγιάσατε.

303. Windisch (*Barnabasbrief*, 381) helpfully draws attention to the language of pure hearts that is found in Herm. *Vis.* 3.9.8 (17.8); 5.7 (25.7); *Sim.* 5.1.5 (54.5).

include "all things" (τὰ σύμπαντα) so that God will complete all things in six days. If a day with the Lord is like 1,000 years and God completed things in six days, Barnabas reasons that all things on earth will be completed in 6,000 years.[304] God's rest on the Sabbath is then taken with reference to the parousia of the Son. The seventh day will be a day for God's true rest as the Son brings the time of the lawless one to an end, judges the ungodly, and changes the sun, moon, and stars (15.5).[305]

Barnabas moves backward in the list of scriptural citations to take up the significance of sanctifying the Sabbath that was mentioned in 15.1. He allows that if it is possible to sanctify the Sabbath in the present, then he and his audience have been deceived (15.6). However, this is only a rhetorical strategy because Barnabas quickly shifts to the alternative in 15.7. He transitions to his interpretation with another conditional sentence: "But if that is not the case" (εἰ δὲ οὐ).[306] If it is impossible to sanctify the Sabbath properly in the present, Barnabas reasons that it will only be possible to rest and sanctify the Sabbath when believers have been justified (δικαιωθέντες) and received the promise (ἀπολαβόντες τὴν ἐπαγγελίαν). This will be a time when lawlessness no longer exists and when all things have been made new by the Lord. To keep the Sabbath holy requires the Son to make lawlessness utterly ineffectual. Since this has not happened and the letter continues to warn readers against lawlessness,[307] Barnabas continues to look forward to the Sabbath.

The author strengthens his argument by appealing to the prophets alongside his interpretations of the Torah. God already told Isaiah that new moons and Sabbaths were unendurable (15.8; Isa 1:13). God's statement is taken to mean that current Sabbath practices fail to please God, but God can still show favor to the Sabbath that God has made. God's words continue to be quoted in the first person even though there is no directly comparable scriptural source. When God has set everything at rest on the Sabbath, that is, when the Son returns to bring justice to the world, then God promises to create the start of an eighth day (15.8). The start of this eighth day is then defined as "the beginning of another world" (ἄλλου κόσμου ἀρχήν). The Sabbath is

---

304. Klevinghaus, *Theologische Stellung*, 26.

305. The opening catena of Hebrews uses Ps 101:26–28 (MT 102:26–28) to describe the Son's permanence in contrast to the Son with the perishability of created works. These works "will also be changed like clothing" (ὡς ἱμάτιον καὶ ἀλλαγήσονται) but the Son remains forever (Heb 1:12). On the textual issues in this psalmic quotation, see Docherty, "Text Form," 361–62.

306. I follow the reading of S at the beginning of 13.7. See also Prigent and Kraft, *Épître de Barnabé*, 186; Prostmeier and Lona, *Epistola Barnabae*, 122.

307. E.g., Barn. 4.1; 10.8; 14.5; 18.2.

thus interpreted with a view to eschatology and is closely tied to new creation. Barnabas moves from this eschatological interpretation in 15.1–8 to allude to current practices in the community. The reason that Barnabas and his community spend the eighth day joyfully is that it is the day on which Jesus was raised from the dead and ascended into heaven (15.9).[308] The majority of Barnabas's Sabbath interpretation puts forward an eschatological interpretation of the Sabbath into which the community will be drawn (15.1–8). However, the final verse links the community's present customs to the discussion to provide further exegetical grounding for differentiating the worship of the true heirs from those who lost the covenant.[309]

Barnabas's reflections on the eschatological Sabbath employ creation themes that were also prominent in the interpretation of Israel's command to enter the land (6.8–19). In both passages, significant Jewish imagery is taken up and reinterpreted in figurative terms. The land is, among other things, a new creation into which people must enter (6.12–16).[310] The Sabbath is a way of conceptualizing the time when God will set all things right when the Son comes again. Barnabas finds signs in both 6.8–19 and 15.1–9 that the promises from the Torah are yet to be completed. While the Lord tells human beings to rule over the fish (Gen 1:26, 28 [Barn. 6.18]), Barnabas is clear that human beings do not have authority over earthly creatures. Likewise, when Barnabas looks for a holy Sabbath and cannot find one, he reasons that there must be a future Sabbath (Exod 20:8; Deut 5:12, 15 [Barn. 15.1, 6–7]). These signs of incompletion in the Torah lead Barnabas to look for future fulfillment (Barn. 6.13; 15.7). The one who will bring things to fruition is the Son of God. The Son was not only present at creation (6.12) but also resides in believers to bring them before the Father (6.16). Likewise, the Son is the one who will bring the time of the lawless one to no effect and will judge the ungodly (15.5). In describing these actions, Barnabas employs traditional apocalyptic imagery of the sun, moon, and stars being changed. Creation will be altered by the eschatological actions of the Son. By reinterpreting traditional Jewish images, illustrating their incompletion in the present, and looking forward to the Son's actions in the eschaton, Barnabas provides cohesion to his interpretation of different theological images in the letter.

---

308. Behr, *John the Theologian*, 88.

309. The community's present custom of worshipping on the eighth day should thus not be viewed as a replacement or a counterpart to the Sabbath on a Barnabean understanding. "Der christliche Sonntag hat mit dem Sabbatgebot unmittelbar nichts zu tun" (Klevinghaus, *Theologische Stellung*, 27).

310. Of course, Barnabas first interprets the land in terms of Jesus (6.9).

The figurative interpretation of the Sabbath has precedents in Jewish Alexandrian exegetes.[311] Aristobulus interprets God's rest with reference to God's continued act of ordering things "for all time" (εἰς πάντα τὸν χρόνον; frag. 5).[312] God gives rest (ἀνάπαυσιν) to human beings on the seventh day, which can be referred to as the first because it is "the beginning of the light in which all things are contemplated" (φωτὸς γένεσις ἐν ᾧ τὰ πάντα συνθεωρεῖται; frag. 5).[313] While Philo links the Sabbath to completion, contemplation, and the perfection of the number seven, he also looks forward to restoration on the Sabbath (*Praem.* 153).[314] The sense of lack that is suggested in a term like restoration is also found in Barn. 15.6–7. The incomplete nature of Sabbath is critical to understanding the discussion of God's rest in Heb 3:7—4:11. The Sinai generation failed to enter into God's rest (Heb 3:11 [Ps 94:11]) or God's Sabbath (Heb 4:4 [Gen 2:2]) so that there is still a Sabbath remaining for those who are faithful to God (Heb 4:8–10).[315] In different ways, Aristobulus, Philo, and Hebrews link Sabbath to creation and find that Sabbath is a time for completion or restoration. Barnabas likewise emphasizes the link between Sabbath and creation. He shares with Hebrews an open-ended understanding of Sabbath that focuses not on keeping Sabbath in the present but on the eschatological fulfillment of Sabbath.

Barnabas's eschatological interpretation of the Sabbath may be linked to creation, but the interpretation of the days as thousand-year lengths of time has led scholars to ask whether Barnabas was a chiliast.[316] Although other ancient texts also linked Ps 89:4 (90:4) to both the days of creation

---

311. Martín, "L'interpretazione allegorica," 176–78.

312. This portion of fragment 5 comes from Eusebius, *Praep. ev.* 3.12.11. Quotations of Eusebius's *Praeparatio evangelica* comes from Mras, *Eusebius*. Translations of Aristobulus's fragmentary writings can be found in Yarbro Collins, "Aristobulus," 837–42. All translations of Aristobulus's works are my own unless otherwise noted.

313. Eusebius, *Praep. ev.* 3.12.9.

314. Philo likewise draws strong connections between the Sabbath, contemplation, and creation (*Decal.* 97–98). Since the seventh day marks the completion of creation (*Decal.* 105; *Fug.* 172–73; *Spec.* 2.58), the Sabbath can be described as the world's birthday (*Opif.* 89; *Spec.* 2.59).

315. God's rest is also mentioned in Heb 3:18; 4:1, 3, 5, 10, 11. The Spirit's continued speech in the present tense may contribute to the sense of current incompleteness in the interpretation of the Sabbath in Hebrews. On the speech of the Spirit, see Pierce, "Hebrews 3.7—4.11," 173–84.

316. For further discussions of chiliasm in the Epistle of Barnabas, see Bauckham, "Sabbath and Sunday," 262–64; Pearson, "Earliest Christianity in Egypt: Further Observations," 102; Rordorf, *Sabbat et dimanche*, 29 n 1; Rordorf, *Sunday*, 93–94.

and to eschatological judgement,[317] early Christian chiliasm refers to "the ancient belief in a thousand-year reign of Christ on earth between his second coming and the last judgment."[318] Irenaeus argues that the resurrection of believers will take place in the flesh and appears to connect the fulfillment of the promise that Abraham's descendants will inherit the land to the saints' reign with Christ during the millennium (*Haer.* 5.30.4–5.32.2).[319] Justin likewise appeals to chiliastic theology (*Dial.* 80–81). Although Barnabas refers both to a millennial Sabbath and to an eighth day in which all things will be set at rest (*Barn.* 15.5, 8), his terminology is not consistent. The Sabbath, which is the seventh day, and the eighth day refer to the same eschatological reality in the letter. The author anticipates a time in the future when all things will be put right as the Son judges the lawless one (15.5). Yet this Sabbath judgement is not strongly delineated from the new creation on the eighth day (15.8). Both days look forward to the time of righteousness that is set to follow the Son's parousia. It is better to regard Barnabas not as a chiliast but instead as someone with a strong hope in new creation after the Son's return.[320]

Eschatological orientations provide a key hinge to the teaching, identity construction, and rationale for acting in the letter. Although Barnabas will emphasize that human beings must act rightly in light of God's future actions, he emphasizes the incompleteness of the eschaton in 15.1–9. God's commandment about Sabbath is yet to be completed and, what is more, is impossible to complete at this time. It is not yet possible to keep the Sabbath holy because this is the age of the lawless one. Believers look forward to the completion of the Sabbath when Jesus returns, and Barnabas urges his audience to read scripture rightly by understanding that the Sabbath commandment describes how God's actions unfold in all of time. For Barnabas, it is important not to reach out and grasp what is still future. This may be one way of conceiving of the error that he finds in Jewish Sabbath practices, namely, that they mistake a future event for

---

317. Second Peter 3:8 appeals to Ps 89:4 (90:4) as an explanation for the perceived slowness in the judgment of the day of the Lord that appears to have existed among some of the author's audience and/or opponents. See further Frey, *Letter of Jude and the Second Letter of Peter*, 402–3. Other ancient writers mirror the Barnabean account insofar as they link the creation of the world in seven days, Ps 89:4 (90:4), and the history of the world into an understanding of the world's timeline as a cosmic week. E.g., 2 En. 33.1–2; *L.A.B.* 28.2; Cyprian, *Fort.* pref. 2; 11; Hippolytus, *Comm. Dan.* 4.23–24; Irenaeus, *Haer.* 5.28.3; Lactantius, *Inst.* 7.14.9.

318. Hill, *Regnum Caelorum*, 1.

319. On Irenaeus's chiliasm, see Hill, *Regnum Caelorum*, 11–20, 254–59; Parvis, "Who Was Irenaeus," 21–22.

320. Bauckham, "Sabbath and Sunday," 263.

present practice. Through believers' practice of celebrating the eighth day in conjunction with Jesus's resurrection (15.9), Barnabas's interpretation of the Sabbath cements his overarching claim that "we" are the true heirs of the covenant and that "we" demonstrate this inheritance by interpreting scripture figuratively and, therefore, rightly.

II.8.b. The Temple (Barn. 16.1–10)

Barnabas turns from an eschatological interpretation of the Sabbath to take up the matter of the temple. He opens the section in 16.1 by introducing a new topic with a rhetorical marker similar to that which was used in 15.1: "Moreover, then" (ἔτι δὲ καί). The topic follows immediately in a prepositional phrase. This section is "about the temple" (περὶ τοῦ ναοῦ; 16.1). Barnabas informs his audience that his opponents are deceived, referring to them as "lousy people" (οἱ ταλαίπωροι). Rather than placing their hope in the creator God, Barnabas accuses them of hoping in a building. They confuse the physical temple with God's house.[321] The author goes so far as to equate their sanctification of God in the temple with gentile worship in their temples. However, God has already declared that he will destroy the temple. In order to support his claim, the author appeals to God's speech through Isaiah. The Lord alone has measured heaven and earth with his hand (Barn. 16.2 [Isa 40:12]). Thus, heaven is the Lord's throne, and the earth serves as a footstool. The Lord taunts the people by asking them what sort of house or place of rest they are able to build for him (Barn. 16.2 [Isa 66:1]). The author urges his audience to recognize that the hope of Israel was vanity.

The destruction of the temple in 70 CE proves the author's exegetical point and is brought to the fore in 16.3–5. Barnabas applies another prophetic word to the current situation in Jerusalem. The prophet saw in advance that those who destroyed the temple would rebuild it (16.3; see also Isa 49:17). Moreover, he claims that the attempt to rebuild the temple is happening during his time and that of his audience.[322] Although the temple was destroyed by Israel's enemies during the war, the servants of the enemies will seek to rebuild it (16.4). Barnabas presses the point about the destruction of the temple further in 16.5, hinting at the continuation of the argument with the word "again" (πάλιν). God also revealed how the city, the temple, and the people of Israel would be handed over. Barnabas appeals to "scripture" (γραφή) to

---

321. Prigent and Kraft, *Épître de Barnabé*, 189n3.

322. The word γίνεται is missing in S and H. It is found only in G and L, which reads *et fiet*. The tensions in the verb tenses that result from including γίνεται make it the more difficult reading.

support his point and employs language and imagery that sound similar to Enochic literature, particularly the Animal Apocalypse (1 En. 85-90).[323] In the citation, the Lord promises to hand over the sheep along with their fold and their tower to be destroyed (1 En. 89.55-56, 66-67).[324] This text has been fulfilled in the destruction of the temple by the Romans (Barn. 16.5). The fall of the temple in 70 CE thus proves Barnabas's point that Israel's decision to place their hope in a building was misplaced.

The reality of the temple is not to be discarded, however. Barnabas turns in 16.6-10 to explore whether there is a temple of God. He again finds the answer to his question in scripture because God said that the temple would be built and brought to completion by divine action. The citation again draws from language that is widely found in Second Temple literature, but the imagery may fit best with the Apocalypse of Weeks in 1 En. 93.1-10 and 91.11-17. God promises that the temple will be gloriously rebuilt "when the seventh day is completed" (τῆς ἑβδομάδος συντελουμένης; 16.6). The reconstruction of the temple provides the hope of the Enochic eighth week (1 En. 91.13), while Tob 14.5 likewise looks forward to the construction of the house when God's people reenter the land after the exile.[325] Thus, Barnabas finds that there is a temple (16.7).

Yet it is not a physical temple found in Jerusalem. Instead, when Barnabas urges his audience to examine how the temple will be built, he appeals to their own human qualities. Prior to their faith in God, the audience was characterized by corrupt and feeble hearts that were full of idolatry and served as houses for demons. All that they did was opposed to God so that "the dwelling of the heart" (τὸ κατοικητήριον τῆς καρδίας) was not a suitable place for God to live. Their hearts thus could not serve as God's temple (16.7). However, their hearts were able to be constructed as God's dwelling place when they were built "in the name of the Lord" (ἐπὶ τῷ ὀνόματι κυρίου; 16.8). The means by which the audience was able to become God's temple was by being renewed and experiencing new creation in Christ.[326] Such a novel experience came to the audience by means of forgiveness of sins and hope in the name.[327] Because this happened, God

---

323. Barnabas has already appealed to Enoch directly in 4.3. Although the citation that follows in 4.3 is not found in extant Enochic literature, Barnabas shows that he is happy to appeal to Enoch as an authority.

324. Black, *Book of Enoch*, 270; Verheyden, "Israel's Fate," 260.

325. Windisch, *Barnabasbrief*, 391.

326. "[T]he argument of 16.6-8 is that, according to the scripture, there is a true temple of God, and this temple is built in us, in the name of the Lord Jesus Christ" (Edwards, *Gospel*, 75).

327. Korn, *Nachwirkungen der Christusmystik*, 44.

dwells "in us" (ἐν ἡμῖν; 16.8).³²⁸ The author's emphasis doubtless lies upon the residence of God within each particular believer, but the ambiguity of the prepositional phrase leaves open the possibility that God is also dwelling "among us," that is, in the community.

Barnabas turns next to the means by which God's dwelling in the community has been revealed. God's abode in believers is evident through the word of faith, God's call of promise, the wisdom of the requirements, the commandments of the teaching, God's own prophecy in believers, and God's dwelling among people who formerly served death but have now had the door of the temple opened to them with an opportunity to enter through the repentance that God brings (16.9). Barnabas emphasizes that people who desire true salvation do not look to themselves (16.10). Reliance upon human actions was Israel's mistake when they set their hope on a building that they constructed (16.1). Rather, salvation is found in the God who dwells and speaks in them. Their salvation should lead to amazement because of what God says. Barnabas draws the audience's focus to the God who indwells them and concludes the argument by stating, "This is the spiritual temple that is being built for the Lord" (τοῦτό ἐστιν πνευματικὸς ναὸς οἰκοδομούμενος τῷ κυρίῳ; 16.10).³²⁹

While constructing an exegetical argument against a physical temple, Barnabas appeals to what he sees as a foolish choice to build the temple again (16.3-4). The prophetic word that Barnabas cites in 16.3 declares that those who destroyed the temple will rebuild it. Barnabas finds that it is happening "now" (νῦν), that is, in his time (16.4). Yet the precise nature of the temple that is in the process of being reconstructed has not been easy for interpreters to determine. Three options present themselves. The temple that will be rebuilt could be spiritual, the temple to Jupiter in Aelia Capitolina, or a third Jewish temple.³³⁰

In favor of understanding the reconstruction in 16.3-4 in terms of a spiritual temple, one can observe that the author eventually comes to this position in 16.6-10. A spiritualized reading of 16.4 simply moves the author's conclusion forward. In addition, the author has already introduced the idea of an incorporeal temple (Barn. 4.11; 6.14-15).³³¹ On this view, the

---

328. Wengst (*Didache*, 185 n 249) draws attention to T. Jos. 10.2-3; T. Benj. 6.4; Herm. Mand. 3.1 (28.1) as examples of other texts in which God dwells among human beings.

329. Lieu, *Christian Identity*, 227-28.

330. On the interpretation of 16.3-4, see the discussion of date in the introduction.

331. Gunther, "Epistle of Barnabas," 151. Other proponents of this view include Prigent and Kraft, *Épître de Barnabé*, 190-91; Williams, "Date," 340-43. Williams ("The Date," 342-43) also raises the possibility that 16.3-4 refers to the destruction of the first

rebuilding of the temple does not refer to a particular historical expectation in Jerusalem but rather to the dwelling of God that sanctifies believers' hearts.[332] However, there are at least two difficulties with this understanding of 16.3–4. First, while a spiritualized reading of these verses coincides with the conclusion of the passage in Barn. 16.6–10, such an understanding of 16.3–4 muddies the structure of the author's argument.[333] Second, if the temple is spiritual, it is not easy to identify the servants of the enemies in 16.4. Prigent tentatively suggests that they are gentile Christians, while Williams identifies them as Roman officials.[334] Yet it is difficult to see quite how either group could be seen as the builder of the temple.[335]

It is thus best to consider other options. Arguments in favor of a physical temple in 16.4 struggle with paltry evidence. If there was hope for a rebuilt temple after the destruction of the second temple in 70, the only known temple was constructed by Hadrian and dedicated to Jupiter around the time of the Bar Kokhba revolt.[336] If the rebuilt temple of Barn. 16.4 refers to the temple of Jupiter that was built on the site of the Jewish temple, the author would disavow the physical building of the temple (16.1–2), highlight its destruction in 70 CE (16.3–4a), and then respond ironically that, by Jove, the temple is being rebuilt in the present (16.4b). Yet the circumstances

---

temple and its rebuilding by Cyrus and his servants. If so, 16.4 might make reference to Ezra 6:13. However, it is difficult to see how this view can account for the present and future tense verbs in 16.3–4.

332. Prigent and Kraft, *Épître de Barnabé*, 191.

333. If the temple that is being rebuilt is a spiritual temple in 16.4, the author would (1) identify the sanctifying of the physical temple as misguided (16.1–2), (2) refer to the destruction of the physical temple (16.3–4a), (3) define a proper understanding of the spiritual temple (16.4b), (4) return to the destruction of the physical temple (16.5), and (5) then detail the significance of the true temple for readers (16.6–10). The spiritual temple in 16.4b would interrupt the otherwise consistent focus on a building and would also result in an unclear argument that is not easy to follow. In addition, this understanding of 16.3–4 would differ from how the author outlines topics at other points in the letter. For example, the author disavows the physical act of fasting in 3.1–2 before defining the true fast in terms of just actions in 3.3–6. This is a two-stage argument that moves from a physical activity to a reinterpretation of the actions.

334. Prigent and Kraft, *Épître de Barnabé*, 191; Williams, "Date," 342.

335. In addition, Horbury (*Jewish War*, 299) points out that it is difficult to see why "they" (αὐτοί) should be the subject of rebuilding a spiritual temple. Since the temple resides in the author and his believing audience, the proper pronoun would more likely be first-person plural.

336. Proponents of understanding the temple that is under construction in 16.3–4 with reference to the temple to Jupiter include Hvalvik, *Struggle for Scripture and Covenant*, 23; Lipsius, "Barnabasbrief," 371–72; Öhler, *Barnabas: Der Mann in der Mitte*, 155–56; Prostmeier, *Barnabasbrief*, 117–19; Prostmeier, "Einleitung," 56; Schwartz, "On Barnabas," 147–53; Vinzent, *Writing*, 222.

under which this temple was planned are difficult to ascertain. Although Dio Cassius dates the temple's construction prior to the Second Jewish War (*Hist.* 69.12), Eusebius claims that the temple was built after Jerusalem was taken again (*Hist. eccl.* 4.6.4).[337] The difficulties with this interpretation are not fatal but neither are the arguments in favor ironclad.

Alternatively, one could imagine hopes for a Jewish temple being rebuilt.[338] Yet it is not clear that there was any time between the destruction in 70 and the first citation of the Epistle of Barnabas at the end of the second century when one could say, "It is happening" (γίνεται; 16.4). The strongest argument in favor of this understanding comes in the grammar of 16.3-4. The pronoun αὐτόν at the end of 16.4 is most naturally understood with reference to τὸν ναὸν τοῦτον in 16.3. The most straightforward reading of the verse is that "this temple," that is, the Jewish temple in Jerusalem, would be rebuilt and that the construction process is now underway at the hands of the servants of Israel's enemies. Identifying the building in these verses as a third, ultimately unrealized Jewish temple makes good sense within the argument of Barn. 16, since it allows the reading and interpretation of the passage to continue without interruption. These hopes may be based on rumors, murmurs, and whispers of information that were not recorded in great detail and no longer remain available to us in a full report, but may appear in fragmentary hints. For example, the Romans are purported to have ordered the temple to be reconstructed in Gen. Rab. 64.10.[339] In Sib. Or. 5.46-50 Hadrian is still viewed positively so that the text was most likely composed prior to the outbreak of the Second Jewish War in 132 CE.[340] Later in the work, there is hope that a messianic figure will appear and rebuild the temple (Sib. Or. 5.422, 433).[341] In a strongly

---

337. Smallwood, *Jews under Roman Rule*, 432-38.

338. For further arguments in favor of interpreting the temple in 16.3-4 as a rebuilt Jewish temple, Shukster and Richardson, "Temple and *Bet Ha-midrash*," 21-23, 24-27; Smallwood, *Jews under Roman Rule*, 435. For a thorough engagement with Shukster and Richardson's arguments, see Henne, "Barnabé, le temple et les pagano chrétiens," 257-76.

339. For the text of Genesis Rabbah, see Theodor and Albeck, *Bereschit Rabba*.

340. On the date of Sib. Or. 5, see Barclay, *Jews in the Mediterranean Diaspora*, 225; Collins, *Sibylline Oracles*, 94-95. Quotations of Sib. Or. 5 come from Geffcken, *Oracula Sibyllina*.

341. On the presence of a messiah in Sib. Or. 5.414-33, see Chester, *Messiah and Exaltation*, 480-81; Horbury, *Jewish Messianism*, 84, 102-3; Oegema, *Gesalbte*, 226; Oegema, *Annointed*, 227. At Sib. Or. 5.422, I follow Collins ("Sibylline Oracles," 1.403 n. 23) in preferring the text of Rzach (*Oracula Sibyllina*, 125) over Geffcken (*Die Oracula Sibyllina*, 124).

polemical passage, John Chrysostom asserts that Jews were thwarted in a third attempt to rebuild the temple (*Adv. Jud.* 5.10).[342]

It is hard to see how the rebuilt temple discussed in 16.3-4 is of a spiritual nature. Barnabas will argue that a spiritual temple is the right way to understand scripture in 16.6-10, but a spiritual temple has not yet been mentioned at 16.3-4 so that a physical building must be in view. A strict determination about whether Barnabas has heard rumors about the construction of a temple to Jupiter or about hopes for a third Jewish temple must be left open. Both options would support his argument, and the evidence is too slight to make a definitive choice.

Barnabas's arguments in favor of the temple of God in 16.6-10 locate the true temple in the community of believers whom God indwells. Barnabas is one of several Jesus-followers in the first and second centuries who defines the temple as something other than the physical building.[343] Jesus's body is defined as a temple (John 2:19-21), while references are made to a heavenly temple in Rev 11:19 and 15:5. Perhaps the best-known examples of the temple metaphor in early Christianity stem from Paul's letters and portray the community of believers in temple terms. The Corinthian community is portrayed as a temple that ought to be united in Paul's argument against divisions in Corinth (1 Cor 3:16-17). Later in the letter, the temple metaphor is applied to individuals in Paul's call for the Corinthians to live holy lives (1 Cor 6:18-20).[344] Believers are referred to as stones that are being constructed into a spiritual house (1 Pet 2:5). The tower visions in Herm. *Vis.* 3 (9.1—21.4); *Sim.* 9 (78.1—110.4) describe believers as stones that have been brought into the tower and united so that the stones appear to Hermas to form one stone (Herm. *Vis.* 3.2.6 [10.6]; *Sim.* 9.9.7 [86.7]). Ignatius of Antioch employs temple imagery in a variety of ways that fit broadly within the early Christian rhetorical motif of defining communities of believers in cultic terms.[345]

Barnabas's definition of the community as a temple that is indwelled by God in 16.8 can thus be situated alongside other texts that employ similar imagery. Likewise, his emphasis on the residence of God within the temple of believers' individual hearts has forerunners in Paul (*Barn.* 16.7; 1 Cor

---

342. For the text of Chrysostom's *Adv. Jud.* see Migne, *Patrologia Graeca*, 48.839-942.

343. The interpretation of the temple without regard to the building in Jerusalem can be found in early Jewish literature as well. See, e.g., 1QS (1Q28) VIII, 5-7; IX, 3-6.

344. Elsewhere in the Pauline corpus, see the temple metaphors in 2 Cor 6:16; Eph 2:19-22.

345. See further Kieffer, "La demeure divine," 287-301; Legarth, *Guds tempel*; Lookadoo, *High Priest and the Temple*, 58-262.

6:19).³⁴⁶ Yet Barnabas goes on to offer further reflections about the means by which God dwells within the temple. God indwells believers by the word of faith, the call of promise, the wisdom of the requirements, and the commandments found in God's teaching (16.9). The construction of the temple within believers is thus a fulfillment of prophecy (16.6). Moreover, Barnabas's understanding of the temple counters the charge that he makes of Jews who constructed and want to rebuild the temple, namely, that it looks to God and is thus not idolatrous (16.10; see also 16.1–2).

Since 16.1–10 castigates both the original builders of the temple and those who seek to rebuild it, the depiction of Barnabas and his audience as a temple fits the anti-Jewish rhetoric that pervades the letter, particularly in 2.1—16.10. The reference to the fall of the temple in 16.3–4 provides a recent event that the author employs to strengthen his case and to bring this portion of the argument to an end. Rather than understanding scripture in physical terms like his opponents, Barnabas urges his audience to read scripture figuratively and christologically. To understand scripture otherwise is idolatrous because it rejects the revelation that God gave to the true people beforehand. The thoroughgoing emphasis on the allegorical significance of cultic passages and the consistent focus on Jesus's suffering on behalf of "us" place Barnabas and his audience in a privileged position as interpreters of scripture because they are "a spiritual temple that is built for the Lord" (πνευματικὸς ναὸς οἰκοδομούμενος τῷ κυρίῳ; 16.10). Although the argument in 2.1—16.10 is far from linear or straightforward, Barnabas's extended exegetical work is designed to strengthen his audience's sense of identity and to clarify the boundary lines between "us" and "them."

---

346. See also Ign. *Eph.* 15.3.

III

Barnabas 17.1–2

Transition

MUCH OF THE ATTENTION that has been devoted to 17.1–2 comes when exploring the matter of the letter's integrity. If *Barnabas* was originally two documents that have now been fused, Barnabas's first-person address in 17.1–2 may have served as the conclusion of 1.1—17.2. If so, the Two Ways Tradition (18.1—20.2) and the conclusion in (21.1–9) may have formed a separate document. However, in addition to the discussion of its purpose and role in determining the letter's integrity, the sentences in 17.1–2 deserve attention for their rhetorical contribution, for the similarities to other rhetorical formulae in the letter, and for the theological themes that are located in this section. For example, Barnabas adds a rhetorical flourish to this section by asserting that he has attempted to clarify matters to his audience "insofar as it was possible" (ἐφ' ὅσον ἦν ἐν δυνατῷ; 17.1). He hopes that he has not left anything out. These words strike a note of humility in the author's rhetoric. Such self-effacing rhetoric has been seen elsewhere in the letter,[1] but the author's modesty gives way in 17.2 to a claim that he has only been able to talk about things that are past.[2] The reason given for this limited scope is because the audience would otherwise not be able to understand. Barnabas's role as a teacher thus comes to the fore, since he knows more than the believers whom he addresses.[3]

---

1. See 1.8; 4.6, 9.

2. Barnabas's assertion to have spoken only about the past contrasts with the past-present-future temporal scheme in 1.7.

3. Barnabas claims that present and future matters "are found in parables" (διὰ τὸ ἐν παραβολαῖς κεῖσθαι; 17.2). Hermas similarly asks the shepherd why the Son of God "appears" (κεῖται) as a slave "in the parable" (ἐν τῇ παραβολῇ; Herm. *Sim.* 5.5.5 [58.5]) of Herm. *Sim.* 5.2.1–11 (55.1–11). See also Herm. *Sim.* 5.6.1 (59.1).

Much of 2.1—16.10 deals with prophetic words that were revealed about Israel's cultic practices and about Israel's figurative role as borne out in history at Sinai. Yet the claim in 17.2 not to have spoken about the present is surprising in light of the description of the prophets in 1.7 and the search for the present that was initiated in 4.1. Barnabas also speaks about the proper authority of human beings over the animals and the eschatological Sabbath that are yet to be completed and are thus in the future (6.18–19; 15.4–8). The repetition of the Sinai narrative (4.6–8; 13.1—14.9) as well as the potent emphasis on Jesus's suffering and death (5.1–8.7) may have influenced Barnabas's depiction of his letter's past, rather than present or future, focus. Nevertheless, his statement in 17.2 creates a tension with what has just been said about the temple (16.3–4).[4] Barnabas's theological emphases in 17.1-2 would cohere more easily with other portions of the letter if the text of S^c and G is accepted. In these manuscripts, Barnabas hopes not to have left out anything "of the things that are necessary for salvation" (τῶν ἀνηκόντων εἰς σωτηρίαν; 17.1).[5] Salvation appears in two transitional statements within the argument of 2.1—16.10 (2.10; 4.1), and the longer reading of 17.1 would more easily connect Barnabas's transition to the rest of the letter. However, the shorter reading is more likely to be the earliest reading, since it is the more difficult reading and is attested in H, S, and L.[6]

Barnabas's thought in 17.1-2 does not contribute a great deal that is new to the argument but neither does it contradict what has come before. The primary role that it plays is as a transition from one set of arguments in 2.1—16.10 to a different set of traditions in 18.1—20.2. Since L does not continue beyond 17.2, it may be possible to view 17.1-2 as a conclusion to a stand-alone letter in 1.1—17.2.[7] However, it is better to see the letter as an integrated whole with 17.1-2 serving as a transition.[8] The strongest argument in favor of viewing 17.1-2 as a transition rather than a conclusion is found in the final sentence of 17.2. The phrase "so much for these things" (ταῦτα μὲν

---

4. For more on the present and future in 17.2, see Prinzivalli and Simonetti, *Seguendo Gesù*, 2.167n179.

5. The reading in the parentheses comes from Sc. The reading in G is slightly longer: anything "of the present things that are necessary for you for salvation" (τῶν ἀνηκόντων ὑμῖν εἰς σωτηρίαν ἐνεστώτων). The text of Sc is accepted by Cunningham, *Dissertation*, 76; Ehrman, *Apostolic Fathers*, 2.74; Holmes, *Apostolic Fathers*, 432; Lindemann and Paulsen, *apostolischen Väter*, 68. The longer ending contains language that is similar to 1 Clem. 45.1. See also Did. 16.2.

6. The shorter reading is accepted by Kraft, *Barnabas*, 133; Prigent and Kraft, *Épître de Barnabé*, 194; Prinzivalli and Simonetti, *Seguendo Gesù*, 2.154; Prostmeier and Lona, *Epistola Barnabae*, 126; Wengst, *Didache*, 186.

7. On the ending of L and its relationship to the Greek manuscripts of the letter, see Dentesano, "La versione latina," 135.

8. Prostmeier, *Barnabasbrief*, 525–29.

οὕτως) may be used as a transitional marker.[9] This phrase is even found in L prior to the doxology that concludes the translation (*haec autem sic sunt*; 17.2).[10] Rather than marking the conclusion of a letter or treatise, Barnabas's sentence signifies the end of one section of the argument and suggests that something is coming afterward. Similar rhetorical formulae can be found in other Greco-Roman writings. For example, Josephus utilizes a variation of this phrase to transition from a description of Gennesaret's geography to the main narrative of Vespasian's attack (*B.J.* 3.521),[11] while Alexander of Aphrodisias says something similar when transitioning between comments on different subjects (*In Metaph.* 500.33).[12] Irenaeus hopes to write both briefly and holistically at the beginning of the *Epideixis* and *Adversus Haereses* (*Epid.* 1; *Haer.* 1.pref.2–3).[13] Like Barnabas, these authors employ similar rhetorical formulae in order to transition to the next section of the argument.

Thus, although 17.1–2 could be interpreted as a conclusion, Barnabas's rhetoric need not be understood in this way. The remark, "so much for these things," is best read as a transition to the Two Ways Tradition. For whatever reason, the Two Ways Tradition was not retained in L, but the Greek witnesses to *Barnabas* continue in 18.1. When these arguments are added to the fact that language about two ways and two peoples characterizes both 2.1—16.10 and 18.1—20.2, there is strong reason to suspect that *Barnabas* was a unified letter from 1.1—21.9. Barnabas shifts in 17.1-2 from a discussion of what can be known about God's revelation to the people of God through scripture (2.1—16.10) to an exhortatory description of the knowledge of God that comes from following the way of light (18.1—20.2). The author's self-portrayal, summary of the contents thus far, and closure of the first body section enable him to transition to what follows.

---

9. Prinzivalli and Simonetti (*Seguendo Gesù*, 2.166) place this phrase in 18.1 rather than 17.2. I follow the verse numbering in Ehrman, *Apostolic Fathers*, 2.74; Prostmeier and Lona, *Epistola Barnabae*, 126.

10. The ending of Barnabas in L is doxological: "You have again something of the majesty of Christ, how all things were made in him and through him. To him be honor and power, and glory, now and forever" (*habes interim de maiestate Christi, quomodo omnia in illum et per illum facta sunt; cui sit honor, uirtus, gloria nunc et in saecula saeculorum*; 17.2 [L]). The text does not continue into 18.1 but rather concludes, "Here ends the Epistle of Barnabas" (*explicit epistola Barnabae*).

11. See also Josephus, *A.J.* 10.130; *C. Ap.* 1.142.

12. Citations from Alexander of Aphrodisias's *In Aristotelis Metaphysica Commentaria* come from Hayduck, *Alexandri Aphrodisiensis* and are cited by page and line number of this edition. For further uses of ταῦτα μὲν οὕτως and variant phrases, see Alexander of Aphrodisias, *In Metaph.* 772.8–9; 786.2; Athanasius, *C. Gent.* 19.34; Origen, *Cels.* 3.38. See also Prostmeier, *Barnabasbrief*, 528–29 and the literature cited there. Citations from Athanasius's *Contra Gentes* come from Thomson, *Athanasius* and are cited by section and line number.

13. Kraft, *Barnabas*, 133; Prigent and Kraft, *Épître de Barnabé*, 195n4.

IV

Barnabas 18.1—20.2

Two Ways: Second Body Section

THE COMMENTARY ON 17.1-2 argued for seeing that passage as a transition between the first and second body sections (2.1—16.10; 18.1—20.2). The letter continues in 18.1 by introducing the Two Ways Tradition. Although some have viewed the Two Ways Tradition as an appendix in the Epistle of Barnabas,[1] this section (18.1-20.2) is better conceived of as a vital part of the letter that is integrated into the rhetorical structure following 17.1-2 and developing themes that were introduced in 1.1—16.10. Barnabas includes the audience in his rhetorical exhortation to "move on" (μεταβῶμεν) to the next section (18.1). The verb indicates that Barnabas and his readers should both be aware of the shift in topic, argument, and rhetorical style that comes in 18.1—20.2.[2] The audience is encouraged to move with Barnabas "on to another knowledge and teaching" (ἐπὶ ἑτέραν γνῶσιν καὶ διδαχήν; 18.1). Noetic (γνω-) terminology has been important throughout the letter,[3] and Barnabas has appealed already to the gift and commandments of teaching in the first body section (9.9; 16.9).[4] The Two Ways Tradition that is utilized in 18.1—20.2 shares other themes with what has come before in the letter. For example, the light that characterizes the way that Barnabas describes in 19.1-12 mirrors the way in which Jesus was described in the Isaianic citations of 14.7-8. The way of darkness (20.1-2) has already been referenced in 5.4 opposite the way of righteousness.[5] Although 18.1—20.2 employs a

---

1. E.g., Hilgenfeld (*Die apostolischen Väter*, 29-30) refers to 18.1—21.9 as "ein paränetischer Anhang."

2. Prostmeier, *Barnabasbrief*, 529.

3. For the central role that knowledge plays in the letter, see especially 1.5, 7.

4. Barnabas also highlights Jesus's teaching of Israel (5.8) while distancing himself—rhetorically, at least—from an intentional teaching role (1.8; 4.9).

5. See also the description of the fish who walk in darkness in Barnabas's discussion

traditional didactic form, Barnabas brings the section into alignment with language found elsewhere in the letter.[6]

Barnabas structures the Two Ways Tradition in a straightforward manner. After the section opens with a note that Barnabas is passing on to a different knowledge and teaching that regards contrasting paths, the dual roads are characterized by light, light-bearing angels, and the Lord, on the one hand, and darkness, the angels of Satan, and the ruler of the present age, on the other (18.1–2). Barnabas then describes the way of light at length (19.1–12). To follow the way of light involves loving, fearing, and glorifying the God who has created and redeemed Barnabas and his audience. It also requires love and right actions toward their neighbors, children, parents, masters, and slaves. The way of light is characterized by humility, righteousness, and generosity as well as hatred for all things related to the evil one. On the other hand, the way of darkness is crooked and cursed (20.1–2). Barnabas's way of darkness is comprised of extensive vice lists, focusing on types of sin (20.1) as well as types of sinners (20.2). This is the path that the righteous have been warned against following in 19.1–12. These final comments in 18.1–20.2 are linked to the earlier portions of the letter because the Two Ways Tradition enables Barnabas to further define the difference between the two peoples.

Barnabas employs a traditional form of teaching to set out these differences. References to alternate ways of living can be found in Greek literature and in texts that are now incorporated into the Hebrew Bible.[7] Barnabas's Two Ways Tradition finds closer parallels in early Jewish literature, such as the *Community Rule* from Qumran or lists from the Testaments of the Twelve Patriarchs.[8] Similarly to Barn. 18.1–2, the *Community Rule* likewise

---

of the food laws (10.10). Barnabas and his audience have been redeemed from darkness by the Son (14.5–6).

6. On connections between 18.1–20.2 with the rest of the letter, see further Hvalvik, *Struggle for Scripture and Covenant*, 63–65; Rhodes, "Two Ways Tradition," 797–816; Smith, "*Epistle of Barnabas*," 465–97.

7. E.g., Hesiod, *Op.* 287–92; *Tab. Ceb.* 4.2–6.3; 24.2–3; Xenophon, *Mem.* 2.1.21–34. Reinhard Feldmeier ("Paideia salvatrix," 150–52) observes the two ways that are set before human beings in the *Tabula Cebetis*, that is, the way of life and the way of deception. Citations from Hesiod's *Works and Days* come from West, *Hesiod*. Citations from *Tabula Cebetis* are drawn from Hirsch-Luipold et al., *Bildtafel des Kebes*. Citations from Xenophon's *Memorabilia* are found in Marchant and Todd, *Xenophon*. Among texts that are now included in the Hebrew Bible, see, e.g., Deut 30:15; Josh 24:15; Ps 1:6; 139:24; Prov 2:8–22; 4:9–10; Jer 21:8. See further Bricker, "Doctrine of the 'Two Ways,'" 501–17; Wilhite, *One of Life*, 285–314. On other forms of ethical digests in the Hebrew Bible, see Barton, *Ethics in Ancient Israel*, 227–44.

8. For the imagery of ways or paths in early Jewish literature, see Sir 15.11–17; CD II, 6; Philo, *Agr.* 101; 2 En. 30.15; 4 Ezra 7.3–12; m. 'Abot 2.1.

sets out the paths available to the community in terms of light and darkness with two spirits that govern each path (1QS III, 13–IV, 26).[9] Beliar masters those who choose the path of evil as they cheat their neighbor and refuse to show mercy (T. Ash. 1.3—6.5).[10] Teachings about opposing paths and angels show up in early Christian texts like the Shepherd of Hermas (Herm. Mand. 6.1.1–6.2.10 [35.1—36.10]; Sim. 6.1.5-6.5.7 [61.5—65.7]).[11] The paths are described in terms of righteousness and unrighteousness (Herm. Mand. 6.1.2 [35.2]), and Hermas is instructed to follow the righteous angel by being modest, gentle, and quiet (Herm. Mand. 6.2.1, 3 [36.1, 3]). Yet the nearest parallels with Barn. 18.1—20.2 can be found in the Didache (Did. 1.1—6.2).[12] In its current form, the Didache opens like *Barnabas*'s Two Ways Tradition by announcing that there are only two ways (Did. 1.1; Barn. 18.1). Yet the Two Ways Tradition in the Didache is not characterized in terms of light and darkness as in Barn. 18.1 but is described instead with regard to life and death (Did. 1.1). The Two Ways Tradition lifts up love for God (Did. 1.1; Barn. 18.2), extols hatred of hypocrisy and things that displease God (Did. 4.12; Barn. 19.2), and insists that those on the way of life should not be double-minded or double-tongued (Did. 2.4; Barn. 19.7–8). Although the Didache's Two Ways Tradition is longer than what is found in *Barnabas* and the Two Ways Tradition continued to be developed and reused in other early Christian texts,[13] the Two Ways Tradition in the Epistle of Barnabas bears witness to an important teaching tool utilized by early Christians to train and form audiences.[14]

This section of the letter has elicited much scholarly attention due to its similarity to Did. 1.1—6.2 and the continuing use of the Two Ways Tradition in other early Christian literature. Much of the focus in the late-nineteenth century through the first half of the twentieth century explored the possibility of literary relationships between *Barnabas*, the

---

9. Dacy, "Epistle to Barnabas," 139–47; Popović, "Anthropology," 58–98; Uusimäki, "Mapping Ideals," 38–39.

10. Nickelsburg, *Jewish Literature*, 311–12. See also 1QM XIII, 12; 1 En. 1.9; 54.3–5; 63.1; 2 En. 10.1–3; T. Levi 3.2–3.

11. One may also note images of paths within Jesus's teachings (Matt 7:13–14; Luke 13:24) as well as references to the way of life and way of the Lord in early Christian discourse (Acts 2:28; 18:25).

12. For a convenient synopsis of the texts, see Kraft, *Barnabas*, 134–60.

13. E.g., Apos. Con. 7.1–19; Aristides, *Apol.* 15; *Vita Shenudi*. On the continued use of the Two Ways Tradition in early Christian literature outside of *Barnabas*, see Aldridge, "Peter and the Two Ways," 233–64; van de Sandt and Flusser, *Didache*, 55–111; Jefford, *Apostolic Fathers and the New Testament*, 217; Stewart-Sykes, *On the Two Ways*, passim; Wilhite, *One of Life*, passim.

14. See further Draper, "Barnabas and the Riddle," 89–113.

Didache, and other examples of the Two Ways Tradition.[15] The discovery of the Dead Sea Scrolls and the *Community Rule* contained in Cave 1 led to a tenuous consensus in which a common source or set of traditions was seen behind the Two Ways Traditions in *Barnabas* and the Didache.[16] More recent studies have examined the function of this material within the Didache or *Barnabas*, while comparing the Two Ways Tradition in these texts to other early Christian literature, exploring theological themes and backgrounds that shed light on *Barnabas* and the Didache, and inquiring into the likely effects of the text for social identity.[17] For the purposes of this commentary, the Two Ways Tradition in 18.1—20.2 should be read first of all within the context of the Epistle of Barnabas. Although reference will be made to similar language and motifs elsewhere in antique literature, the first priority in what follows will be to illuminate Barnabas's words within the context of his own letter.

IV.1. Introduction (Barn. 18.1–2)

As Barnabas transitions to the Two Ways Tradition, he introduces the reflections on diverging paths as "another knowledge and teaching" (ἑτέρα γνῶσις καὶ διδαχή; 18.1). Barnabas's description of these metaphorical roads will be characterized by a series of statements about how his audience should live rather than the exegetical arguments about the true people of God, the revelation of Jesus's suffering and death, or the significance of cultic actions described in scripture. When Barnabas refers to knowledge (γνῶσις), the term is not limited to exegetical statements or to understanding God's revelation that was given beforehand. Knowledge has implications for the present. Indeed, knowledge may be found by following the instructions that Barnabas gives in 18.1—20.2 so that the two pathways are the content of a kind of knowledge with which Barnabas wants his readers to be closely acquainted.[18] Something similar can be said when comparing Barnabas's use of teaching language. The teaching that was revealed to Abraham when circumcising 318 men in his household leads to a teaching that guides one along the right path (9.9; 18.1).

---

15. E.g., Robinson, *Barnabas*; Taylor, "Two Ways," 243–58; Windisch, *Barnabasbrief*, 404–6.

16. E.g., J. P. Audet, "Affinités," 219–38, 41–82; Barnard, "'Epistle of Barnabas' and Its Contemporary Setting," 190–203; Barnard, *Studies in the Apostolic Fathers*, 87–107.

17. E.g., Rordorf and Tuilier, *La doctrine*, 22–34; Wilhite, *Didache*, 99–162.

18. Hvalvik, *Struggle for Scripture and Covenant*, 65.

The divergence described in the Two Ways Tradition is further defined in terms of teaching and authority (διδαχῆς καὶ ἐξουσίας). Both words occur as genitive descriptions that modify the two ways (ὁδοὶ δύο). It is possible that the genitives function epexegetically and thereby describe the same phenomenon. If so, the phrase may be translated, "There are two ways of teaching, that is, of authority." Teaching and authority would be used synonymously to describe the same reality. Yet it is preferable to interpret the words as characterizing the ways slightly differently. The divergent paths in the Two Ways Tradition provides a teaching from the author that guides the people in how they should live. By speaking in this manner, the author extends the description of teaching from his introductory statement about knowledge and teaching. Yet the dual paths do not only offer teaching but also indicate alternative authorities. The reference to authority gives Barnabas's Two Ways Tradition an eschatological emphasis that is aware of heavenly realities. Both paths have authorities who govern them, and Barnabas lays before the audience two options from which they must choose. The choice to walk along one path is simultaneously a choice to obey a ruler.

The opening clauses of 18.1 speak of the dual roads together, but Barnabas quickly begins to differentiate them in what follows. The respective paths are differentiated in terms of opposites: light and darkness, the angels who provide company on each path, and the authority who rules over each path (18.1–2). Between the first and second of these opposing characteristics, Barnabas summarily puts the alternatives before his audience when he writes, "There is a great difference between the two ways" (διαφορὰ δὲ πολλὴ τῶν δύο ὁδῶν; 18.1).[19] The difference will be illustrated in more detail throughout the list of traits and actions that will follow in 19.1—20.2. For example, the way of light is characterized by believers' love for the one who made them (19.2), while the first vice listed on the way of darkness is idolatry (20.1). Yet the paired alternatives in the Two Ways Tradition mirrors strong divisions made by the author throughout the letter. Barnabas argues that circumcision can be rightly accepted as an act related to the ears or can be misunderstood as a physical sign (9.1–9).[20] Although the covenant was received by Moses as a servant, it was rejected by Israel at Sinai and given to the true heirs, Barnabas and his audience (14.1–5). The difference between the paths that is mentioned in 18.1 mirrors Barnabas's argumentative style elsewhere. There are only two options, and the audience is exhorted to choose the right one.

---

19. See also Did. 1.1; *Doctr.* 1.1 (*distantio autem magna est duarum uiarum*). Citations from the *Doctrina apostolorum* come from Rordorf and Tuilier, *La doctrine*.

20. Yuh, "Do as I Say," 273–95.

Barnabas employs light and dark imagery to emphasize the great difference. He has already utilized the contrast between light and dark in his description of the Son's redemption in 14.5–9. Darkness characterizes the realm from which Barnabas and his audience were rescued (14.5–7). The author's Isaianic citations depict the Son as the light of the nations (φῶς ἐθνῶν; 14.7–8),[21] while the darkness in which Barnabas's opponents dwell prevents them from understanding the christological significance of the red heifer (8.7).[22] Darkness is the realm of the fish who swim in the deep and with whom the people are not to associate (10.10). Although the Didachist uses life and death as the opposing characteristics in its Two Ways Tradition,[23] Barnabas is not alone among early Christian authors in employing contrasts between light and dark.[24] Light and dark are also significant motifs in Pauline and Johannine literature. Paul tells the Corinthians that the god of this age has blinded unbelievers so that they cannot see the light. God brought light to believers' hearts so that they could see God's glory displayed in the face of Christ (2 Cor 4:4–6).[25] The Johannine Jesus refers to himself as the light of the world (John 8:12; 9:5) and urges his followers to walk and believe in the light so that they can become children of light (John 12:35–36).[26] The author of 1 John similarly weaves together God

21. Light is also the consequence of the true fast that breaks unjust bonds and liberates the oppressed (3.4).

22. The darkness experienced by Barnabas's opponents when interpreting scripture contrasts with the open (φανερά) nature with which Barnabas and his audience understand due to the revelation that they have received (8.7).

23. See Did 1.1 where the two ways are portrayed in terms "of life" (τῆς ζωῆς) and "of death" (τοῦ θανάτου).

24. E.g., Aristides describes the teaching of God as the door of light (*Apol.* 17.3). On Aristides, *Apol.* 17.3, see Lattke, *Aristides Apologie*, 370–71. Citations from Aristides's *Apology* come from Pouderon and Pierre, *Aristide: Apologie*.

25. Later in the letter, Paul asks believers what fellowship light can have with darkness (2 Cor 6:14). The implicit answer is that light cannot fellowship with darkness. Satan, however, masquerades as an angel of light (2 Cor 11:14). Paul uses light and darkness to contrast two different ways of living in expectation of the parousia in 1 Thess 5:4–5. The Romans are exhorted to lay aside deeds associated with darkness and to put on the armor of light (Rom 13:12). Similar imagery and contrasts between light and dark are found in Eph 6:10–17 (see also Eph 5:8–9). While Romans and Ephesians make use of battle imagery rather than paths, the rhetorical aims are similar to Barn. 18.1—20.2. Paul sets out to encourage believers to live rightly and cautions them against living in ways that run counter to what God has revealed in Christ.

26. Light and darkness also play a significant role among the key themes of the gospel that are introduced in the Johannine prologue (John 1:4–9). Jesus employs light imagery in his discussion with Nicodemus, which takes place at night (John 3:19–21). John the Baptist is also associated with light (John 1:6–8; 5:35). Belief in Jesus is connected with light, while rejection of Jesus keeps people in darkness (John 1:9; 12:46).

as light, the need to walk in the light, and warnings against living in the dark (1 John 1:5–7).[27] By associating the Two Ways Tradition with light and darkness (Barn. 18.1), Barnabas participates in a tradition of early Christian discourse that not only coheres with what he has said earlier in the letter but also urges his readers to walk actively along the way of light.

Barnabas's second description of the difference between the dual paths concerns the spiritual beings that are likewise found along the paths. The contrast is emphasized by Barnabas's use of the same introductory formulae and the repetition of the word "angels" (ἄγγελοι; 18.1). The angels are appointed over the roads, and Barnabas introduces the two groups of angels by placing the prepositional phrases (ἐφ' ἧς) at the beginning of each clause. The μέν . . . δέ construction heightens the contrast, while the twofold use of "angels" drives the point home. The angels along the path of light are "light-bearing" (φωταγωγοί), while the angels along the path of darkness belong to Satan. Barnabas's mention of the angels along the two streets is reminiscent of the Community Rule (1QS), which also highlights the role of the prince of light and angel of darkness (1QS III, 20–21) in its discussion of the opposing ways.[28] The Shepherd of Hermas likewise refers to the angels of righteousness and evil that guide human beings, and Hermas is urged to be faithful in trusting the works of the angel of righteousness (Mand. 6.2.1–10 [36.1–10]).[29]

Barnabas saves the most important contrast between the opposing ways of living for the final position. "The Lord from eternity and for eternity" (ὁ κύριος ἀπ' αἰώνων καὶ εἰς τοὺς αἰῶνας) is associated with the way of light, while "the ruler of the present age of lawlessness" (ὁ ἄρχων καιροῦ τοῦ νῦν τῆς ἀνομίας; 18.2) is linked to the dark path. The use of temporal language is prevalent in Barnabas's description of the two rulers. The Lord is described as eternal. He exists as Lord from the beginning of the ages until their end. By using the word αἰών, Barnabas places the emphasis in 18.2 on the furthest extents of God's eternality, that is, the beginning and the end. On the other hand, the ruler of this present age (καιροῦ τοῦ νῦν) is elsewhere described as Satan.[30] Barnabas employs terminology that is reminiscent of the Johannine tradition (John 12:31; 14:30; 16:11) and thereby acknowledges that the chief evil being has some authority in the present.[31] The true God who has

27. Light is also associated with love and the new commandment, while darkness is aligned with hatred in the Johannine epistles (1 John 2:8–10).

28. See also the reference to the "angel of truth" (1QS III, 25).

29. For further comparison of angels in *Barnabas's* Two Ways Tradition and angels discussed in other texts that contain Two Ways Traditions, see Kraft, *Barnabas*, 135–36.

30. Farrar, "Intimate and Ultimate Adversary," 539.

31. For further references, see Windisch, *Barnabasbrief*, 397.

revealed Godself to believers and who has acted to redeem Barnabas and his audience in Christ rules over the light path. On the other hand, the ruler of the present lawless age governs the path of darkness. Believers are thereby challenged to follow the path of light and to associate themselves with the God who rules over that path.

The Two Ways Tradition that is set out in 18.1—20.2 mirrors Barnabas's discussion elsewhere of the two peoples: "this people" and "that people"; the true heirs and Israel; "us" and "them."[32] Although Barnabas does not mention Israel in 18.1—20.2 and employs traditional forms that are used without reference to Israel elsewhere in early Christian literature, he associates the way of light with the audience and himself, while connecting his opponents to the way of darkness. Israel's idolatry that was typified at Sinai has resulted in them walking along the path of darkness under the influence of Satan's angels and the ruler of this present age. Yet Barnabas is not deterministic. While the peoples who are in view may be regarded as types, the individuals whom Barnabas addresses must choose which path they will walk along. The Two Ways Tradition in *Barnabas* thus functions to build up the boundary walls between Barnabas's audience and his opponents while simultaneously drawing the audience together into a more cohesive group that collectively seeks to pursue the way of the Lord. This topic is introduced in general terms in 18.1-2, but the discussion continues through 20.2, by which point each path will have been characterized in further detail.

IV.2. The Way of Light (Barn. 19.1–12)

Barnabas moves in 19.1-12 to describe the way of light more fully. In terms of length, the discussion of the way of light swamps both the introduction and the characterization of the way of darkness. Barnabas puts forward a positive portrayal of what it looks like to live in faithful obedience to the Lord who rules over the way of light. While the exhortations, imperatives, and warnings that follow contribute coherently to urge Barnabas's audience to live rightly, it is not easy to find a framework within which to understand how the individual statements are organized. The introduction to the way of light is found in 19.1. Some of the following exhortations can be linked together. For example, Barnabas urges the audience to be rightly related to God with a series of instructions in 19.2, while he collects exhortations pertaining to how children should be treated in 19.5. Yet the

---

32. Yuh ("Do as I Say," 280, 287) helpfully locates Barnabas's use of the Two Ways Tradition alongside other attempts to identify his audience as a distinct and identifiable social group.

characterization of the way of light is effective not because of its structure but due to the effect that it can have on readers when the power of the paraenetic cascade is absorbed in its dizzying and uplifting call to act rightly as true heirs of the covenant.

The first sentence in 19.1 clearly introduces the topic and may even function like a title for what follows: "This, then, is the way of light" (ἡ οὖν ὁδὸς τοῦ φωτός ἐστιν αὕτη; 19.1). A nearly identical statement is found in Did. 1.2 that describes the way of life.[33] Barnabas transitions clearly from setting two options before his audience to explaining what actions lie along the light path. His next statement provides the audience with further motivation for continuing along this route. If there are any in the audience who want to make their way "to the determined place" (ἐπὶ τὸν ὡρισμένον τόπον), they should be diligent with respect to their actions. The place that is appointed for Barnabas's audience is an eschatological reference. Ignatius utilizes the language of a place that is set apart for certain people when speaking about alternative kinds of deeds, namely, those that lead to death and those that lead to life (Ign. *Magn.* 5.1).[34] Barnabas sets the way of light before the audience in the hope that they will receive all that they hope for from following the Son of God. This hope in final eschatological redemption provides the rationale for continuing to follow the way of light.

The author likewise insists that the way of light is a form of knowledge (Barn. 19.1).[35] This knowledge is described in three ways at the end of 19.1. First, it is knowledge that was "given to us" (δοθεῖσα ἡμῖν; 19.1) just as knowledge about Jesus's identity and death on the cross was given to Abraham (9.8). Second, it is knowledge that is given for the purpose of walking in it. The knowledge that Barnabas puts forward is dynamically oriented. Finally, the knowledge is "such as follows" (τοιαύτη). This adjective points forward to the rest of the material that follows in 19.2–12. Yet one may also notice that this adjective can be used elsewhere in the context of an implicit warning if the following instruction is not followed.[36]

After the opening sketch of the way of light in 19.1, Barnabas shifts to specific paraenetic statements in 19.2–12. The author urges the audience

---

33. The Didache introduces the way of life with the following words: "This, then, is the way of life" (ἡ μὲν οὖν ὁδὸς τῆς ζωῆς ἐστιν αὕτη; 1.2). The use of μέν enhances the contrast with the way of death that is introduced by δέ in Did 5.1.

34. The word τόπος is also employed with similar eschatologically final connotations in Acts 1:25; 1 Clem. 5.4, 7; 44.5; Pol. *Phil.* 9.2. See further Prigent and Kraft, *Épître de Barnabé*, 196n4; Wengst, *Didache*, 187n262; Prinzivalli and Simonetti, *Seguendo Gesù*, 2.546n183.

35. See also 18.1.

36. E.g., Acts 16:24; Rom 1:32; 1 Cor 5:1.

to be properly related to God and to stand against all that opposes God in 19.2. Right relation to God demonstrates itself in three actions: love, fear, and glorification.[37] The words θεός and κύριος do not appear at this point. Rather, God is identified by creative and redemptive actions. The reference to "the one who redeemed you" may refer to the Father because the Father is more clearly in view with regard to the preceding creation statements. Alternatively, the phrase may be a reference to the Son, since redemption language is used with regard to the Son in 14.5-8.[38] Although it is difficult to identify precisely who is meant by "the one who redeemed you from death" (τὸν σε λυτρωσάμενον ἐκ θανάτου), all works that lead to the goal that God established assume "that a person's existence is founded upon God and his salvific actions from the beginning as well as with a view to their eschatological goal."[39]

Concomitant with right relation to God are two dispositions that Barnabas desires to see in his audience. They are instructed to be "single-minded in heart and rich in spirit" (19.2). Barnabas's instruction to be rich in spirit echoes language that was used in the introduction of the letter. The audience was praised for their connection to the rich requirements of the Lord and for receiving the wealth of the Spirit of the Lord poured on them (1.2-3). Barnabas thus urges the audience to become what they have already received from God so that the instructions in the Two Ways Tradition follow from what God alone has done for Barnabas and his audience.[40] On the other hand, the audience must not be joined with those who walk in the way of death. In calling his readers to avoid joining with his opponents, Barnabas repeats language that he has already employed when outlining the food laws in 10.3-5.[41] That the way of death (19.2) or the way of

---

37. Although the textual situation in Sir 7.29-31 is complex, Ben Sira records a concentration of language about loving, fearing, and glorifying or honoring that is similar to Barn. 19.2. Hermas is likewise given a threefold set of instructions told to believe in God, to fear God, and to be self-controlled due to this fear (Herm. Mand. 1.2 [26.2]; 6.1.1 [35.1]).

38. Fuller discussions of this ambiguity may be found in Prostmeier, *Barnabasbrief*, 537-39.

39. Prostmeier, *Barnabasbrief*, 539. Prostmeier's full sentence runs as follows: "Entscheidend ist, daß alle Werke, die zu dem von Gott festgesetzten Ziel führen, das Bekenntnis voraussetzen, daß die Existenz des Menschen von Anfang an sowie mit Blick auf ihr eschatologisches Ziel auf Gott und seinem Heilswillen gründet."

40. A similar phenomenon is found within Barn. 1 as Barnabas tells the audience about the wealth that they have received from God (1.2-3) before urging them to act richly in fear of God (1.7).

41. Barnabas speaks comparably in 10.8 and 11. See also Hvalvik, *Struggle for Scripture and Covenant*, 162.

darkness (18.1) is particularly associated with Barnabas's Jewish opponents and not generic evil people can be illustrated by comparing the juxtaposition of the path of righteousness and the dark path in 5.4. Barnabas's Two Ways Tradition furthers his attempt to establish strong borders separating his community from his opponents. For this reason, the audience is told to hate all that fails to please God and all hypocrisy (19.2). Their hatred of what opposes God contrasts with the love that they are called to show for their creator. Barnabas continues warning the audience by urging them not to neglect the Lord's commandments.

The instructions in 19.3 center upon instructions to avoid arrogance. Barnabas continues to allow negative adverbs to drive his teaching in 19.3. The audience is counselled not to exalt themselves.[42] Instead, they should be humble "in every way" (κατὰ πάντα; 19.3). The call to humility is not limited to relationships with particular individuals or with other people in general. Rather, Barnabas's Two Ways Tradition demands humility in every aspect of believers' lives.[43] The audience is then advised not to take up glory for themselves. Glory rightly belongs to God (19.2), so the claim of glory for oneself takes something that is rightfully God's and misapplies it to the self (19.3). Believers are taught not to accept evil counsel against their neighbor.[44] This instruction stands slightly apart from the other three instructions in 19.3 because it is not immediately clear how evil counsel can be connected to the pride against which Barnabas warns in the rest of the verse. Yet Barnabas's placement of the commandment here may demonstrate his concern to live humbly even when someone finds information that may be embarrassing to their neighbors or advantageous to themselves. Finally, Barnabas calls the audience to keep their souls from arrogance. The active verb indicates that believers should take the initiative in guarding themselves from becoming arrogant or entering into actions that are characteristic of arrogant people.

Barnabas turns to more traditional language at the beginning of 19.4, urging the audience not to engage in sexual immorality, adultery, or the corruption of children. Similar concern for sexual purity was evident in 10.6. The command not to commit adultery can be found in the Ten Words (Exod 20:14; Deut 5:18), and Barnabas's additional instructions extend the force of this command. A link between sexual promiscuity and idolatry may also implicitly provide the rationale for Barnabas's next admonition. The audience should not allow the Word of God to go out from any who

---

42. The same instruction is found in Did. 3.9.
43. Becker, *Begriff der Demut*, 201.
44. See Did. 2.6.

are impure. God's Word is rightly associated only with purity on the way of light. Partiality when encountering sin is next on the agenda. There should not be any favoritism when it comes to rebuking someone for a transgression. Believers are called instead to be gentle, quiet, and to fear the words that they hear. These are the first positive instructions that Barnabas has given since the command to be humble (19.3). Rather than defining the audience by what they should not be, Barnabas portrays believers who are walking along the way of light as gentle and attentive to the words that are spoken to them. With this in mind, he warns them not to hold grudges against brothers and sisters. Grudges tend to disrupt the gentleness by which the community should be described.

If grudges and gentleness are the key instructions at the conclusion of 19.4, Barnabas urges his audience to right choices and speech in the opening instructions of 19.5. They are commanded not to be double-minded. While double-mindedness could be used by early Christians with regard to various phenomena, Barnabas is particularly concerned about the audience's perception of the future as well as the decisions that they will make.[45] Readers are not to be of two minds about "whether something will be or not" (πότερον ἔσται ἢ οὔ; 19.5). Nor should the audience take the Lord's name in vain. Taking the Lord's name in vain returns the Two Ways Tradition to the Ten Words that Barnabas may have already alluded to when discussing adultery.[46] To take the name of the Lord in vain is not only a misuse of speech but may also be an idolatrous act because it does not recognize the Lord's identity and worthiness of worship. In 19.5, believers are not only taught with regard to their minds or their speech but also with regard to how they act toward their neighbors. They must love their neighbor. As with the instruction to be gentle and quiet, this command is one of a minority of admonitions that is given without a negative adverb. To love one's neighbor may be regarded as a summary of the second table of the Ten Words. Its repetition in the early Christian Jesus traditions makes its appearance in 19.5 unsurprising.[47] However, given the prominent place of this instruction within the Two Ways Tradition that is recorded in the Didache (1.2; 2.7), one may wonder why the

---

45. Double-mindedness is elsewhere connected to doubts in prayer (Jas 1:8; Herm. Mand. 9.5–7 [39.5–7]), to wealth (Herm. Vis. 3.6.5 [14.5]; Sim. 8.8.1–2 [74.1–2]), to susceptibility to false prophets (Herm. Mand. 11.1–2 [43.1–2]), and is left open to interpretation within broader contexts (Jas 4:8; 1 Clem. 23.2–4; 2 Clem. 11.2–5; Did. 4.4; Herm. Vis. 3.7.1 [15.1]; Sim. 8.7.1–3 [73.1–3]; 8.8.3, 5 [74.3, 5]). On double-mindedness in early Christianity, see further List, "Δίψυχος," 85–104.

46. See Exod 20:7; Deut 5:11.

47. See Matt 22:39; Mark 12:31; Luke 10:27; Rom 13:9; Gal 5:14; Jas 2:8; Gos. Thom. 25.1; Justin, Dial. 93.2–3. All quotations from the Gospel of Thomas come from Gathercole, Gospel of Thomas.

instruction is mixed into Barn. 19.5 and not given a more significant location within Barnabas's description of the way of light.

The final paraenetical statements in 19.5 concern the audience's interaction with children. As some of the most vulnerable in Roman society, these instructions draw the audience's eyes to demonstrate concern for those whose voice is weak or nonexistent. Barnabas teaches readers that they should not kill a child "in corruption" (ἐν φθορᾷ) or do away with a child "after it is born" (γεννηθέν). To do away with children after birth is most likely a reference to the exposure of unwanted or burdensome children in the Roman world. Barnabas urges the audience to cut off such practices within the walls of their own community. It is most likely that the phrase "in corruption" refers to attempts to abort children prior to birth. The prepositional phrase may be used to speak of this practice indirectly, but it also illustrates that Barnabas viewed the practice as detestable. Barnabas's concern for children extends beyond birth, however. The next instruction urges readers not to take their hand away from their son or daughter. Rather, they have a responsibility to teach their children to fear God from youth.[48] The Two Ways Tradition in Barnabas aims to have children not only survive but learn the fear of God.

Barnabas then returns to consider how believers relate to their neighbors. Believers are warned not to desire "your neighbor's belongings" (τὰ τοῦ πλησίον σου; 19.6). The admonition in 19.6 again sounds similar to a command that is found in the Ten Words (Exod 20:17; Deut 5:21).[49] Barnabas adds the closely related command not to be greedy. There is a close relation between desire for the possessions of one's neighbor and greed. Readers should not be joined "by your soul" (ἐκ ψυχῆς σου) to those who are exalted. Rather, they should live with the just and the humble. To be joined by the soul envisions an intimate connection by which one closely associates with those who are exalted. Those who walk along the way of light should instead characteristically link their lives to people who are of low repute and who are fair. The conjunction that precedes Barnabas's injunction against joining with those who are exalted (οὐδέ) indicates a

---

48. Barnabas's consistent use of prepositions in 19.5 helps to underline his point. Readers should not remove their hand "from your son or from your daughter" (ἀπὸ τοῦ υἱοῦ σου ἢ ἀπὸ τῆς θυγατρὸς σου). Rather, they should teach them "from youth" (ἀπὸ νεότητος). The repetition of ἀπό as well as the placement of all three prepositions between the two verbs makes the statement more memorable.

49. In both renditions of the commandment found in the Torah, the Israelite are instructed "not to desire" (οὐκ ἐπιθυμήσεις) "anything that belongs to your neighbor" (ὅσα τῷ πλησίον σου). The Ten Words are more specific than the sentence from Barn. 19.6 examined here, because it also indicates that one should not desire their neighbor's wife, house, slave, or ox. Yet the Two Ways Tradition runs close to the Ten Words here.

link between this teaching and the instruction not to be greedy. The author connects not desiring another's possessions, not being greedy, and not associating with those who are exalted. Barnabas next shifts the point of view regarding these instructions by appealing to God's sovereignty. Those on the way of light should receive all things that happen to them "as good things" (ὡς ἀγαθά). This difficult teaching is then explained with reference to God's transcendence. The reason that all things can be accepted as good is that believers know that nothing happens without God. This theological clause may ground believers' relationship to their neighbors in the instructions throughout 19.6 and thus enable them to live without undue desire for their neighbor's possessions or status.

Barnabas continues to reflect on relationships with others but turns the attention closer to home in 19.7. Similarly to 19.5, believers are warned against being double-minded and are given instructions about how to interact in the home. Barnabas adds here that believers should not be "double-minded or double-tongued" (διγνώμων οὐδὲ δίγλωσσος; 19.7). Speech will continue to play an important role in the instructions to slaves and masters. However, slaves are first instructed simply to submit to their masters in shame and fear. By doing this, their submission is like "a pattern of God" (τύπῳ θεοῦ).[50] Slaves' submission to their masters may conform to the pattern of God insofar as believers are called to fear God (1.7; 2.2; 4.11; 10.11; 11.5) or in the same way as the Son of God endured suffering (5.1—6.4). Conversely, masters are warned against ordering their male or female slaves around "bitterly" (ἐν πικρίᾳ; 19.7). Barnabas's instruction is directed toward believers, since he envisions the slaves hoping in the same God as their masters. The admonition in 19.7 comes with a warning, namely, that hostile commands may result in slaves' failing to fear "the God who is over both" (τὸν ἐπ' ἀμφοτέροις θεόν). The God who rules over both slaves and masters did not come to call people "according to reputation" (κατὰ πρόσωπον). He came instead to call those whom the Spirit prepared.[51] Whether Barnabas's believing audience is slave or master, then, they are called to relate well to one another within the confines of societal expectations of slave and master. All the while, Barnabas reminds readers that there is only one absolute ruler,

---

50. A similar instruction is given in Did. 4.11. See further Wilhite, *Didache*, 146–47.

51. Although Barnabas does not set out a clear statement of how the Father, Son, and Spirit relate to one another, the Spirit's agency in preparing believers whom God calls in 19.7 provides strong evidence for proto-Trinitarian inclinations in the letter. Svigel ("Trinitarianism," 28–29) points to functional parallels in the preparatory work of the Son and Spirit (3.6; 19.7) to strengthen arguments in favor of an incipient Trinitarianism within the Epistle of Barnabas.

thereby introducing a relativizing or perhaps even destabilizing note into the slave-master relationship.[52]

In 19.8, Barnabas picks up the theme of relating to the neighbor that was also described in 19.6. He begins with a positive command to do something rather than the negative commands that have characterized so much of 19.3–7. Believers are instructed to share in all things with their neighbors and not to claim that anything is their own. These statutes reverse the order of negative instruction followed by positive corollary that was found in 19.3, 5, and 6. Separatist tendencies with regard to anything that one owns are disavowed. Rather, those on the way of light are to share all things with their neighbors. Barnabas argues that believers should share in perishable matters if they share imperishable things in common. Since those on the way of light have been brought into relation with the immortal God, Barnabas reasons *a fortiori* that corruptible matters should likewise be shared. He then warns believers not to be "quick to speak" (πρόγλωσσος). He again offers a reason for his admonition, namely, that the mouth is a trap of death. Rather than find themselves ensnared, believers should be slow to speak. Believers are thus called to be pure insofar as they are able "for the sake of your soul" (ὑπὲρ τῆς ψυχῆς σου). Purity is not only right in relation to God but also has benefits for believers.

Two vivid images come to the fore related to the issue of giving and caring for others in 19.9. The first instruction is associated with the teaching about holding things in common with others in the community in 19.8. Barnabas urges his audience not to stretch out their hands when it is time to receive but close their hands when it is time to give. The focus on the hand draws believers' attention to a specific behavior rather than limiting the teaching to a way of thinking that underlies such behaviors. It is not a characteristic of the way of light to stretch one's hands in order to be ready to receive but to fail to be equally ready to give when the time comes.[53] Barnabas returns to his more common way of ordering opposing instructions, namely, with the negative admonition in the first position followed by the positive advice. He again turns to the love that his audience

---

52. On these tensions in the instructions to slaves, see Koch, *Geschichte des Urchristentums*, 60. Also writing in the second century, Aristides further destabilizes the relationship between masters and slaves without dissolving the relationship entirely. Aristides claims that Christians refer to their slaves and children as brothers (*Apol.* 15.5). For further similarities between Aristides's account of Christians (*Apol.* 15–17) and other early Christian literature including *Barnabas*, see Lattke, "Wahrheit der Christen," 226–32.

53. The same sentence is found in Did 4.5. Similar imagery is utilized in Sir 4:31. See further Jefford, "Wisdom of Sirach," 17–19; Skehan, "Didache 1,6 and Sirach 12,1," 533–36.

should demonstrate toward one another.⁵⁴ Readers are called to show love particularly to someone "who speaks the word of the Lord to you" (τὸν λαλοῦντά σοι τὸν λόγον κυρίου; 19.9). The author of Hebrews likewise urges his audience to remember their leaders "who spoke the word of God to you" (οἵτινες ἐλάλησαν ὑμῖν τὸν λόγον τοῦ θεοῦ; Heb 13:7).⁵⁵ Barnabas teaches the audience to love such leaders with a second image. Believers should look after those who proclaim the word "like the pupil of your eye" (ὡς κόρην τοῦ ὀφθαλμοῦ σου; Barn. 19.9). Similar to the more common English expression "the apple of one's eye," Barnabas's instruction is to love those who proclaim the Lord's word as the most valuable, precious, and perhaps vulnerable members of the body.⁵⁶

While the eschatological framework in which Barnabas gives his instructions never disappears entirely from the Two Ways Tradition, it becomes more explicit again in 19.10. The audience should remember the day of judgement as they walk along the way of light. Night and day form a merism indicating that the day of the Lord should be on believers' minds at all times. Alongside this instruction to remember the day of the Lord as they go about their daily lives, the audience is likewise instructed to seek out other saints each day. Barnabas's image of seeking "the faces of the saints" (τὰ πρόσωπα τῶν ἁγίων) suggests direct or intimate contact with other believers.⁵⁷ There are two modes by which believers can join another's presence: by laboring in words or in works. Barnabas says more about the way in which words can be used. Those on the way of light should work through their words to encourage others while also giving careful thought to the salvation of lives "by word" (τῷ λογῷ). Believers' speech should bring encouragement and align with the purposes of salvation. Barnabas's second suggestion draws attention to the works that believers do with their hands. These works should be offered as a ransom price (λύτρον) for the sins that one has committed. By including these statements in the Two Ways Tradition, Barnabas makes clear that believers continue to be called to live out their place as the true heirs who have received revelation from God and that

---

54. Instructions to love have already been found in Barnabas's Two Ways Tradition in 19.2, 5. For believers' act of love elsewhere in the letter, see 1.4; 4.1.

55. For further instructions to care for leaders, see also 1 Cor 9:8–12; 1 Thess 5:12; 1 Tim 5:17–22; Heb 13:17.

56. For other uses of this image, see Deut 32:10; Ps 16:8 (MT 17:8); Zech 2:12; Odes Sol. 2.10; Gos. Thom. 25.2.

57. Although τὰ πρόσωπα τῶν ἁγίων does not appear in S and H, I have followed G and Sc in retaining the phrase. See also Lona and Prostmeier, *Epistola Barnabae*, 132.

the actions by which they demonstrate their place within the people of God should be taken up within the community of believers.[58]

The eschatological context that imbibes 19.10 is continued in the instructions of 19.11. Believers should not be hesitant when they give, nor should they grumble while giving. Instead, those who give while walking on the way of light may trust that the one who pays the wage knows that they have given. This reference to God's eschatological payback is predicated on the presupposition that God is a good (καλός) paymaster.[59] Barnabas's instruction may also serve as an example of how believers are to constantly remember the day of the Lord (19.10). The audience is likewise told to keep what has been passed down to them. The traditions that they have received from Barnabas and other teachers should be valued and kept. Moreover, the people are not to add to or take away from what has been given to them. The command not to add or subtract from authoritative collections has longstanding roots, particularly in apocalyptic literature.[60] The focus on the end of things continues into Barnabas's command that believers should hate evil "completely" (εἰς τέλος; 19.11).[61] Finally, believers should judge righteously (δικαίως; 19.11), just as the Lord will judge the world without partiality (ἀπροσωπολήμπτως; 4.12). Utter hatred of evil things and righteous judgement are thus to characterize members of the community who are walking along the way of light.

Barnabas's closing instructions in 19.12 take up how to live on the way of light within the community of Christ-followers.[62] Believers should not cause division (σχίσμα) but should instead make peace (εἰρηνεύσεις).[63] Barnabas's instruction follows the pattern of other instructions in 19.1–12 that come in the form of a contrast. Here the contrast is between division and peace. Believers should make peace by "bringing together those who are fighting" (μαχουμένους συναγαγών). Peace is not sought in a flowery ideal but in the restoration of parties who have lived with conflict between them. Barnabas moves from this topic to admonish the audience also to confess

---

58. Tugwell, *Apostolic Fathers*, 43.

59. In 19.11, Barnabas again utilizes a contrasting form of teaching in which the negative instruction precedes the positive. See also 19.3, 5, 6, 9.

60. E.g., Deut 4:1–2; 12:32; Jer 33:2 (26:2 MT); Rev 22:18–19; 1 En. 104.10–13; Let. Aris. 310–11; Josephus, *A.J.* 1.17.

61. See the similar telic language about hating evil in 4.10.

62. Windisch, *Barnabasbrief*, 402.

63. A nearly identical instruction appears in Did. 4.3. The Barnabean Two Ways Tradition contains the participle συναγαγών, which does not appear at this point in the Didache.

their sins within the community.[64] Although the confession of wrongdoing may have multiple healing benefits, it is placed after the instructions regarding peaceful living in order to guard against division. Confession then gives way to prayer as Barnabas warns his audience against entering into prayer "with an evil conscience" (ἐν συνειδήσει πονηρᾷ; 19.12).[65] Evil consciences are not characteristic of people who walk along the way of light.

Barnabas offers instructions to his audience regarding how to live on the way of light in 19.1–12 in ways that should provide for cohesion in the community, a loving relationship with the God who rules over the way of light, and distinction from their counterparts on the way of darkness. This form of knowledge and instruction illustrates that Barnabas views γνῶσις as an active pursuit that extends beyond the life of the mind. The Two Ways Tradition thus complements what Barnabas has already said regarding inheritance, covenant, and God's revelation in scripture and the Son. There is a question about how Barnabas brings this section of the letter to an end. In S and H, 19.12 closes by urging people not to pray with an evil conscience. However, G and a corrector of S (S[c]) add, "This is the way of light" (αὕτη ἐστὶν ἡ ὁδὸς τοῦ φωτός). The sentence provides a clear conclusion to Barnabas's description of the way of light, and the attestation in multiple manuscripts makes it tempting to think that the longer reading is earlier.[66] However, in light of the discrepancy in the manuscript tradition, the longer reading may have been added to balance 19.12 with the opening of the way of light in 19.1.[67] In addition, S and H may collectively provide marginally stronger evidence. On balance, then, the evidence tips the scales slightly in favor of the shorter reading as the earlier reading.[68] Regardless of which reading is accepted, however, Barnabas's description of the way of light is intended to draw his readers to live rightly in light of the revelation that they have received from scripture and the Son. The way of light is the path along which the true heirs of the covenant should walk.

---

64. See similarly Did. 4.14.

65. Teaching about confession and a warning against praying with an evil conscience are found not only in Barn. 19.12 but also in Did. 4.14. The link with the Didache is significant because, just as in *Barnabas*, it comes at the end of the Didachist's teaching regarding the way of light.

66. The longer reading of Barn. 19.12 is accepted by Ehrman, *Apostolic Fathers*, 2.78; Holmes, *Apostolic Fathers*, 438; Lindemann and Paulsen, *Apostolischen Väter*, 70; Prostmeier and Lona, *Epistola Barnabae*, 132; Windisch, *Barnabasbrief*, 402.

67. The Didache's description of the way of life ends similarly: "This is the way of life" (αὕτη ἐστὶν ἡ ὁδὸς τῆς ζωῆς; Did. 4.14).

68. The shorter reading is accepted by Prigent and Kraft, *Épître de Barnabé*, 210; Wengst, *Didache*, 190; Prinzivalli and Simonetti, *Seguendo Gesù*, 2.170.

IV.3. The Way of the Black One (Barn. 20.1–2)

Barnabas turns now to the second of the paths that he introduced in 18.1-2. While the way of light was described in the same terms in both the introduction and in its elaboration (18.1; 19.1), the name of the way of darkness shifts between the introduction and its description in 20.1. In 18.1, the opposing way was characterized as "the way of darkness" (ἡ [ὁδός] τοῦ σκότους). Barnabas now names the path "the way of the Black One" (ἡ τοῦ μέλανος ὁδός; 20.1), a term that has already been used to refer to the devil in 4.10.[69] Although the name has shifted, one may observe a loose link between darkness and blackness so that Barnabas's presentation of the Two Ways Tradition remains conceptually coherent. His portrayal of the way with regard to the Black One may also be linked to the close association between the way of darkness and the ruler of the present age of lawlessness (18.2). In referring to the way of the Black One, Barnabas reminds his readers of the ruler of the second way. The Two Ways Tradition in *Barnabas* is not simply a virtue and vice list. Each path exists in relation to specific beings who reign over the path, the people who walk on it, and the way of life that the path symbolizes.

The second way's association with the Black One is not the only way in which Barnabas warns his audience to live rightly. The path is described as "crooked" (σκολιά; 20.1), a term that is associated with an improper lifestyle in proverbial literature.[70] Likewise, it is a lifestyle that is "full of cursing" (κατάρας μεστή).[71] Barnabas follows a Deuteronomic way of thinking as he closes his letter with two paths in which his audience can choose to walk.[72] If the audience, whom Barnabas has already argued are the rightful heirs of the covenant (13.1–14.9), leave the way of light, they will find themselves cursed along the way of the Black One. Moreover, Barnabas characterizes the way of the Black One as a way "of eternal death" (θανάτου αἰωνίου; 20.1). Although Jesus nullified death and redeemed his followers from its power (5.6; 14.5; 19.2), death is elsewhere associated with Barnabas's Jewish opponents (5.11; 10.5). Likewise, the end of the

---

69. Prinzivalli and Simonetti, *Seguendo Gesù*, 2.548 n 198. Although τοῦ μέλανος could be grammatically neuter and thus designate "the way of blackness." This is the interpretation of Farrar, "Intimate and Ultimate Adversary," 525 n 33. Barnabas's previous personalized use of the term in 4.10 and the references to Satan in 18.1–2 incline me to see the way in 20.1 as the way that belongs to the Black One.

70. E.g., Prov 21:8; 22:5, 14. See further Kraft, *Barnabas*, 156.

71. See also Did. 5.1; Niederwimmer, *Didache*, 114.

72. See the blessings and curses in Deut 26:16–28:68. For "way" language in Deuteronomy, see Deut 5:33; 8:6; 9:12, 16; 26:17; 28:9; 30:16; 31:29.

letter offers a fresh emphasis on the various features that demonstrate how the way of the Black One is a way of death and also of punishment. In line with these descriptions, the way is further described as one "in which are the things that destroy their soul" (ἐν ᾗ ἐστὶν τὰ ἀπολλύντα τὴν ψυχὴν αὐτῶν). To follow the way of the Black One is a destructive act, but the loss from such devastating practices ultimately turns back on those who follow the way of the Black One. Barnabas thus sets this way in front of his readers in the hope that they will reject this path.

What follows in 20.1-2 is a series of two vice lists that make the way of the Black One sound particularly unenticing. Seventeen vices are highlighted in the first list (20.1). These are primarily abstract nouns naming practices that should be abhorrent to Barnabas and his audience. This account is followed by a list of twenty-two attributes or types of people who exist on the way of the Black One (20.2). First on the list of vices is idolatry (εἰδωλολατρεία; 20.1).[73] Barnabas's reference to idolatry would presumably include worship of pagan gods that other Jewish and Christian authors warn against when discussing idolatry.[74] However, Barnabas elsewhere in the letter refers to his Jewish opponents in terms that suggest idolatry. For example, Jewish temple worship is portrayed in terms that nearly equate it with the worship of other nations' gods in temples (16.1-2).[75] Barnabas's choice to give idolatry the first place on his list of vices that characterize the way of the Black One along with his use of the concept at other points in the letter signify that the way of the Black One is the way along which Barnabas understands his Jewish opponents to be walking. Their idolatry has led them astray so that the one who governs their path is not the God who created them but rather the Black One who rules over the present age of lawlessness.[76]

The remaining sixteen vices in 20.1 must be read with Barnabas's Jewish opponents in mind. Indeed, the final vice on the list complements idolatry's initial position. The way of the Black One is characterized by a lack of fear of God (ἀφοβία θεοῦ).[77] The way of darkness is also characterized by a failure to observe some of the Ten Words, namely, the instructions against

---

73. Smith, "Epistle of Barnabas," 483

74. E.g., Exod 20:2-6; Deut 5:6-10; Ps 115:4-8; 135:15-18; Wis 14.12-13, 27; 1QS IV, 9-11; Rom 1:23-24; Theophilus, *Autol.* 2.34. Citations from Theophilus's *Ad Autolycum* come from Grant, *Theophilus of Antioch*.

75. See also 4.6-8; 11.1; 14.1-5.

76. On the privileged place of idolatry in the vice list of 20.1, see Prigent and Kraft, *Épître de Barnabé*, 212 n 2; Prinzivalli and Simonetti, *Seguendo Gesù*, 2.548n199.

77. Rhodes, *Epistle of Barnabas*, 98-99.

adultery and murder.[78] Those who inhabit the way of the Black One misuse and misunderstand their power. Their way of life can be described in terms of audacity (θρασύτης), the elevation of power (ὕψος δυνάμεως), robbery (ἁρπαγή), pride (ὑπερηφανία), and contumacy (αὐθάδεια). Like the ruler of the dark way (18.2; 20.1), they elevate their own power as they act deceitfully and lawlessly among themselves and others. The deceit (δόλος) that is found along the dark way is complemented by double-heartedness (διπλοκαρδία) and hypocrisy (ὑπόκρισις). Barnabas portrays this path as inconsistent, just as he warned his audience along the way of light to avoid similar self-divided vices (19.5, 7).[79] Much of the way of darkness is thus directly opposed to the way of light that has been illumined in 19.1-12. However, Barnabas adds that magic (φαρμακεία) and sorcery (μαγεία) are found along the way of the Black One. Magical terms have a traditional place in early Christian vice lists, but there is no opposing parallel in 19.1-12.[80]

Barnabas continues to outline how the way of darkness twists all that is good from the way of light when he lists twenty-two types of people who walk in darkness. Such people are described as "persecutors of the good, haters of truth, and lovers of lies" (διῶκται τῶν ἀγαθῶν, μισοῦντες ἀλήθειαν, ἀγαπῶντες ψεῦδος; 20.2). Their sense of goodness and their abilities to determine what is worthy of love are corrupt and run opposite to what is outlined in 19.1-12. In contrast to Jesus and the actions that Barnabas demands of his own audience, gentleness and endurance remain "far and distant" (μαρκρὰν καὶ πόρρω) from the way of darkness.[81] Although Barnabas is adamant that those on the way of light must acknowledge God's creative actions in love (19.2), those on the path of darkness "do not know the one who made them" (οὐ γινώσκοντες τὸν ποιήσαντα αὐτούς; 20.2). Accordingly, they become murderers of children and corrupters of what God formed.[82] Because those on the way of darkness have rejected God's authority in favor of that of Satan, they fail to care for the children that God has made. This disposition may also be tied to Barnabas's assertions of idolatry as God's authority has been

---

78. Conversely, those walking along the way of light are warned against committing adultery in 19.4.

79. Barnabas's stark division between two paths and two peoples does not allow for division inside of a person. Warnings against a doubled soul, mind, tongue, and heart reflect a desire for a holistic and unified understanding of the person (19.5, 7; 20.1).

80. On magical terminology, see Gal 5:20; Did 3.4; Rev 9:21. See also Ign. *Eph.* 19.3, where magic is among the things destroyed "when God appears humanly" (θεοῦ ἀνθρωπίνως φανερουμένου).

81. On Jesus's endurance, see 5.1, 5-6, 12; 14.4. Barnabas's audience is likewise called to endure (2.2; 21.5). On gentleness among Barnabas's audience, see 19.4.

82. These descriptions contrast with warnings against corrupting children (19.4) and murdering children in corruption (19.5).

replaced by others. Those on the way of darkness can thus be described as "all-sinful" (πανταμάρτητοι). This adjective not only links to his descriptions of "the completion of sins" (τὸ τέλειον τῶν ἁμαρτημάτων; 5.11) though the active agency of Barnabas's Jewish opponents in the deaths of Jesus and the prophets but also brings the dreary list of vices and vicious persons to an end with a final, all-encompassing thud.

Barnabas's outline of the way of darkness in 20.1–2 offers a stark warning to the audience to stay away from the actions that are described in these extended vice lists. The links between the way of darkness and descriptions of Jewish opponents are also intended to associate the opponents with the way of darkness. The actions in Barnabas's vice list will destroy the soul by turning it away from God in order to serve idols. Those who inhabit the way of darkness are to be regarded as covenant breakers. Whatever claim to God's inheritance they may assert, Barnabas presumes it to be false. If the opponents fail to recognize God's revelation and do not walk in the way of light, they must be grouped with those who walk along the way of darkness. Barnabas and his audience are thereby urged to avoid this negative example and to hold to the way of light.

V

Barnabas 21.1–9

Closing

HAVING SET OUT AN extended case both for how God has revealed Godself in scripture and for how people may choose to walk in response to what God has done, Barnabas turns to conclude his letter with a series of exhortations to hear and act rightly. The closing of the letter begins with a transition from the Two Ways Tradition that further integrates the Two Ways Tradition and the letter closing into the rhetoric of the entire letter by insisting that it is good to learn, reiterating the importance of the Lord's requirements, and encouraging people to walk in accordance with the right eschatological path (21.1). The closing paraenesis targets those in the community who are in high positions, but much of the advice can be accepted by all readers (21.2–8). The frame of the Barnabean admonitions is eschatologically oriented, and his imperatives anticipate an eventual τέλος that draws ever nearer.[1] Readers should thus act rightly while they can, remember that it is God who rules over the world, and recall Barnabas and his words. The latter instructions give way to Barnabas's formal conclusion, which shares traits found in other ancient Greek letters (21.9). In the closure of the letter (21.1–9), the author thus looks to encourage his audience, to solidify social solidarity, and to enhance his own memory within the community.

V.1. Transition from Two Ways (Barn. 21.1)

A concluding statement from the Two Ways Tradition brings together a final encouragement for readers to bear in mind as they move away from the virtue and vice lists of 19.1—20.2. The conjunction "therefore" (οὖν; 21.1) illustrates the close connection that Barnabas envisions between the Two

---

1. Prigent and Kraft, *Épître de Barnabé*, 214n2.

Ways Tradition and what follows in 21.1. The audience is told that it is good to walk (περιπατεῖν)—a verb that fits nicely with the imagery of diverging paths.[2] The lifestyle that Barnabas upholds in 21.1 is not only based on walking but also on learning (μαθόντα).[3] The insistence that the audience learn is reminiscent of the repeated references to knowledge throughout *Barnabas*. The audience is called to learn "the requirements of the Lord that have been written" (τὰ δικαιώματα τοῦ κυρίου ὅσα γέγραπται). By repeating language found elsewhere in the letter, Barnabas adds cohesion to his conclusion with this reference. The requirements of the Lord refer to everything that Barnabas has said about the interpretation of scripture, the practices that follow thereon, and the two paths between which the audience must choose to walk. The combination of "requirements," a relative pronoun, and a verb indicating communication is found throughout Deuteronomy.[4] The effect of rehearsing the "requirements" at this point is, therefore, not only to bring cohesion to the letter but also to place Barnabas within a Deuteronomistic way of speaking.[5]

After the initial transition statement from the Two Ways Tradition to the conclusion, Barnabas strengthens the eschatological connections between 18.1—20.2 and the transition in 21.1. In so doing, he also provides an eschatological motivation for action. In response to the Two Ways Tradition, the diverging options lead to starkly different results. Barnabas refers to walking in the way of light without reference to light. Instead, he speaks about the one who does "these things" (ταῦτα; 21.1). The rationale that Barnabas provides for walking along the way of light is that the person who acts in this way "will be glorified in the kingdom of God" (ἐν τῇ βασιλείᾳ τοῦ θεοῦ δοξασθήσεται). The kingdom of God is a future-oriented reality that has yet to come to fulfillment. God's kingdom provides a source of hope for Barnabas's audience that ethical action will

---

2. Hvalvik (*Struggle for Scripture and Covenant*, 201) notes similarities between the instruction to walk in these things in the conclusion (21.1) and to seek out the Lord's requirements in the exordium (2.1).

3. Several translators render the participle (μαθόντα) and the infinitive (περιπατεῖν) as parallel infinitives. The opening of the sentence would thus be translated more or less as follows: "It is good to learn and to walk." See the translations in Ehrman, *Apostolic Fathers*, 2.81; Holmes, *Apostolic Fathers*, 439; Prigent and Kraft, *Épître de Barnabé*, 215; Lindemann and Paulsen, *Apostolischen Väter*, 73; Prinzivalli and Simonetti, *Seguendo Gesù*, 2.173; Prostmeier and Lona, *Epistola Barnabae*, 135.

4. E.g., Deut 4:40, 45; 5:1, 31; 6:1, 2, 4, 17, 20; 7:11; 8:11; 27:10; 28:45. Deuteronomy, however, uses verbs of speaking (λαλέω; ἐντέλλομαι) rather than a verb of writing (γράφω) in Barn. 21.1.

5. Rhodes (*Epistle of Barnabas*, 99–101) helpfully highlights the Deuteronomistic posture of *Barnabas* in its rehearsal of retribution and reward.

be rewarded. Barnabas contrasts the audience's option not with reference to darkness but with reference to choosing "those things" (ἐκεῖνα). The far demonstrative pronoun is again employed to indicate the choice that the audience should avoid.[6] The choice to walk along the way of darkness is made with one's works, and the one who chooses this way "will destroy themselves" (συναπολεῖται). Future reward or punishment thus serves as a motivation for ethical activity in the letter. Barnabas confirms this with an emphatic repetition of the phrase "for this reason" (διὰ τοῦτο). Resurrection (ἀνάστασις) and recompense (ἀνταπόδομα) exist in order to motivate people to act rightly. Barnabas's eschatological statements in 21.1 are uniformly directed toward the future, and this future orientation is intended to warn, reward, and motivate Barnabas's audience to walk in accordance with the things that he has written in the letter.

V.2. Concluding Paraenesis (Barn. 21.2–8)

The concluding paraenesis contains a series of ethical statements that bring the letter toward its close by urging the audience to act rightly. Barnabas begins by imploring the audience with two main requests in 21.2–4. In both requests, the author addresses the audience directly with the word, "I ask" (ἐρωτῶ; 21.2, 4). Although the advice in 21.2 may be appropriate for a broad swath of believers, the first request is particularly directed to those who are in high positions (21.2). The second request opens to include the entire audience (21.4).

Barnabas's request to those who are in elevated positions is that they would accept some well-intentioned advice (συμβουλία) (21.2). The advice that follows is based on the premise that there are people among them to whom they can do good. The phrase "to do good" (ἐργάσεσθε τὸ καλόν) may call to mind other early Christian texts that describe charitable actions that believers can do.[7] When Barnabas urges those in high positions to do good, it is likely that charitable actions are similarly in view. However, when this instruction is placed in the immediate aftermath of the Two Ways Tradition, the meaning of "to do good" in 21.2 should be expanded beyond acts of mercy. Rather, it includes not only acts of mercy

---

6. For other uses of ἐκεῖνος, see 2.9; 3.6; 8.7; 10.12; 13.1, 3.

7. See particularly Mark 14:7, where Jesus tells his hearers that they have the poor with them (τοὺς πτωχοὺς ἔχετε μεθ' ἑαυτῶν) to whom they can "do good" (εὖ ποιῆσαι). Immediately before this, Jesus told the woman whom he was addressing that she "did a good work" (καλὸν ἔργον ἠργάσατο) for him (Mark 14:6). See also Matt 26:10–11.

but also the sorts of actions along the way of light.[8] They should not fail in this action. The rationale for Barnabas's request is again eschatologically oriented in 21.3. Barnabas appeals to the day of the Lord and its approach in order to motivate those in elevated positions to act rightly. The day is described as "the day in which all things associated with the evil one will be destroyed" (ἡ ἡμέρα ἐν ᾗ συναπολεῖται πάντα τῷ πονηρῷ; 21.3). Yet it is not the day alone that is drawing closer. The Lord and his wage are likewise coming.[9] With these things in mind, those in high position are called to maintain their path on the way of light.

Although one could imagine that believers may interpret 21.2–3 with a wide lens, Barnabas directs his counsel particularly to the more elevated members of the community. His second request is self-consciously reiterated with a wider audience in view. He introduces it with the phrase, "again and again" (ἔτι καὶ ἔτι). What follows in 21.4 is related both to the immediately preceding advice in 21.2–3 and also to themes that are found in the Two Ways Tradition. Three imperatives follow that should characterize believers in the community. The audience is first instructed to be good lawgivers (νομοθέται ἀγαθοί) among themselves. They should also remain as "faithful advisers" (σύμβουλοι πιστοί) within their community. Lastly, Barnabas commands them to remove "all hypocrisy" (πᾶσαν ὑπόκρισιν) from them. The call to live rightly is not limited to those in high positions but extends to the entire audience. All believers in the community should join together in walking on the way of light.

The focus shifts slightly from the audience's direct actions in 21.2–4 to a prayer for God's gifts and the community's ongoing link to the Lord in 21.5–6. God's role among believers in the community is explicitly named in 21.5–6. Barnabas's prayer occurs in a wish-formula that invokes God's gifts for the community in the third-person. Barnabas addresses God with a view to God's authority. God "rules over all the world" (ὁ τοῦ παντὸς κόσμου κυριεύων; 21.5). The Son has already been described as the Lord of the world (5.5). Barnabas now employs a similar participial phrase to describe God, that is, the Father. The relation of Father and Son is intimate and unique in the letter. The prayer that God would give (δώῃ) something to his audience mirrors the description of God's gifts in 1.2 and 9.9. The list of terms that follows likewise shares similarities with other portions of the letter. Barnabas's wish is for the audience to receive wisdom, understanding, insight, knowledge of his requirements, and endurance. Barnabas's characteristic emphasis on knowing and understanding is evident

8. Prostmeier, *Barnabasbrief*, 567–68.
9. Edwards, *Gospel*, 76–77.

in his prayer for the audience. The list bears marked similarities to 2.1–3; each of the terms in 21.5 are found together in the earlier transition. The author's attention turns to wisdom, endurance, and the Lord's requirements at both transition points, but human agency is emphasized in the earlier passage while Barnabas concludes with a prayer that God would give these things to the audience. His prayer formula for God to give the audience "knowledge of his requirements" (γνῶσιν τῶν δικαιωμάτων αὐτῶν) resounds particularly strongly with the repeated use of both the γνω-stem and of the language of requirements.

Barnabas's next imperative urges the believers to be taught directly by God, that is, to be "God-taught" (θεοδίδακτοι; Barn. 21.6). Barnabas's compound relies on the same sort of eschatological hope that is expressed in Isa 54:13, in which the children of God's people anticipate being taught by God (διδακτοὺς θεοῦ) without mediation.[10] The word also appears in Paul's instructions to the Thessalonians to show love toward brothers and sisters in the community. Paul does not need to teach them because they are "God-taught" (θεοδίδακτοι; 1 Thess 4:9).[11] Barnabas's audience should likewise be taught by God. While they might start by giving attention to what Barnabas has written, the author instead situates the command in the context of what God is seeking from them. Barnabas's readers are to seek (ἐκζητοῦντες) what the Lord seeks from them (τί ζητεῖ κύριος ἀφ' ὑμῶν; Barn. 21.6). The audience has been told before to seek to walk in the right way (2.1; 4.1; 19.10).[12] Their pursuit is now situated opposite to God's own search to find something in them. Barnabas urges them to act when they find what God desires from them.[13] He offers a purpose to the audience that explains a rationale for acting in this way, namely, "in order that you may be found on the day of judgement" (ἵνα εὑρεθῆτε ἐν ἡμέρᾳ κρίσεως; 21.6).[14] By seeking what God desires from them, the audience

---

10. Jesus likewise appeals to this tradition when identifying himself as the bread of life that the ancestors ate in the wilderness (John 6:45).

11. Ignatius of Antioch likewise employs a large number of compound words including θεοδρόμος (Ign. Phld. 2.2), θεοπρεσβευτής (Ign. Smyrn. 11.2), and θεοπρεπής (Ign. Pol. 7.2). See further Brent, "Ignatius of Antioch in Second Century, Asia Minor," 64; Schoedel, *Ignatius*, 7.

12. See also 2.9; 11.1; 14.1; 16.6.

13. Hvalvik, *Struggle for Scripture and Covenant*, 201–2.

14. A textual variant occurs with regard to the verb εὑρεθῆτε in 21.6. The word εὑρεθῆτε is found in S, while εὕρητε is found in H and Clement of Alexandria, and σωθῆτε is found in G. Given the correspondence between the readings in S, H, and Clement of Alexandria (*Strom.* 2.84.3 [18]), the reading in G may be regarded as the most likely to be late. G may thus be dismissed when trying to determine the earliest reading. Although εὕρητε is attested already in Clement of Alexandria and is accepted

can trust that God will find them on the day of judgement. While the imperatives are directed to the audience, the focus of both Barnabas and his readers is directed toward God.[15]

As Barnabas continues to draw the letter to a close, the emphasis of 21.7–8 lies on memory and the author. Thus Barnabas urges the audience to "remember me" (μνημονεύετέ μου; 21.7). Believers are to remember the author if there is any "remembrance of what is good" (ἀγαθοῦ μνεία). The good that the audience recollects can be understood in two senses. They may think of the good things that Barnabas has written in the letter and that ultimately come from God. Alternatively, since Barnabas instructs his readers to remember him, the audience may recall good memories about the author himself. At the end of the letter, it may be best to allow both meanings to stand side-by-side and not to differentiate too strongly. Nevertheless, the good things that have been revealed by God and may be found on the way of light are emphasized more strongly as Barnabas calls the audience to meditate (μελετῶντες) on things that are good. Meditation is an act that is associated with those who understand things rightly, walk on the way of light, and fear the Lord.[16] The good things that the audience is to recall thus include not only Barnabas but the things that have been revealed by God through his letter. Barnabas again provides a rationale for the act to which he is calling them. In 21.7, the reason that they should recall what is good is so that "both desire and sleeplessness" (καὶ ἡ ἐπιθυμία καὶ ἡ ἀγρυπνία) may result in something good. Although no pronoun modifies the nouns, the context indicates that at least Barnabas's desire and sleeplessness are in view. Barnabas reiterates his request formula from 21.2 and 4: "I ask you, requesting a favor" (ἐρωτῶ ὑμᾶς, χάριν αἰτούμενος; 21.7).[17]

Having urged the audience to remember what is good, Barnabas offers a negative imperative in 21.8. The audience should not fail to do any of the things contained in the Two Ways Tradition or in the rest of the letter. Yet this negative command is conceptually connected with what precedes it in

---

by Prigent and Kraft (*Épître de Barnabé*, 217 n 7), the passive verb may be preferred on the supposition that the ΕΘ in ΕΥΡΕΘΗΤΕ was lost in an early textual corruption. See the discussion in Prostmeier, *Barnabasbrief*, 562; Windisch, *Barnabasbrief*, 408. See also Ehrman, *Apostolic Fathers*, 2.82; Holmes, *Apostolic Fathers*, 440; Lindemann and Paulsen, *Apostolischen Väter*, 72; Prinzivalli and Simonetti, *Seguendo Gesù*, 2.172; Prostmeier and Lona, *Epistola Barnabae*, 136; Wengst, *Didache*, 192.

15. Prostmeier, *Barnabasbrief*, 572–74.

16. See 4.11; 10.11; 11.5; 19.10.

17. I follow the verse numbering in Ehrman, *Apostolic Fathers*, 2.82; Holmes, *Apostolic Fathers*, 440; Lindemann and Paulsen, *Apostolischen Väter*, 74; Prostmeier and Lona, *Epistola Barnabae*, 136; Wengst, *Didache*, 192. The sentence appears in 21.8 in Prigent and Kraft, *Épître de Barnabé*, 216; Prinzivalli and Simonetti, *Seguendo Gesù*, 2.172.

21.7 by the use of another word drawing the audience's attention to what is good. In 21.8, they are warned against failing "as long as the good vessel is still with you" (ἕως ἔτι τὸ καλὸν σκεῦός ἐστιν μεθ' ὑμῶν). Barnabas has already described the sacrifice and glorification of Jesus's body by referring to the body as "the vessel of the spirit" (τὸ σκεῦος τοῦ πνεύματος; 7.3; 11.9). The reference to the vessel in 21.8 thus urges the audience not to fail as long as their flesh is with them or, in other words, as long as they live.[18] Rather, the audience is told again to seek out (ἐκζητεῖτε) the things that Barnabas has described and to fulfill (ἀναπληροῦτε) every commandment. Barnabas then offers a rationale for instructing his audience to undertake this action: "for it is worthy" (ἔστιν γὰρ ἄξια). The inherent value of the things that Barnabas has described in the letter thus provides another rationale for why the audience should accept what is contained in its pages.

V.3. Letter Closing (Barn. 21.9)

The letter concludes with the eschatocol in 21.9. The closing protocol works in three parts. Barnabas initially repeats his eagerness to write to his audience and reminds them of the purpose of the letter.[19] He has written to them in the best way that he can, and the reason for this letter is ultimately "in order that you may rejoice" (εἰς τὸ εὐφρᾶναι ὑμᾶς). The initial formula maintains the author's appearance of humility by indicating that he has done his best. The second part of the letter closing reiterates the close relationship that he has with the audience while simultaneously placing himself in an authoritative position. The audience is greeted by the multivalent word, "farewell" (σώζεσθε).[20] The description of them as children of love and peace not only places them in a closely related position to Barnabas but also serves to characterize them positively. Finally, Barnabas ends the letter with a benediction: "May the Lord of glory and all grace be with your spirit" (ὁ κύριος τῆς δόξης καὶ πάσης χάριτος μετὰ τοῦ πνεύματος ὑμῶν).[21]

Barnabas's conclusion draws together themes that have been found elsewhere in his letter. Joy is connected to the three teachings of the Lord (1.6) and has already been mentioned as a Barnabean motivation for

18. Prostmeier, *Barnabasbrief*, 575; Windisch, *Barnabasbrief*, 408.

19. Barnabas has already emphasized his eagerness and haste to write in 1.5 and 4.9.

20. The word has a formulaic meaning at this point in the letter, but its significance within early Christian literature and particularly in *Barnabas* make a multivalent meaning likely. See further Hvalvik, *Struggle for Scripture and Covenant*, 203; Prostmeier, *Barnabasbrief*, 576; Windisch, *Barnabasbrief*, 408.

21. See the similar doxological forms in Gal 6:18; Phil 4:23; 2 Thess 3:18; 2 Tim 4:22.

writing (1.8).²² The multivalence of σώζεσθε in 21.9 is particularly interesting. The word can be used as a greeting that wishes someone well at the end of a conversation or letter, and it should be understood in this way at 21.9.²³ However, the word can be used in early Christian texts to describe the means by which people are rescued and made alive by God.²⁴ Barnabas has likewise used the word in this latter sense earlier in the letter. The audience has been encouraged to seek out things that can save them (4.1), and the focus on the covenant, the true people of God, and Jesus's suffering and endurance repeatedly calls to mind salvation throughout the letter. Indeed, Prostmeier identifies soteriology as the primary theme in the letter.²⁵ In light of *Barnabas*'s emphasis on salvation and the right relation of Barnabas's audience as the true heirs of the covenant, the choice to end this letter with such a multivalent term provides another subtle reminder for the audience to come to deeper knowledge of the things that are able to save them.²⁶ God's unique ability to grant salvation and grace then provides a fitting benediction and conclusion to a letter that set out to show the ways in which God revealed Godself through the prophets and the Son.

---

22. Other references to joy in the letter are found in 4.11 and 10.11.

23. Windisch, *Barnabasbrief*, 408.

24. E.g., Matt 10:22; 18:11; 19:25; Mark 10:26; Luke 19:10; John 3:17; Acts 15:1; 16:31; Rom 5:9; 11:26; 1 Cor 1:18; 7:16; Eph 2:8; 1 Tim 2:4; Heb 7:25 Jas 1:21; 4:12; 5:20; 1 Pet 3:21; 4:18; Jude 23.

25. "Die Soteriologie ist das theologische Thema des Barnabasbriefes; Christologie, Ekklesiologie und Eschatologie sind ihr funktional zugeordnet" (Prostmeier, *Barnabasbrief*, 85). See also Prostmeier, "Einleitung," 47.

26. Hvalvik, *Struggle for Scripture and Covenant*, 203.

Bibliography

Aasgaard, Reidar. "Brothers and Sisters in the Faith: Christian Siblingship as an Ecclesiological Mirror in the First Two Centuries." In *The Formation of the Early Church*, edited by Jostein Ådna, 285-316. WUNT 183. Tübingen: Mohr/Siebeck, 2005.

Adams, Sean A., and Seth M. Ehorn. "What Is a Composite Citation? An Introduction." In *Composite Citations in Antiquity*, Vol. 1, Jewish, Graeco-Roman, and Early Christian Uses, edited by Sean A. Adams and Seth M. Ehorn, 1-16. LNTS 525. London: Bloomsbury T. & T. Clark, 2016.

Aland, Kurt, Christian Hannick, and Klaus Junack. "Bibelhandschriften II: Neues Testament." *TRE* 6 (1980) 114-31.

Albl, Martin C. "The *Testimonia* Hypothesis and Composite Citations." In *Composite Citations in Antiquity*, Vol. 1, Jewish, Graeco-Roman, and Early Christian Uses, edited by Sean A. Adams and Seth M. Ehorn, 182-202. LNTS 525. London: Bloomsbury T. & T. Clark, 2016.

Aldridge, Robert E. "Peter and the 'Two Ways.'" *VC* 53 (1999) 233-64.

Alexander, Philip. "The Image of Jews and Judaism in the Apostolic Fathers." In *The Cambridge Companion to the Apostolic Fathers*, edited by Michael F. Bird and Scott D. Harrower, 29-49. Cambridge: Cambridge University Press, 2021.

Audet, J. P. "Affinités littéraires et doctrinales du Manuel de Discipline." *RB* 59 (1952) 219-38; 60 (1953) 41-82.

Aune, David E. "Justin Martyr's Use of the Old Testament." *BETS* 9.4 (1966) 179-97.

Ayres, Lewis. "Continuity and Change in Second-Century Christianity: A Narrative against the Trend." In *Christianity and the Second Century: Themes and Developments*, edited by James Carleton Paget and Judith Lieu, 106-21. Cambridge: Cambridge University Press, 2017.

Backhaus, Knut. "Das Bundesmotiv in der frühchristlichen Schwellenzeit: Hebräerbrief, Barnabasbrief, Dialogus cum Tryphone." In *Der Sprechende Gott: Gesammelte Studien zum Hebräerbrief*, 153-73. WUNT 240. Tübingen: Mohr Siebeck, 2009.

Barclay, John M. G. "'I Will Have Mercy on Whom I Have Mercy': The Golden Calf and Divine Mercy in Romans 9-11 and Second Temple Judaism." *EC* 1 (2010) 82-106.

———. *Jews in the Mediterranean Diaspora from Alexander to Trajan (323 BCE to 117 CE)*. Edinburgh: T. & T. Clark, 1996.

———. *Paul and the Gift*. Grand Rapids: Eerdmans, 2015.

Bardy, Gustave. *Eusèbe de Césarée: Histoire ecclésiastique*. 4 vols. SC 31, 41, 55, 73. Paris: Cerf, 1952-60.

———. *La question des langues dans l'église ancienne*. ÉTH, Vol. 1. Paris: Beauchesne, 1948.
Barnard, Leslie W. "The Background of Judaism and Christianity in Egypt." In *Studies in Church History and Patristics*, 27–51. Analecta Vlatadon 26. Thessaloniki: Patriarchal Institute for Patristic Studies, 1978.
———. "The Date of the Epistle of Barnabas: A Document of Early Egyptian Christianity." *JEA* 44 (1958) 101–7.
———. "The Epistle of Barnabas—A Paschal Homily?" *VC* 15 (1961) 8–22.
———. "The 'Epistle of Barnabas' and Its Contemporary Setting." *ANRW* 27.1: 154–207. Part 2, *Principat*, 27.1. Edited by Wolfgang Haase. Berlin: De Gruyter, 1992.
———. "The Epistle of Barnabas in Its Jewish Setting." *Studies in Church History and Patristics*, 52–106. Analecta Vlatadon 26. Thessaloniki: Patriarchal Institute for Patristic Studies, 1978.
———. *Justin Martyr: His Life and Thought*. Cambridge: Cambridge University Press, 1967.
———. "A Note on *Barnabas* 6,8–17." StPatr 4 (1961) 263–67.
———. "The Old Testament and Judaism in the Writings of Justin Martyr." *VT* 14 (1964) 395–406.
———. *Studies in the Apostolic Fathers and Their Background*. Oxford: Blackwell, 1966.
Bartlet, James Vernon. *The Apostolic Age: Its Life, Doctrine, Worship, and Polity*. Edinburgh: T. & T. Clark, 1902.
———. "Barnabas." In *The New Testament in the Apostolic Fathers*, edited by a Committee of the Oxford Society of Historical Theology, 1–23. Oxford: Clarendon, 1905.
Barton, John. *Ethics in Ancient Israel*. Oxford: Oxford University Press, 2014.
Batovici, Dan. "The Apostolic Fathers in Codex Sinaiticus and Codex Alexandrinus." *Bib* 97 (2016) 581–605.
———. "The Less-Expected Books in *Codex Sinaiticus* and *Alexandrinus*: Codicological and Palaeographical Considerations." In *Comment le Livre s'est fait livre: La fabrication des manuscrits bibliques (IVe–XVe siècle): Bilan, résultats, perspectives de recherches*, edited by Chiara Ruzzier and Xavier Hermand, 39–50. Turnhout: Brepols, 2015.
———. "Textual Revisions of the *Shepherd of Hermas* in Codex Sinaiticus." *ZAC* 18 (2014) 443–70.
———. "Two B Scribes in Codex Sinaiticus?" *BASP* 54 (2017) 197–206.
Batovici, Dan, and Joseph Verheyden. "Digitizing the Ancient Versions of the Apostolic Fathers: Preliminary Considerations." In *Digital Humanities and Christianity: An Introduction*, edited by Tim Hutchings and Claire Clivaz, 103–23. Introductions to Digital Humanities—Religion 4. Berlin: De Gruyter, 2021.
Bauckham, Richard. "Barnabas in Galatians." *JSNT* 2 (1979) 61–70.
———. "Sabbath and Sunday in the Post-Apostolic Church." In *From Sabbath to Lord's Day: A Biblical, Historical and Theological Investigation*, edited by D. A. Carson, 291–98. Grand Rapids: Zondervan, 1982.
Bauer, Thomas J. *Paulus und die kaiserzeitliche Epistolographie: Kontextualisierung und Analyse der Briefe an Philemon und an die Galater*. WUNT 276. Tübingen: Mohr Siebeck, 2012.
Baumstark, Anton. "Der Barnabasbrief bei den Syrern." *OrChr* NS 2 (1912) 235–40.

———. Review of *A Catalogue of the Syriac Manuscripts Preserved in the Library of the University of Cambridge*, by William Wright and of *Catalogue of Early Christian Antiquities and Objects from the Christian east in the Department of British and Mediaeval Antiquities and Ethnography in the British Museum*, by G. M. Dalton. *OrChr* 2 (1902) 204–23.

Beatrice, Pier Franco. "Une citation de l'Évangile de Matthieu dans l'Épître de Barnabé." In *The New Testament in Early Christianity: La reception des écrits néotestamentaires dans le christianisme primitif*, edited by Jean-Marie Sevrin, 231–45. BETL 86. Leuven: Leuven University Press, 1989.

Becker, Eve-Marie. *Der Begriff der Demut bei Paulus*. Tübingen: Mohr Siebeck, 2015.

Behr, John. *John the Theologian and His Paschal Gospel: A Prologue to His Theology*. Oxford: Oxford University Press, 2019.

———. *On the Apostolic Preaching: St. Irenaeus of Lyons*. PPS 17. Crestwood, NY: St. Vladimir's Seminary, 1997.

———. *Origen: On First Principles*. 2 vols. OECT. Oxford: Oxford University Press, 2017.

Berger, Klaus. "Apostelbrief und apostolische Rede: Zum Formular frühchristlicher Briefe." *ZNW* 65 (1974) 190–231.

Bergren, Theodore A. *Fifth Ezra: The Text, Origin and Early History*. SCS 25. Atlanta: Scholars, 1990.

Bettini, Maurizio. *Women and Weasels: Mythologies of Birth in Ancient Greece and Rome*. Translated by Emlyn Eisenach. Chicago: University of Chicago Press, 2013.

Black, Matthew. *The Book of Enoch or 1 Enoch: A New English Edition*. SVTP 7. Leiden: Brill, 1985.

Blackman, Philip. *Mishnayoth*. 6 vols. London: Mishna, 1951–55.

Blumell, Lincoln H., and Thomas A. Wayment. "The 'Number of the Beast:' Revelation 13:18 and Early Christian Isopsephies." In *Book of Seven Seals: The Peculiarity of Revelation, Its Manuscripts, Attestation, and Transmission*, edited by Thomas J. Kraus and Michael Sommer, 119–35. WUNT 363. Tübingen: Mohr Siebeck, 2016.

Bobichon, Philippe. *Justin Martyr: Dialogue avec Tryphon—Édition critique, traduction, commentaire*. 2 vols. Paradosis 47. Fribourg: Academic Press Fribourg, 2003.

Bockmuehl, Markus. "The Son of David and His Mother." *JTS* 62 (2011) 476–93.

Bonwetsch, G. Nathanael, and Hans Achelis. *Hippolytus' Werke*. 2 vols. GCS 1. Leipzig: Hinrichs, 1897.

Borret, Marcel. *Origène: Contre Celse*. 5 vols. SC 132, 136, 147, 150, 227, 238. Paris: Cerf, 1967–77.

Boulenger, Fernand. *Grégoire de Nazianze: Discourse funèbres*. TDÉHC. Paris: Librairie Alphonse Picard, 1908.

Bovon, François. "Beyond the Canonical and Apocryphal Books, the Presence of a Third Category: The Books Useful for the Soul." *HTR* 105 (2012) 125–37.

———. "Canonical, Rejected, and Useful Books." In *New Testament and Christian Apocrypha: Collected Studies II*, edited by Glenn E. Snyder, 318–22. WUNT 237. Tübingen: Mohr Siebeck, 2009.

———. "Names and Numbers in Early Christianity." *NTS* 47 (2001) 267–88.

———. "'Useful for the Soul': Christian Apocrypha and Christian Spirituality." In *The Oxford Handbook of Early Christian Apocrypha*, edited by Andrew F. Gregory and Christopher M. Tuckett, 185–95. Oxford: Oxford University Press, 2015.

Bowker, John. *The Targums and Rabbinic Literature: An Introduction to Jewish Interpretations of Scripture.* Cambridge: Cambridge University Press, 1969.
Bradshaw, Paul F., Maxwell E. Johnson, and L. Edward Phillips. *The Apostolic Tradition: A Commentary.* Hermeneia. Minneapolis: Fortress, 2002.
Braun, F. M. "La 'Lettre de Barnabé' et l'Évangile de saint Jean." *NTS* 4 (1958) 119–24.
Bray, Gerald. *God Has Spoken: A History of Christian Theology.* Wheaton, IL: Crossway, 2014.
Breytenbach, Cilliers. *Paulus und Barnabas in der Provinz Galatien: Studien zu Apostelgeschichte 13f.; 16,6; 18,23 und den Adressaten des Galaterbriefes.* AGJU 38. Leiden: Brill, 1996.
———. "Zeus und der lebendige Gott: Anmerkungen zu Apostelgeschichte 14,11–17." *NTS* 39 (1993) 396–413.
Breytenbach, Cilliers, and Christiane Zimmermann. *Early Christianity in Lycaonia and Adjacent Areas: From Paul to Amphilochius of Iconium.* AGJU 101. ECAM 2. Leiden: Brill, 2018.
Bricker, Daniel P. "The Doctrine of the 'Two Ways' in Proverbs." *JETS* 38 (1995) 501–17.
Brox, Norbert. *Der Hirt des Hermas.* KAV 7. Göttingen: Vandenhoeck & Ruprecht, 1991.
Brooks, James A. "Clement of Alexandria as a Witness to the Development of the New Testament Canon." *SecCent* 9 (1992) 41–55.
Bryennios, Philotheos. Διδαχὴ τῶν δώδεκα Ἀποστόλων. Constantinople: 1883.
———. Τοῦ ἐν ἁγίοις πατρὸς ἡμῶν Κλήμεντος ἐπισκόπου Ῥώμης αἱ δύο πρὸς Κορινθίους ἐπιστολαί. Constantinople: 1875.
Bulhart, Vinzenz and Jan Willem Philip Borleffs. *Tertullianus: Ad martyras, Ad Scapulam, De fuga in persecutione, De monogamia, De virginibus velandis, De pallio, De paenitentia.* CSEL 76. Vienna: Hölder-Pichler-Tempsky, 1957.
Burger, J.-D. "L'Énigme de Barnabas." *MH* 3 (1946) 180–93.
Burke, Jonathan. "Satan and Demons in the Apostolic Fathers." *SEÅ* 81 (2016) 127–68.
Canellis, Aline. *Débat entre un lucifèrien et un orthodoxe.* SC 473. Paris: Cerf, 2003.
Carleton Paget, James. "Antijudaism and Early Christian Identity." *ZAC* 1 (1997) 195–225.
———. "*Barnabas* 9.4: A Peculiar Verse on Circumcision." *VC* 45 (1991) 242–54.
———. "Barnabas' Anti-Jewish Use of Some New Testament Texts: Fact or Fiction?" In *The 'New Testament' as a Polemical Tool*, edited by Hagit Amirav and Riemer Roukema, 91–112. NTOA 118. Göttingen: Vandenhoeck & Ruprecht, 2018.
———. "The *Epistle of Barnabas.*" In *The Writings of the Apostolic Fathers*, edited by Paul Foster, 72–80. London: T. & T. Clark Continuum, 2007.
———. *The Epistle of Barnabas: Outlook and Background.* WUNT 2.64. Tübingen: Mohr Siebeck, 1994.
———. "The *Epistle of Barnabas* and the Writings that Later Formed the New Testament." In *The Reception of the New Testament in the Apostolic Fathers*, edited by Andrew F. Gregory and Christopher M. Tuckett, 229–49. Oxford: Oxford University Press, 2005.
———. "Egypt." In *Redemption and Resistance: The Messianic Hopes of Jews and Christians in Antiquity*, edited by Markus Bockmuehl and James Carleton Paget, 183–97. London: T. & T. Clark Continuum, 2007.
———. "Jewish Proselytism at the Time of Christian Origins: Chimera or Reality?" *JSNT* 62 (1996) 65–103.

———. "Jews and Christians in Ancient Alexandria—From the Ptolemies to Caracalla." In *Jews, Christians and Jewish Christians in Antiquity*, edited by James Carleton Paget, 123–47. WUNT 251. Tübingen: Mohr Siebeck, 2010.
———. "The Old Testament in the Apostolic Fathers." In *Studies on the Text of the New Testament and Early Christianity: Essays in Honor of Michael W. Holmes on the Occasion of His 65th Birthday*, edited by Daniel M. Gurtner, Juan Hernández Jr., and Paul Foster, 453–76. NTTSD 50. Leiden: Brill, 2015.
———. "Paul and the Epistle of Barnabas." *NovT* 38 (1996) 359–81.
———. "Paul and the *Epistle of Barnabas*." In *The Apostolic Fathers and Paul*, edited by Todd D. Still and David E. Wilhite, 79–100. PPSD 2. London: T. & T. Clark Bloomsbury, 2017.
———. "The Vision of the Church in the Apostolic Fathers," In *A Vision for the Church: Studies in Early Christian Ecclesiology in Honour of J. P. M. Sweet*, edited by Markus Bockmuehl and Michael B. Thomson, 193–206. Edinburgh: T. & T. Clark, 1997.
Cary, Earnest E. *Dio Cassius: Roman History*. 9 vols. LCL. Cambridge: Harvard University Press, 1914–27.
Chadwick, Henry. *Origen: Contra Celsum*. Cambridge: Cambridge University Press, 1953.
Chandler, Karen K. "The Rite of the Red Heifer in the Epistle of Barnabas VIII and Mishnah Parah." In *Approaches to Ancient Judaism V: Studies in Judaism and Its Greco-Roman Context*, edited by William Scott Green, 99–114. Atlanta: Scholars, 1985.
Charlesworth, James H., and Craig A. Evans. "Jesus in the Agrapha and Apocryphal Gospels." In *Studying the Historical Jesus: Evaluations of the State of Current Research*, edited by Bruce D. Chilton and Craig A. Evans, 479–533. NTTSD 19. Leiden: Brill, 1994.
Chester, Andrew. *Messiah and Exaltation*. WUNT 207. Tübingen: Mohr Siebeck, 2007.
Cho, Ho Hyung. "ὁ νόμος τοῦ Χριστοῦ Reconsidered: A Fresh Look at Galatians 6:2, Barnabas 2:6, and Magnesians 2." *Canon & Culture* 13.1 (2019) 263–94.
Cohn, Leopold, and Paul Wendland. *Philonis Alexandrini opera quae supersunt*. 6 vols. Berlin: Reimerus, 1896–1915.
Cole, Zachary J. "P45 and the Problem of the 'Seventy(-two)': A Case for the Longer Reading in Luke 10.1 and 17." *NTS* 63 (2017) 203–21.
Collins, John J. "Sibylline Oracles." In *The Old Testament Pseudepigrapha*, edited by James H. Charlesworth, 2 vols, 1: 317–472. Garden City, NY: Doubleday, 1983–85.
———. *The Sibylline Oracles in Egyptian Judaism*. SBLDS 13. Missoula: Scholars, 1974.
Cosaert, Carl P. *The Texts of the Gospels in Clement of Alexandria*. NTGF 9. Atlanta: Society of Biblical Literature, 2008.
Cotton, Hannah M., and Ada Yardeni. *Discoveries in the Judaean Desert XXVII*. Oxford: Clarendon, 1997.
Cunningham, William. *A Dissertation on the Epistle of S. Barnabas, Including a Discussion of Its Date and Authorship*. London: Macmillan, 1877.
Curley, Michael J. *Physiologus: A Medieval Book of Nature Lore*. Chicago: University of Chicago Press, 2009.
Cysouw, Michael. *The Paradigmatic Structure of Person Marking*. OSTLT. Oxford: Oxford University Press, 2003.
———. "Inclusive/Exclusive Distinction in Independent Pronouns." In *The World Atlas of Language Structures Online*, edited by Matthew S. Dryer and Martin Haspelmath, chapter 39. Leipzig: Max Planck Institute for Evolutionary Anthropology, 2013. (Available at http://wals.info/chapter/39, accessed on December 12, 2020.)

Dacy, Marianne. "The Epistle to Barnabas and the Dead Sea Scrolls." In *The Dead Sea Scrolls Fifty Years after Their Discovery: Proceedings of the Jerusalem Congress, July 20–25, 1997*, edited by Lawrence H. Schiffmann, Emanuel Tov, and James C. VanderKam, 139–47. Jerusalem: Israel Exploration Society, 2000.

Danker, Frederick W., Walter Bauer, William F. Arndt, and F. Wilbur Gingrich. *Greek-English Lexicon of the New Testament and Other Early Christian Literature*. 3rd ed. Chicago: University of Chicago Press, 2000.

Dawson, David. *Allegorical Readers and Cultural Revision in Ancient Alexandria*. Berkeley: University of California Press, 1992.

———. *Christian Figural Reading and the Fashioning of Identity*. Berkeley: University of California Press, 2001.

de Boer, E. A. "Tertullian on 'Barnabas' Letter to the Hebrews' in *De pudicitia* 20.1–5." *VC* 68 (2014) 243–63.

Dentesano, Annalisa. "La versione latina dell'epistola di Barnaba: Analisi linguistica e della tecnica di traduzione." *FO* 52 (2015) 133–44.

Derry, Ken. "One Stone on Another: Towards an Understanding of Symbolism in the *Epistle of Barnabas*." *JECS* 4 (1996) 515–28.

Dibelius, Martin. *Der Hirt des Hermas*. HNT. Tübingen: Mohr, 1923.

Dobschütz, Ernst von. *Das Kerygma Petri: Kristisch untersucht*. TUGAL 11.1 Leipzig: Hinrichs, 1893.

Docherty, Susan. "The Text Form of the OT Citations in Hebrews Chapter 1 and the Implications for the Study of the Septuagint." *NTS* 55 (2009) 355–65.

Dods, Marcus. "Barnabas." *The Biblical World* 25.5 (1905) 334–46.

Dodson, Joseph R. "Rejection and Redemption in the Wisdom of Solomon and the Letter of Barnabas." *CBQ* 80 (2018) 45–61.

Doutreleau, Louis. *Didyme l'Aveugle: Sur Zacharie*. 3 vols. Sources chrétiennes 83–85. Paris: Cerf, 1962.

Downs, David J. *Alms: Charity, Reward, and Atonement in Early Christianity*. Waco, TX: Baylor University Press, 2016.

Draper, Jonathan A. "Barnabas and the Riddle of the Didache Revisited." *JSNT* 58 (1995) 89–113.

Dunn, Geoffrey D. "Tertullian and Rebekah: A Re-Reading of an 'Anti-Jewish' Argument in Early Christian Literature." *VC* 52 (1998) 119–45.

Dunn, James D. G. *Beginning from Jerusalem*. Christianity in the Making 2. Grand Rapids: Eerdmans, 2009.

———. *Jesus Remembered*. Christianity in the Making 1. Grand Rapids: Eerdmans, 2003.

———. *Neither Jew nor Greek: A Contested Identity*. Christianity in the Making 3. Grand Rapids: Eerdmans, 2015.

Eberhart, Christian A. *Kultmetaphorik und Christologie: Opfer- und Sühneterminologie im Neuen Testament*. WUNT 306. Tübingen: Mohr Siebeck, 2013.

Edwards, J. Christopher. "The Epistle of Barnabas." In *The Reception of Jesus in the First Three Centuries*, Vol. 2, edited by Chris Keith, Helen K. Bond, Christine Jacobi, and Jens Schröter, 27–40. London: Bloomsbury T. & T. Clark, 2020.

———. *The Gospel according to the Epistle of Barnabas: Jesus Traditions in an Early Christian Polemic*. WUNT 2.503. Tübingen: Mohr Siebeck, 2019.

———. "Identifying the Lord in the Epistle of Barnabas." *StPatr* 93 (2017) 51–60.

Ehorn, Seth M. "Abraham in the Apostolic Fathers." In *Abraham in Jewish and Early Christian Literature*, edited by Sean A. Adams and Zanne Domoney-Lyttle, 149–63. LSTS 93. London: Bloomsbury T. & T. Clark, 2019.
Ehrman, Bart D. *The Apostolic Fathers*. 2 vols. LCL 24–25. Cambridge: Harvard University Press, 2003.
———. "The New Testament Canon of Didymus the Blind." *VC* 37 (1983) 1–21.
Ehrman, Bart D., and Zlatko Pleše. "Agrapha." In *The Apocryphal Gospels: Texts and Translations*, edited by Bart D. Ehrman and Zlatko Pleše, 351–67. Oxford: Oxford University Press, 2011.
Elliott, J. K. *The Apocryphal New Testament*. Oxford: Clarendon, 1993.
Engelhardt, Moritz von. *Das Christenthum Justin des Märtyrers: Eine Untersuchung über die Anfänge der katholischen Glaubenslehre*. Erlangen: Deichert, 1878.
Evans, Ernest. *Tertullian: Adversus Marcionem*. OECT. Oxford: Clarendon, 1972.
———. *Tertullianus: Treatise against Praxeas*. London: SPCK, 1948.
Ewald, Heinrich. *Geschichte des Volkes Israel*. 3rd ed. Göttingen: Dietrich, 1868.
Farrar, Thomas J. "The Intimate and Ultimate Adversary: Satanology in Early Second-Century Christian Literature." *JECS* 26 (2018) 517–46.
Feldmeier, Reinhard. "*Paedeia salvatrix*: Zur Anthropologie und Soteriologie der *Tabula Cebetis*." In *Die Bildtafel des Kebes: Allegorie des Lebens*, edited by Rainer Hirsch-Luipold, Reinhard Feldmeier, Barbara Hirsch, Lutz Koch, and Heinz-Günther Nesselrath, 149–63. SAPERE 8. Darmstadt: Wissenschaftliche Buchgesellschaft, 2005.
Fontaine, Jacques. *Tertullien, De corona*. Paris: Presses Universitaires de France, 1966.
Foster, Paul. *Colossians*. BNTC. London: Bloomsbury T. & T. Clark, 2016.
———. *The Gospel of Peter: Introduction, Critical Edition and Commentary*. TENTS 4. Leiden: Brill, 2010.
Frey, Jörg. *The Letter of Jude and the Second Letter of Peter: A Theological Commentary*. Translated by Kathleen Ess. Waco, TX: Baylor University Press, 2018.
Funk, F. X. "Der Codex Vaticanus gr. 859 und seine Descendenten." *ThQ* 62 (1880) 629–37.
———. *Patres apostolici*. Vol. 1. Tübingen: Laupp, 1901.
Gallagher, Edmon L., and John D. Meade. *The Biblical Canon Lists from Early Christianity: Texts and Analysis*. Oxford: Oxford University Press, 2017.
Gallaher Branch, Robin. "Barnabas: Early Church Leader and Model of Encouragement." *IDS* 41 (2007) 295–322.
Gathercole, Simon. *The Gospel of Thomas: Introduction and Commentary*. TENTS 11. Leiden: Brill, 2014.
Gaventa, Beverly Roberts. *Acts*. ANTC. Nashville: Abingdon, 2003.
Geffcken, Johannes. *Die Oracula Sibyllina*. GCS 8. Leipzig: Hinrichs, 1902.
Giambelluca Kossava, Alda, Claudio Leonardi, Lorenzo Perrone, Enrico Norelli, and Paolo Bettiolo. *Ascensio Isaiae: Textus*. CCSA 7. Turnhout: Brepols, 1995.
Ginsburger, Moses. *Pseudo-Jonathan: Thargum Jonathan ben Usiel zum Pentateuch*. Berlin: Calvary, 1903.
Gleede, Benjamin. *Parabiblica Latina: Studien zu den griechisch-lateinischen Übersetzungen parabiblischer Literatur unter besonderer Berücksichtigung der apostolischen Väter*. VCSup 137. Leiden: Brill, 2016.
Goltz, Eduard von der. *Ignatius von Antiochien als Christ und Theologe: Eine dogmengeschichtliche Untersuchung*. TUGAL 12.3. Leipzig: Hinrichs, 1894.

Gombis, Timothy G. *The Drama of Ephesians: Participating in the Triumph of God.* Downers Grove, IL: IVP Academic, 2010.
Goodspeed, Edgar J. "The Salutation of Barnabas." *JBL* 34 (1915) 162–65.
Grant, Robert M. *Theophilus of Antioch: Ad Autolycum.* OECT. Oxford: Oxford University Press, 1970.
Gregory, Andrew F., and Christopher M. Tuckett. "Reflections on Method: What Constitutes the Use of the Writings that Later Formed the New Testament in the Apostolic Fathers." In *The Reception of the New Testament in the Apostolic Fathers*, edited by Andrew F. Gregory and Christopher M. Tuckett, 61–82. Oxford: Oxford University Press, 2005.
Grenfell, Bernard P., and Arthur S. Hunt. *The Oxyrhynchus Papyri.* Vol. 6. London: Egyptian Exploration Society, 1908.
Grenfell, Bernard P., Arthur S. Hunt, and David G. Hogarth. *Fayum Towns and Their Papyri.* London: Egyptian Exploration Society, 1900.
Gunther, John J. "The Association of Mark and Barnabas with Egyptian Christianity." *EvQ* 54 (1982) 219–34; 55 (1983) 21–29.
———. "The Epistle of Barnabas and the Final Rebuilding of the Temple." *JSJ* 7 (1976) 143–51.
Gwatkin, Henry Melvill. *Early Church History to A.D. 313.* 2 vols. London: Macmillan, 1909.
Hall, Stuart G. *Melito of Sardis: On Pascha and Fragments.* OECT: Oxford: Oxford University Press, 1979.
Hanson, A. T. "The Activity of the Pre-Existent Christ as Reflected in the Epistle of Barnabas." StPatr 18.3 (1990) 155–59.
Hanson, R. P. C. *Allegory and Event: A Study of the Sources and Significance of Origen's Interpretation of Scripture.* London: SCM, 1959.
Hardy Ropes, James. *Die Sprüche Jesu, die in den kanonischen Evangelien nicht überliefert sind: Eine kritische Bearbeitung des von D. Alfred Resch gesammelten Materials.* TUGAL 14.2. Leipzig: Hinrichs, 1896.
Harland, Philip A. "Familial Dimensions of Group Identity: 'Brothers' (ΑΔΕΛΦΟΙ) in Associations of the Greek East." *JBL* 124 (2005) 491–513.
von Harnack, Adolf. *The Acts of the Apostles.* Translated by J. R. Wilkinson. London: Williams & Norgate, 1909.
———. *Geschichte der altchristlichen Literatur bis Eusebius.* 2nd ed. 2 vols. Leipzig: Hinrichs, 1958.
Harrisville, Roy A. "ΠΙΣΤΙΣ ΧΡΙΣΤΟΥ: Witness of the Fathers." *NovT* 36 (1994) 233–41.
Hartog, Paul. "The Good News in Old Texts? The 'Gospel' and the 'Archives' in Ign. Phld. 8.2." StPatr 93 (2017) 105–21.
———. *Polycarp's* Epistle to the Philippians *and the* Martyrdom of Polycarp: *Introduction, Text, and Commentary.* Oxford: Oxford University Press, 2013.
Hatch, Edwin. *Essays in Biblical Greek.* Oxford: Clarendon, 1889.
Hayduck, Michael. *Alexandri Aphrodisiensis: In Aristotelis Metaphysica Commentaria.* CAG 1. Berlin: Reimer, 1891.
Heer, Joseph Michael. "Der lateinische Barnabasbrief und die Bibel." *RQ* 23 (1909) 215–45.
———. *Die versio latina des Barnabasbriefs und ihr Verhältnis zur lateinischen Bibel.* Freiburg im Breslau: Herder, 1908.

Hegedus, Tim. "Midrash and the Letter of Barnabas." *BTB* 37 (2007) 20–26.
———. "Midrash in the Letter of Barnabas," StPatr 45 (2010) 331–35.
Hengel, Martin. *The Atonement: The Origins of the Doctrine in the New Testament.* Translated by John Bowden. Philadelphia: Fortress, 1981.
———. "Der stellvertretende Sühnetod Jesu: Ein Beitrag zur Entstehung des urchristlichen Kerygmas." *IKaZ* 9 (1980) 1–25, 135–47.
Henne, Philippe. "Barnabé, le temple et les pagano-chrétiens." *RB* 103 (1996) 257–76.
———. "Justin, la Loi, et les Juifs." *RTL* 26 (1995) 450–62.
Hernández, Juan, Jr. *Scribal Habits and Theological Influences in the Apocalypse: The Singular Readings of Sinaiticus, Alexandrinus, and Ephraemi.* WUNT 2.218. Tübingen: Mohr Siebeck, 2006.
Hilgenfeld, Adolph. *Die apostolischen Väter: Untersuchungen über Inhalt und Ursprung der unter ihrem Namen erhaltenen Schriften.* Halle: Pfeffer, 1853.
———. *Barnabae Epistula: Integram graece iterum edidit.* 2nd ed. Leipzig: Weigel, 1877.
———. *Barnabae Epistula: Integram graece primum edidit.* Leipzig: Weigel, 1866.
Hill, Charles E. "'In These Very Words': Methods and Standards of Literary Borrowing in the Second Century." In *The Early Text of the New Testament*, edited by Charles E. Hill and Michael J. Kruger, 261–81. Oxford: Oxford University Press, 2012.
———. *Regnum Caelorum: Patterns of Millennial Thought in Early Christianity.* 2nd ed. Grand Rapids: Eerdmans, 2001.
Hirsch-Luipold, Rainer, Reinhard Feldmeier, Barbara Hirsch, Lutz Koch, and Heinz-Günther Nesselrath. *Die Bildtafel des Kebes: Allegorie des Lebens.* SAPERE 8. Darmstadt: Wissenschaftliche Buchgesellschaft, 2005.
Hoek, Annewies van den. "Clement and Origen as Sources on 'Noncanonical' Scriptural Traditions during the Late Second and Earlier Third Centuries." In *Origeniana Sexta: Origène et la Bible*, 93–113. BETL 118. Leuven: Peeters, 1995.
———. "Techniques of Quotation in Clement of Alexandria: A View of Ancient Literary Working Methods." *VC* 50 (1996) 223–43.
Hofius, Otfried. "Versprengte Herrenworte." In *Neutestamentliche Apokryphen in deutscher Übersetzung*, edited by Wilhelm Schneemelcher, 2 vols. 1.76–79. 5th ed. Tübingen: Mohr Siebeck, 1987.
Hogg, Michael A., and Dominic Abrams. *Social Identifications: A Social Psychology of Intergroup Relations and Group Processes.* London: Routledge, 1998.
Holtzmann, H. J. "Barnabas und Johannes." *ZWT* 14 (1871) 336–51.
Hooper, W. D., and Harrison Boyd Ash. *Cato and Varro: On Agriculture.* LCL 283. Cambridge: Harvard University Press, 1934.
Horbury, William. "Jewish-Christian Relations in Barnabas and Justin." In *Jews and Christians: The Parting of the Ways A.D. 70 to 135*, edited by James D. G. Dunn, 315–45. WUNT 66. Tübingen: Mohr Siebeck, 1992.
———. *Jewish Messianism and the Cult of Christ.* London: SCM, 1998.
———. *Jewish War under Trajan and Hadrian.* Cambridge: Cambridge University Press, 2014.
———. *Jews and Christian: In Contact and Controversy.* Edinburgh: T. & T. Clark, 1998.
Horrell, David G. "From ἀδελφοί to οἶκος θεοῦ: Social Transformation in Pauline Christianity." *JBL* 120 (2001) 293–311.
———. *The Making of Christian Morality: Reading Paul in Ancient and Modern Contexts.* Grand Rapids: Eerdmans, 2019.
Hoselton, Luke R. "'You Have Been Raised with Christ': Investigating the Spatial Portrait of New Creation in Ephesians." *JBTS* 5.1 (2020) 24–39.

Houghton, H. A. G. *The Latin New Testament: A Guide to Its Early History, Texts, and Manuscripts*. Oxford: Oxford University Press, 2016.

Hude, Karl. *Xenophōntos apomnēmoneumata: Xenophontis commentarii*. BSGRT. Leipzig: Teubner, 1934.

Hunt, Arthur S. *The Oxyrhynchus Papyri*. Vol. 7. London: Egyptian Exploration Society, 1910.

———. *The Oxyrhynchus Papyri*. Vol. 8. London: Egyptian Exploration Society, 1911.

Hurtado, Larry W. *The Early Christian Artifacts: Manuscripts and Christian Origins*. Grand Rapids: Eerdmans, 2006.

———. *Lord Jesus Christ: Jesus Devotion in Earliest Christianity*. Grand Rapids: Eerdmans, 2003.

———. "The Origin of the *Nomina Sacra*: A Proposal." *JBL* 117 (1998) 655–73.

Hvalvik, Reidar. "Barnabas 9.7–9 and the Author's Supposed Use of *Gematria*." *NTS* 33 (1987) 276–82.

———. "Christ Proclaiming His Law to the Apostles: The *Traditio Legis*-Motif in Early Christian Art and Literature." In *The New Testament and Early Christian Literature in Greco-Roman Context: Studies in Honor of David E. Aune*, edited by John Fotopoulos, 405–37. NovTSup 122. Leiden: Brill, 2006.

———. "The *Epistle of Barnabas*." In *The Cambridge Companion to the Apostolic Fathers*, edited by Michael F. Bird and Scott D. Harrower, 268–89. Cambridge: Cambridge University Press, 2021.

———. *The Struggle for Scripture and Covenant: The Purpose of the Epistle of Barnabas and Jewish-Christian Competition in the Second Century*. WUNT 2.82. Tübingen: Mohr Siebeck, 1996.

Jacobson, Howard. *A Commentary on Pseudo-Philo's Liber Antiquitatum Biblicarum: With Latin Text and English Translation*. 2 vols. AGJU 31. Leiden: Brill, 1996.

Jaubert, Annie. *Clément de Rome: Épître aux Corinthiens*. SC 169. Paris: Cerf, 1971.

———. *Origène: Homélies sur Josué*. SC 71. Paris: Cerf, 1960.

Jeremias, Joachim. *Unknown Sayings of Jesus*. 2nd ed. Translated by Reginald H. Fuller. London: SPCK, 1964.

Jefford, Clayton N. *The Apostolic Fathers and the New Testament*. Peabody, MA: Hendrickson, 2006.

———. "The Wisdom of Sirach and the Glue of the Matthew-Didache Tradition." In *Intertextuality in the Second Century*, edited by D. Jeffrey Bingham and Clayton N. Jefford, 8–23. BAC 11. Leiden: Brill, 2016.

Johnson, A. E. "Interpretive Hierarchies in Barnabas I–XVII." *StPatr* 17.2 (1993) 702–6.

Jones, W. H. S. and H. Rackham. *Pliny: Natural History*. 10 vols. LCL. Cambridge: Harvard University Press, 1938–62.

Jongkind, Dirk. *Scribal Habits of Codex Sinaiticus*. TS 5. Piscataway, NJ: Gorgias, 2007.

Joosten, Jan. "The Date and Provenance of the *Gospel of Barnabas*." *JTS* 61 (2010) 200–15.

Junod, Eric, and Jean-Daniel Kaestli. *Acta Johannis*. 2 vols. CCSA 1.1–2. Turnhout: Brepols, 1983.

Kayser, Johannes. *Ueber den sogenannten Barnabas-Brief: Eine patristische Abhandlung*. Paderborn: Tunsermann, 1866.

Kieffer, René. "La demeure divine dans le temple et sur l'autel chez Ignace d'Antioche." In *La cité de Dieu: Die Stadt Gottes*, edited by Martin Hengel, Siegfried Mittmann, and Anna Maria Schwemer, 287–301. WUNT 129. Tübingen: Mohr Siebeck, 2000.

Kirk, Alexander N. "Ignatius' Statements of Self-Sacrifice: Intimations of an Atoning Death or Expressions of Exemplary Suffer." *JTS* 64 (2013) 66–88.
Kister, Menahem. "Barnabas 12:1; 4:3 and 4Q Second Ezekiel." *RB* 97 (1990) 63–67.
Klauck, Hans-Josef. *Ancient Letters and the New Testament: A Guide to Context and Exegesis*. Waco, TX: Baylor University Press, 2006.
Klevinghaus, Johannes. *Die theologische Stellung der Apostolischen Väter zur alttestamentlichen Offenbarung*. BFCT 44.1. Gütersloh: Bertelsmann, 1948.
Koch, Dietrich-Alex. *Geschichte des Urchristentums: Ein Lehrbuch*. Göttingen: Vandenhoeck & Ruprecht, 2013.
———. "Taufinterpretation bei Ignatius und im Barnabasbrief: Christologische und soteriologische Deutungen." In *Ablution, Initiation, and Baptism: Waschungen, Initiation und Taufe*, edited by David Hellholm, Tor Vegge, Øyvind Norderval, and Christer Hellholm, 817–48. BZNW 176. 3 vols. Berlin: De Gruyter, 2011.
Koester, Helmut. *Introduction to the New Testament*. 2nd ed. 2 vols. New York: De Gruyter, 1995–2000.
Kok, Michael. "The True Covenant People: Ethnic Reasoning in the Epistle of Barnabas." *SR* 40 (2011) 81–97.
Kollmann, Bernd. *Joseph Barnabas: Leben und Wirkungsgeschichte*. SBS 175. Stuttgart: Katholisches Bibelwerk, 1998.
Kollmann, Bernd, and Werner Deuse. *Alexander Monachus: Laudatio Barnabae— Lobrede auf Barnabas*. Turnhout: Brepols, 2007.
König, Jason. *Saints and Symposiasts: The Literature of Food and the Symposium in Greco-Roman and Early Christian Culture*. Greek Culture in the Roman World. Cambridge: Cambridge University Press, 2012.
Korn, Helmut. *Die Nachwirkungen der Christusmystik des Paulus in den Apostolischen Vätern*. Leipzig: Robert Noske, 1928.
Kraft, Robert A. *Barnabas and the Didache: A New Translation and Commentary*. Apostolic Fathers 3. New York: Thomas Nelson, 1965.
———. "Barnabas' Isaiah Text and Melito's *Paschal Homily*." *JBL* 80 (1961) 371–73.
———. "Barnabas' Isaiah Text and the 'Testimony Book' Hypothesis." *JBL* 79 (1960) 336–50.
———. "The Epistle of Barnabas: Its Quotations and Their Sources." PhD diss., Harvard University, 1961.
———. "An Unnoticed Papyri Fragment of Barnabas." *VC* 21 (1967) 150–63.
Kraus, Thomas J., and Tobias Nicklas. *Das Petrusevangelium und die Petrusapokalypse: Die griechischen Fragmente mit deutscher und englischer Übersetzung*. GCS 11. Berlin: De Gruyter, 2004.
Kühneweg, Uwe. "Das neue Gesetz: Zur christlichen Selbstdefinition im 2. Jahrhundert." *StPatr* 21 (1989) 129–36.
Lake, Kirsopp. *The Apostolic Fathers*. LCL 24–25. Cambridge: Harvard University Press, 1912–13.
Lampe, Geoffrey W. H. L. *Patristic Greek Lexicon*. Oxford: Clarendon, 1961.
Lattke, Michael. *Aristides "Apologie."* KfA 2. Freiburg: Herder, 2018.
———. "Die Wahrheit der Christen in der Apologie des Aristides: Vorstudie zu einem Kommentar." In *Ein neues Geschlecht? Entwicklung des frühchristlichen Selbstbewusstseins*, edited by Markus Lang, 215–35. NTOA 105. Göttingen: Vandenhoeck & Ruprecht, 2014.
Legarth, Peter V. *Guds tempel: Tempelsymbolisme og kristologi hos Ignatius von Antiokia*. MVS 3. Århus: Kolon, 1992.

Liddell, Henry George, Robert Scott, and Henry Stuart Jones. *A Greek-English Lexicon*. 9th ed. with revised supplement. Oxford: Clarendon, 1996.
Lieu, Judith M. *Christian Identity in the Jewish and Graeco-Roman World*. Oxford: Oxford University Press, 2004.
———. "Self-Definition vis-à-vis the Jewish Matrix." In *The Cambridge History of Christianity: Origins to Constantine*, edited by Margaret M. Mitchell and Frances M. Young, 214–29. Cambridge: Cambridge University Press, 2006.
Lightfoot, J. B. *The Apostolic Fathers: Revised Texts with Introductions, Notes, Dissertations, and Translations*. 2nd ed. 2 parts in 5 vols. London: Macmillan, 1889–91.
Lincicum, David. "Against the Law: The *Epistle of Barnabas* and Torah Polemic in Early Christianity." In *Law and Lawlessness in Early Judaism and Early Christianity*, edited by David Lincicum, Ruth Sheridan, and Charles Stang, 105–21. WUNT 420. Tübingen: Mohr Siebeck, 2019.
———. "Paul and the *Testimonia*: Quo Vademus?" *JETS* 51 (2008) 297–308.
Lincicum David, Ruth Sheridan, and Charles Stang. "Introduction." In *Law and Lawlessness in Early Judaism and Early Christianity*, edited by David Lincicum, Ruth Sheridan, and Charles Stang, 1–8. WUNT 420. Tübingen: Mohr Siebeck, 2019.
Lindars, Barnabas. *The Theology of the Letter to the Hebrews*. Cambridge: Cambridge University Press, 1991.
Lindemann, Andreas, and Henning Paulsen, eds. *Die Apostolischen Väter: Griechisch-deutsche Parallelausgabe*. Tübingen: Mohr Siebeck, 1992.
Lindeskog, Gösta. "Schöpfer und Schöpfung in den Schriften der apostolischen Vätern." *ANRW* 27.1:588–648. Part 2, *Principat*, 27.1. Edited by Wolfgang Haase. Berlin: De Gruyter, 1992.
Lipsius, R. A. "Barnabasbrief." In *Bibel-Lexikon*, Vol. 1, edited by Daniel Schenkel, 363–73. Leipzig: Brockhaus, 1869.
Lipsius, R. A., and Maxmilian Bonnet. *Acta Apostolrum Apocrypha*. Vol. 2. Leipzig: Mendelssohn, 1903.
List, Nicholas. "Δίψυχος: Moving beyond Intertextuality." *NTS* 67 (2021) 85–104.
Löhr, Winrich A. "La doctrine de dieu dans la lettre à Flora de Ptolémée." *RHPR* 75 (1995) 177–91.
Longenecker, Bruce W. *The Cross before Constantine: The Early Life of a Christian Symbol*. Minneapolis: Fortress, 2015.
Lookadoo, Jonathon. "Barnabas in History and Memory." *KNTS* 26 (2019) 1121–62.
———. "The Form and Function of the Psalter in *Barnabas* 6." *CanCul* 14.2 (2020) 211–46.
———. *The High Priest and the Temple: Metaphorical Depictions of Jesus in the Letters of Ignatius of Antioch*. WUNT 2.473. Tübingen: Mohr Siebeck, 2018.
———. "Ignatius of Antioch and Scripture." *ZAC* 23 (2019) 201–27.
———. *The Shepherd of Hermas: A Literary, Historical, and Theological Handbook*. London: T. & T. Clark Bloomsbury, 2021.
Lowy, Simeon. "The Confutation of Judaism in the Epistle of Barnabas." *JJS* 11 (1960) 1–33.
Luckritz Marquis, Timothy. "Perfection Perfected: The Stoic 'Self-Eluding Sage' and Moral Progress in Hebrews." *NovT* 57 (2015) 187–205.
Madden, Frederic W. *Coins of the Jews*. London: Trübner, 1903.

Malik, Peter. "The Corrections of Codex Sinaiticus and the Textual Transmission of Revelation: Josef Schmid Revisited." *NTS* 61 (2015) 595–614.
———. "The Earliest Corrections in Codex Sinaiticus: A Test Case from the Gospel of Mark." *BASP* 50 (2013) 207–54.
Marchant, E. C., and O. J. Todd. *Xenophon: Memorabilia, Oeconomicus, Symposium, Apology*. LCL. Cambridge: Harvard University Press, 1923.
Marcovich, Miroslav. *Iustini Martyris apologiae pro Christianis: Iustini Martyris dialogus cum Tryphone*. PTS 38/47. Berlin: De Gruyter, 2005.
Markschies, Christoph. *Christian Theology and Its Institutions in the Early Roman Empire: Prolegomena to a History of Early Christian Theology*. Translated by Wayne Coppins. BMSEC 3. Waco, TX: Baylor University Press, 2015.
———. "New Research on Ptolemaeus Gnosticus." *ZAC* 4 (2000) 225–54.
———. "Die valentinianische Gnosis und Marcion—einige neue Perspektiven." In *Marcion und seine kirchengeschichtliche Wirkung: Marcion and His Impact on Church History*, edited by Gerhard May and Katharina Greschat, 159–75. TU 150. Berlin: De Gruyter, 2002.
Martín, José Pablo. "L'interpretazione allegorica nella *Lettera di Barnaba* e nel guidaismo alessandrino." *SSR* 6 (1982) 173–83.
McDonald, Lee Martin. *Forgotten Scriptures: The Selection and Rejection of Early Religious Writings*. Louisville, KY: Westminster John Knox, 2009.
Ménard, Hugo. *Sancti Barnabae apostoli (ut fertur) epistola catholica*. Paris: Piget, 1645.
Menken, Maarten J. J. "Old Testament Quotations in the Epistle of Barnabas with Parallels in the New Testament." In *Textual History and the Reception of Scripture in Early Christianity: Textgeschichte und Schriftrezeption im frühen Christentum*, edited by Johannes de Vries and Martin Karrer, 295–321. SCS 60. Atlanta: Society of Biblical Literature, 2013.
Meshorer, Ya'akov. *Jewish Coins of the Second Temple Period*. Translated by I. H. Levine. Tel-Aviv: Am Hassefer, 1967.
Metzger, Bruce M. "Seventy or Seventy-Two Disciples." *NTS* 5 (1958–59) 299–306.
Metzger, Marcel. *Les constitutions apostoliques*. 3 vols. SC 320, 329, 336. Paris: Cerf, 1985–87.
Micaelli, Claudio. *Tertullien: La pudicite*. 2 vols. SC 394–95. Paris: Cerf, 1993.
Migne, J.-P. *Patrologia Graeca*. Vol. 48. Paris, 1862.
Miller, Frank Justus. *Ovid: Metamorphoses*. 2 vols. LCL 42–43. Cambridge: Harvard University Press, 1916.
Milne, H. J. M., and T. C. Skeat. *Scribes and Correctors of the Codex Sinaiticus*. London: British Museum, 1938.
Minns, Denis, and Paul Parvis. *Justin, Philosopher and Martyr*: Apologies. OECT. Oxford: Oxford University Press, 2009.
Mor, Menahem. *The Second Jewish Revolt: The Bar Kokhba War, 132–136 CE*. BRLA 50. Leiden: Brill, 2016.
Moreschini, Claudio, and Enrico Norelli. *Manuale di letteratura cristiana antica greca e latina*. Brescia: Morcelliana, 1999.
Morgan, Teresa. *Roman Faith and Christian Faith: Pistis and Fides in the Early Roman Empire and Early Churches*. Oxford: Oxford University Press, 2015.
Mras, Karl. *Eusebius Werke: Die Praeparatio Evangelica*. 2 vols. GCS 43.1–2. Eusebius Werke 8.1–2. Berlin: Akademie, 1956.

Muilenburg, James. "The Literary Relations of the Epistle of Barnabas and the Teaching of the Twelve Apostles." PhD diss., Yale University, 1929.

Murray, Michele. *Playing a Jewish Game: Gentile Christian Judaizing in the First and Second Centuries, CE*. SCJ 13. Waterloo, ON: Wilfrid Laurier University Press, 2004.

Myrshall, Amy C. "Codex Sinaiticus, Its Correctors, and the Caesarean Text of the Gospels." PhD diss., University of Birmingham, 2005.

———. "The Presence of a Fourth Scribe?" In *Codex Sinaiticus: New Perspectives on the Ancient Biblical Manuscript*, edited by Scott McKendrick, David Parker, Amy Myshrall, and Cillian O'Hogan, 139-48. London: British Library, 2015.

Nesselrath, Heinz-Günther. *Gegen falsche Götter und falsche Bildung: Tatian, Rede an die Griechen*. SAPERE 28. Tübingen: Mohr Siebeck, 2016.

Neusner, Jacob. *The Babylonian Talmud: A Translation and Commentary*. 22 vols. Peabody, MA: Hendrickson, 2005.

Nickelsburg, George W. E. "Abraham the Convert: A Jewish Tradition and Its Use by the Apostle Paul." In *Biblical Figures Outside the Bible*, edited by Michael E. Stone and Theodore A. Bergren, 151-75. Harrisburg, PA: Trinity Press International, 1998.

———. *Jewish Literature between the Bible and the Mishnah: A Historical and Literary Introduction*. 2nd ed. Minneapolis: Fortress, 2005.

Nicklas, Tobias. *Jews and Christians? Second Century "Christian" Perspectives on the "Parting of the Ways."* Tübingen: Mohr Siebeck, 2014.

Niederwimmer, Kurt. *The Didache*. Translated by Linda M. Maloney. 2nd ed. Hermeneia. Minneapolis: Fortress, 1998.

Niehoff, Maren. *Jewish Exegesis and Homeric Scholarship in Alexandria*. Cambridge: Cambridge University Press, 2011.

Niese, Benedict. *Flavii Iosephi opera*. 6 vols. Berlin: Weidmann, 1885-95.

Norelli, Enrico. "Il dibattito con il giudaismo nel II secolo: *Testimonia*; Barnaba; Giustino." In *La Bibbia nell'antichità cristiana*, Vol. 1, edited by Enrico Norelli, 199-233. Bologna: EDB, 1993.

Norris, Richard A. "The Apostolic and Sub-Apostolic Writings: The New Testament and the Apostolic Fathers." In *The Cambridge History of Early Christian Literature*, edited by Frances Young, Lewis Ayres, and Andrew Louth, 11-19. Cambridge: Cambridge University Press, 2004.

Oegema, Gerbern. *The Anointed and His People: Messianic Expectations from the Maccabees to Bar Kochba*. JSPSup 27. Sheffield, UK: Sheffield Academic Press, 1998.

———. *Der Gesalbte und sein Volk: Untersuchungen zum Konzeptualisierungsprozeß der messianischen Erwartungen von den Makkabäern bis Bar Koziba*. SIJD 2. Göttingen: Vandenhoeck & Ruprecht, 1994.

Öhler, Markus. *Barnabas: Der Mann in der Mitte*. BG 12. Leipzig: Evangelische Verlagsanstalt, 2005.

———. *Barnabas: Die historische Person und ihre Rezeption in der Apostelgeschichte*. WUNT 156. Tübingen: Mohr Siebeck, 2003.

O'Neil, J. C. "The Origins of Monasticism." In *The Making of Orthodoxy: Essays in Honour of Henry Chadwick*, edited by Rowan Williams, 270-87. Cambridge: Cambridge University Press, 1989.

Osborn, Eric F. *Clement of Alexandria*. Cambridge: Cambridge University Press, 2005.

———. *Justin Martyr*. BHT 47. Tübingen: Mohr Siebeck, 1973.

Osburn, Carroll D. "Methodology in Identifying Patristic Citations in NT Textual Criticism." *NovT* 47 (2005) 313–43.
Parvis, Paul. "Who Was Irenaeus? An Introduction to the Man and His Work." In *Irenaeus: Life, Scripture, and Legacy*, edited by Paul Foster and Sara Parvis, 13–24. Minneapolis: Fortress, 2012.
Paulsen, Henning. *Studien zur Theologie des Ignatius von Antiochien*. FKDG 29. Göttingen: Vandenhoek & Ruprecht, 1978.
Parker, David C. *Codex Sinaiticus: The Story of the World's Oldest Bible*. London: British Library, 2010.
———. *An Introduction to the New Testament Manuscripts and Their Texts*. Cambridge: Cambridge University Press, 2008.
Pearson, Birger A. "Earliest Christianity in Egypt: Further Observations." In *The World of Early Egyptian Christianity: Language, Literature, and Social Context*, edited by James E. Goehring and Janet A. Timbie, 97–112. CUASEC. Washington, DC: Catholic University of America Press, 2007.
———. "Earliest Christianity in Egypt: Some Observations." In *The Roots of Egyptian Christianity*, edited by Birger A. Pearson and James E. Goehring, 132–59. SAC. Philadelphia: Fortress, 1986.
———. "Egypt." In *The Cambridge History of Christianity: Origins to Constantine*, edited by Margaret M. Mitchell and Frances M. Young, 331–50. Cambridge: Cambridge University Press, 2006.
Peck, Arthur Leslie. *Aristotle: Generation of Animals*. LCL 366. Cambridge: Harvard University Press, 1942.
Pelletier, André. *Lettre d'Aristée à Philocrate*. SC 89. Paris: Cerf, 1962.
Pendergraft, Mary. "'Thou Shalt Not Eat the Hyena': A Note on 'Barnabas' *Epistle* 10.7." *VC* 46 (1992) 75–79.
Peterson, David. *Hebrews and Perfection: An Examination of the Concept of Perfection in the 'Epistle to the Hebrews.'* SNTSMS 47. Cambridge: Cambridge University Press, 1982.
Pierce, Madison N. "Hebrews 3.7—4.11 and the Spirit's Speech to the Community." In *Muted Voices of the New Testament: Readings in the Catholic Epistles and Hebrews*, edited by Katherine M. Hockey, Madison N. Pierce, and Francis Watson, 173–84. LNTS 587. London: Bloomsbury T. & T. Clark, 2017.
Popović, Mladen. "Anthropology, Pneumatology, and Demonology in Early Judaism: The Two Spirits Treatise (1QS III, 13–IV, 26) and Other Texts from the Dead Sea Scrolls." In *Dust of the Ground and Breath of Life (Gen 2:7): The Problem of a Dualistic Anthropology in Early Judaism and Christianity*, edited by Jacques van Ruiten and George van Kooten, 58–98. TBN 20. Leiden: Brill, 2016.
Porter, Stanley E. *Constantine Tischendorf: The Life and Work of a 19th Century Bible Hunter, Including Constantine Tischendorf's* When Were Our Gospels Written? London: Bloomsbury T. & T. Clark, 2015.
Pouderon, Bernard, and Marie-Joseph Pierre. *Aristide, Apologie*. SC 470. Paris: Cerf, 2003.
Preuschen, Erin. *Der Johanneskommentar*. GCS 10. Origenes Werke 4. Leipzig: Hinrichs, 1903.
Prigent, Pierre, and Robert A. Kraft. *Épître de Barnabé*. SC 172. Paris: Cerf, 1971.
Prinzivalli, Emanuela, and Manlio Simonetti. *Seguendo Gesù: Testi christiani delle origini*. 2 vols. Milan: Mondadori, 2010–15.

Prostmeier, Ferdinand R. "Antijudaismus im Rahmen christlicher Hermeneutik: Zum Streit über christliche Identität in der Alten Kirche, Notizen zum Barnabasbrief." *ZAC* 6 (2002) 38–58.

———. *Der Barnabasbrief*. KAV 8. Göttingen: Vandenhoeck & Ruprecht, 1999.

———. "Der Barnabasbrief." In *Die Apostolischen Väter: Eine Einleitung*, edited by Wilhelm Pratscher, 39–58. Göttingen: Vandenhoeck & Ruprecht, 2009.

———. "Einleitung." In *Epistola Barnabae, Ad Diognetum: Barnabasbrief, An Diognet*, edited by Horacio E. Lona and Ferdinand R. Prostmeier, 9–70. FonChr 72. Freiburg: Herder, 2018.

———. "The Epistle of Barnabas." In *The Apostolic Fathers: An Introduction*, edited by Wilhelm Pratscher, 27–45. Translated by Elisabeth E. Wolfe. Waco, TX: Baylor University Press, 2010.

———. "Zur handschriftlichen Überlieferung des Polykarp- und des Barnabasbriefes: Zwei nicht beachtete Deszendenten des Cod. Vat. Gr. 859." *VC* 48 (1994) 48–64.

Prostmeier, Ferdinand R., and Horacio E. Lona. *Epistola Barnabae, Ad Diognetum: Barnabasbrief, An Diognet*. FonChr 72. Freiburg: Herder, 2018.

Punt, Jeremy. "*He Is Heavy . . . He's My Brother*: Unravelling Fraternity in Paul (Galatians)." *Neot* 46.1 (2012) 153–71.

Quispel, Gilles. *Ptolémée, Lettre à Flora: Analyse, texte critique, traduction, commentaire et index grec*. 2nd ed. SC 24. Paris: Cerf, 1966.

Rabassini, Andrea. "L'ombra della iena: Un animale magico nella cultura filosofica del Rinascimento." *Bruniana & Campanelliana* 10 (2004) 87–104.

Rahlfs, Alfred. *Psalmi cum Odis*. 3rd ed. SVTG 10. Göttingen: Vandenhoeck & Ruprecht, 1979.

Rahlfs, Alfred, and Robert Hanhart. *Septuaginta*. 2nd ed. Stuttgart: Deutsche Bibelgesellschaft, 2006.

Ramsay, William Mitchell. *The Church in the Roman Empire before A.D. 170*. 10th ed. London: Hodder & Stoughton, 1897.

Rehm Bernhard, and Georg Strecker. *Die Pseudoklementinen I: Homilien*. 3rd ed. GCS 42 Berlin: Akademie, 1992.

———. *Die Pseudoklementinen II: Rekognitionen*. 2nd ed. GCS 51. Berlin: Akademie, 1994.

Reinach, Théodore, Wilhelm Spiegelberg, and Seymour de Ricci. *Papyrus grecs et démotiques recueillis en Égypte*. Paris: Ernest Leroux, 1905.

Rhodes, James N. "Barnabas 4.6b: The Exegetical Implications of a Textual Problem." *VC* 58 (2004) 365–92.

———. *The Epistle of Barnabas and the Deuteronomic Tradition: Polemics, Paraenesis, and the Legacy of the Golden-Calf Incident*. Tübingen: Mohr Siebeck, 2004.

———. "The Two Ways Tradition in the *Epistle of Barnabas*: Revisiting an Old Question." *CBQ* 73 (2011) 797–816.

Ribbens, Benjamin J. *Levitical Sacrifice and Heavenly Cult in Hebrews*. BZNW 222. Berlin: De Gruyter, 2016.

Richard, Marcel. "Les fragments du Commentaire de S. Hippolyte sur les Proverbes de Salomon." In *Opera Minora*, Vol. 1, edited by Eligius Dekkers et al., 339–44. Turnhout: Brepols, 1976.

Richardson, Ernest Cushing. *Hieronymus, Liber de viris illustribus: Gennadius, Liber de viris illustribus*. TUGAL 14.1. Leipzig: Hinrichs, 1896.

Richardson, Peter, and Martin B. Shukster. "Barnabas, Nerva, and the Yavnean Rabbis." *JTS* 34 (1983) 31–55.
Roberts, W. Rhys. *Demetrius On Style: The Greek Text of Demetrius* De elocutione *Edited after the Paris Manuscript*. Cambridge: Cambridge University Press, 1902.
Robillard, Edmond. "L'Épître de Barnabé: Trois époques, trois théologies, trois rédacteurs." *RB* 78 (1971) 184–209.
Robinson, J. Armitage. *Barnabas, Hermas, and the Didache*. London: SPCK, 1920.
Roller, Otto. *Das Formular der Paulinischen Briefe: Ein Beitrag zur Lehre vom Antiken Briefe*. BWA(N)T 4.6. Stuttgart: Kohlhammer, 1933.
Rordorf, Willy. *Sabbat et dimanche dans l'Eglise ancienne*. TC. Neuchâtel: Delachaux & Niestlé, 1972.
———. *Sunday: The History of the Day of Rest and Worship in the Earliest Centuries of the Christian Church*. Translated by A. A. K. Graham. Philadelphia: Westminster, 1968.
Rordorf, Willy, and André Tuilier. *La doctrine des douze apôtres (Didachè)*. SC 248. Paris: Cerf, 1978.
Rothschild, Clare K. "The Apostolic Mothers." In *The Cambridge Companion to the Apostolic Fathers*, edited by Michael F. Bird and Scott D. Harrower, 175–85. Cambridge: Cambridge University Press, 2021.
———. "Down the Rabbit Hole with Barnabas: Rewriting Moses in Barnabas 10." *NTS* 54 (2018) 410–34.
———. "Epistle of Barnabas and Secession through Allegory." In *New Essays on the Apostolic Fathers*, 191–212. WUNT 375. Tübingen: Mohr Siebeck, 2017.
———. "Ethiopianising the Devil: ὁ μέλας in Barnabas 4." *NTS* 65 (2019) 223–45.
Rousseau, Adelin. *Démonstration de la prédication apostolique*. SC 406. Paris: Cerf, 1995.
Rousseau, Adelin, Louis Doutreleau, Bertrand Hemmerdinger, and Charles Mercier. *Irénée de Lyon: Contres les hérésies*. 10 vols. SC 100.1–2, 152–53, 210–11, 263–64, 293–94. Paris: Cerf, 1965–82.
Runge, Steven E. *Discourse Grammar of the Greek New Testament: A Practical Introduction for Teaching and Exegesis*. LBRS. Peabody, MA: Hendrickson, 2010.
Runia, David T. *Philo in Early Christian Literature: A Survey*. CRINT 3. Assen: Van Gorcum, 1993.
Ruwet, Jean. "Les apocryphes dans les œuvres d'Origene." *Bib* 25 (1944) 143–66, 311–34.
———. "Clément d'Alexandrie: Canon des écritures et apocryphes." *Bib* 29 (1948) 77–99, 240–68, 391–408.
Rzach, Aloisius. Χρησμοὶ Σιβυλλιακοί: *Oracula Sibyllina*. Prague: Tempsky, 1891.
Sanders, James A. *Torah and Canon*. Philadelphia: Fortress, 1972.
Sandt, Huub van de, and David Flusser. *The Didache: Its Jewish Sources and Its Place in Early Judaism and Christianity*. CRINT 3.5. Assen: Van Gorcum, 2002.
Schaff, Philip. *The Oldest Church Manual Called the Teaching of the Twelve Apostles*. New York: Scribner, 1885.
Schenke, Hans-Martin. "Der Barnabasbrief im Berliner 'Koptischen Buch' (P. Berol. 20915)." In *Der Same Seths: Hans Martin Schenkes Kleine Schriften* zu *Gnosis, Koptologie und Neuem Testament*, edited by Gesine Schenke Robinson, Gesa Schenke, and Uwe-Karsten Plisch, 911–34. NHS 78. Leiden: Brill, 2012.

Schenke Robinson, Gesine, Hans-Martin Schenke, and Uwe-Karsten Plisch. *Das Berliner "Koptische Buch" (P. 20915): Eine Wiederhergestellte frühchristlich-theologische Abhandlung*. 2 vols. CSCO 610–11. Leuven: Peeters: 2004.

Schille, Gottfried. "Zur urchristlichen Tauflehre: Stilistische Beobachtungen am Barnabasbrief." *ZNW* 49 (1958) 31–52.

Schliesser, Benjamin. "Faith in Early Christianity: An Encyclopedic and Bibliographical Outline." In *Glaube: Das Verständnis des Glaubens im frühen Christentum und in seiner jüdischen und hellenistisch-römischen Umwelt*, edited by Jörg Frey, Benjamin Schliesser, and Nadine Ueberschaer, with the help of Kathrin Hager, 3–50. WUNT 373. Tübingen: Mohr Siebeck, 2017.

Schneider, Horst. "Einführung in den Physiologus." In *Christus in natura: Quellen, Hermeneutik und Rezeption des Physiologus*, edited by Zbyněk Kindschl Garský and Rainer Hirsch-Luipold, 5–13. SBR 11. Berlin: De Gruyter, 2019.

Schnelle, Udo. *Die ersten Jahre des Christentums: 30–130 n. Chr*. 2nd ed. UTB. Göttingen: Vandenhoeck & Ruprecht, 2016.

Schnider, Franz, and Werner Stenger. *Studien zum neutestamentlichen Briefformular*. NTTS 11. Leiden: Brill, 1987.

Schoedel, William R. "Ignatius and the Archives." *HTR* 71 (1978) 97–106.

———. *Ignatius of Antioch*. Hermeneia. Philadelphia: Fortress, 1985.

Scholfield, A. F. *Aelian: On the Characteristics of Animals*. 3 vols. LCL. Cambridge: Harvard University Press, 1958–59.

Schrage, Wolfgang. *Der erste Brief an die Korinther*. 4 vols. EKK 7. Neukirchen-Vluyn: Neukirchener, 1991–2001.

Schwartz, Daniel R. "On Barnabas and Bar-Kokhba." In *Studies in the Jewish Background of Christianity*, 147–53. WUNT 60. Tübingen: Mohr Siebeck, 1992.

Scott, Alan. "The Date of the *Physiologus*." *VC* 52 (1998) 430–41.

Scully, Jason. "Redemption for the Serpent: The Reception History of Serpent Material from the *Physiologus* in the Greek, Latin, and Syriac Traditions." *ZAC* 22 (2018) 422–55.

Sheppard, G. T. "Canon." In *The Encyclopedia of Religion*, Vol. 3, edited by Mircea Eliade, 62–69. New York: Macmillan, 1987.

Shotwell, Willis A. *The Biblical Exegesis of Justin Martyr*. London: SPCK, 1965.

Shukster, Martin B., and Peter Richardson. "Temple and *Bet Ha-midrash* in the Epistle of Barnabas." In *Andi-Judaism in Early Christianity: Separation and Polemic*, edited by Stephen G. Wilson, 17–31. ESCJ 2. Waterloo, ON: Wilfrid Laurier University Press, 1986.

Skarsaune, Oskar. "Baptismal Typology in *Barnabas* 8 and the Jewish Background." StPatr 18.3 (1990) 221–28.

———. "The Development of Scriptural Interpretation in the Second and Third Centuries—Except Clement and Origen." In *Hebrew Bible, Old Testament: The History of Its Interpretation*, Vol. 1.1, 373–442. Göttingen: Vandenhoeck & Ruprecht, 1996.

———. "Ethnic Discourse in Early Christianity." In *Christianity and the Second Century: Themes and Developments*, edited by James Carleton Paget and Judith Lieu, 250–64. Cambridge: Cambridge University Press, 2017.

———. "Jewish Christian Sources Used by Justin Martyr and Some Other Greek and Latin Fathers." In *Jewish Believers in Jesus: The Early Centuries*, edited by Oskar Skarsaune and Reidar Hvalvik, 379–416. Peabody, MA: Hendrickson, 2007.

———. *The Proof from Prophecy—A Study in Justin Martyr's Proof-Text Tradition: Text-Type, Provenance, Theological Profile.* NovTSup 56. Leiden: Brill, 1987.
Skehan, Patrick W. "Didache 1,6 and Sirach 12,1." *Bib* 44 (1963) 533–36.
Smallwood, E. Mary. *The Jews under Roman Rule: From Pompey to Diocletian.* SJLA 20. Leiden: Brill, 1976.
Smith, Julien C. "The Epistle of Barnabas and the Two Ways of Teaching Authority." *VC* 68 (2014) 465–97.
Song, Jae Jung. *Linguistic Typology.* OTLing. Oxford: Oxford University Press, 2018.
Speigl, Jakob. "Ignatius in Philadelphia: Ereignisse und Anliegen in den Ignatiusbriefen." *VC* 41 (1967) 360–76.
Stählin, Otto. *Clemens Alexandrinus: Protrepticus und Paedagogus.* GCS 12. Leipzig: Hinrichs, 1905.
———. *Clemens Alexandrinus: Stromata Buch I–VI.* GCS 15. Leipzig Hinrichs, 1906.
———. *Clemens Alexandrinus: Stromata Buch VII und VIII, Excerpta ex Theodoto, Eclogae propheticae, Quis dives salvetur, Fragmente.* GCS 17. Leipzig: Heinrichs, 1909.
Standhartinger, Angela. "Ptolemaeus und Justin zur Autorität der Schrift." In *Ein neues Geschlecht? Entwicklung des frühchristlichen Selbstbewusstseins,* edited by Markus Lang, 122–49. NTOA 105. Göttingen: Vandenhoeck & Ruprecht, 2014.
Stewart-Sykes, Alistair. *On the Two Ways: Life or Death, Light or Darkness: Foundational Texts in the Tradition.* PPS 41. Crestwood, NY: St. Vladimir's Seminary Press, 2011.
Steyn, Gert J. *A Quest for the Assumed LXX Vorlage of the Explicit Quotations in Hebrews.* FRLA(N)T 235. Göttingen: Vandenhoeck & Ruprecht, 2011.
Stökl Ben Ezra, Daniel. "The Biblical Yom Kippur, the Jewish Fast of the Day of Atonement and the Church Fathers." StPatr 34 (2001) 493–502.
———. "Fasting with Jews, Thinking with Scapegoats: Some Remarks on Yom Kippur in Early Judaism and Christianity, in Particular 4Q541, *Barnabas* 7, Matthew 27 and Acts 27." In *The Day of Atonement: Its Interpretations in Early Jewish and Christian Traditions,* edited by Thomas Hieke and Tobias Nicklas, 165–87. TBN 15. Leiden: Brill, 2012.
———. *The Impact of Yom Kippur on Early Christianity: The Day of Atonement from Second Temple Judaism to the Fifth Century.* WUNT 163. Tübingen: Mohr Siebeck, 2003.
Stühlmacher, Peter. *Reconciliation, Law, and Righteousness: Essays in Biblical Theology.* Translated by Everett R. Kalin. Philadelphia: Fortress, 1986.
Sundberg, Albert C. "Canon Muratori: A Fourth Century List." *HTR* 66 (1973) 1–41.
Svigel, Michael J. *The Center and the Source: Second Century Incarnational Christology and Early Catholic Christianity.* GSECP 66. Piscataway, NJ: Gorgias, 2016.
———. "Trinitarianism in *Didache, Barnabas,* and the *Shepherd*: Sketchy, Scant, or Scandalous?" *Perichoresis* 17 (2019) 23–40.
Tarvainen, Olavi. *Faith and Love in Ignatius of Antioch.* Translated by Jonathon Lookadoo. Eugene, OR: Pickwick, 2016.
———. *Glaube und Liebe bei Ignatius von Antiochien.* SLAG 14. Helsinki: Luther-Agricola-Gesellschaft, 1967.
Taylor, Charles. "The Two Ways in Hermas and Xenophon." *JP* 21 (1893) 243–58.
Taylor, Miriam S. *Anti-Judaism and Early Christian Identity: A Critique of the Scholarly Consensus.* StPB 46. Leiden: Brill, 1995.
Theodor, Julius, and Chanoch Albeck. *Bereschit Rabba.* VAWJ. Berlin: Poppelauer, 1927.

Thomson, Robert W. *Athanasius: Contra Gentes and De Incarnatione*. OECT. Oxford: Clarendon, 1971.
Tischendorf, Constantine. *Bibliorum Codex Sinaiticus Petropolitanus: Auspiciis augustissimis imperatoris Alexandri II. ex tenebris protraxit in Europam transtulit ad invandas atque illustrandas sacras litteras*. 4 vols. St. Petersburg, 1862.
———. *Codex Claromontanus*. Leipzig: Brockhaus, 1852.
Tite, Philip L. "How to Begin and Why? Diverse Functions of the Pauline Prescript within a Greco-Roman Context." In *Paul and the Ancient Letter Form*, edited by Stanley E. Porter and Sean A. Adams, 57–99. Pauline Studies 6. Leiden: Brill, 2010.
Torrance, Thomas F. *The Doctrine of Grace in the Apostolic Fathers*. Edinburgh: Oliver & Boyd, 1948.
Tovey, Derek Morton Hamilton. "The Narrative Structure and Flow of the Prologue to John's Gospel." In *Johannine Christology*, edited by Stanley E. Porter and Andrew W. Pitts, 155–68. Johannine Studies 3. Leiden: Brill, 2020.
Tränkle, Hermann. *Edition de QSF Tertulliani Aduersus Iudaeos*. Wiesbaden: Steiner, 1964.
Trapp, Michael. *Greek and Latin Letters: An Anthology, with Translation*. Cambridge: Cambridge University Press, 2003.
Trebilco, Paul R. *Self-Designations and Group Identity in the New Testament*. Cambridge: Cambridge University Press, 2012.
———. *Outsider Designations and Boundary Construction in the New Testament: Early Christian Communities and the Formation of Group Identity*. Cambridge: Cambridge University Press, 2017.
Treu, Ursula. "Zur Datierung des *Physiologus*." *ZNW* 57 (1966) 101–4.
Trever, John. *Scrolls from Qumran Cave I*. Jerusalem: Albright Institute of Archaeology and the Shrine of the Book, 1972.
Tucker, J. Brian, and Coleman A. Baker. *T. & T. Clark Handbook to Social Identity in the New Testament*. London: Bloomsbury T. & T. Clark, 2014.
Tugwell, Simon. *The Apostolic Fathers*. London: Continuum, 1989.
Uusimäki, Elisa. "Mapping Ideal Ways of Living: Virtue and Vice Lists in 1QS and 4Q286." *JSP* 30 (2020) 35–45.
Van der Horst, Pieter W. "Did the Gentiles Know Who Abraham Was?" In *Abraham, the Nations, and the Hagarites: Jewish, Christian, and Islamic Perspectives on Kinship with Abraham*, edited by Martin Goodman, George H. van Kooten, and Jacques T. A. G. M. van Ruiten with editorial assistance from Albertina Oegema, 61–75. TBN 13. Leiden: Brill, 2010.
van Unnik, W. C. "De la règle Μήτε προσθεῖναι μήτε ἀφελεῖν dans l'histoire du canon." *VC* 3 (1949) 1–36.
Vanhoozer, Kevin J. *Remythologizing Theology: Divine Action, Passion, and Authorship*. CSCD 18. Cambridge: Cambridge University Press, 2010.
Venter, Dirk J. "The Implicit Obligations of Brothers, Debtors and Sons (Romans 8:12–17)." *Neot* 48.2 (2014) 283–302.
Verheyden, Joseph. "Israel's Fate in the Apostolic Fathers: The Case of 1 Clement and the Epistle of Barnabas." In *Q in Context I: The Separation between the Just and the Unjust in Early Judaism and in the Sayings Source*, edited by Markus Tiwald, 237–62. Göttingen: Vandenhoeck & Ruprecht, 2015.
Vesco, Jean-Luc. "La lecture du Psautier selon l'Épître de Barnabé." *RB* 93 (1986) 5–37.

Vielhauer, Philipp. *Geschichte der urchristlichen Literatur: Einleitung in das Neue Testament, die Apokryphen und die Apostolischen Väter*. Berlin: De Gruyter, 1975.
Vinzent, Markus. *Writing the History of Early Christianity: From Reception to Retrospection*. Cambridge: Cambridge University Press, 2019.
Vitelli, Girolamo. *Papiri greco-egizii, papiri Fiorentini*. Vol. 3. Milanç Ulrico Hoepla, 1915.
———. *Papiri greci e latini (n. 731-870)*. Vol. 7. Florence: Pubblicazioni della Società Italiana, 1925.
Vitelli, Girolamo, and Medea Norsa. *Papiri greci e latini*. Vol. 3. Florenceç Enrico Ariani, 1914.
Vööbus, Arthur. *The Didascalia Apostolorum in Syriac*. Vol. 2. CSCO 408. Leuven: Peeters, 1979.
Wake, William. *The Genuine Epistles of the Apostolical Fathers*. London: Sare, 1693.
Wendel, Susan J. *Scriptural Interpretation and Community Self-Definition in Luke-Acts and the Writings of Justin Martyr*. NovTSup 139. Leiden: Brill, 2011.
Wengst, Klaus. "Barnabasbrief." In *TRE*, Vol. 5, edited by Gerhard Müller et al., 238-41. Berlin: De Gruyter, 1980.
———. *Didache (Apostellehre), Barnabasbrief, Zweiter Klemensbrief, Schrift an Diognet*. SUC 2. Munich: Kösel, 1984.
———. *Tradition und Theologie des Barnabasbriefes*. AKG 42. Berlin: De Gruyter, 1971.
West, Martin L. *Hesiod: Works and Days*. Oxford: Oxford University Press, 1978.
Westcott, B. F. *A General Survey of the History of the Canon of the New Testament*. 4th ed. London: Macmillan, 1875.
Wevers, John William. *Genesis*. SVTG 1. Göttingen: Vandenhoeck & Ruprecht, 1974.
———. *Deuteronomium*. SVTG 3.2. Göttingen: Vandenhoeck & Ruprecht, 1977.
———. *Leviticus*. SVTG 2.2. Göttingen: Vandenhoeck & Ruprecht, 1982.
———. *Notes on the Greek Text of Genesis*. SCS 35. Atlanta: Scholars, 1993.
White, John L. "Ancient Greek Letters," In *Greco-Roman Literature and the New Testament: Selected Forms and Genres*, edited by David E. Aune, 85-105. SBLSBS 21. Atlanta: Scholars, 1988.
Whitenton, Michael R. "After ΠΙΣΤΙΣ ΧΡΙΣΤΟΥ: Neglected Evidence from the Apostolic Fathers." *JTS* 61 (2010) 82-109.
Whitfield, Bryan J. *Joshua Traditions and the Argument of Hebrews 3 and 4*. BZNW 194. Berlin: De Gruyter, 2013.
———. "Pioneer and Perfecter: Joshua Traditions and the Christology of Hebrews." In *A Cloud of Witnesses: The Theology of Hebrews in Its Ancient Contexts*, edited by Richard Bauckham, Daniel Driver, Trevor Hart, and Nathan MacDonald, 80-87. LNTS 387. London: T. & T. Clark Continuum, 2008.
Whittaker, John. "The Value of Indirect Tradition in the Establishment of Greek Philosophical Texts or the Art of Misquotation." In *Editing Greek and Latin Texts: Papers Given at the Twenty-Third Annual Conference on Editorial Problems, University of Toronto 6-7 November 1987*, edited by J. Grant, 63-95. New York: AMS, 1989.
Wilhite, Shawn J. *The Didache: A Commentary*. AFCS 1. Eugene, OR: Cascade, 2019.
———. *"One of Life and One of Death:" Apocalypticism and the Didache's Two Ways*. GSECP 70. Piscataway, NJ: Gorgias, 2019.
Williams, Arthur Lukyn. "The Date of the Epistle of Barnabas." *JTS* 34 (1933) 337-46.

Windisch, Hans. *Der Barnabasbrief.* HNT Ergänzungsband. Tübingen: Mohr Siebeck, 1920.
Wolter, Michael. *Das Lukasevangelium.* HNT 5. Tübingen: Mohr Siebeck, 2008.
Wright, William. *A Catalogue of the Syriac Manuscripts Preserved in the Library of the University of Cambridge.* 2 vols. Cambridge: Cambridge University Press, 1901.
Yarbro Collins, Adela. "Aristobulus." In *The Old Testament Pseudepigrapha,* Vol. 2, edited by James H. Charlesworth, 831–42. Garden City, NY: Doubleday, 1983–85.
Young, Douglas. *Theognis Megarensis indicibus ad Theognidem Adiectis.* BSGRT. Stuttgart: Teubner, 1998.
Yuen-Collingridge, Rachel. "Hunting for Origen in Unidentified Papyri: The Case of P.Egerton 2 (=Inv. 3). In *Early Christian Manuscripts: Examples of Applied Method and Approach,* edited by Thomas J. Kraus and Tobias Nicklas, 39–57. TENTS 5. Leiden: Brill, 2010.
Yuh, Jason N. "Do as I Say, Not as They Do: Social Construction in the Epistle of Barnabas through Canonical Interpretation and Ritual." *HTR* 112 (2019) 273–95.
Zañartu, Sergio. "Les concepts de vie et de mort chez Ignace d'Antioche." *VC* 33 (1979) 324–41.
Zetterholm, Magnus. *The Formation of Christianity in Antioch: A Social-Scientific Approach to the Separation between Judaism and Christianity.* London: Routledge, 2003.
Ziegler, Joseph. *Duodecim Prophetim.* SVTG 13. Göttingen: Vandenhoeck & Ruprecht, 1943.
———. *Ieremias, Baruch, Threni, Epistula Ieremiae.* 4th ed. SVTG 15. Göttingen: Vandenhoeck & Ruprecht, 2013.
———. *Isaias.* 3rd ed. SVTG 14. Göttingen: Vandenhoeck & Ruprecht, 1983.

Author Index

Aasgaard, Reidar, 74
Abrams, Dominic, 38
Achelis, Hans, 142
Adams, Sean A., 90, 116
Aland, Kurt, 14
Albeck, Chanoch, 188
Albl, Martin C., 89, 120
Aldridge, Robert E., 196
Alexander, Philip, 63
Ash, Harrison Boyd, 146
Audet, J. P., 197
Aune, David E., 41
Ayres, Lewis, xii, 54

Backhaus, Knut, 62, 172
Baker, Coleman A., 38
Barclay, John M. G., 80, 138, 168, 188
Bardy, Gustave, 9, 14
Barnard, Leslie W., 19, 21–22, 26–27, 41, 63, 71, 118, 121, 197
Bartlet, James Vernon, 22, 49, 106
Barton, John, 195
Barton, Stephen C., xiii
Bastow, Sarah, xi
Bates, Matthew W., 158
Batovici, Dan, x, 5, 10, 15
Bauckham, Richard, 28, 182–83
Bauer, Thomas J., 71
Baumstark, Anton, 10
Beatrice, Pier Franco, 29, 106
Becker, Eve-Marie, 204
Behr, John, 13, 45, 181
Berding, Kenneth, xii
Berger, Klaus, 73
Bergren, Theodore A., 90

Bettini, Maurizio, 145
Bettiolo, Paolo, 86
Bingham, D. Jeffrey, x, xiii
Black, Matthew, 185
Blackman, Philip, 128
Blumell, Lincoln H., 142
Bobichon, Philippe, 41
Bonwetsch, G. Nathanael, 142
Borchardt, C. F. A., xii
Borlefs, Jan Willem Philip, 45
Borret, Marcel, 13
Boulenger, Fernand, 28
Bounds, Christopher Todd, xiii
Bovon, François, 16, 142
Bowker, John, 141
Bradshaw, Paul F., 121
Braun, F. M., 159
Bray, Gerald, 52
Brent, Allen, 220
Breytenbach, Cilliers, 28
Bricker, Daniel P., 195
Brooks, James A., 13
Brox, Norbert, 92
Bryennios, Philotheos, 6
Buitenwerf, Rieuwerd, xiv
Bulhart, Vinzenz, 45
Burger, J.-D., 27
Burke, Jonathan, xiii, 86

Canelis, Aline, 121
Carleton Paget, James, 12, 15–17, 19, 21, 23, 27, 35–38, 47–49, 54, 63, 73, 90–92, 98–99, 120–21, 126, 138–39, 141–42, 150, 153, 159
Cary, Earnest E., 24

AUTHOR INDEX

Chadwick, Henry, 13
Chandler, Karen K., 42, 132, 134
Charlesworth, James H., 48
Chester, Andrew, 188
Cho, Ho Hyung, 62, 92–93
Cohn, Leopold, 18
Cole, Zachary J., 12
Collins, John J., 188
Cosaert, Carl P., 13
Cotelier, J. B., x
Cotton, Hannah M., 26
Cunningham, William, 9, 21, 24, 77, 81, 94, 99, 109, 111, 192
Curley, Michael J., 149
Cysouw, Michael, 96

Dacy, Marianne, 196
Dahl, Nils A., 119, 121
Dawson, David, 39, 127
De Boer, E. A., 14, 28
Dentesano, Annalisa, 9–10, 192
Derry, Ken, 115, 119, 154
Deuse, Werner, 29
Dibelius, Martin, 82
Dobschütz, Ernst von, 92
Docherty, Susan, 180
Dods, Marcus, 28
Dodson, Joseph R., 64, 116
Doutreleau, Louis, 13, 90
Downs, David J., 80, 89
Draper, Jonathan A., 3, 59, 196
Dunn, Geoffrey D., 168
Dunn, James D. G., 28, 39, 48

Eberhardt, Christian A., 130
Edwards, J. Christopher, 49, 53–54, 63, 74–75, 82, 95, 99, 102, 106, 123, 141, 160, 169, 185, 219
Ehorn, Seth M., 90, 116, 169–70
Ehrman, Bart D., xi, 4, 13, 15, 48, 76, 81, 83, 94, 99, 109, 111, 127, 166, 192, 211, 217, 221
Elliott, J. K., 48
Emmenegger, Gregor, xi
Engelhardt, Moritz von, 41
Evans, Craig A., 48
Evans, Ernest, 121
Ewald, Heinrich, 22

Farrar, Thomas J., xiii, 86, 200, 212
Feldmeier, Reinhard, 195
Fischer, J. A., x
Flusser, David, 196
Fontaine, Jacques, 121
Foster, Paul, ix, xii–xiii, 28, 113
Frey, Jörg, 183
Funk, F. X., 8, 17, 23

Gallagher, Edmon L., 16
Gallaher Branch, Robin, 28
Gallandi, Andreas, xi
Gathercole, Simon, 205
Gaventa, Beverly, 28
Gazal, André A., xi
Geffcken, Johannes, 188
Giambelluca Kossava, Alda, 86
Ginsburger, Moses, 141
Gleede, Benjamin, 9–10
Goltz, Eduard von der, 18
Gombis, Timothy, 86
Goodspeed, E. J., 72–73
Grant, Robert, ix
Greenfell, Bernard P., 72
Gregory, Andrew F., xii–xiii, 44
Gunther, John J., 17, 24, 186
Gwatkin, Henry Melvill, 15, 23

Hainthaler, Theresia, xi
Hall, Stuart G., 108
Hanhart, Robert, 108
Hannick, Christian 14
Hanson, R. P. C., 122, 144, 152, 172, 175
Hardy Ropes, James, 48, 127
Harland, Philip A., 74
Harnack, Adolf von, 15, 83
Harrisville, Roy A., 103
Hartog, Paul A., xi, xiii, 7, 18
Hatch, Edwin, 91, 120
Hauser, J. Alan, xiii
Hayduck, Michael, 193
Heer, Joseph Michael, 9–10
Hegedus, Tim, 118, 128, 132, 134, 142
Hemmerdinger, Bertrand, 90
Henne, Philippe, 188
Hengel, Martin, 130
Henne, Philippe, 41
Hernández, Juan, Jr., 5
Hilgenfeld, Adolph, 20, 22, 75, 97, 194

Hill, Charles E., 44, 183
Hirsch, Barbara, 195
Hirsch-Luipold, Rainer, 195
Hoek, Annewies van den, 12–13, 44
Hoffius, Otfried, 48
Hogarth, David G., 72
Hogg, Michael A., 38
Hollander, Harm W., xiv
Holmes, Michael W., xi, 4, 7, 21, 76, 81, 83, 94, 99, 109, 111, 166, 192, 211, 217, 221
Holtz, H. J., 159
Hooper, W. D., 146
Horbury, William, 26, 41, 63, 187–88
Horrell, David G., 74
Hoselton, Luke R., 86
Houghton, H. A. G., 14
Hude, Karl, 58
Hunt, Arthur S., 72
Hurtado, Larry W., 38, 100, 127, 129, 141–42
Hvalvik, Reidar, xviii, 19, 21–24, 26–27, 30, 35, 59, 72–74, 78–80, 83, 88, 91–93, 99, 102, 112, 119, 122, 142, 157, 177, 187, 195, 197, 203, 217, 220, 222–23

Ittig, Thomas, x

Jacobson, Howard, 128
Jaubert, Annie, 15, 108
Jefford, Clayton N., ix–xii, 17, 19, 22, 49, 59, 64, 106, 196, 208
Jeremias, Joachim, 48
Johnson, A. E., 39, 64, 127
Johnson, Maxwell E., 121
Jones, W. H. S., 146
Jongkind, Dirk, 5
Junack, Klaus, 14
Junod, Eric, 82

Kannengiesser, Charles, 39
Kastelli, Jean-Daniel, 82
Kayser, Johannes, 27
Khomych, Taras, xi
Kieffer, René, 189
Kirk, Alexander N., 103
Kister, Menahem, 47, 160
Klauck, Hans-Josef, 71

Klevinghaus, Johannes, 92, 112, 147, 167, 171, 174, 176, 180–81
Kloppenborg, John S., xiii
Koch, Dietrich-Alex, 119, 121, 152, 155, 208
Koch, Lutz, 195
Koester, Helmut, xii, 29
Kok, Michael, 63–64, 167
Kollmann, Bernd, 28–29
König, Jason, 150
Korn, Helmut, 53, 67, 119, 185
Kraft, Robert A., xviii, xxi, 4–5, 7–10, 13–14, 18–19, 24, 27, 35, 41, 57, 66, 76, 81, 83, 86, 90–92, 94–95, 98–99, 109, 111, 116, 121, 123, 125, 133–34, 140, 157, 180, 184, 186–87, 192–93, 196, 200, 202, 211–13, 216–17, 221
Kraus, Thomas J., 50
Kühneweg, Uwe, 89

Lake, Kirsopp, 21
Lanfranchi, Pierluigi, xiv
Lattke, Michael, 199, 208
Lawson, J., xiii
Legarth, Peter V., 189
Leonardi, Claudio, 86
Lieu, Judith M., 63–64, 102, 140, 186
Lightfoot, J. B., xi, 6–7, 17, 19
Lincicum, David, x, 41–42, 62–63, 147
Lindars, Barnabas, 96
Lindemann, Andreas, xiii, 4, 7, 17, 21, 76, 81, 83, 94, 109, 111, 166, 192, 211, 217, 221
Lindeskog, Gösta, 122
Lipsius, R. A., 24, 187
List, Nicholas, 205
Löhr, Winrich A., 41
Lona, Horacio E., 4, 6, 66, 74, 76, 81, 83, 96, 99, 109, 111, 124, 166–67, 180, 192–93, 209, 211, 217, 221
Longenecker, Bruce W., xiii, 142, 158
Lookadoo, Jonathon, xiii, 18, 28, 45, 59, 115, 120, 189
Louth, Andrew, xii
Lowy, Simeon, 63
Luckritz Marquis, Timothy, 96

Madden, Frederic W., 26
Mali, Franz, xi
Malik, Peter, 5
Marchant, E. C., 195
Marcovich, Miroslav, 39, 92
Markschies, Christoph, 41, 91
Marshall, I. Howard, xiii
Martín, José Pablo, 17, 122, 159, 182
McDonald, Lee Martin, 16
McGuckin, John A., xiii
Meade, John D., 16
Menken, Maarten J. J., 116
Mercier, Charles, 90
Ménard, Hugo, 74
Menken, Maarten J. J., 35
Meshorer, Ya'akov, 26
Metzger, Bruce M., 12
Metzger, Marcel, 59
Micaelli, Claudio, 14
Migne, J.-P., 189
Miller, Frank Justus, 146
Milne, H. J. M., 5
Minns, Denis, 19
Mor, Menahem, 26
Moreschini, Claudio, 26, 64
Morgan, Teresa, 135
Moss, Candida R., ix
Mras, Karl, 182
Muilenburg, James, 30, 73
Murray, Michele, 19, 22, 63–64
Myrshall, Amy C., 5

Nesselrath, Heinz-Günther, 88, 195
Neusner, Jacob, 129
Nickelsburg, George W. E., 169, 196
Nicklas, Tobias, xii, 18, 50
Niederwimmer, Kurt, 212
Niehoff, Maren, 17
Norelli, Enrico, 26, 41, 64, 86
Norris, Richard A., xii, 17

Oegema, Gerbern, 188
Öhler, Markus, 12, 15, 26, 28–29, 187
O'Neil, J. C., 104
Osborn, Eric F., 11, 41
Osburn, Carroll D., 35

Parker, David C., 5, 14
Parvis, Paul, 19, 183
Paulsen, Henning, 4, 7, 17–18, 21, 76, 83, 93, 109, 111, 166, 192, 211, 221
Pearson, Birger A., 17, 65, 182
Peck, Arthur Leslie, 146
Pelletier, André, 149
Pendergraft, Mary, 146
Perrone, Lorenzo, 86
Peterson, David, 96
Phillips, L. Edward, 121
Pierce, Madison N., 182
Pierre, Marie-Joseph, 130, 199
Pleše, Zlatko, 48, 127
Plisch, Uwe-Karsten, 11
Popović, Mladen, 196
Porter, Stanley E., 5
Pouderon, Bernard, 130, 199
Pratscher, Wilhelm, xi–xii
Presuchen, Erin, 45
Prigent, Pierre, 4–5, 7–10, 13, 18–19, 21, 24, 27, 66, 76, 81, 83, 86, 90–92, 94, 98–99, 109, 111, 125, 130, 144, 166, 180, 184, 186–87, 192–93, 202, 211, 213, 216–17, 221
Prinzivalli, Emanuela, 4, 6, 19, 35, 37, 61, 66, 73, 75–76, 81, 83, 86, 92, 94, 99, 101, 109, 111, 115, 166, 192–93, 202, 211–13, 217, 221
Prostmeier, Ferdinand R., xviii, 4–10, 12–13, 16–17, 19, 24, 49, 56, 63, 66, 73–78, 81–83, 86–88, 90, 92, 94, 96, 99, 105, 107, 109, 111–12, 116–17, 124, 157–58, 166–67, 180, 187, 192–94, 203, 209, 211, 217, 219, 221–23
Punt, Jeremy, 74

Quispel, Gilles, 39, 140

Rabassini, Andrea, 146
Rackham, H., 146
Rahlfs, Alfred, 91, 108, 115
Ramsay, William Mitchell, 22
Ranson, Angela, xi
Rehm, Bernhard, 28, 86

Reinach, Théodore, 72
Rhodes, James N., xviii–xix, 3, 20, 73–74, 78–79, 88, 92, 94, 99, 101–2, 107, 124, 149, 153, 195, 213, 217
Ribbens, Benjamin J., 96
Richard, Marcel, 130
Richardson, Ernest Cushing, 14
Richardson, Peter, 18–19, 21, 22, 24–25, 63, 65, 98, 188
Roberts, W. Rhys, 80
Robillard, Edmond, 29, 142
Robinson, J. Armitage, 197
Robinson, Thomas A., xiv
Roller, Otto, 71–72
Rordrof, Willy, 182, 197–98
Rothschild, Clare K., x, 13, 39, 63, 99, 101, 105, 127, 140, 145–46, 174, 177
Rousseau, Adelin, 45, 90
Runge, Steven E., 37, 64
Runia, David T., 17
Ruwet, Jean, 12–13, 16
Rzach, Aloisius, 188

Sanders, James A., 16
Sandt, Huub van de, 196
Schaff, Philip, 6
Schenke, Hans-Martin, 10–11
Schenke Robinson, Gesine, 11
Schille, Gottfried, 121
Schliesser, Benjamin, 103, 135
Schneider, Horst, 149
Schnelle, Udo, 28
Schnider, Franz, 71
Schoedel, William R., 18, 82, 220
Schrage, Wolfgang, 28
Schwartz, Daniel R., 24, 187
Scott, Alan, 149
Scully, Jason, 149
Sheppard, G. T., 16
Sheridan, Ruth, 42
Shotwell, Willis A., 41
Shukster, Martin B., 18–19, 21, 22, 24–25, 63, 65, 98, 188
Simonetti, Manlio, 4, 6, 19, 21, 35, 37, 61, 66, 73, 75–76, 80, 83, 86, 92, 94, 99, 101, 109, 111, 115, 166, 192–93, 202, 211–13, 221

Skarsaune, Oskar, 41, 110, 120, 130–31, 133–34, 166
Skeat, T. C., 5
Skehan, Patrick W., 208
Smallwood, E. Mary, 24, 188
Smith, Julien C., 3, 78, 195, 213
Song, Jae Jung, 96
Speigl, Jakob, 18
Stählin, Otto, 11–12, 82
Standhartinger, Angela, 40, 138, 178
Stang, Charles, 42
Stanton, Graham N., xiii
Stark, A. R., xiii
Steenberg, M. C., ix
Stenger, Werner, 71
Stewart-Sykes, Alistair, 196
Steyn, Gert J., 120
Still, Todd D., xiii
Stökl Ben Ezra, Daniel, 128–29
Strecker, Georg, 28, 86
Streeter, B. H., 17
Stühlmacher, Peter, 130
Sundberg, Albert C., 16
Svigel, Michael J., 54–55, 111, 154, 162, 207

Taylor, Charles, 197
Taylor, Miriam S., 63, 168
Theodor, Julius, 188
Thomson, Robert W., 193
Tischendorf, Constantine, 5, 14–15
Tite, Philip L., 71
Todd, O. J., 195
Torrance, Thomas F., xiii, 67
Tovey, Derek Morton Hamilton, 37–38, 64
Tränkle, Hermann, 130
Trapp, Michael, 71
Trebilco, Paul R., 38, 74
Treu, Ursula, 149
Trevett, Christine, xii
Trever, John, 128
Trigg, Joseph W., xiii
Tromp, Johannes, xiv
Tucker, J. Brian, 38
Tuckett, Christopher M., xii–xiii, 44
Tugwell, Simon, xii, 27, 210
Tuilier, André, 197–98

Uusimäki, Elisa, 196

Vanhoozer, Kevin J., 52
van der Horst, Pieter W., 168
van Unnik, W. C., 16
Venter, Dirk J., 74
Verheyden, Joseph, xii–xiii, 10, 63, 109, 146, 152, 158, 185
Vesco, Jean-Luc, 45, 116, 154
Vielhauer, Philipp, 26–27, 71, 127, 157
Vinzent, Markus, 26, 187
Vitelli, Girolamo, 8–9, 72–73
Vööbus, Arthur, 113

Wake, William, x, 81
Wallace, Daniel B., xiii
Watson, Duane F., xiii
Wayment, Thomas A., 142
Wendel, Susan J., 41
Wendland, Paul, 18
Wengst, Klaus, xxi, 18–19, 21, 24, 29, 34, 66, 71, 74, 77, 81, 83, 87, 90, 94, 98–99, 109, 111, 113, 117, 121, 130, 159, 166, 186, 192, 202, 211, 221
West, Martin L., 58, 195
Westcott, B. F., 14–15
Wevers, John William, 120, 148

White, John L., 71
Whitenton, Michael R., xiii, 103
Whitfield, Bryan J., 163
Whittaker, John, 44
Wilhite, David E., xiii
Wilhite, Shawn J., 6, 29, 58, 195–96, 207
Williams, Arthur Lukyn, 19, 21, 24, 186
Windisch, Hans, xviii, xxi, 11, 67, 72, 77–78, 81, 83, 90, 92, 99, 103, 105, 112, 117, 121, 142, 179, 185, 197, 200, 210–11, 221–23
Wolter, Michael, 12
Wright, William, 10

Yarbro Collins, Adela, 182
Yardeni, Ada, 26
Young, Douglas, 150
Young, Frances M., xii
Young, Stephen E., xii
Yuen-Collingridge, Rachel, 9
Yuh, Jason N., 37, 137, 139, 198, 201

Zahn, Theodor, xi
Zamfir, Korinna, xii
Zañartu, Sergio, 82
Zetterholm, Magnus, 18
Ziegler, Joseph, 90
Zimmermann, Christiane, 28

Ancient Document Index

Old Testament/Hebrew Bible

Genesis

1:1	34, 110
1:26–28	45, 122
1:26	36, 110, 113, 119, 122–23, 181
1:28	36, 110, 119–20, 123, 181
2:2–3	45, 179
2:4–24	118
3:1–7	159
14	140
14:14	140–41
15:6	167
17:1–14	140
17:4–5	167
17:23–27	140
17:23	141
17:27	141
25:21–23	45, 166
25:29–34	168
27:1–40	168
32:28	168
48:8–20	169
48:9	45
48:11–19	166
48:11	45

Exodus

17:8–16	158, 160, 164
17:8–13	35
17:14	163
20	179
20:2–6	213
20:4–5	159
20:7	46, 205
20:8	179, 181
20:14	46, 204
20:17	46, 206
29:32–33	125
31:13–17	179
31:18	46, 100
32–34	100
32:7	46, 100
33:1–3	34
33:1	44, 46, 118, 123
33:3	44, 46, 118, 123
34:28	46, 100

Leviticus

11	46, 148
11:4–6	148
11:4	148
11:5	148
11:8	148
11:12–19	148
11:29	148
11:42	148
16	125, 129
16:7–10	129
16:7–9	35
16:7	126
16:9	126
16:21	129

Leviticus (continued)

16:27	128
20:24	34, 44, 46, 118, 123
23:29–30	114, 125, 128
26:1	159, 162

Numbers

13–14	163
13:16	163
19	35, 42, 132, 134–36
19:9	134
19:11	134
19:13	134
19:16	134
21:4–9	162, 164
21:4–8	35
21:8–9	56, 159
29:11	125

Deuteronomy

1:25	34, 44, 46, 118, 123
4:1–2	210
4:1	60, 148
4:5	60, 148
4:40	217
4:45	217
5	179
5:1	217
5:6–10	213
5:8–9	159
5:11	46, 205
5:12	179, 181
5:15	179, 181
5:18	46, 204
5:21	46, 206
5:31	217
5:33	212
6:1	217
6:2	217
6:4	217
6:17	217
6:20	217
7:11	217
8:6	212
8:11	217
9:7–21	100
9:9–17	100
9:12	100, 212
9:16	212
10:16	139
12:32	210
14	46, 148
14:7	148
14:8	148
14:10	148
14:12–17	148
14:12	148
14:19	148
14:21	148
21:3	130
26:16—28:68	212
26:17	212
27:10	217
27:15	159, 162
28:9	212
28:45	217
30:15	195
30:16	212
31:29	212
32:10	209

Joshua

1:1	163
2:1–24	126
6:17	126
6:22–25	126
24:15	195

Ezra

4:21	92
5:5	92
6:8	92
6:13	187

Psalms

1	155–56

1:1	45, 147–48, 150
1:3–6	154, 164
1:3	45
1:6	195
16:8	209
17:45	138
21:17	35, 45, 116–17, 158
21:19	35, 45, 116–17
21:21	34, 45, 113, 117, 158
21:23	36, 45, 119–20, 123
23:4	179
41:3	36, 45, 119, 123
50:19	45, 89–91
68	129
68:22	129
89:4	45, 179, 182–83
95:10	133
101:26–28	180
107:4	36, 45, 120, 123
109:1	35, 45, 49, 163–64
115:4–8	213
117	115
117:12	35, 45, 117
117:22	35, 45, 52, 115, 117
117:24	35, 45, 115
118:120	45, 113, 158
135:14–18	213
138:24	195

Proverbs

1:7	82
1:17	108
2:8–22	195
4:9–10	195
21:8	212
22:5	212
22:14	212
30:31	130

Isaiah

1:11–13	44, 88, 90
1:12	90
1:13	90, 180
3:9–10	116–17
3:10	116
5:21	105
16:1–2	45, 152
16:1	153
28:16	35, 45, 115, 117
33:13	138
33:18	156
40:12	44, 184
42:6–7	45, 58, 175
42:6	66
43:18–19	123
45:1	35, 164
46:10	123
49:5	123
49:6–7	45, 58, 175
49:6	66
49:17	44, 184
50:6–7	44, 114, 129
50:6	34
50:7	34–35, 45, 113, 115
50:8–9	34–35, 61, 114
53	110
53:5	34, 44, 108–9, 113–14
53:6–7a	109
53:7	34, 44, 108–9, 114
54:13	220
58	36, 93–94
58:4–10	44, 94–95
58:4–7	12
58:4–5	93
58:4	94
58:5	94
58:6	94–95
58:7	94–95
58:8	66
61:1–2	45, 58, 175
65:2	60, 158
66:1	44, 184

Jeremiah

2:12–13	45
2:13	152
4:3–4	41, 45, 139
7:22–23	45, 89–90
9:24–25	41
9:26	139
12:9	148
17:24–25	179
21:8	195
33:2 (26:2 MT)	210

Ezekiel

11:19	36, 45, 119, 123
20:25	139
36:26	36, 45, 119, 123
40–48	48, 160
47:1–12	155
47:9	155

Daniel

7	98
7:7–8	21, 26, 98
7:24	21, 26, 98

Zechariah

2:12	209
7:9–10	45, 89–90
8:17	45, 89–90
13:7	34, 45, 114
13:8	113

Apocrypha

1 Esdras

6.8	72
8.9	72

1 Maccabees

10.18	72
10.25	72
11.30	72
11.32	72
12.6	72
12.20	72
13.36	72
14.20	72
15.2	72
15.16	72

2 Maccabees

	72
1.10	72
9.19	72
11.16	72
11.22	72
11.27	72
11.34	72
14.35	88

3 Maccabees

1.3	81
2.9	88
3.12	72
7.1	72

4 Maccabees

10.2	81

Sirach

4.31	208
7.29–31	203
13.18	148
15.11–17	195

Tobit

14.5	185

Wisdom of Solomon

2.12	116
14.12–13	213
14.27	213

Pseudepigrapha

Apocalypse of Abraham

1–8	169

2 Baruch

57.2	82

1 Enoch

1.9	196
54.3–5	196
63.1	196
85–90	185
89.55–56	185
89.66–67	185
89.56	47
89.61–64	98
89.66	47
90.17–18	98
91.11–17	185
91.13	185
93.1–10	185
104.10–13	210

2 Enoch

10.1–3	196
30.15	195
33.1–2	183

4 Ezra

4.33	47, 159
5.4–9	47
5.5	47, 106, 160
6.21–24	47
7.3–12	195
8.3	49, 106
9.15	49, 106
11.36–46	21

5 Ezra

1.31	90
2.33–34	153
2.33	153

Jubilees

11–12	169
19.15–31	168

Letter of Aristeas

144	149
146–47	149
150	149
165–66	149
165	146
168–69	149
310–11	210

Liber antiquitatum biblicarum

13.6	128
28.2	183

Martyrdom and Ascension of Isaiah

2.4	86
4.1–3	86
4.2	86
9.5	100
9.13	100
10.7–8	100

Odes of Solomon

2.10	209

Sibylline Oracles

3.388–400	21
5.46–50	188
5.414–33	188
5.422	188
5.433	188

Testament of Asher

1.3–6.8	58
1.3–6.5	196

Testament of Benjamin

6.4	186

Testament of Joseph

10.2–3	186

Testament of Levi

3.2–3	196

New Testament

Matthew

7:7	15
7:13–14	196
9:13	49, 112
10:22	223
18:11	223
18:13	73
19:25	223
22:14	49, 105–6
22:39	205
22:44	164
26:10–11	218
26:31	45
26:49	72
27:25	113, 131
27:35	116
27:48	129
28:9	72

Mark

2:17	112
10:26	223
12:31	205
12:36	164
14:6	218
14:7	218
15:24	116
15:36	129
16:14	86

Luke

1:28	72
4:6	86
5:32	112
6:23	73
10	12
10:1	12
10:27	205
12:5	86
13:24	196
19:10	223
20:42–43	164
23:34	116
23:36–37	129

John

1:1–18	37, 64
1:4–9	199
1:6–8	199
1:9	199
1:29	130
1:34	130
2:19–21	189
3:13–14	159
3:14–15	49
3:17	223
3:19–21	199
3:29	73
5:35	199
6:45	220
8:12	199
9:5	199
12:31	200
12:35–36	199
12:46	199
14:30	86, 200
16:11	200
19:24	116
19:28–30	129
20:25	113

Acts

1:25	202
2:28	196
2:34	164

ANCIENT DOCUMENT INDEX

4:36	28
5:41	73
8:32–33	108
9:26–30	28
13:1–14:28	12
13:1–12	28
14:8–20	28
15:1	223
15:23	72
16:18	75
16:24	202
16:31	223
17:25	88
18:25	196
23:26	71–72
26:17–18	86
26:18	86
27:9	128

Romans

1:1–7	71
1:16–17	135
1:23–24	213
1:32	202
2:25–3:2	140
3:3	92
3:21–26	135
3:25–26	130
3:31	92
4	169
4:10–12	167
4:11	49, 169
4:12	169
4:13–25	135
4:14	92
4:17	169
5:9	223
7:1	74
9–11	168
9:10–13	168
9:32–33	115
10:20–21	158
11:26–28	168
11:26	223
11:36	159
12:1	74
12:12	73
13:9	205
14:1—15:13	150

1 Corinthians

1:10	74
1:18	223
1:28	92
3:16–17	189
4:13	103
4:15	73
5:1	202
5:4	75
6:18–20	189
6:19	190
7:1	107
7:16	223
7:18–19	140
8:1—10:33	150
8:1	107
8:6	159
9:2	92
9:6	12, 14, 28
9:8–12	209
10:1	74
12:1	107
13:12	199
13:13	82
15:25	164
16:1	107

2 Corinthians

1:1	71
2:16	189
4:4–6	199
6:14	199
8:1	74
11:14	199

Galatians

1:4	86
2:1–14	28
2:11–14	27–28
2:13	27

Galatians *(continued)*

2:16–20	135
3:10–14	130
3:17	92
3:19	139
4:19	73
4:28	74
5:11–12	140
5:14	205
5:20	214
5:22–23	82
6:2	62, 92
6:18	222

Ephesians

2:2	86
2:5–6	86
2:8–9	135
2:8	223
2:15	92
2:17	86
2:19–22	189
5:8–9	86, 199
5:16	86
5:20	75
6:10–17	199
6:11	86

Philippians

3:2	140
3:9	135
4:4	73

Colossians

1:16	159
3:17	75
4:11	140
4:23	222

1 Thessalonians

1:1	73
4:9	220
4:10	74
5:4–5	199
5:12	209

2 Thessalonians

2:7	86
3:6	75
3:13	74
3:18	222

1 Timothy

2:4	223
5:17–22	209

2 Timothy

4:22	222

Hebrews

1:3	49
1:12	180
1:13	49, 164
2:12	120
3:1–6	172
3:7—4:13	163
3:7—4:11	182
3:11	182
3:12	74
3:18	182
4:1–11	49
4:1	182
4:3	182
4:4	182
4:5	182
4:8–10	182
4:10	182
4:11	182
5:1—10:18	130
7:25	223
8:1	49
10:12	49
12:24	109
13:7	209
13:17	209
13:22	80

James

1:1	72
1:2–5	82
1:8	205
1:21	223
2:8	205
3:1	74
4:8	205
4:12	223
5:20	223

1 Peter

1:1	71
1:2	109
1:14	73
2:4–10	115
2:5	189
2:21–24	108
2:22–24	130
3:21	223
4:5	86
4:7–9	86
4:13	73
4:14	75
4:18	223
5:12	80

2 Peter

1:5–7	82, 200
3:8	183
3:10	74

1 John

2:1–2	130
2:8–10	200
3:13	74
4:10	130

2 John

1	71
10–11	72

Jude

23	223

Revelation

9:21	214
13:2	86
17:7–14	21
19:7	73
22:18–19	210

Dead Sea Scrolls

CD

II, 6	195

1QM

XIII, 12	196

1QpHab

XI, 7–8	128

1QS

III, 13–IV, 26	58, 196
III, 20–21	200
III, 25	200
IV, 9–11	213
VIII, 5–7	189
IX, 3–6	189

XHev/SE

30	26

Early Jewish Writings

Aristobulus

Frag. 5	182

Genesis Rabbah

64.10	188

Josephus

Antiquitates iudaicae

1.17	210
1.154–57	169
1.257–58	168
17.165	128
17.167	128
18.94	128

Bellum judaicum

3.521	193

Philo

De agricultura

101	195

De congressu eruditionis gratia

129	168

De decalogo

50–51	178
97–98	182
105	182
154	178
159	128

De fuga et inventione

172–73	182

De migration Abrahami

89–93	18
89–90	140
92	138, 140

De opificio mundi

89	182
128	178
172	81

De praemiis et poenis

153	182

De sacrificiis Abelis et Caini

4	168
17	168

De specialibus legibus

1.1	178
1.2	139
1.3–7	140
1.5	139
1.8–11	140
1.8–10	138
1.190	128
1.304–6	138
2.58	182
2.59	182
4.101	149
4.103	149
4.106–7	149
4.107	81
4.108	149

De vita Mosis

2.23	128

Legum allegoriae

2.78–81	159

Quaestiones et solutiones in Genesin

3.46–47	138

Quis rerum divinarum heres sit

168	178

Rabbinic Writings

m. 'Abot

2.1	195

m. Menahor

11.7	128

b. Nedarim

32a	141

m. Parah

3.3–4	135
3.4	135

b. Yoma

62b	129

m. Yoma

4.2	129
6.1	129
6.4	129

Greco-Roman Writings

Aelian

De natura animalium

1.25	146
13.15	145

Alexander of Aphrodisias

In libros metaphysicos Aristotelis

500.33	193
772.8–9	193
786.2	193

Aristotle

De generatione animalium

3.6 (756b)	146
3.6 (757a)	146

Demetrius

De elocutione

228	80

Dio Cassius

Historia romana

69.12	188
69.12.1–2	24
69.18.3	72

Hesiod

Opera et dies

287–92	58, 195

Ovid

Metamorphoses

15.408–10	146

Pliny the Elder

Naturalis historia

8.81 (217–19)	145

Tabula Cebetis

4.2–6.3	195
24.2–3	195

Theognis

1.35–36	150

Varro

De re rustica

3.12.4	145

Xenophon

Memorabilia

2.1.21–39	58
2.1.21–34	195

Early Christian Writings

Acts of Barnabas

24	28
26	28

Acts of John

109	82

Aristides

Apology

14.4	130
15–17	208
15	196
15.5	208
17.3	199

Athanasius

Contra gentes

19.34	193

1 Clement

1.1	71
4.7	74
4.12	172
5.4	202
5.7	202
12	126
12.7–8	126
13.1	74
16.3–14	108
23.2–4	205
36.5	164
44.5	202
45.1	192
51.3	172
51.5	172
52.1	88

2 Clement

1.1	74
2.4	112
11.2–5	205
13.1	74

Clement of Alexandria

Paedagogus

1.59.1 (7)	12
2.17.1 (1)	12
2.83.4–5 (10)	13, 15
3.1 (1)	73
3.75.3—76.1 (10)	12
3.89.4–5 (12)	94
3.90.1–2 (12)	12
3.90.3—91.4 (12)	91
3.90.3 (12)	90

Stromateis

1.182.3 (29)	92
2.31.2 (6)	27, 80
2.31.3 (6)	12
2.35.5 (7)	12
2.67.1—69.4 (15)	13, 15
2.68.2 (15)	92
2.84.3 (18)	220
2.105.1–3 (20)	12
2.116.2 (20)	15
2.116.3—2.117.4 (20)	15
2.116.3 (20)	11–12, 28
5.51.2—52.1 (8)	12
5.51.4–5 (8)	150
5.52.1–2 (8)	150
5.52.4 (8)	150

ANCIENT DOCUMENT INDEX

5.63.1–6 (10)	119
5.63.1 (10)	27
6.65.2 (8)	119
6.84.2–3 (11)	142
7.16.5 (3)	92
7.55.6 (10)	82

Constitutiones apostolicae

7.1.1–19	59, 196

Cyprian

Ad Fortunatum

Pref. 2	183
11	183

Didache

1.1—6.3	29
1.1—6.2	50, 58, 196
1.1	196, 198–99
1.2	202, 205
1.4	209
2.2	145
2.4	196
2.6	204
2.7	205
3.4	214
3.9	204
4.1	209
4.3	210
4.4	205
4.5	208
4.11	207
4.12	196
4.14	211
5.1	202, 212
5.2	145
11.3	81
16.2	105, 192

Didascalia

5.17	113

Didymus the Blind

Commentarii in Zachariam

234	13, 105
259	13, 15, 28, 73
355	13, 105

Doctrina apostolorum

1.1	198

Epistle to Diognetus

5.1—6.10	4
5.3	81
9.2	113

Epistle of Barnabas

1.1—21.9	30, 193
1.1—17.2	10, 30, 35, 191
1.1—16.10	194
1.1—5.7	8
1.1–8	29, 61, 71, 85, 87
1.1	5, 13, 71–75, 84
1.2–8	78, 83
1.2–4	75–79
1.2–3	38, 73, 77, 80, 82, 104, 203
1.2	52, 60–61, 75–76, 87, 141, 219
1.3	53, 56, 75–77
1.4–5	83
1.4	30, 38, 42, 53, 60, 75, 77–78, 80, 82–83, 107
1.5–8	79–84
1.5	xxi, 34, 56, 61, 65, 79–84, 97, 147, 169–70, 194, 222
1.6–7	81
1.6	67, 78–83, 97, 148, 169, 222
1.7	34, 36, 40, 52, 56, 79–83, 88, 93, 96–97, 108, 129, 157, 191–92, 194, 203, 207

Epistle of Barnabas
(continued)

1.8	78–79, 84, 103, 191, 194, 223
2.1—16.10	30, 85–190, 192–94
2.1—3.6	90
2.1–10	29
2.1–3	85–87, 220
2.1	53, 60–61, 65, 86–87, 90, 97, 217, 220
2.2–3	87
2.2	87, 207, 214
2.3	87, 169
2.4—16.10	33, 59
2.4—4.14	108, 165
2.4—3.6	30, 35, 51, 87–97, 106, 112, 135, 143, 177
2.4–10	35, 40, 43, 88–93
2.4–8	89
2.4–6	87–88
2.4	36, 88, 96–97
2.5	35, 44, 53, 88–90
2.6	xx, 49, 62, 89, 92–93
2.7–10	38, 59
2.7–8	35, 45, 62, 88–90
2.7	36, 89, 93
2.8	89, 93
2.9–10	88, 92
2.9	37, 53, 89, 218, 220
2.10	35–36, 45, 57, 66, 89–90, 93, 192
3.1–6	35, 40, 88, 93–96
3.1–5	35, 38, 44, 59, 94–96
3.1–3	12
3.1–2	88, 93, 187
3.1	36, 64, 93–95
3.2	94
3.3–6	187
3.3–5	43, 88
3.3	36, 64, 93–95
3.4	66, 94–95, 199
3.5	94
3.6	30, 37, 49, 62, 93–94, 96, 107, 157, 207, 218
4.1–14	35, 96–107, 113, 174
4.1–6a	97–98, 101
4.1–5	20, 97
4.1–2	97, 102, 104, 106, 173
4.1	56–57, 65, 93, 97–98, 169–70, 180, 220, 223
4.2	98
4.3–5	20, 25–26, 98, 173
4.3	20, 36, 46–47, 52, 65, 82, 97–98, 102, 106–7, 160, 169–71, 185
4.4–5	20–21, 23, 46
4.4	21, 36, 98
4.5	21–23, 36, 46, 98
4.6–10	20
4.6–9	143
4.6–9a	97
4.6b–9a	98–104, 112, 116, 165
4.6–8	30, 40–43, 60, 64, 100, 112, 173–74, 177–78, 192
4.6b–8	101–3
4.6	63, 78, 98–101, 103, 110, 133, 178, 191
4.7–8	46, 62–63, 100, 146, 173–74
4.7	30, 36, 97, 100–101, 169, 174
4.8–9	103
4.8	36, 38, 43, 59, 100–103, 174
4.9–14	104–6
4.9b–14	97, 101, 104–6
4.9	20, 57, 65, 78, 86, 102–6, 173, 191, 194, 222

4.10	30, 49, 60, 66, 97, 102, 104–5, 169, 212	5.7	7–8, 55, 110, 116–17
4.11	36, 39, 60–61, 65–67, 97, 102, 104–5, 119, 122, 156, 169, 186, 207, 221, 223	5.8–9	58, 110, 112, 117
		5.8	34, 46, 111–12, 194
		5.9	13, 34, 49, 53, 107, 111–12
		5.10	10, 56, 58, 107, 111
4.12	105, 210	5.11–14	43, 55, 108, 131
4.13	57, 102, 105	5.11b–6.4	121
4.14	36, 46, 49, 102, 104–6	5.11–12	117
5.1—8.7	35, 38, 53, 106–36, 143, 165, 173, 177, 192	5.11	34, 37, 53, 97, 107, 113–14, 133, 169, 212, 215
5.1—7.11	127	5.12	34, 36, 45, 52, 107, 113–14, 214
5.1—6.19	122		
5.1—6.7	45, 107–17, 119, 175	5.13—6.7	117
		5.13—6.4	154
5.1—6.4	52, 207	5.13—6.2	114
5.1–14	103, 106–7, 113, 115, 118, 124	5.13–14	113–14, 124–25, 154
5.1–4	107–9	5.13	34, 36, 45, 53, 107, 113, 117, 122
5.1–2	107, 110		
5.1	43, 53, 57, 107–9, 116, 214	5.14	34, 36, 44, 113, 115, 129, 154
5.2	34, 36, 38, 44, 46, 55, 59, 64, 107–9, 112–14, 116, 122, 133, 136	6.1–4	106, 108, 114–15, 117, 122
		6.1–2	34, 114
		6.1	36, 61, 114
5.3–4	109–10	6.2–4	115
5.3	34, 37, 56, 108	6.2–3	35, 44
5.4	30, 36, 46, 60, 66, 108, 169, 194, 204	6.2	36, 117
		6.3	35–36, 67, 115, 135, 154
5.5–11	110		
5.5–10	108, 112–13	6.4	35–36, 45, 52, 115, 117
5.5–7	121		
5.5–6	43, 214	6.5–7	108, 116–18
5.5	34, 45, 52–53, 55, 59, 107, 110, 113, 116, 122, 219	6.5	78, 115–16
		6.6–7	116, 121
		6.6	35–36, 45, 115–17, 158
5.6–9	111		
5.6–7	110	6.7	36, 45–46, 53, 116–17, 119, 122
5.6	35, 37, 56–57, 92, 107, 110, 112, 116, 172, 212		
		6.8–19	34, 36, 106–7, 110, 117–24, 131, 181
5.7–10	55		
5.7–8	131		

Epistle of Barnabas
(continued)

6.8	36, 44, 46, 52, 117–18, 121, 123	7.4	36, 125, 138
		7.5	49, 53, 125, 129
		7.6–11	125
6.9–16	118	7.6–8	129–30
6.9	34, 36, 46, 57, 67, 118, 120, 122–23, 135, 169–70, 172, 181	7.6–7	35, 129
		7.6	61, 125–26, 131
		7.7–10	131
		7.7	126–28, 130
		7.8	126, 129
		7.9–10	126
6.10	34, 36, 118, 123	7.9	53, 126, 131
6.11–19	121	7.10–11	53
6.11–13	11	7.10	107, 126–28
6.11	57, 119, 122, 128	7.11	48, 126–28, 131
6.12–16	181	8.1–7	35, 40, 42, 107, 132–36
6.12–13	119–20, 122		
6.12	35–36, 45, 53, 55, 119–20, 122–23, 181	8.1	46, 57, 97, 132–34, 136, 169
		8.2–4	133
6.13	36, 66, 107, 119, 123, 181	8.2	132–33, 138
		8.3	46, 57, 133–36
6.14–16	120, 122	8.4	46, 133, 135–36
6.14–15	66, 186	8.5–6	65
6.14	36, 45, 66, 119, 123	8.5	57, 67, 133–36
		8.6	134, 136
6.15	39, 67, 119, 122	8.7	30, 37–38, 40, 64, 133–34, 136–37, 155, 199, 218
6.16	36, 45, 48, 118, 120, 123, 181		
6.17–19	120	9.1—12.11	165, 173
6.17–18	11	9.1—10.12	35, 51, 106, 136–51, 177
6.17	120, 123		
6.18–19	123, 192	9.1–9	39–40, 43, 137–43, 147, 155, 169, 198
6.18	36, 45, 120, 122–23, 181		
		9.1–6	8–9, 142
6.19	97, 120, 123, 169–70	9.1–5	142–43
		9.1–3	137, 139, 142
7.1—8.7	117, 119, 124, 138	9.1–3a	8
7.1–11	107, 124–32	9.1	30, 36, 107, 134, 137–39, 165
7.1–2	131		
7.1	37, 124, 127	9.2	36, 46, 52, 138–39
7.2	53, 59, 121, 124, 127, 133	9.3b–6	9
		9.3	30, 36, 138–39
7.3–11	39–40	9.4–6	137, 142
7.3–5	125, 129, 131	9.4–5	41
7.3–4	125, 130	9.4	37, 43, 92, 139–40, 142, 151
7.3	36, 61, 97, 114, 124–25, 127–29, 169, 222		

ANCIENT DOCUMENT INDEX 269

9.5	36, 45, 52, 61, 114, 138–39	10.11	12, 36, 43, 46, 60–62, 137, 147, 150, 156, 203, 207, 221, 223
9.6–9	142		
9.6	18, 30, 105, 139, 142	10.12	30, 37, 133, 137, 144, 147, 151, 218
9.7–9	137		
9.7–8	39, 41, 46, 142, 148	11.1—12.11	35, 38, 151–65
		11.1–11	152–57
9.7	55, 140, 142–43, 172	11.1	36, 45, 53, 107, 151–53, 155–58, 164–65, 220
9.8	36, 135, 138, 140–41, 169, 172, 202	11.2–7	154
		11.2–5	154
9.9	34, 38, 42, 76, 78, 133, 141–42, 194, 197, 219	11.2	36, 43, 152–53, 156
		11.3	153–54
10.1–12	12–13, 27, 43, 117, 137, 143–51, 155	11.4–5	153
		11.4	36, 153–55, 169
		11.5	153–54, 156, 207, 221
10.1–11	137		
10.1–9	148	11.6–8	45, 151, 164
10.1–8	137	11.6–7	154–55
10.1–5	144	11.6	36, 154–56
10.1–2	46	11.7	30, 154, 156
10.1	144, 147–48	11.8	36, 57, 67, 156–57
10.2	36, 55, 60–61, 144, 151, 158, 161	11.9–11	48, 160, 164
		11.9	36, 155, 222
10.3–8	46	11.10–11	151
10.3–5	144, 147, 203	11.10	36, 155–57
10.3–4	12	11.11	55, 57, 67, 155–57
10.3	7, 144, 147	12.1–11	133, 156–64
10.4	144, 147, 150	12.1–7	157
10.5	97, 144, 147, 169, 212	12.1	36, 46, 48, 151, 158–60, 165
10.6–8	144–46, 148	12.2–7	53
10.6	144–45, 148, 204	12.2–4	46
10.7–8	145	12.2–3	57, 135, 157, 160, 164
10.7	13, 144–45		
10.8	144–46, 149, 180, 203	12.2	35–36, 46, 55, 57, 158, 160–62
10.9–10	137, 144	12.3	10, 158, 170
10.9	36, 46, 55, 144, 146–47, 151, 158, 161	12.4	30, 36, 158
		12.5–7	35, 49, 157, 159–60, 164
10.10	13, 30, 45–46, 65, 97, 144, 147–48, 169, 195, 199	12.5	46, 159–62
		12.6	46, 159, 161–62
		12.7	56, 159, 161–62
10.11–12	144	12.8–11	157

Epistle of Barnabas
(continued)

12.8–9	74, 157, 163
12.8	36, 46, 53, 163
12.9	36, 53, 162, 163
12.10–11	157, 163
12.10	35–36, 45, 49, 53, 163
12.11	35–36, 46, 163–64
13.1—14.9	30, 35, 38, 40, 165–78, 192, 212
13.1–7	165–71, 173
13.1	64, 165–66, 170–71, 218
13.2–7	46, 135, 165–66, 170–71
13.2–6	167–68
13.2–3	169–70
13.2	36, 45, 165–67
13.3	166, 169, 218
13.4–6	170
13.4	36, 45, 166
13.5	36, 55, 167
13.6	167, 169–71
13.7	36, 46, 49, 64, 97, 167, 169–70, 180
14.1–9	171–77
14.1–5	41–43, 62–64, 165, 173–74, 178–79, 198
14.1	30, 165–66, 171–72, 174, 220
14.2–3	46, 172–73, 178
14.2	30, 36, 55, 172, 174
14.3	63, 172, 174
14.4–5	59, 172, 174–77
14.4	59, 170, 172, 174–76, 178, 214
14.5–9	176, 199
14.5–8	203
14.5–7	66, 199
14.5–6	176, 195
14.5	37, 43, 57, 61, 97, 107, 113, 169–71, 173–76, 180, 212
14.6–9	165, 175
14.6–8	58
14.6	36, 57, 175–76
14.7–9	45, 175
14.7–8	66, 194, 199
14.7	36, 175–76
14.8	36, 175–76
14.9	36, 175–76
15.1—16.10	30, 35, 51, 106, 177–90
15.1–9	40, 49, 117, 122, 177–84
15.1–8	181
15.1–3	179
15.1	36, 46, 178–79, 181, 184
15.2	36, 179
15.3	36, 45, 52, 179
15.4–8	192
15.4–7	179
15.4–5	66
15.4	36, 45, 52, 179
15.5	53, 66, 180–81, 183
15.6–7	181–82
15.6	36, 180
15.7	67, 180–81
15.8	36, 180, 183
15.9	181, 184
16.1–10	12, 29, 39, 43, 117, 122, 177, 184–90
16.1–5	27
16.1–2	52, 187, 190, 213
16.1	23, 43, 52, 92, 178, 184, 186
16.2–3	44
16.2	10, 23, 36, 92, 184
16.3–5	91, 184
16.3–4	xx, 19–20, 23–26, 186–90
16.3–4a	187
16.3	25, 36, 184, 188
16.4	24–26, 184, 186–88
16.4b	187
16.5–6	65
16.5	36, 46–47, 184, 187

16.6–10	24, 66–67, 185–87, 189	19.8–9	59
16.6–8	52, 74, 185	19.8	10, 208
16.6	36, 74, 166, 185, 190, 220	19.9	208–10
16.7–9	15	19.10	57, 67, 156, 209–10, 220–21
16.7	67, 185, 189	19.11	67, 97, 169, 210
16.8	57, 67, 74, 185–86, 189	19.12	210–11
16.9	36, 60–61, 114, 186, 190, 194	20.1–2	59, 66, 194–95, 212–15
16.10	56, 186, 190	20.1	10, 43, 52, 66, 86, 195, 198, 212–14
17.1–2	29, 191–94	20.2	195, 201, 213–14
17.1	191–92	21.1–9	29, 191, 216–23
17.2	29, 56, 191–93	21.1	52, 60–61, 67, 216–18
18.1—21.9	10, 29, 194	21.2–8	216, 218–22
18.1—20.2	xxi, 29–30, 35, 50, 58–59, 77, 191–215, 217	21.2–4	218
		21.2–3	219
18.1—19.12	66	21.2	218, 221
18.1–2	37, 58, 195, 197–201, 212	21.3	57, 66–67, 219
		21.4	62, 218–19, 221
18.1	13, 66, 86, 170, 193–94, 196–98, 200, 202, 204, 212	21.5–6	219
		21.5	52, 56, 60–61, 170, 214, 219–20
18.2	40, 53, 57, 65, 180, 196, 200, 212, 214	21.6	52, 67, 220
		21.7–8	221
19.1–12	43, 194–95, 201–11, 214	21.7	156, 221–22
		21.8	5, 61, 221–22
19.2–12	202	21.9	29, 56, 73, 216, 222–23
19.1–2	10		
19.1	56, 65, 170, 201–2, 211–12		

Eusebius of Caesarea

Historia ecclesiastica

1.12.1	13
2.1.4	13
3.25.4	13
3.25.6	15
4.6.4	24, 188

Praeparatio evangelica

3.12.9	182
3.12.11	182

19.2	52, 57, 59, 61, 196, 198, 201, 203–4, 212, 214
19.3–7	208
19.3	204–5, 208, 210
19.4	46, 52, 145, 204–5, 214
19.5	46, 201, 205–8, 210, 214
19.6	46, 206–8, 210
19.7–8	196
19.7	55, 67, 207, 214

Gospel of Peter

1.1–2	131
3.6	131
3.9	50
5.16	49, 129
5.17	113, 129
6.21	113
6.23	131
7.25	131

Gospel of Thomas

25.1	205
25.2	209

Gregory of Nazianzus

Orationes

43.32.3	28

Hippolytus

Commentarius in Danielem

4.23–24	183

De Antichristo

50	142

Ignatius

Ephesians

3.2—4.1	104
7.2	40
8.1	103
14.1	82
15.3	190
17.1	86
18.1	103
19.3	214

Magnesians

1.2	86
2	62, 92
5.1	202
7.2	104
8.2	110
13.1	81–82

Romans

inscr.	71
7.1	86
8.2	80

Philadelphians

2.2	220
3.3	74
6.2	86
8.2	18

Smyrnaeans

6.1	82
11.2	220

Polycarp

6.1	104
7.2	220

Irenaeus

Adversus Haereses

1.pref.2–3	193
1.15.2	11
2.6.1	158
4.15.1	139
4.17.1	90
4.20.4	11
4.21–23	168
5.28.3	183
5.30.3	142
5.30.4–32.2	183

Epideixis

1	193
46	161
48	164
49	164
76	45
79	158
92	158

Jerome

Altercatio Luciferiani

4	121

De viris illustribus

5–6	28
6	14–15, 28

John Chrysostom

Adversus Judaeos

5.10	189

Justin

1 Apology

1.1	19
13.1	88
15.7–8	112
31–33	11
37.5–8	90
41.4	133
50.5–10	108
52	11
63–64	11

Dialogue with Trypho

11–47	41
11.2	92
13.1–7	108
15	94
20.3–4	150
23.2	88
24.4	158
28.2–3	41
40.4–5	131
40.4	130–31
43.1	92
45.4	41
47.2–5	41
48–107	41
49.7–8	163
73.1	133
73.2	108
90–81	183
89.3	108
91	161
93.2–3	205
98.5	120
106.2	120
108–41	41
110.3	82
112	161
123.8	168
131	161
134.6	168
137.3	116

Kerygma Petri

1a	92
1b	92

Lactantius

Institutiones divinae

7.14.9	183

Martyrdom of Polycarp

2.4–3.1	86

Melito

Peri Pascha

64	108–9
72	116

Origen

Commentarii in evangelium Joannis

32.61	45

Contra Celsum

1.62–63	112
1.63	13, 28, 112
3.38	193
7.20	139

De principiis

3.2.4	13

In Jesu Nave homiliae

7.1	15

Physiologus

33	150
35	149
38	149

Polycarp

Philippians

inscr.	71
3.3	82
9.2	8, 202
9.2–14.1	8

Pseudo-Clement

Homilies

1.9.1	28
2.38–40	139
3.42–51	139
15.7.4	86

Recognitions

1.7.7	28

Ptolemy

Letter to Flora

33.3.1	40
33.3.2–5	40
33.3.2	139–40
33.3.3	140
33.3.8	40
33.4.1–2	40
33.4.7	40
33.5.2	40
33.5.3	178
33.5.8–15	40
33.5.11	138
33.7.2–7	40
33.7.6	40
33.7.10	40

Shepherd of Hermas

Visions

1.1.4 (1.4)	72
1.2.2 (2.2)	72
3 (9.1–21.4)	189
3.1.4 (9.4)	74
3.2.6 (10.6)	189
3.3.2 (11.2)	73
3.6.5 (14.5)	205
3.7.1 (15.1)	205
3.8.2–8 (16.2–8)	82
3.9.8 (17.8)	179
4.2.2 (23.2)	72
5.7 (25.7)	179

Mandates

1.2 (26.2)	203
3.1 (28.1)	186
4.3.4 (31.4)	86
4.3.6 (31.6)	86
6.1.1—6.2.10 (35.1—36.10)	196
6.1.1 (35.1)	203
6.1.2 (35.2)	196
6.2.1–10 (36.1–10)	59, 200
6.2.1 (36.1)	196
6.2.3 (36.3)	196
9.5-7 (39.5-7)	205
11.1-2 (43.1-2)	205
12.5.1—12.6.5 (49.1—50.5)	86

Similitudes

5.1.5 (54.5)	179
5.2.1-11 (55.1-11)	191
5.5.5 (58.6)	191
5.6.1 (59.1)	191
6.1.5—6.5.7 (61.5—65.7)	196
6.2.1—6.5.7 (62.1—65.7)	59
8.3.2 (69.2)	92
8.7.1-3 (73.1-3)	205
8.8.1-2 (74.1-2)	205
8.8.3 (74.3)	205
8.8.5 (74.5)	205
9 (78.1—110.4)	189
9.9.7 (86.7)	189
9.15.2 (92.2)	82
9.19.1 (96.1)	13

Tatian

Oratio ad Graecos

4.5	88

Tertullian

Adversus Judaeos

1.3–8	168
7.2	164
10.11	133
14.9-10	130
14.9	130

Adversus Marcionem

1.14.3	121
2.18.2–3	150
3.7.7–8	130
3.7.7	130–31
3.19.1	133

Adversus Praxean

11.8	164
28.11	164

De corona militis

3.3	121

De fuga in persecutione

11.3	45

De pudicitia

20.2	14, 28

Theophilus of Antioch

Ad Autolycum

2.34	213

Traditio apostolica

21.28	121
21.33-37	121